Essential Ideas for the Reform of American Schools

A volume in
Research and Theory in Educational Administration

Series Editors:
Wayne K. Hoy, *The Ohio State University*
Cecil Miskel, *University of Michigan*
Michael F. DiPaola, *The College of William and Mary*

Research and Theory in Educational Administration

Wayne K. Hoy, Cecil Miskel, and Michael F. DiPaola, Series Editors

Essential Ideas for the Reform of American Schools

edited by

Wayne Hoy
Ohio State University

and

Michael DiPaola
College of William and Mary

INFORMATION AGE
PUBLISHING

Charlotte, North Carolina • www.infoagepub.com

Library of Congress Cataloging-in-Publication Data

Essential ideas for the reform of American schools / edited by Wayne Hoy and Michael DiPaola.
   p. cm. -- (Research and theory in educational administration)
   Includes bibliographical references.
   ISBN 978-1-59311-687-3 (hardcover) -- ISBN 978-1-59311-686-6 (pbk.) 1. School improvement programs--United States. 2. Educational change--United States. I. Hoy, Wayne K. II. DiPaola, Michael F., 1947-
   LB2822.82.E77 2007
   371.200973--dc22

                                                                    2007006597

ISBN 13: 978-1-59311-686-6 (pbk.)
        978-1-59311-687-3 (hardcover)
ISBN 10: 1-59311-686-1 (pbk.)
        1-59311-687-X (hardcover)

Printed in the United States of America

CONTENTS

PART V: ON ORGANIZATIONAL TRUST

PART VI: ON COLLECTIVE EFFICACY

PART VII: ON ACADEMIC OPTIMISM

PART VIII: ON ORGANIZATIONAL CITIZENSHIP

PART IX: ON ORGANIZATIONAL JUSTICE

ABOUT THE EDITORS

Wayne K. Hoy is the Novice Fawcett Chair in educational administration at The Ohio State University. His research interests include school properties that enhance teaching and learning.

Michael F. DiPaola is a professor in educational policy, planning, and leadership at The College of William & Mary. His research interests include school leadership and the social processes that contribute to school effectiveness.

EDITORS' COMMENTS

Wayne K. Hoy and Michael F. DiPaola

Essential Ideas for the Reform of American Schools is the sixth in a series dedicated to advancing our understanding of schools through empirical study and theoretical analysis. Wayne Hoy and Cecil Miskel edited the first five editions of the series. Cecil has retired and is marching to the beat of a different drummer these days; Michael DiPaola of the College of William and Mary has joined the editorial team.

This book is different than its predecessors in that it identifies and synthesizes 11 key constructs that have important implications for both administrators and researchers; these constructs guide administrators engaged in meaningful school improvement efforts and provide researchers an agenda for future study. The articles of the book capture decades of theoretical and research work.

The book series on *Theory and Research in Educational Administration* is about understanding schools. In future issues we will welcome articles and analyses that explain school organizations and their administration. We are interested in the "why" questions about schools. To that end, case analyses, surveys, large database analyses, experimental studies, and theoretical analyses are all welcome. Space will be provided for authors to do comprehensive analyses when it is appropriate and useful. We believe that the *Theory and Research in Educational Administration Series* has the potential to make an important contribution to our field, but we will be successful only if our colleagues continue to join us in this mission.

Wayne K. Hoy, The Ohio State University
Michael F. DiPaola, The College of William and Mary
November 2006

ACKNOWLEDGMENTS

We thank the following journals for permission to republish the articles of this book:

- *American Educational Research Journal*
- *Educational Researcher*
- *Elementary School Journal*
- *Educational Administration Quarterly*
- *Journal of Educational Administration*
- *Journal of Research and Development in Education*
- *Journal of School Leadership*
- *International Journal of Educational Management*
- *The High School Journal*

Part I

INTRODUCTION AND OVERVIEW

INTRODUCTION AND OVERVIEW

Wayne K. Hoy and Michael F. DiPaola

Essential Ideas for the Reform of American Schools identifies and synthesizes key constructs that have important implications for the improvement of schools. The articles have been written over a period of more than a decade and are grounded in theoretical analysis and empirical research. Together they form a coherent body of literature for both practitioners interested in improving schools and researchers committed to the study of school effectiveness.

ELEVEN KEY CONCEPTS FOR SCHOOL IMPROVEMENT

The chapters are organized around constructs that have been identified as critical aspects of schooling and schools in the United States; all have been published in scholarly national and international journals, and all are analyses we have done alone, together, or with our colleagues and former students. The research and theory demonstrates how a body of work by a group of researchers can build and expand to new areas as old questions are answered and as new ones shape future inquiry.

Pupil Control

The book begins with the analysis of the saliency of *pupil control* in the life of public schools. Pupil control is conceived along a continuum from custodial to humanistic control, and four decades of analysis and research are summarized as the reader is guided through the conceptualization of pupil control, the development of theory, the use of that theory to generate hypotheses, and the importance of testing theory. In the end, the evidence strongly supports the conclusion that a humanistic pupil control perspective in schools is a necessary condition for the healthy socio-emotional development of students.

Organizational Climate

The *organizational climate* of schools is the next important construct. Organizational climate is the relatively enduring quality of the school that is experienced by participants, affects their actions, and is based on their collective perceptions of behavior in schools. The climate of the school depicts its "personality," that is, climate is to a school as personality is to an individual. In chapter 2, Hoy and Clover provide a basis for conceptualizing and measuring the openness of school climate, the Organizational Climate Description Questionnaire (OCDQ). Through factor analytic techniques, they identify three aspects of principal behavior and three dimensions of teacher behavior, which determine the extent to which schools are open or closed in their professional interactions. Like humanistic pupil control, subsequent research has demonstrated that the openness of the school climate is related to encouraging student outcomes (e.g., lower student alienation) as well as positive professional relations (e.g., shared decision making, loyalty, and commitment). Although the Hoy and Clover article describes a climate measure for elementary schools, subsequent research has added middle and high school versions of the OCDQ (see www.coe.ohio-state.edu/whoy). This Web site also has norms for comparing the climate of your school with a typical public school.

Organizational Health

The *organizational health of schools* is another perspective on the atmosphere or character of the school; however, instead of focusing on the openness of interpersonal relationships, here the emphasis is upon healthy interpersonal dynamics. Moreover, the Organizational Health Inventory (OHI) developed, described, and measured by Hoy and Feldman in chapter 3 extends the notion of climate to include students as well as principals and teachers. In fact, the academic emphasis of the school is positively related to student achievement even when socioeconomic status is being controlled. The subsequent article in chapter 4 by Goddard, Sweetland, and Hoy uses hierarchical linear modeling demonstrating the importance of academic emphasis in facilitating higher levels of student achievement. The OHI and its subtests, including Academic Emphasis, along with norms for computing the health of a school can be found at www.coe.ohio-state.edu/whoy.

One of the challenges facing administrators and researchers is to find the critical properties of schools that make a difference in student achievement. One school factor that consistently is demonstrated to be related to student achievement is socioeconomic status (SES); in fact, SES is so strongly related to school achievement that it simply overwhelms most other school properties and therein lies the rub—there is little educators can do to change the SES of the school population. What other characteristics of schools, which are more amenable to change, facilitate student achievement in schools holding SES constant? They are hard to find. We have shown that the academic emphasis of the school does make a positive difference in student achievement even controlling for SES (see chapter 4). Are there other similar school characteristics that make such a difference in school achievement?

Organizational Trust

The notion of *organizational trust* seemed another possibility. Hoy and Tschannen-Moran define, conceptualize, and measure school trust in chapter 5 as they develop and validate an Omnibus Trust Scale. Five facets of trust are gleaned from the literature and measured in schools. Organizational trust is the faculty's willingness to be vulnerable to others based on confidence that the other party is benevolent, reliable, competent, honest, and open. Trust in schools is embedded in relationships and the referent of trust influences its meaning. In schools, organizational trust has three important referents—faculty trust in the principal, faculty trust in colleagues, and faculty trust in students and parents. Surprisingly, faculty trust in students and trust in parents are essentially the same; you don't have the one without the other. Moreover, only faculty trust in students and parents is directly and positively related to school achievement, controlling for SES. Chapter 6 demonstrates the significance of faculty trust in students and parents in facilitating school achievement.

Collective Efficacy

Self-efficacy is an individual belief in one's capacity to organize and execute courses of action needed to accomplish a specific task. Self-efficacy evolves from Bandura's social cognitive theory and is a powerful factor in human learning, motivation, and performance in many arenas. For example, students with strong self-efficacy perform at higher levels and teachers with high self-efficacy are likewise successful in their teaching. Not surprisingly, a faculty belief about the *collective efficacy* of their school is a potent force for student achievement. In chapter 7, Goddard, Hoy, and Woolfolk Hoy provide strong evidence that the collective efficacy of urban elementary schools facilitates student learning controlling for SES. Subsequent research at the middle and secondary level supports the importance of collective efficacy in improving school achievement. In Chapter 8, the same authors review subsequent research on sense of efficacy and propose a model of the formation, influence, and change of perceived collective efficacy in schools. They also suggest ways to organize to foster collective agency.

Academic Optimism

Why are academic emphasis, trust, and collective efficacy consistently related to student achievement when controlling for SES whereas other school properties are not? Is there some latent construct that under girds these three properties? In chapter 9, Hoy, Tarter, and Woolfolk Hoy probe this question. They explain that academic emphasis, collective efficacy beliefs, and faculty trust shape the normative and behavioral environment of the school and provide a potent cultural force to influence behavior. These school properties work together in a unified fashion to create a positive academic environment, which they call *academic optimism.*

Their conception of academic optimism has cognitive, affective, and behavioral elements. Collective efficacy is a *cognitive* group belief or expectation. Faculty trust in parents and students is an *affective* response, and academic emphasis is the press for particular *behaviors* in the school workplace. Thus academic optimism is conceived as a latent variable with three basic properties—efficacy, trust, and academic emphasis. These researchers provide empirical evidence to support the conclusion that academic optimism is a powerful latent construct that promotes student achievement, even controlling for SES, previous achievement, and other demographic variables.

Organizational Citizenship

Organizational citizenship is the voluntary and discretionary behavior of the faculty that exceeds the formal requirements of the job. In chapter 10, DiPaola, Tarter, and Hoy identify the conceptual underpinnings of organizational citizenship and then develop a reliable and valid operational measure for the concept in schools. Collegial leadership of the principal, teacher professionalism, academic press, school mindfulness, and school effectiveness as perceived by teachers are all positively and significantly related to organizational citizenship. In chapter 11, DiPaola and Hoy continue this line of inquiry by identifying school characteristics that promote organizational citizenship, and in chapter 12, they provide evidence that links faculty citizenship with student achievement.

Organizational Justice

There is little doubt that justice has become a touchstone in contemporary American society. Thus, the system of justice that educational leaders are responsible for creating bears scrutiny. Organizational justice is not a new topic in the management literature, but it is rare to find discussions or analyses of organizational justice in schools. *Organizational justice* refers to individual's perceptions of fairness. In chapter 13, Hoy and Tarter review the literature and identify 10 principles of organizational justice that highlight the tenets of distributive justice (fairness of who gets what) and procedural justice (fairness of the mechanisms of distribution). Then they demonstrate empirically the symbiotic relationship between organizational justice and trust, concluding that there can be no justice without trust in schools.

Organizational Mindfulness

Just as individuals can be mindless, so too can schools; the rigid adherence to all rules is just one example of mindlessness that imbues some schools. Managing the unexpected to avert major crises by careful attention to ongoing operations is the hallmark of successful organization. *Organizational mindfulness* is a set of school properties characterized by a preoccupation with failure, a reluctance to simplify interpretations, a sensitivity to basic operations, commitment to resilience, and deference to expertise—all of which enable the school to manage effectively and deal with the unexpected by both anticipation and resilience. Mindfulness in schools is a paradox; it sees problems as opportunities and views successes as problems; it is both optimistic and skeptical. In chapter 14, Hoy, Gage, and Tarter first examine the elements of mindful school organization and administration, and then define and measure both in the school. An empirical analysis reveals the pivotal importance of trust in the development and operation of mindful schools. The authors conclude that school mindfulness and faculty trust are necessary conditions for each other.

Enabling School Structures

Like it or not schools are bureaucratic structures with hierarchies, division of labor, impersonality, objective standards, and rules and regulations. Most people react to the mere mention of bureaucracy in negative terms; the term is pejorative. Yet the research on bureaucratic structures reveals a more complicated pattern. Although some studies describe the negative consequences of structure in terms of alienation, hostility, inefficiency, and dissatisfaction, other research suggests such positive consequences as clarity of responsibility, efficiency, and effectiveness. In chapter 15, Hoy and Sweetland theoretically reconcile these two contrasting views of structure and offer a functional organizational model that they call *enabling structure*. This construct is developed and operationalized using factor analytic methods and then related to such variables as role conflict, principal trust, and truth spinning. The evidence suggests that such structures enable teachers to do their jobs more creatively and effectively.

Chapter 16 examines the concepts of enabling and mindful school structures in more detail, looking at similarities and differences and providing a richer description with examples of each framework. The chapter concludes with a series of hypotheses to illustrate the utility of the two perspectives.

Empowerment

The book ends with a normative model of shared decision making that answers the questions: under what conditions and how should administrators should teachers in making decisions? Three criteria in the form of questions are proposed to guide administrators in making such decisions: (1) Do the teachers have the expertise to contribute to the decision?; (2) Do the teachers have a personal stake in the situation?; and (3) Can the teachers be trusted to make a decision in the best interests of the school? The answers to these questions define six situations that call for differing strategies and levels of involvement. *Empowerment* is more than a slogan; it is a thoughtful approach to enhance decision making and share power in constructive ways. The proposed model of shared decision making is a reflective basis for empowering teachers.

Summary and Conclusions

The theory and research in this book support the following generalizations:

- Humanistic pupil-control in schools is a positive feature of school life that facilitates the healthy socioemotional development of students.
- Open organization climates are important to teachers and students alike; such atmospheres are conducive to positive student self concepts, meaningful student-teacher interactions, teacher loyalty, commitment, shared decision making, and authentic behavior.
- A healthy school climate depicts positive relationships between the school and community, between administrators and teachers, and between teachers and students.
- A strong academic emphasis in the climate of a school facilitates high levels of student achievement in spite of SES.
- Organizational trust is an important aspect of school life because it is positively related to a host of important school outcomes, including student achievement.
- Collective efficacy of schools is also an important force in the achievement of students regardless of the SES of the student population.
- Organizational citizenship behaviors of the faculty are significantly related to collegial leadership of the principal, teacher professionalism, academic press, school mindfulness, and school effectiveness as perceived by teachers.
- It is difficult to find organizational variables that predict student achievement that go beyond the influence of SES, but academic emphasis, faculty trust, and collective efficacy are three exceptions. They form a latent general variable, called academic optimism, which is a potent predictor of school achievement controlling for many variables including previous achievement and SES.
- Organizational citizenship behaviors of the faculty have a significant relationship to student achievement even when controlling for SES.

- Organizational justice in schools promotes trust, and trust nurtures organizational justice.
- Ten principles of organizational justice provide a model for fair treatment of teachers in schools.
- Organizational mindfulness and enabling structures are two properties of schools that help teachers do their jobs more effectively.
- Teacher trust in both administrators and each other, however, is likely a necessary condition for the development of mindful and enabling structures.
- Finally, successfully empowering teachers to share in important decision making depends upon their expertise, the relevance of the decision to them, and the extent to which teachers are willing to subordinate their own interests for what is best for the group.

PART II

ON PUPIL CONTROL

CHAPTER 1

THE PUPIL CONTROL STUDIES

A Historical, Theoretical, and Empirical Analysis

Wayne K. Hoy

The pupil control ideology (PCI) studies originated at The Pennsylvania State University under the direction of Professor Donald J. Willower. The article describes the beginning and evolution of the PCI studies and the role of theory in their development. PCI inquiry is now in its fourth decade and the concept of pupil control ideology and its measure (PCI form) continue to be useful to researchers as they analyze in school organizations.

The Pennsylvania State University Pupil Control Studies began with a case study of a junior high school in central Pennsylvania (Willower & Jones, 1963, 1965). Professor Donald J. Willower put together a research team composed of himself, an educational sociologist, and several graduate students. For more than a year, they did a comprehensive ethnographic case study of a junior high school—spending hundreds of hours observ-

Reprinted by permission from the *Journal of Educational Administration*, Vol. 39, pp. 424-441. Copyright © 2001. All rights reserved.

Essential Ideas for the Reform of American Schools, pp. 3–23
Copyright © 2007 by Information Age Publishing
All rights of reproduction in any form reserved.

ing and recording student-teacher, teacher-teacher, and administrator-teacher interactions in places of high visibility such as the faculty lounge, faculty meetings, assemblies, and the cafeteria. Pupil control was the dominant motif and integrative theme that gave meaning too much of what was happening in the school. Indeed the researchers were struck by the saliency of pupil control, a fact that was vividly demonstrated by a host of examples:

- the widespread suspicion of teachers that the guidance counselors were undermining their authority when they dealt with students,
- the fear that the new principal would be weak on discipline,
- the continuous, and often emotional discussions, about student discipline in the faculty lounge,
- the cafeteria and assembly halls that served as "proving grounds" for new
- teachers to demonstrate they could "handle" difficult students, and
- the single role of toilet paper padlocked and chained to the wall in the boys' lavatory that was a symbol of coercive control that pervaded the school.

Ever the theorist, Professor Willower asked for an explanation. He and fellow graduate student, Terry Eidell, and I read and probed the literature. Why was pupil control so important? How should we conceptualize pupil control? Those were two of the questions that framed our readings and subsequent discussions. They were theoretical questions, so we read theoretical literature, analyzed it, and together with Don Willower, we developed some tentative answers.

THEORETICAL UNDERPINNINGS

Richard Carlson's (1964) theoretical analysis of service organizations was especially useful in explaining why control was so salient in schools. Schools, like prisons and public mental hospitals, are service organizations in which clients have no say in their participation—they must participate; and the organization has no choice in selecting clients—they must take them all. It is not surprising that in service organizations with mandatory participation and unselected clients, some participants may not want to take advantage of the services offered by the organization; hence, control is a problem. Not surprisingly, client control is a central feature of life in public mental hospitals and prisons as well as in schools. To be sure, there are dramatic differences among prisons, public mental hospitals, and schools, but mandatory participation and unselected clients inevitably insure that client control is central in all these organizations.

Pupil Control: Custodial to Humanistic

Our next challenge was to conceptualize pupil control. We reviewed a number of frameworks. We considered Etzioni's (1962) notion of coercive and normative control, Lewin, Lippitt, and White's (1939) authoritarian and democratic control, and Rotter's (1954) notion of internal and external locus of control among others, but eventually we settled on the work of Gilbert and Levinson (1957) in their study of patients in public mental hospitals (service organizations with unselected clients and mandatory participation). They conceptualized client control along a continuum of custodial to humanistic and so did we. There were two compelling reasons for selecting Gilbert and Levinson's framework over the others. First, a custodial approach was theoretically consistent with the problems of control of unselected clients in service organizations. Second, the framework was a good fit with the extant theory of teaching and learning; that is, humanistic pupil control was consistent with the discovery method of teaching and learning and other educational reforms popular in the 1960s. Even today a humanistic perspective on pupil control fits current constructivist approaches (Hoy & Miskel, 2001).

The model for the *custodial orientation* is the traditional school in which behavior is rigid and tightly controlled; maintenance of order is a primary concern. Students are stereotyped in terms of their appearance, behavior, and parents' social status. Teachers with a custodial orientation of pupil control view students as irresponsible and undisciplined individuals who must be controlled by punitive sanctions. Teachers do not attempt to understand student behavior; in fact, they view misbehavior in moralistic terms and as a personal affront. Teachers conceive of the school as an autocratic organization with a rigid pupil-status hierarchy. Students must accept the decisions of teachers without question. The flow of power and communication is unilateral and downward, and cynicism, impersonality, and watchful mistrust imbue the custodial orientation.

The model for the *humanistic orientation* is the school as a learning community in which members learn by cooperative interaction and experience. Interpersonal relationships are close, warm, and friendly. Learning and behavior are interpreted in psychological and sociological terms, not moralistic ones. Self-discipline and self-regulation are substituted for rigid and strict teacher control. Teachers conceive of the school as a democratic organization with two-way communication between students and teachers and increased self-determination of students. A humanistic orientation is marked by optimism, openness, flexibility, understanding, and increased student self-determination. Both teachers and students are willing to act upon their own volition and then accept responsibility for their actions.

The custodial and humanistic orientations on pupil control are ideological extremes. They are analytic abstractions, that is, pure types that may or may not be found in such form in experience. The perspectives, however, are useful to compare, contrast, and analyze patterns of controlling students in school.

THE PCI FORM

The development of a measure of pupil control using the custodial-humanistic framework was a critical ingredient in the Penn State Pupil Control Ideology Studies. The Pupil Control Ideology Form (PCI) is a 20-item Likert-type scale with five response categories for each item ranging from strongly agree to strongly disagree. The instrument was designed to tap the custodial-humanistic framework described above (Willower, Eidell, & Hoy, 1967). The following items are examples:

- Pupils often misbehave in order to make the teacher look bad (C).
- Pupils should not be permitted to contradict the statements of teachers in class (C).
- A few pupils are just young hoodlums and should be treated accordingly (C).
- Pupils can be trusted to work together without supervision (H).
- Teachers should consider revision of their teaching methods if these are criticized by their pupils (H).

All the items are scored and summed such that the higher the score, the more custodial the orientation. Although the custodial-humanistic framework implies that both behavior and ideology vary along the control continuum, the PCI Form measures ideology, not behavior.

The details of the development of the PCI, its reliability, and validity are found in the original Penn State monograph (Willower, Eidell, & Hoy, 1967). The reliability coefficients of the PCI have been consistently high both in the original and subsequent studies (Packard, 1989). Similarly, construct validity of the scores on the measure has been demonstrated many times in a variety of contexts (Appleberry & Hoy, 1969; Hoy, 1967; Willower, Eidell, & Hoy, 1967), but the scale is not without its critics (Packer, 1989). The PCI, however, has stood the test of time. It has been used in over 200 published studies, and attempts to refine and improve upon the PCI have fallen short (Moretz, 1997; Finkelstein, 1998). Moreover, the PCI continues to be used productively to study control perspectives of educators (Denig, 1999; Finkelstein, 1998; Hall, Hall, & Abaci, 1997; Lunnenberg, 2000; Morrison, Wilcox, Madrigal, & McEwan, 1997; Morrison, Wilcox, Madrigal, Roberts, & Hintze, 1999; Saad & Hendrix, 1993; Weinstein, Woolfolk, Dittmeir, & Shanker, 1994).

THEORY AND HYPOTHESIS GENERATION

The Penn State Studies on pupil control were theoretically based. Not only was the framework grounded in theory but so also were the original hypotheses. We were as interested in substantiating the theory on which the hypotheses rested as we were testing the hypotheses themselves.

Theoretical Assumptions

One general assumption of the original study was that both social and psychological factors influenced attitudes and behavior of educators; hence, in trying to explain the pupil control ideology of teachers and principals, we were concerned with both role and personality factors.

Another assumption of our work was that much of what happens in schools is a function of attempts of individuals to maintain and enhance their status relative to others. Further, we assumed that when status is threatened, the natural tendency is for people to protect themselves by adopting a stance that they believe will help them control the threat. There is ample evidence of teachers who try to maintain their status relative to students. Just consider the mode of address and dress as well as the use of punishment such as detention, verbal reprimands, and sending unruly students to the office. These are common mechanisms used by teachers to maintain and enhance their status. Finally, the status of teachers and principals is grounded in the nature of the school and in the requirements of the role. That is, many status problems for public school educators are accentuated by the fact that schools are service organizations with mandatory participation and unselected clients. Teachers in particular are affected by the requirement that they deal directly with these unselected student clients, many of whom do not what to be in school. We postulated that when the status of educators is threatened, they turn to custodial means to gain control over the situation.

Theoretical Rationale and Hypotheses

The theoretical arguments developed above led to the first set of hypotheses. In developing these hypotheses we considered role factors that would enhance or reduce the threat to the status of teachers, administrators, and guidance counselors.

Roles. First, we assumed that elementary students, compared with secondary students, pose less threat to teacher status. The smaller, younger, and less mature elementary students pose neither the physical nor the intellectual threat that their larger, older, and more mature counterparts do. Indeed, some secondary students are larger and smarter than their teachers. Secondary students also are moving toward identification with peers, not adults. They are concerned with self in the eyes of their peers and thus are more concerned with saving face with peers than either parents or teachers. If our theory is correct, then so should be our hypothesis that secondary teachers are more custodial in their pupil control ideology than elementary teachers; moreover, secondary principals should be more custodial than elementary principals.

What about teachers compared to principals? Here we assumed that those individuals who had to deal directly with unselected student clients would be more threatened and thus more custodial in their pupil control ideology. When a student misbehaves in the classroom, the teacher is on stage. Twenty or more students are watching to see what the teacher will do. Typically, teachers perform. They act angry. They demonstrate they are in charge. Their response is often punishment. The situation is not right to probe the causes of the misbehavior in front of the class. On the other hand, the principal usually sees an unruly student in the privacy of the office. The privacy in itself makes the interaction less threatening, and the situation is more amenable to an analysis of the causes of the misbehavior. Contrary to the common sense notion that the principal is in charge and needs to demonstrate his or her authority and power, our theory suggests that the principal's status is less threatened by the students than the teacher's status; hence, we hypothesized that teachers are more custodial in their pupil control ideology than principals. Similarly, we predicted that teachers are more custodial than guidance counselors, who also have the luxury of meeting with students in private.

Next, we considered the roles of guidance counselor and principal. Which group is more custodial? Both roles are one step removed from the direct control of the students; hence, the threat to status is not salient in either case. Counselors, however, have an expressive role; their job is primarily one of helping students with their socio-emotional development. Principals, on the other hand, have a more instrumental role; they are concerned that the school achieves its goals. The press for principals is more task-oriented whereas for counselors, it is more relations-oriented; thus, we hypothesized that principals are more custodial in pupil control ideology than guidance counselors.

Socialization. Teachers learn the appropriate role requirements for teaching through the socialization process. They are socialized to the requisite roles and behavior both formally and informally, that is, through education and experience. New teachers, receive much of their initial socialization to teaching in their preparation programs, which are for the most part idealistic, and humanistic (Hoy, 1967, 1968, 1969; Hoy & Woolfolk, 1990). Experience is also a strong socialization agent; in fact, we assumed that the most significant socialization takes place on the job. Evidence from a number of studies (Coleman, 1961; Hoy & Woolfolk, 1990; Waller, 1932; Willower & Jones, 1965) consistently demonstrates that the teacher subculture in public schools tends to be custodial. Good teaching is often equated with good control. New teachers spend a great deal of their time trying to convince older teachers that they can handle the students and are not weak on discipline (Willower & Jones, 1965). Hence, we predicted that beginning teachers are more custodial in their pupil control ideology than experienced teachers.

Personality. In addition to how social and role factors influenced pupil control ideology, we were interested with the impact of personality. Beginning with the classic studies of Adorno and colleagues (1950) on facism, the authoritarian personality has been a major focus of study for many years, but it remains a puzzle to contemporary social scientists (Altemeyer, 1996). In the early studies, authoritarianism was conceived of as a right-wing affliction, but others have viewed it as a personality characteristic that varies across the spectrum of political and religious beliefs (Altemeyer, 1996; Rokeach, 1960).

The underlying theory of the authoritarian personality suggests that custodial control is a facet of the authoritarian personality; indeed, Gilbert and Levinson (1957) provided support for that proposition in their study of public mental hospitals. We were concerned with a more general notion of authoritarianism, which was not limited to the political right but was general and unrelated to political ideology. To that end, we selected Rokeach's framework of dogmatism, which refers to the structure of one's beliefs rather than the content of the beliefs. Dogmatism deals with how one believes rather than with what one believes. It is a general notion of authoritarianism conceptualized along a continuum from closed mindedness (authoritarian) to open mindedness (nonauthoritarian). We assumed that those who have a personality disposition toward authoritarianism, that is, who want things concrete, who disdain ambiguity, and who revere authority, would also embrace custodial control; hence, we predicted that, regardless of school level or role, closed-minded educators are more custodial in their pupil control ideology than open-minded ones.

FINDINGS AND OBSERVATIONS

Not surprisingly, all of the hypotheses developed above were supported (Willower, Eidell, & Hoy, 1967). I say "not surprisingly" because they were anchored in sound theory. Willower insisted that every hypothesis developed and tested have a strong theoretical base. In the press to solve practical problems, much of contemporary research is without theoretical foundation, and the consequence is that much of it is not significant. I personally find it appalling and a step backwards that so much of the research published in our better journals is atheoretical; indeed, it is sometimes difficult to find the hypotheses guiding the studies let alone the theoretical rationale and explanation for the relationships. Since the end of the so-called theory movement in educational administration, researchers have turned to more "practical" concerns often at the expense of theory building.

I have long argued that theoretical research in the end is most practical (Hoy, 1978, 1982, 1994). In the PCI studies, for example, we were concerned first and foremost with theoretical explanations. I repeat—we were concerned with testing the underlying theory of the hypotheses as much as the hypotheses themselves. Why are secondary teachers more custodial then elementary ones? Why are teachers more custodial than principals? The why questions are the theoretical issues. They demand more general explanation rather the superficial conclusion that the facts speak for themselves, which almost never is the case.

Our explanation was supported. Much of what happens in schools is a function of attempts of people to maintain and enhance their status relative to others. When status is threatened, individuals attempt to protect their status by adopting a stance they believe gives them more control. When students threaten the status of teachers, a custodial response is a typical way that teachers use to gain more control. Teachers in particular are vulnerable to threat because they must deal directly with student clients who are unselected and have little desire to take advantage of schooling. Moreover, the threat to the status of teachers is increased as students get bigger, harder to control, and smarter because students can better challenge teachers, a conclusion supported by the finding that secondary teachers are more custodial than elementary ones. The fact that principals and counselors do not have to deal routinely with students directly in a group context is structural feature of schools that gives these individuals more freedom to interact humanistically with pupils, a conclusion supported by the finding that principals and counselors are more humanistic in their pupil control than teachers.

The fact that schools are service organizations with mandatory participation and unselected clients virtually guarantees that pupil control will be a salient aspect of school life. Teacher education programs that spout idealistic and humanistic ideology are not sufficient to change the cultures of schools. As long as the teacher subculture of public schools is custodial, beginning teachers will likely become more custodial in perspective as they are socialized into the roles as teachers. The finding that experienced teachers are more custodial than elementary teachers supports the socialization hypothesis that neophytes are socialized into a custodial school culture. This original hypothesis was tested and supported using cross sectional data. A better test of the hypothesis demands longitudinal data, and these data were collected in the series of studies described next.

The socialization hypotheses has been confirmed and refined in a series of longitudinal studies (Hoy, 1967, 1968, 1969; Hoy & Rees, 1977; Hoy & Woolfolk, 1990).[1] Student teachers, both elementary and secondary, become more custodial in ideology as they experience student teaching. The finding was supported in the 1960s (Hoy, 1967, 1968, 1969) and then reconfirmed two decades later with a new group of student teachers (Hoy & Woolfolk, 1990). Apparently, student teachers are still typically faced with a relatively custodial teacher subculture, and their socialization during student teaching makes them more custodial in their pupil control.

The longitudinal studies refine the socialization hypothesis. Teachers become more custodial during student teaching and again during their first year of teaching, but after these two initial years of socialization, the pupil control orientation of teachers becomes stable; they do not become more custodial with subsequent experience. We suspect a number of things are at work. First, the overly idealistic and humanistic teachers probably drop out of teaching. Second, two years of socialization and experience provides enough change and reality adjustment to enable even the most humanistic teachers to cope successfully with discipline problems. After a year on the job, most of those teachers who continue to teach have found an orientation toward pupil control that is comfortable and functional in their roles.

Finally, we return to the general assumption of the PCI studies—that both social and psychological factors influence attitudes and behavior of educators. Thus far we have discussed how the social factors of role and structure influence pupil control ideology. Now we turn to the personality factor of dogmatism. Our theoretical assumption was that custodial control ideology was a facet of an authoritarian personality. Hence, we expected closed-minded educators would be more custodial than open-minded ones regardless of role. Indeed, that was the case. Both structure and personality were predictors of custodial pupil control ideology, a finding consistent with the general theories of Getzels and Guba (1957) and Bandura (1977, 1997).

NEW DIRECTIONS

The major theoretical assumptions of the pupil control studies continue to be supported in contemporary research. For example, Lunnenberg (2000) did a study on bureaucratic structure and pupil control with a sample of 297 teachers and 7,376 students in 20 urban schools. The results were consistent with the findings in the original PCI study. Structure was related to pupil control in schools: the more bureaucratic the structure, the more custodial the pupil control ideology and behavior of teachers. Let's review the rationale and theory of this finding. Unselected student clients and mandatory participation in public schools produce students who are resistant to schooling; hence, pupil control becomes a salient feature of school life. School organizations react to the pupil control problems with bureaucratic structures that have a rigid hierarchy ($r = .67$, $p < .01$), a plethora of rules and regulations to control ($r = .81$, $p < .01$), centralization of control ($r = .78$, $p < .01$), and impersonality ($r = .61$, $p < .01$), all features that help the school organization control it members. These are strong correlations between PCI and bureaucratic structure reported by Lunnenberg (2000). Further, he also found similar relationships between structure and pupil control behavior; in fact, he demonstrates a strong relationship between pupil control ideology and pupil control behavior ($r = .73$, $p < .01$), a finding that has been substantiated in a number of PCI studies (Packard, 1989)—the more the custodial the ideology of teachers, the more custodial their behavior.

Lunnenburg (2000) also found that a professional perspective was negatively related to custodialism of teachers; the more the technical competence of teachers and the more subject matter specialization, the less custodial the ideology and behavior of teachers. Teacher professionalism may well be an antidote to custodial control. Bureaucratic structures, however, with their patent control features are consistent with custodial pupil control. In fact, just as custodial ideology is a facet of an authoritarian personality, custodial ideology may also be a facet of authoritarian bureaucratic structure.

How can the degree of custodial pupil control in schools be reduced? Public schools will remain service organizations with mandatory participation and unselected clients for the foreseeable future so pupil control will likely remain a central problem in public schools. The selection of teachers with strong professional orientations and the selection of open-minded teachers are likely to be helpful in muting the custodial edge of bureaucratic school structures. It certainly is easier to select individuals with personal attributes more conducive to a humanistic ideology than it is to change personality of a teacher or to change school structure. But such selection attempts at the individual level will be tempered by existing custodial teacher cultures, bureaucratic socialization, and authoritarian structures in many schools not to mention the legal challenges for denying people their work. In the end, if schools are to be less custodial and more humanistic, then the basic structure and culture of schools must be changed. But what kind of structure is functional for schools?

A DIFFERENT PERSPECTIVE ON
BUREAUCRATIC STRUCTURE IN SCHOOLS

Two conflicting views of the consequences of bureaucracy emerge from the literature. Some studies demonstrate that bureaucracy alienates (Aiken & Hage, 1968; Hoy, Blazovsky, & Newland, 1983; Scott, 1998), frustrates (Anderson, 1968; Arches, 1991), stifles innovation (Hage & Aiken, 1970), and is unresponsive to its publics (Coleman, 1974; Scott, 1998), while other research finds bureaucracy increases satisfaction (Michaels, Cron, Dubinsky, and Joachimsthaler, 1988), facilitates innovation (Craig, 1995; Damanpour, 1991), and reduces role conflict (Senatra, 1980), There have been several recent attempts to reconcile these divergent findings (Adler, 1999, Adler & Borys, 1996; Hoy & Sweetland, 2000; Hoy and Sweetland, 2001).

Building on the work of Adler and Borys (1996, 1999), Hoy and Sweetland (2000, 2001) propose a different kind of bureaucratic structure for schools, one that enables rather than controls. The ubiquitous control mentality that pervades most hierarchies produces teacher dissatisfaction, alienation, and hostility (Hoy & Sweetland, 2001; Mintzberg, 1989). In schools, custodial control is a facet of coercive structures, and structure in schools is likely to persist for a variety of reasons. For example, the accountability movement in schools demands more not less structure, and structure is a critical ingredient of coordination and efficiency. A key to avoiding the dysfunctions of bureaucratic structure is to change the kind of structure rather than trying to eliminate structure itself. We need to develop structures in schools that facilitate and enable rather than control and coerce. The issue is not the *amount* of structure but rather the *kind* of structure.

School Structure: Enabling to Hindering

In our recent work, we conceptualized school structure along a continuum from enabling at one extreme to hindering at the other pole. Moreover, this construct has been tested and verified in three different samples of schools (Hoy & Sweetland, 2000; Hoy & Sweetland, 2001).

The prototype of the *enabling structure* is a hierarchy that helps rather than hinders and a system of rules and regulations that guides problem solving rather than controls and punishes. Although hierarchy often hinders, that need not be the case; in fact, in enabling structures, principals and teachers work cooperatively across recognized authority boundaries while retaining their distinctive roles. Likewise, rules and regulations are flexible guides to help solve problems rather than constraints that create them. Formalization and centralization work hand in hand to enable and support the work of teachers. Thus, both the authority hierarchy and the rules and procedures are mechanisms to support the work of the teachers rather than vehicles to enhance power and control.

The prototype for a *hindering structure* is the classic authoritarian bureaucracy, a structure and system of rules and regulation that controls and coerces. The hierarchy has as its basic goal the control of teachers. In such schools, teacher behavior is closely supervised and tightly regulated. The hierarchy of authority is used to gain disciplined compliance and the system of rules and regulations is used to buttress and support that control. In hindering structures, formalization and centralization work hand in hand to control, coerce, and discipline teachers. The role of both the system of authority and the system of rules and regulations is to assure that potentially reluctant and irresponsible teachers do what is prescribed

Table 1.1. Contrasting Characteristics of Enabling and Hindering School Structures

Characteristics of Enabling Structure	Characteristics of Hindering Structure
Facilitates problem solving	Frustrates problem solving
Enables cooperation	Promotes control
Is flexible	Is rigid
Learns from mistakes	Punishes mistakes
Values difference	Demands consensus
Fosters trust	Fosters distrust

by the school organization. The power of the administration is enhanced and the work of the teachers is hindered. The distinguishing features of these contrasting school structures are summarized in Table 1.1.

Rationale and Hypothesis

In schools with enabling structures, the orientation should shift away from control, including the custodial control of students. It is more likely that enabling schools will be able to examine student misbehavior in terms of problems to be solved rather than issues to be controlled. Students' threat to status of teachers should be reduced because the teacher's colleagues and the administration are more attuned to understanding, cooperation, and problem solving. A "cascading effect" has been postulated in coercive school structures: unconditional and harsh rules imposed on teachers lead to unconditional and harsh rules imposed on students (Hoy & Sweetland, 2001). The cascading effect of coercive administrative rules should be reduced in enabling structures, that is, teachers will be less likely to turn their frustrations with administrators and rigid rules toward their students. Thus, it is predicted *that teachers in enabling school structures should be less custodial in pupil control ideology than those with hindering school structures*. Indeed, the expectation is a moderate negative relationship between enabling school structure and pupil control ideology. We turn to a test of this hypothesis.

Method

To test the hypothesis, data were collected from a fairly representative sample of high schools in Ohio. The sample, measures, and procedures are briefly described below.

Sample. The sample for the study consisted of 97 high schools in Ohio. Although procedures were not used to ensure a random sample from the population of high schools, care was taken to select urban, suburban, and rural schools from diverse geographic areas of the state. One hundred fifty high schools were contacted and invited to participate, but only about two thirds agreed to take part. The high schools were defined by grade span levels that included grades 9-12 and grades 10-12. Schools in the sample represented the entire range of socioeconomic status (SES); in fact, data from the Ohio Department of Education support the representatives of the sample in terms of both SES and urban-rural balance._

Data Collection. Data were collected from the teachers in each school at a regularly scheduled faculty meeting. A trained researcher administered research instruments during regular faculty meetings. All responses were anonymous. Because the unit of analysis of this study was the school, faculty members were selected at random and were asked to respond to questionnaires. Their responses were aggregated at the school level for each variable to provide school scores.

Measures. Two instruments were administered to a random sample of teachers in all schools—a short form of the PCI and an Enabling Bureaucracy Scale (EBS).[2] A 5-item scale constructed from the original 20-item PCI form measured the pupil control ideology of teachers. The five items selected for the short form were those PCI items that had high discriminate power in the original study. The items included: "Pupils often behave in order to make the teacher look bad," "Too much time is spent on guidance and activities and too little time on academic preparation," "Pupils are usually not capable of solving their problems through logical reasoning," "Student governments are a good safety valve but should not have much influence on school policy," and "Being friendly with pupils often leads them to become too familiar." All the items are custodial items; hence, the higher the score, the more custodial the pupil control ideology. The alpha coefficient of reliability was .66.

The enabling bureaucracy scale (EBS) is composed of 12 Likert-type items. Teachers are asked to respond along a 6-point scale indicating the extent to which each item characterized their school. The scale is balanced with items measuring enabling formalization (EF), coercive formalization (CF), enabling centralization (EC), and hindering centralization (HC). Sample items include, "Administrative rules in this school are guides to solutions rather than rigid procedures (EF)," "Administrative rules in this school are used to punish teachers (CF)," "The administrative hierarchy of this school enables teachers to do their job (EC)," and "In this school the authority of the principal is used to undermine teachers (HC)." The 12 items form one strong factor measuring enabling school structure with an alpha coefficient of reliability of .95. The validity of the scores on the scale has been supported in three separate factor analytic studies described by Hoy and Sweetland (2001).

Findings and Discussion

The hypothesis that enabling school structure is negatively related to custodial pupil control ideology of teachers was supported ($r = -.26, p < .01$); the more enabling the school structure, the less custodial the pupil control ideology of the faculty. A moderate correlation between enabling structure and PCI was anticipated, but the correlation, although statistically significant, was weaker than expected. Part of the reason for the smaller than expected correlation was the use of the short form for the PCI. Its reliability coefficient was only .66, which attenuated the correlation in this study.

Nevertheless, the results, demonstrate that school bureaucracies need not be custodial structures. In fact, school structures can be created to encourage humanism in pupil control ideology rather than custodialism; such schools have enabling structures in which the both the administrative hierarchy and system of rules and regulations facilitate problem solving, are flexible, enhance professional cooperation, value differences, foster trust, and create a climate where teachers and administrators are not punished for mistakes but rather use mistakes as opportunities to learn and grow.

It also seems reasonable to propose that one way to change the custodial school cultures that exist in many public schools is to begin by changing the school structure from hindering to enabling. As teachers continue to become more professional and expert in their teaching, administrators need to become more flexible, cooperative, and enabling in both their leadership and in the development of rules and procedures that guide school activities. Principals in enabling schools find ways to help teachers succeed rather than monitor their behavior to ensure compliance. In fact, it seems likely that transformational leadership is critical in the creation of enabling and humanistic school structures, but of course that remains an empirical question in need of further study.

CONCLUDING COMMENTS

I have tried to tell the PCI story beginning with its inception and purpose and continuing by sketching a few of the natural paths of the research. The PCI studies are part of the rich legacy of Professor Donald J, Willower, a legacy grounded in scholarship, theory, and research in education. The aim of the current analysis was to examine the historical and theoretical underpinnings of the PCI studies and then demonstrate the vitality of the concept by discussing the results of an original, contemporary pupil control study. Table 1.2 is an overview of some key PCI studies; the figure presents a chronology, provides a few sample studies, notes the key variables, and summarizes the methods.

The PCI studies are important in a number of ways. First, the sheer volume makes this line of inquiry notable and rare in education; well over 200 studies have been done and the beat goes on. Second, the effort should serve as a model for those interested in theoretical research. The inquiry began with an exploratory case study. Based on the case study, the salience of pupil control in schools was highlighted and theoretical explanations were proposed. Next, pupil control was conceptualized along a custodial-humanistic continuum and a valid and reliable measure of the concept (the PCI Form) was created to test the proposed explanations, which were offered as a set of hypotheses. Finally, the hypotheses were tested and the results were published. They were published to subject the findings and explanations to critical appraisal of other scholars and researchers. Many have taken the challenge and reacted, refined, and expanded on the PCI studies. The research serves as a sound model for advancing the inquiry and knowledge in our field; unfortunately, however, it is a road less traveled by some of our colleagues.

The original PCI hypotheses were anchored in sound theory that considered both social and psychological factors. Threat to status was a critical concept used to explain the tendency of educators to adopt a custodial stance when dealing with pupils. Other things being equal, threat to teacher status by students often leads to custodial action in an effort to protect one's status and gain control over the situation. Thus, roles in the organization condition perspectives on pupil control and explain, for example, why teachers are usually more custodial than principals. Not only are social roles important in understanding the pupil control of educators but so too are personality factors. A custodial pupil control perspective seems to be a facet of an authoritarian personality, whether personality is measured as right-wing ideology (Adorno et al., 1959; Nachtscheim & Hoy, 1976) or as a more general notion of dogmatism (Rokeach, 1960; Willower, Eidell, & Hoy, 1967). Indeed, it seems clear that one's pupil control perspective is a function of role interacting with personality.

The PCI studies demonstrate the role of theory in generating hypotheses and the importance of testing theory. What is missing in much of the research in education and educational administration are the theoretical linkages that explain the relationships. It is important, for example, not only to know that climate is related to student achievement or that teacher empowerment is good, but why. What are the key organizational concepts, generalizations, and mechanisms that explain higher achievement? These are critical questions and they are theoretical ones; their answers will provide a deeper understanding of the dynamics of organizational life in schools and suggest more effective and lasting solutions to the problems of practice.

I end this paper on a personal note. I was fortunate to be one of Don Willower's early students; he shaped my career and professional life. His interests in scholarship, research, theory, and writing were contagious. The PCI studies were the beginning of not only an important line of inquiry but also the genesis of my own scholarship and writing; they provided me with a sound model for scholarship, one that has stood the test

Table 1.2. Overview of the History and Development of the PCI Studies

	Exploratory Analysis	Theoretical and Instrument Development	Socialization Studies	Personality Studies	Climate Studies	Student Outcome Studies
Example Studies	Initial Study (Willower & Jones, 1963; 1967)	(Willower, 1965; Willower, Eidell, & Hoy, 1967)	(Hoy, 1967, 1968, 1969; Hoy & Woolfolk, 1990; McAuthur, 1978, 1979)	(Blankenship & Hoy 1967; Helsel, 1971; Leppert & Hoy, 1972; Nachtscheim & Hoy, 1976; Lunnenburg, 1992)	(Appleberry & Hoy,1969; Bean & Hoy, 1974; Hoy & Henderson, 1982; Lunnenberg, 1991b, 2000,; Hoy & Sweetland, 2001)	(Hoy, 1972; Deibert & Hoy, 1977; Lunnenberg, 1983, 1989, 1991a, 2000; Finkelstein, 1998)
Key Variables	Descriptive, Exploratory analysis of the school. Thick and rich description. Pupil Control.	Roles—teacher, principal, counselor, experience Personality—dogmatism	Socialization of student teachers and beginning teachers in the U.S. and Australia.	Authoritarianism Dogmatism Traditional values Status obeisance Orderliness Self-assertion Locus of control	Openness Authenticity Instruction Robustness Structure	Alienation Self actualization Self concept Vandalism Disruptive behavior Quality of school life
Methods	Ethnographic Case Study	Survey Correlational Cross sectional	Quasi-Experimental Longitudinal	Correlational Multiple regression Cross sectional	Correlational Multiple regression Cross sectional	Correlational Multiple regression Cross sectional

of time. Many of us owe much to Donald J. Willower; he was an extraordinary scholar, mentor, and friend.

NOTES

1. I have cited only studies that I have done. There are dozens of other studies that are consistent with these results in the United States (see Packard, 1989) and Australia (for example, see McAuthur, 1978, 1979).
2. This study is part of a larger study to measure and validate the construct of enabling school structure (Hoy & Sweetland, 2001).

REFERENCES

Adler, P. S. (1999). Building better bureaucracies. *The Academy of Management Executive, 13*, 36-49.

Adler, P. S., & Borys, B. (1996). Two types of bureaucracy: Enabling and coercive. *Administrative Science Quarterly, 41*, 61-89.

Adorno, T. W., Brunswick, E. F., Levinson, D. J., & Sanford, N. (1950). *The authoritarian personality.* New York: Harper.

Aiken, M. and Hage, J. (1968). Organizational interdependence and intra-organizational structure. *American Sociological Review, 33*, 912–930.

Altemeyer, B. (1996). *The Authoritarian Specter.* Cambridge, MA: Harvard University Press.

Anderson, J. G. (1968). *Bureaucracy in education,* Baltimore: Johns Hopkins Press.

Appleberry, J. B., & Hoy, W. K. (1969). The pupil control ideology of professional personnel in "open" and "closed" elementary schools." *Educational Administration Quarterly, 5*, 74-85.

Arches, J. (1991). Social structure, burnout, and job satisfaction. *Social Work, 36*, 202-206.

Bandura, A. (1977). Self-efficacy: Toward a unifying theory of behavioral change. *Psychological Review, 84*, 191-215.

Bandura, A. (1997). *Self-efficacy: The exercise of control.* New York: Freeman.

Bean, J. S., & Hoy, W. K. (1974). Pupil control ideology of teachers and instructional climate in the classroom. *High School Journal, 58*, 61-69.

Blankenship, J., & Hoy, W. K. (1967). An analysis of the relationship between open- and closed-mindedness and capacity for independent thought and action. *Journal of Research in Science Teaching, 5*, 69-72.

Carlson, R. O. (1964). Environmental constraints and organizational consequences: The public school and its clients. In D. E. Griffiths (Ed.), *Behavioral science and educational administration* (pp. 262–276). Chicago: University of Chicago Press.

Coleman, J. S. (1961). *The adolescent society* New York: Free Press.

Coleman, J. S. (1974). *Power and structure of society.* New York: Norton.

Craig, T. (1995). Achieving innovation through bureaucracy. *California Management Review, 38,* 8-36.

Damanpour, F. (1991). Organizational innovation. *Academy of Management Journal, 34,* 555-591.

Denig, S. J. (1999). Discipline in public and religious elementary and secondary schools: A comparative analysis. *The Journal of Research on Christian Education, 8,* 51-74.

Deibert, J. P., & Hoy, W. K. (1977). Custodial high schools and self-actualization of students. *Educational Research Quarterly, 2,* 24-31.

Etzioni, A. (1962), *A comparative analysis of complex organizations.* New York: Free Press.

Finkelstein, R. (1998), *The effects of organizational health and pupil control ideology on the achievement and alienation of high school students.* Unpublished doctoral dissertation, St. John's University, Jamaica, New York.

Getzels, J. W., & Guba, E. G. (1957). Social behavior and the administrative process. *School Review, 65,* 423-441.

Gilbert, D. C., & Levinson, D. J. (1957). Custodialism and humanism in mental hospital structure and staff ideology. In M. Greenblatt (Ed.), *The patient and the mental hospital* (pp. 20-34). Glencoe, IL: The Free Press.

Hall, E., Hall, C., & Abaci, R. (1997). The effects of human relations training on reported teacher stress, pupil control ideology, and locus of control. *British Journal of Educational Psychology, 19,* 488-496.

Hage, J., & Aiken, M. (1970). *Social change in complex organizations.* New York: Random House.

Helsel, A. R. (1976). Personality and pupil control behaviour. *Journal of Educational Administration, 14,* 79-86.

Hoy, W. K. (1967). Organizational socialization: The student teacher and pupil control ideology. *Journal of Educational Research, 61,* 153-155.

Hoy, W. K. (1968). Pupil control and organizational socialization: The influence of experience on the beginning teacher. *School Review, 76,* 312-323.

Hoy, W. K. (1969). Pupil control ideology and organizational socialization: A further examination of the influence of experience on the beginning teacher., *School Review, 77,* 257-265.

Hoy, W, K, (1972). Dimensions of student alienation and characteristics of public high schools. *Interchange, 3,* 38-52.

Hoy, W. K. (1978). Scientific research in educational administration. *Educational Administration Quarterly, 14,* 1-12.

Hoy, W. K. (1982). Recent developments in theory and research in educational administration." *Educational Administration Quarterly, 18,* 1-10.

Hoy, W. K. (1994). Foundations of educational administration: Traditional and emerging perspectives. *Educational Administration Quarterly, 30,* 178-198.

Hoy, W. K., & Henderson, J. E. (1983). Principal authenticity, school climate, and pupil-control orientation. *Alberta Journal of Educational Research, 2,* 123-130.

Hoy, W. K., & Miskel, C. G. (2001). *Educational administration: Theory, research, and practice* (6th ed.). New York: McGraw Hill.

Hoy, W. K., & Rees, R. (1977). The bureaucratic socialization of student teachers. *Journal of Teacher Education, 28,* 23-26.

Hoy, W. K., & Sweetland, S. R. (2000). Bureaucracies that work: Enabling not coercive. *Journal of School Leadership*, *10*, 525-541.

Hoy, W. K., & Sweetland, S. R. (2001). Designing better schools: the meaning and measure of enabling school structures. Retrieved from http://www.coe.ohio-state.edu/whoy/cases_5.htm

Hoy, W. K., & Woolfolk, A. E. (1990). Socialization of student teachers. *American Educational Research Journal*, *27*, 279-300.

Hoy, W. K., Blazovsky, R., & Newland, W. (1983). Bureaucracy and alienation: a comparative analysis. *The Journal of Educational Administration*, *21*, 109–121.

Leppert, E., & Hoy, W. K. (1972). Teacher personality and pupil control ideology. *The Journal of Experimental Education*, *40*, 57-59.

Lunnenberg, F. C. (1983). Pupil control ideology and self concept as a learner. *Educational Research Quarterly*, *8*, 33-39.

Lunnenberg, F. C. (1991a). Educators' pupil-control ideology as a predictor of educators' reactions to pupil disruptive behavior. *High School Journal*, *74*, 81-87.

Lunnenberg, F. C. (1991b). Pupil control ideology and behavior as predictors of environmental robustness: public and private schools compared. *Journal of Research and Development in Education*, *24*, 14-19.

Lunnenberg, F. C. (1992). Locus of control, pupil control ideology, and dimensions of teacher burnout. *Journal of Instructional Psychology*, *19*, 13-22.

Lunnenberg, F. C. (2000). *School bureaucratization, pupil control ideology, and pupil control behavior.* Paper presented at the annual meeting of the American Educational Research Association, New Orleans, LA.

Lunnenberg, F. C., & Schmidt, L. J. (1989). Pupil control ideology, pupil control behavior, and quality of school life. *Journal of Research and Development in Education*, *22*, 35-44.

Michaels, R. E., Cron, W. L., Dubinsky, A. J., & Joachimsthaler, E. A. (1988). Influence of formalization on the organizational commitment and work alienation of salespeople and industrial buyers. *Journal of Marketing Research*, *25*, 376-383.

McAuthur, J. T. (1978). What does teaching do to teachers? *Educational Administration Quarterly*, *14*, 89-103.

McAuthur, J. T. (1979). Teacher socialization: the first five years. *Alberta Journal of Educational Administration*, *25*, 264-274.

Mintzberg, H. (1989). *Mintzberg on management.* New York: Free Press.

Moretz, S. A. (1997) *Trust, autonomy, and teacher's student control ideology.* Unpublished doctoral dissertation, Rutgers University, New Brunswick, NJ.

Morrison, T. G., Wilcox, B., Madrigal, J. L., & McEwan, B. (1997). Development of teachers' theoretical orientations toward reading and pupil control ideology. *Reading and Research Instruction*, *36*, 141-156.

Morrison, T. G., Wilcox, B., Madrigal, J. L., Roberts, S., & Hintze, E. (1999). Teachers' theoretical orientations toward reading and pupil control ideology: a national survey. *Reading Research and Instruction*, *38*, 333-350.

Nachtscheim, N., & Hoy, W. K. (1976). Authoritarian personality and control ideologies of teachers. *The Alberta Journal of Educational Research*, *22*, 173-177.

Packard, J. S. (1989). The pupil control studies. In N. Boyan (Ed.), *Handbook of research on educational administration* (pp. 185-207). New York: Longman.

Rokeach, M. (1960). *The open and closed mind*. New York: Basic Books.

Saad, I. A., & Hendrix, V. L. (1993). Pupil control ideology in a multicultural society: Arab and Jewish teachers in Israeli elementary schools. *Comparative Education Review, 37*, 21-30.

Scott, W. R. (1998). *Organizations: rational, natural, and open systems* (4th ed.). Englewood Cliffs, NJ: Prentice-Hall.

Senatra, P. T. (1980). Role conflict, role ambiguity, and organizational climate in a public accounting firm. *Accounting Review, 55*, 594-603.

Waller, W. (1932). *The sociology of teaching*. New York: Wiley.

Weinstein, C. S., Woolfolk, A. E., Dittmeir, L., & Shanker, U. (1994). Protector or prison guard; using metaphors and media to explore student teachers' thinking about classroom management. *Action in Teacher Education, 16*, 41-54.

Willower, D. J., & Jones, R. G. (1963). When pupil control becomes and institutional theme. *Phi Delta Kappa, 45*, 107-109.

Willower, D. J. (1965). Hypotheses on the school as a social system. *Educational Administration Quarterly, 1*, 40-51.

Willower, D. J., & Jones, R. G. (1967). Control in an educational organization. In J. D. Raths, J. R. Pancella, & J. S. V. Ness (Eds.), *Studying teaching* (pp. 424–428). Englewood Cliffs, NJ: Prentice-Hall.

Willower, D. J., Eidell, T. L., & Hoy, W. K. (1967). *The school and pupil control ideology*. Monograph No. 24, Pennsylvania State University, University Park.

PART III

ON ORGANIZATIONAL CLIMATE

CHAPTER 2

ELEMENTARY SCHOOL CLIMATE

A Revision of the OCDQ[1]

Wayne K. Hoy and Sharon I. R. Clover

The Organizational Climate Description Questionnaire is evaluated and refined in light of an investigation of the construct, organizational climate. The authors outline the development and testing of the revised instrument and report the empirical data collected in this process.

In a pioneering study more than two decades ago, Halpin and Croft mapped the domain of the organizational climate of elementary schools with the development of the Organizational Climate Description Questionnaire (OCDQ).[2] Ever since, the OCDQ has been a popular research instrument among students of educational organizations; in fact, it remains the most well-known conceptualization and measure of school climate.

Although Halpin and Croft themselves urged future researchers to revise, modify, and expand the OCDQ, there has been remarkably little

Reprinted by permission from the *Educational Administration Quarterly*, Vol. 22, pp. 93-110. Copyright © 1986. All rights reserved.

Essential Ideas for the Reform of American Schools, pp. 27–45

movement in that direction as time, school conditions, and society have changed. The purposes of the present inquiry are to examine the general notion of organizational climate, to evaluate the OCDQ as a measure of climate, and to refine and test empirically a contemporary version of the OCDQ.

ORGANIZATIONAL CLIMATE

Schools feel different. As one moves from school to school, each has a "personality" of its own. It is this feel or personality that Halpin and Croft use to explain analogously the idea of organizational climate; that is, "personality is to the individual what organizational climate is to the organization."[3]

School climate is the teachers' perceptions of the work environment. More specifically, climate is a set of measurable properties of the work environment of teachers and administrators based on their collective perceptions. These perceptions are strongly influenced by the leadership practices of administrators; indeed, the single most important individual in affecting the climate of the school is the principal. It is the principal who is given control of the formal organization, and it is the principal whose leadership practices set the stage for the normative and behavioral structure of the informal organization.

Climate has a major impact on organizational performance because it affects the motivations of individuals.[4] Interpersonal relationships among teachers and between principals and teachers directly shape motivation and behavior. The task of conceptualizing and classifying different climates is not an easy one; in fact, because of their perceptual nature, there may be an infinite variety of organizational climates. What are the important dimensions of school climate that motivate behavior? Again, there are no simple answers, but Halpin and Croft provide one answer; they define eight dimensions of teacher-teacher and principal-teacher interactions. All eight dimensions are measurable, and describe the school situation and differentiate among schools. Whether these aspects of climate represent symptoms or causes is less important to administrators than their usefulness in describing the situation accurately, in relating the dimensions to specific motivations and behavior, and in enabling one to measure changes in the situation.[5]

In brief, the concept of organizational climate can be summarized as a relatively enduring quality of the school environment that (a) is affected by the principal's leadership, (b) is experienced by teachers, (c)

influences members' behavior, and (d) is based on collective perceptions.

THE ORGANIZATIONAL CLIMATE DESCRIPTION QUESTIONNAIRE

Although the OCDQ is still a widely used measure of school climate, it has
a number of weaknesses that need attention. First, as has already been
suggested, the instrument has not undergone any revision despite
changes in society and schools during the past twenty years. In one of the
few comprehensive empirical attempts to appraise the OCDQ, Hayes concluded that many of the items of the OCDQ were no longer measuring
what they were intended to measure, that some of the subtests were no
longer valid (e.g., aloofness), that the reliabilities of some of the subtests
were low, and that the instrument needed a major revision.[6] In fact, a
close examination of Halpin and Croft's original study reveals that even
in their analyses the reliabilities of some of the subtests were low, and
many of the items had weak construct validity.[7]

Another limitation of the OCDQ is that it describes the climate of the
school without dealing with students. Concern is restricted to social interactions among professional personnel. To exclude the student from the
analysis of school climate is to restrict the scope of the climate measure.

Silver also is critical of the conceptual underpinnings of the OCDQ for
other reasons; she argues that the framework lacks clear underlying
logic.[8] For example, she notes that although the hindrance subtest is
defined by Halpin and Croft as one dimension of teacher's behavior, the
concept refers to administrative demands rather than interpersonal
behavior of teachers.

Similarly, other conceptual problems become apparent. Halpin and
Croft themselves question the adequacy of their concept of consideration
by suspecting that two or more facets of considerate behavior have been
confounded within a single measure. Moreover, the concept of production
emphasis seems poorly labeled; the measure clearly taps close supervision
and autocratic behavior, not an emphasis on high production standards.
Directive behavior seems a more apt description of their aspect of principal behavior.

After Halpin and Croft had identified the eight dimensions of school
climate, they attempted to classify schools into one of six climate types
based on the school's profile of scores. School climates were conceived
along a continuum of open to closed—open climates distinguished by
functional flexibility and closed climates marked by functional rigidity.
The meaning of the middle climates, however, is vague. This ambiguity is
in large part a function of the operational construction of the continuum,

a very rough one at best. Three independent criteria were used to classify school climates, a fact that led Silver to conclude there are three continuums, not one.[9] Subsequent attempts to replicate the original six climate types have often failed, again raising some question about the usefulness of the six climate types.[10] Indeed, Andrews has concluded that the designation of the discrete climates along an open to closed continuum adds nothing to the meaning that is not already present in the subtests, and in fact detracts from the OCDQ.[11]

The unit-of-analysis problem is another important issue to consider in developing climate measures. Most researchers acknowledge the issue when using existing climate scales to test hypotheses regarding the correlates of these measures; that is, they aggregate the data at the school level when the constructs are viewed as organizational characteristics. Ironically, however, concerns relating to the appropriate analytic units during instrument development are rare.[12] Halpin and Croft are no exception. Although they were concerned with the dimensions of school climate as characteristics of the organization, OCDQ data gathered from individual teachers in all schools were factor analyzed at the item level without regard to school as the researchers sought to map the basic dimensions of teacher and principal interaction. Thus, in identifying the dimensions of climate, the initial analysis was performed at an individual level, not an organizational one. That is, the sample for analysis was 1151 individuals, not 71 schools. Such an analysis ignores a basic conceptual assumption of climate measures—they are organizational characteristics, not individual ones. Conceptual consistency and clarity require that climate analyses should be performed at the system or group level; the focus throughout should be on properties of schools.[13]

In sum, the OCDQ needs revision. The instrument remains unchanged after more than twenty years. Questions about the reliability and validity of both items and subtests persist. Moreover, conceptual problems abound: there is a lack of underlying logic to the framework; the meanings of some of the dimensions are vague; the climate continuum is ambiguous and likely not a single continuum; and the conceptualization excludes students. Finally, the unit of analysis in the development of the OCDQ dimensions was the individual; the appropriate analytic unit is the school.

DEVELOPMENT OF THE REVISED OCDQ

The development of the revised instrument involved two steps, each of which will be described in some detail. First, the original items of the OCDQ were evaluated and new items were generated. Next, a pilot study was performed to deal with the unit-of-analysis issue, reduce the number of items, refine the items, and identify the factor structure of the revised OCDQ.

Item Generation

The first step in revising the OCDQ was to evaluate the existing items in the OCDQ by examining Halpin and Croft's rotated item factor matrix for the original 64 items of the OCDQ. Factor loadings for all items within each subtest were compared, and items with relatively low loadings were either revised or discarded; eventually twenty-four items were discarded.

Next, it was decided to broaden the scope of the OCDQ by developing items focused on students and teacher-student interactions. In particular, items were written to measure the pupil control behavior and the academic press of the school. Pupil control is a basic problem faced by public schools and academic press has emerged from the school effectiveness literature as a critical ingredient of effective schools.[14]

Some items were developed by the researchers independently and others jointly, but no item was included unless there was consensus on the following criteria: (1) the statement reflected a property of the school (the unit of analysis was the school); (2) the statement was clear and concise; (3) the statement had content validity; and (4) the statement had discriminatory potential. Fourteen items were developed to measure the academic press of the school; 17 items were generated to measure pupil control behavior, and new items were added to subtests with only a few items, such as hindrance, intimacy, and consideration.

Special attention was given to hindrance, production emphasis, and aloofness because of the lack of conceptual clarity of these dimensions. Although Halpin and Croft considered hindrance a teacher dimension, the present effort identified the concept as a principal characteristic. Items that described the principal's behavior as directing and controlling supplemented the remaining "production emphasis" items that focused on autocratic behavior. Aloofness was probably the weakest of the original OCDQ subtests and in view of Hayes' evidence and conclusion that the items simply no longer measured aloofness, an entire new set of items was written.[15]

In the tradition of the original OCDQ, all items were simple statements and respondents were asked to indicate the extent that each statement characterized their school along a four-point Likert scale as rarely occurs, sometimes occurs, often occurs, or very frequently occurs. Samples of the new items added to the instrument included the following:

- The principal checks lesson plans.
- The principal treats teachers as equals.
- Teachers are burdened with busywork.
- Faculty meetings are useless.
- Teachers socialize with each other.
- Teachers help and support each other.
- Teachers are friendly with teachers.
- Teachers praise pupils who do good work.
- The learning environment is orderly and serious.

Pilot Study

The preliminary revised OCDQ now contained 131 potential, mostly untested items. Therefore, reduction of the number of items became an initial task as the factor structure of the revised instrument was explored. A decision was made to use a preliminary sample of schools for this purpose.

Pilot Sample

A pilot sample of 38 elementary schools was identified for exploration and refinement of the instrument. The sample included urban, suburban, and rural schools and represented a diverse subset of elementary schools. Only schools with 10 or more teachers were included in the sample. The researchers collected data from four teachers selected at random in each of the 38 schools. Since the unit of analysis was the school, individual data were aggregated at the school level for each item and the exploratory procedures were performed to reduce the number of items and determine the factor structure of the revised instrument.

Unit of Analysis

Sirotnik has identified three types of analyses that have been used in climate studies—total analysis, within school-analysis, and between-school analysis.[16] Total analysis examines relationships among variables across individuals, ignoring possible relevant grouping factors. Within-school analysis is also an individual approach; however, in this case the group effect is removed from the individual score before analysis. Finally, between-school analysis uses the group as the unit of analysis; mean scores are aggregated at the school level to form the variables for analysis. When the property is viewed as fundamentally intrinsic to the group, as it is in school climate, then between-school analysis is most appropriate.

Unfortunately, total analysis is most frequently used, or more accurately misused, in studies of organizational climate. Halpin and Croft used the total analysis approach to determine the eight basic dimensions of school climate. They factored an item-correlation matrix for the OCDQ based on 1151 individuals ignoring the fact that the individuals came from 71 different schools.[17] A more appropriate procedure would have been to aggregate the scores at the school level and then factor analyze the item matrix, but then, of course, the size of the group would have been much smaller ($n = 71$ schools).

The correction of the flaw in the unit of analysis produces a major dilemma: the number of items of the original OCDQ (64) was almost as large as the sample (71). Although the minimum allowable ratio of cases to items (variables) is still a matter of debate, the number of cases should exceed the number of items; and in general, the number of cases to items should be as large as possible.[18] In the present study, the preliminary instrument had 131 items with only 38 schools, nearly more than three times as many items as cases. Since it was not feasible to increase drastically the size of the sample, the strategy was to use this small pilot sample simply to refine and to reduce substantially the length of the revised OCDQ so that subsequent analysis of the revised OCDQ could more closely meet the minimum criterion for the ratio of cases to items.

Factor Analyses

Three criteria were used to reduce the total number of items in the revised OCDQ. First, the criterion of simple structure was employed in all factor analyses; only items that loaded high on one factor and low on all others were retained. Second, in addition to their mathematical contribution to the factor, items were evaluated for conceptual clarity and fit with primary items in the factor. Finally, items were eliminated if they reduced substantially the internal consistency of the subtest as measured by Cronbach's coefficient alpha.

A series of exploratory factor analyses of the pilot data was performed. School mean scores were generated for each item and the item-correlation matrices were factored. A 10-factor solution with a varimax rotation was performed, based on the expectation that there would be the eight original factors and two new dimensions of academic press and pupil control. Immediately 56 items were eliminated because of their low loading ($< .3$) across all factors. A second factor analysis was conducted with the remaining 75 items, and nine additional items were dropped before a mini factor analysis was performed with the remaining 66 items. Along with each factor analysis, reliability analyses were performed for each subtest to refine each subtest.

In the process of performing the exploratory factor analyses, several conclusions were drawn that influenced the interpretation and further refinement of the revised instrument. First, using the criterion of simple structure, there were fewer than 10 interpretable factors. The aloofness dimension was never sufficiently distinct in any of the factor solutions; hence, following Hayes' recommendation, the aloofness subtest was eliminated.[19] Next, most of the items measuring consideration and trust consistently loaded together on the same factor; consequently, only the nine items which most strongly clustered together were retained. Finally, the academic press items and pupil control items lost their conceptual identity as the analyses became more refined; that is, neither emerged as distinct factors. Instead, these items were interwoven into many dimensions of both principal and teacher behavior. Thus, it was reluctantly decided to remove academic press and pupil control items from the instrument. As a consequence, only 42 items remained in the revised OCDQ, and after another series of iterations, a six-factor solution was selected as the best solution.

Discussion

The six dimensions of school climate that finally emerged were grouped into two categories. Three of the dimensions described principal behavior and three depicted teacher behavior.

Those items on the original consideration and trust subtests that came together to form one common factor all reflected cognitive and affective aspects of supportive principal behavior; hence, this factor was termed "supportive leader behavior." The original and new "production emphasis" items also clustered together and formed a factor that was called "directive leader behavior." Finally, the last dimension of leader behavior was a revised version of hindrance, which was more appropriately labeled "restrictive leader behavior." In brief, the leader behavior of elementary principals was conceived in terms of supportive, directive, and restrictive behaviors.

Similarly, there were changes in the teacher dimensions in the revised OCDQ. The original esprit subtest changed dramatically; in fact, only two of the original items remained. The new set of items described teachers as colleagues committed to each other, their work, and their school, a factor called "collegial teacher behavior." With minor revisions, two of the original OCDQ subtests, "intimacy" and "disengagement," remained. Thus, the interaction patterns of elementary teachers were described in terms of collegial, intimate, and disengaged teacher behaviors.

The revised instrument, OCDQ-RE, was now ready for further analysis. It contained 42 items that mapped six dimensions of school climate—

three at the administrative level and three at the teacher level. There is little question that this is a new instrument. Although the OCDQ-RE builds upon the original OCDQ, it is more parsimonious; it has different dimensions; and one-half the items are new. The six dimensions are defined and summarized in Table 2.1.

A TEST OF THE REVISED INSTRUMENT (OCDQ-RE)

Having completed the data reduction and reconceptualization of the new questionnaire in the pilot study, the 42-item instrument (OCDQ-RE) was ready to be tested with a new separate data set of 70 schools in order to demonstrate the stability of the factor structure, to confirm the validity and stability of the subtests, and to check for a second-order factor of openness.

Sample

Seventy elementary schools in New Jersey agreed to participate in the study. A separate, new random sample of at least six teachers was drawn from each of the 38 pilot schools and 32 new schools were added to that

Table 2.1.   The Six Dimensions of the OCDQ-RE

Principal's Behavior

(1) *Supportive* behavior reflects a basic concern for teachers. The principal listens and is open to teacher suggestions. Praise is given genuinely and frequently, and criticism is handled constructively. Supportive principals respect the professional competence of their staffs and exhibit both a personal and professional interest in each teacher.

(2) *Directive* behavior is rigid, close supervision. Principals maintain close and constant control over all teacher and school activities, down to the smallest details.

(3) *Restrictive* behavior hinders rather than facilitates teacher work. The principal burdens teachers with paper work, committee requirements, routine duties, and other demands that interfere with their teaching responsibilities.

Teachers' Behavior

(4) *Collegial* behavior supports open and professional interactions among teachers. Teachers are proud of their school, enjoy working with their colleagues, and are enthusiastic, accepting, and mutually respectful of the professional competence of their colleagues.

(5) *Intimate* behavior reflects a cohesive and strong network of social support among the faculty. Teachers know each other well, are close personal friends, socialize together regularly, and provide strong support for each other.

(6) *Disengaged* behavior refers to a lack of meaning and focus to professional activities. Teachers are simply putting in time and are non-productive in group efforts or team-building; they have no common goal orientation. Their behavior is often negative and critical of their colleagues and the organization.

final sample. Although the school sample was not a random one, it was a diverse one representing a broad range of schools from urban, suburban, and rural areas, and spanning the entire range of socio-economic status. Extremely small elementary schools were not included in the sample; in fact, only schools with ten or more faculty members were considered candidates for the sample. Schools that participated came from 12 of the 21 counties in the state. Thirty-nine percent were located in the six counties having the least number of school districts; 37% of the schools came from the six counties with the largest number of districts; and 24% of the schools were gathered from the remaining nine middle counties.

In most cases, data were collected by a researcher at a regular faculty meeting.[20] Two-thirds of the faculty selected at random responded to the revised OCDQ and the remaining one-third completed an instrument of similar length, which was not part of the OCDQ development. In total, 1071 teachers and principals in 70 schools participated in the study.

Factor Analysis

School mean scores were calculated for each item, and the item-correlation matrix from the 70 schools was factor analyzed. Six factors with eigenvalues from 12.9 to 1.62 explaining 67.2% of the variance were retained. The six-factor solution, after varimax rotation, is summarized and presented in Table 2.2.

The results strongly supported the factor structure uncovered in the pilot study. The items loaded on the appropriate subtest and generally loaded highly on only one factor. Moreover, the reliability scores for subtests for the new data set remained high; the alpha coefficients were as follows: Directive (.89), Supportive (.95), Restrictive (.80), Disengaged (.75), Collegial (.90), and Intimate (.86). Finally, a comparison was made between the factor loadings on the six factors for the pilot data and for the final data set. The results are remarkably similar; in fact, the factor structures for both data sets are virtually identical.[21] Sample items for each subtest are provided in Figure 2.1.

The stability of the factor structure also supports the construct validity of the six dimensions of climate. Factor analyses enable the researcher to study the constitutive meanings of constructs and thus, their construct validity.[22] In the present study, six hypothetical entities, dimensions of school climate, were constructed. The relations among the items consistently held up as theoretically expected; that is, the items (variables) measuring each dimension were systematically related to each other as expected in the test of the OCDQ-RE.

Table 2.2.   Six-Factor Varimax Solution for the 42 Items of the OCDQ-RE

Subtest	Item	I	II	III	IV	V	VI
	1	.82	-.07	.15	-.20	-.60	-.24
	2	.82	-.11	.24	.08	-.13	.13
	3	.82	-.28	.17	.09	-.17	.06
Supportive	4	.90	.10	.09	.09	.02	.02
	5	.83	-.10	.07	.15	-.23	-.08
	6	.74	.08	.27	-.10	.00	-.15
	7	.73	.02	.06	.03	-.16	-.13
	8	.78	-.04	.26	.13	-.07	.10
	9	.84	-.07	.09	.13	-.07	-.22
	10	-.45	.68	-.18	-.19	.20	-.06
	11	-.09	.53	-.05	.08	.06	-.02
	12	-.38	.66	-.06	.08	-.02	.17
Directive	13	-.13	.64	-.19	-.11	.05	-.18
	14	.18	.84	-.12	-.05	.12	-.13
	15	.04	.67	.03	.05	.02	.21
	16	-.58	.61	-.24	-.15	.11	-.14
	17	-.08	.81	-.01	-.16	.05	.23
	18	.04	.87	.01	-.09	.10	.02
	19	.13	.11	.62	.01	.19	.00
	20	.03	-.25	.70	-.18	-.17	-.10
	21	.00	-.02	.64	.27	-.38	-.10
Collegial	22	.32	-.08	.64	.51	-.18	-.04
	23	.20	-.17	.76	.17	.03	-.24
	24	.26	-.10	.73	.32	-.09	.00
	25	.28	-.05	.70	.32	-.25	.00
	26	.41	-.06	.46	.39	-.25	-.29
	27	.20	.17	.08	.62	-.04	.15
	28	.04	-.08	.08	.80	-.08	-.13
Intimate	29	-.04	-.22	.34	.58	.11	.21
	30	-.14	-.20	.21	.52	-.24	-.12
	31	.00	-.15	-.01	.82	-.03	-.21
	32	.05	.04	.10	.83	-.03	-.11
	33	.29	.00	.14	.72	-.16	-.29
	34	-.19	.39	.05	.10	.65	.26
Restrictive	35	-.17	-.02	-.06	.17	.78	.12
	36	-.34	.20	-.47	.19	.52	.06
	37	-.15	.28	-.26	-.14	.54	.09
	38	-.38	.19	.03	-.09	.58	.54
	39	-.39	.04	.11	-.30	.24	.49
Disengaged	40	.04	.11	-.42	.13	.03	.57
	41	-.10	.11	-.46	.14	-.24	.52
	42	-.07	.15	-.31	-.33	.18	.62

SUPPORTIVE PRINCIPAL BEHAVIOR

The principal uses constructive criticism.
The principal complements teachers.
The principal listens to and accepts teachers' suggestions.

DIRECTIVE PRINCIPAL BEHAVIOR

The principal monitors everything teachers do.
The principal rules with an iron fist.
The principal checks lesson plans.

RESTRICTIVE PRINCIPAL BEHAVIOR

Teachers are burdened with busywork.
Routine duties interfere with the job of teaching.
Teachers have too many committee requirements.

COLLEGIAL TEACHER BEHAVIOR

Teachers help and support each other.
Teachers respect the professional competence of their colleagues.
Teachers accomplish their work with vim, vigor, and pleasure.

INITMATE TEACHER BEHAVIOR

Teachers socialize with each other.
Teachers' closest friends are other faculty members at this school.
Teachers have parties for each other.

DISENGAGED TEACHER BEHAVIOR

Faculty meetings are useless.
There is a minority group of teachers who always oppose the majority.
Teachers ramble when they talk at faculty meetings.

Figure 2.1.   Selected Items for Each of Subscale of the OCDQ-RE.

Each of the dimensions of organizational climate represents a property of the organization; therefore, each climate aspect was examined further to confirm that the measures represented organizational rather than individual phenomena. Such an analysis seemed particularly important since each subtest score was derived by averaging responses at the item level for each school. Thus, each measure was studied by analysis of variance to determine whether the schools or the individuals in them constituted the primary source of variation. Table 2.3 presents the results of the analysis for collegial teacher behavior. The results showed that the between-school variance was far greater than the within-school variance. The ratio of 4.29 was statistically significant beyond the .001 level. The results confirmed the expectation that collegial behavior can be conceived as an organizational property rather than an individual one. Analyses of each of the six

Table 2.3. Analysis of Variance on Collegial Behavior

F Source Ratio	D.F.	Sum of Squares	Mean Squares	
Between groups	69	51.7379	.7498	4.2968*
Within groups	444	77.4807	.1745	
Total	513	129.2186		

*$p < .001$

measures produced similar results; between-school variance was significantly greater than within-school variance on all dimensions.

Second-Order Factor Analysis

Thus far, the analysis of data has been concerned with identifying the
items that formed the basic dimensions of climate. Now, attention turned
to an analysis of the six dimensions or subtest scores. To compute each
school's scores on the six factors, item scores were summed within each
subtest, and subtest scores were computed for each school.

Halpin and Croft proposed the following useful standards for con-
structing a battery of subtests: First, each subtest should measure a relatively different type of behavior, second, the battery as a whole should tap
enough common behavior to permit researchers to find a pattern of more
general factors; and third, the general factors extracted should not be dis-
cordant with those already reported in the literature.[23] Since an examination of the subtest correlations in Table 2.4 revealed six variables that
were relatively independent, a second-order factor analysis was performed on the subtest correlation matrix searching for a few underlying
general factors.

A two-factor solution with a varimax rotation is given for the six subtests in Table 2.5.[24] Disengaged, intimate, and collegial teacher behavior
load strongly only on Factor I, while restrictive, directive, and supportive
principal behavior load strongly only on Factor II. Factor I is characterized by teachers' interactions that are meaningful and tolerant (low disengagement); that are friendly, close, and supportive (high intimacy); and
that are enthusiastic, accepting, and mutually respectful (high collegial
relations). In general, this factor denotes an openness and functional flexibility in teacher relationships. Accordingly, it was labeled "openness in
faculty relations."

Factor II is defined by principal behavior that is characterized by the
assignment of meaningless routines and burdensome duties to teachers

Table 2.4. **Correlations Between Subtest Scores of the OCDQ-RE**

	Sup	*Dir*	*Res*	*Col*	*Int*	*Dis*
Supportive	1.00					
Directive	-.30	1.00				
Restrictive	-.49	.44	1.00			
Collegial	.44	-.29	-.48	1.00		
Intimate	.28	-.20	-.28	.48	-.63	
Disengaged	-.31	.16	.41	-.63	-.45	1.00

Table 2.5. **Two-Factor Varimax Solution for the Six Dimensions of the OCDQ-RE**

Subtest	*I* *Openness*	*II* *Closedness*
Supportive	.33	-.65
Directive	.01	.83
Restrictive	-.34	.75
Collegial	.77	-.36
Intimate	.76	-.11
Disengaged	-.84	.15

(high restrictiveness); by rigid, close, and constant control over teachers (high directiveness); and by a lack of concern and openness for teachers and their ideas (low supportiveness). In general, the second factor depicts a functional rigidity and closedness in the principal's leadership behavior, hence, Factor II was named "closedness in principal behavior." Thus, both second-order factors are viewed along an open-closed continuum.

Summary and Discussion

The Organizational Climate Description Questionnaire has been revised. The result, the OCDQ-RE, is a 42-item instrument with six subtests that describe the behavior of elementary teachers and principals. The revised instrument measures three aspects of principal leadership— supportive, directive, and restrictive behavior. The aloofness dimension of the original OCDQ was eliminated; it simply could not be identified in the present study. Moreover, trust and consideration merged to form one dimension of leadership, supportive behavior. Finally, hindrance was reformulated and measured as restrictive principal behavior. These three dimensions of principal behavior provided the components of a second-order construct, closedness; that is, principal-teacher interactions were conceived along a continuum from open to closed. Open principal behavior is reflected in genuine relationships with teachers where the principal is interested in creating an environment that supports teachers' efforts, encourages their participation and contributions, and frees teachers from routine busywork so they can concentrate on teaching tasks as contrasted with closed principal behavior that is rigid, close, controlling, and nonsupportive.

The OCDQ-RE also measures three dimensions of teacher interactions— collegial, intimate, and disengaged behavior. The esprit subtest of the original OCDQ was replaced by the concept of collegial teacher behavior. Collegial teachers not only take pleasure in their work and pride in their school, but they work together and respect each other as competent professionals. Halpin and Croft's original intimacy and disengagement dimensions remain basic subtests of the OCDQ-RE, but both subtests were refined to improve their internal consistency. Like the three subtests of principal behavior, the three characteristics of teacher behavior provided the elements of a second-order construct, openness; that is, teacher-teacher interactions were conceived along an open to closed continuum. Open teacher behavior is characterized by sincere, positive, and supportive relationships among the teaching staff; interactions are close, friendly, and warm; and teachers have mutual respect for each other and are tolerant of divergent ideas and behaviors. Closed teacher behavior, in contrast, is marked by meaninglessness, divisiveness, apathy, isolation, nonsupport, and intolerance.

The conceptual underpinnings of the OCDQ-RE seem consistent and clear. Unlike the original OCDQ, the revised instrument has two general factors—one a measure of openness of teacher interactions and the other a measure of openness of teacher-principal relations. Moreover, these two openness factors are orthogonal. That is, it is quite possible to have open faculty interactions and closed principal ones or vice versa. Thus, theoretically, four contrasting types of school climate are possible. First, both general factors of the school can be open producing a congruence of openness between the principal's and teachers' behavior. Second, both factors can be closed producing a congruence of closedness. There are also two incongruent patterns. The principal may be open with the faculty, but teachers may be closed with each other, or the principal may be closed with teachers, while the teachers are open with each other. The four possibilities are depicted in Figure 2.2 and form the bases of four school climate types.

When both teacher and principal behaviors are open, the school climate has been termed an *Open Climate*; and when both sets of behaviors are closed, the school climate has been termed a *Closed Climate*. Since openness in teacher interactions can be independent of openness in principal behavior, it should not be surprising for some schools to have principals who are supportive, concerned, flexible, facilitating, and non-controlling (i.e., open) and yet the faculty is divisive, intolerant, apathetic, and uncommitted (i.e., closed). Such a climate is one where the faculty is simply unwilling to accept a principal who seems likely to be effective. At worst, the faculty will immobilize and sabotage the principal's leadership attempts; at best, the faculty simply ignores such a principal. Despite the leadership of the principal, the faculty is uncommitted to the task at hand in what has been termed a *Disengaged Climate*, Finally, some schools have rigid principals who attempt to be restrictive and controlling (i.e., closed), yet the faculty is cohesive, committed, and supportive of and open to each other. The faculty simply ignores the restrictive and controlling behavior of an ineffective principal as they engage themselves in the process of teaching; hence, the climate is termed an *Engaged Climate*.

The properties of the six subtests of the OCDQ-RE are impressive. All of thee scales have high reliability coefficients, much higher than those in the original OCDQ. The subtests are reasonably pure; that is, the items load high on one subtest and relatively low on the others when subjected to factor analysis. Moreover, the stability of the factor structures in two separate samples provided evidence of the construct validity of each subtest. Finally, the unit of analysis in all phases of the present investigation was appropriately the school, not the individual. The six aspects of school climate are organizational properties, not individual ones.

One limitation of the OCDQ, however, was not overcome. The OCDQ-RE, like the original OCDQ, is restricted to social interactions among professional personnel. Initially, an attempt was made to include items in the new instrument that measured student-oriented behaviors, but unfortunately, the items did not fit into the conceptual perspective that eventually emerged. This is not to say that student variables are not related to the climate of schools. The authors believe that they are. For example, those items that described student-student and teacher-student interactions were correlated with items in virtually all the subtests; and that was the rub. They did not form any independent factor; hence, the items were eliminated from the instrument. It is interesting, however, to note that an academic press index (alpha = .71) was later constructed that tapped the extent to which the school stressed academic performance, an orderly and serious learning environment, and high, but achievable student goals. Not surprisingly, both openness in teacher-teacher relations ($r = .52, p <$

PRINCIPAL BEHAVIOR

		OPEN	CLOSED
T E A C H E R	O P E N	OPEN CLIMATE	ENGAGED CLIMATE
B E H A V I O R	C L O S E D	DISENGAGED CLIMATE	CLOSED CLIMATE

Figure 2.2. Typology of school climates.

.01) and openness in teacher-principal relations ($r = .43$, $p < .01$) were significantly correlated with the academic press.

It seems reasonable to predict that openness in both teacher and principal behavior may be related *to* positive student outcomes, but it also seems likely that open principal behavior will not lead to effective student performance unless it is coupled with open teacher behavior. The key to successful principal leadership is to influence teachers. But open, supportive, non-directive, and non-controlling principal behavior does not guarantee an impact on the teachers' behavior. In fact, a more structured and controlling pattern of principal behavior may be necessary with some faculties (e.g., Disengaged Climate) until the faculty matures and becomes more engaged. Under what conditions does openness in leader behavior produce openness in teacher behavior? The findings of this study suggest that no *one* leadership pattern, not even an open one, is successful in all settings. Rather a contingency approach to leadership is once again reaffirmed.

The typology of school climates developed here seems to have both theoretical and practical significance. It provides a framework for study of leadership, motivation, and school effectiveness, as well as a perspective for developing change strategies and school improvement programs. The instrument itself, however, should be subjected to further analysis to insure that its factor structure is stable over a wide range of populations and samples.

CONCLUSION

The OCDQ-RE is a parsimonious and reliable research tool ready for further testing. This contemporary set of measures maps the domain of organizational climate for elementary schools. The six subtests of the OCDQ-RE can be grouped into two categories: characteristics of the principal's leadership and characteristics of faculty behavior. Each set of behaviors is defined by a more general construct of openness, but openness in principal behavior was independent of openness in faculty behavior, hence, two continuums of openness underlie the climate of elementary schools and provide the basis for a four-celled typology of organizational climate: Open, Closed, Engaged, and Disengaged Climates.

NOTES

1. We would like to thank our colleague, Professor Joel Caldwell, for his helpful critiques of several earlier drafts of this article.
2. A. W. Halpin and D. B. Croft. *Thee Organizational Climate of Schools* (Washington, D.C.: U.S. Office of Education, Research Project, Contact *SAE 543-8629, August 1962).
3. A. W. Halpin, *Theory and Research in Administration* (New York: Macmillan, 1966). p. 131.
4. G. H. Litwin and R. A. Stringer, Jr., *Motivation and Organizational Climate* (Boston: Harvard Business School, 1968), pp. 1-44.
5. Ibid., p. 46.
6. A. E.Hayes, "A Reappraisal of the Halpin-Croft Model of the Organizational Climate of Schools," (Paper presented at the Annul Meeting of the American Educational Research Association, New Orleans, 1973).
7. Halpin and Croft, Organizational donate, p. 66.
8. P. Silver, *Educational Administration; Theoretical Perspectives on Practice and Research* (New York: Harper & Row, 1983), pp. 188-190.
9. Ibid., pp. 191-192.
10. For example, see R. J. Brown, *Organizational Climate of Elementary Schools*, Research Monograph No. 2 (Minneapolis: Educational Research and Development Council, 1965); and Hayes, "A Reappraisal."
11. J. H. M. Andrews, "School Organizational Climate: Some Validity Studies," *Canadian Educational Research Digest, S* (1965), p. 333.
12. K. A. Sirotnik, "Psychometric Implications of the Unit of Analysis Problem Examples From the Measurement of Organizational Climate)," *Journal of Educational Measurement*, 17 (Winter 1980), p. 256.
13. For a comprehensive analysis of the unit of analysis dilemma faced by researchers studying group properties such as climate, see Sirotnik (Ibid.: 245-284). See also T. R. Knapp, "The Unit and the Context of Analysis for

Research in Educational Administration," *Educational Administration Quarterly,* 18,1 (Winter 1982): 1-13; and T. R. Knapp, "The Unit Analysis Problem in Applications of Simple Correlational Analysis in Educational Research," *Journal of Educational Statistics 2 (Fall* 1977): 171-186.

14. D. J. Willower, T. L. Eidell, and W. K. Hoy, *The School and Pupil Control Ideology* (University Park: Perm State University Studies Monograph No. 24,1967); and S. Bossert et al., "The Instructional Management Role of the Principal," *Educational Administration Quarterly.* 18, 3 (Summer 1982): 34-64.

15. Hayes, "A Reappraisal."

16. Sirotnik," Psychometric Implications."

17. Halpin and Croft, *Organizational Climate,* pp. 181-183.

18. R. J. Rummel, *Applied Factor Analysis* (Evanston: Northwestern University Press, 1970), p. 220. See also R. B. Cattell, *Factor Analysis: An Introduction and Manual for the Psychologist and Social Scientist* (New York: Harper & Row, 1952).

19. Hayes, "A Reappraisal."

20. In several schools a faculty member collected the anonymous questionnaires.

21. A specific comparison of the two factor structures from the two samples is available upon request.

22. F. N. Kerlinger, *Foundations of Behavioral Research,* 2nd ed. (New York: Holt, Rinehart & Winston, 1976), pp. 685-686.

23. Halpin, "A Reappraisal" p. 156.

24. The eigenvalue of the third factor was less than one. Before rotation, the eigenvalues for the two factors were 2.92 and 1.01.

Wayne K. Hoy *is Professor and Associate Dean far Academic Affairs in the Graduate School of Education, Rutgers University.*

Sharon I. R. Clover *is the Assistant Superintendent at Parsippany-Troy Hills Township in* Parsippany, New Jersey.

PART III

ON ORGANIZATIONAL HEALTH

CHAPTER 3

ORGANIZATIONAL HEALTH

The Concept and its Measure

Wayne K. Hoy and John A. Feldman

The concept of the organizational health of schools was defined and conceptualized using the theoretical foundations of Talcott Parsons. Then an
Organizational Health Inventory (OHI) was developed to measure the
health of schools along seven dimensions of student-teacher, teacher-
teacher, and teacher-administrator interactions. The instrument was
devised and refined in a pilot study. Then the 44-item OHI was tested, and
the stability of the factor structure and the validity of the construct were
evaluated with a sample of 78 secondary schools. The results were positive;
stability of the factor structure, and the reliability and validity of the subtests
were supported. Prototypes of very healthy and unhealthy schools were
developed, and the practical and theoretical consequences of the research
were discussed.

The notion of the health of an organization is not new. Two decades ago,
Matthew Miles (1969) proposed a model for the analysis of the organiza-

Reprinted by permission from the *Journal of Research and Development in Education*, Vol.
20, pp. 30-38. Copyright © 1987. All rights reserved.

tional health of schools. He defined a healthy organization as one that "...
not only survives in its environment, but continues to cope adequately
over the long haul, and continuously develops and extends its surviving
and coping abilities" (Miles, 1969, p. 378). Miles goes on to postulate 10
properties of healthy organizations, which are concerned with the task,
maintenance, and growth needs of organizations. These needs are summarized in Table 3.1. The characteristics of organizational health are cast
within the framework of the organization as an open social system; they
are a fairly durable set of system properties.

Miles (1969) argues that a steadily ineffective organization would not
be healthy. Although short-run operations on any given day may be effective or ineffective, health implies a summation of effective short-run coping. Miles' framework is a heuristic one for thinking about schools, but
unfortunately, attempts to operationalize the model have been less than
successful. Kimpston and Sonnabend (1978), for example, tried to
develop an instrument that measured each of the 10 dimensions of health
described by Miles. They were unsuccessful. Their instrument was a very
short form, with questionable psychometric properties, which measured
only 6 of Miles' 10 factors of school health.

SCHOOL HEALTH

School health is used to conceptualize the organizational climate of
schools, a concept that has been identified as an important variable
related to school effectiveness (Brookover et al., 1978). The purpose of
this paper is to define school health, identify its dimensions, and
describe the procedures and results used to develop its measure. After
an initial attempt to operationalize Miles' 10 dimensions of organizational health was unsuccessful, attention turned to the theoretical analyses of Parsons et al. (1953) and Etzioni (1975) as well as the empirical
literature on school effectiveness for a scheme to conceptualize and
measure school health.

All social systems must solve four basic problems if they are to survive,
grow, and develop. Parsons et al. (1953) refers to these as the imperative
functions of adaptation, goal attainment, integration, and latency. In
other words, schools must solve:

1.   the problem of acquiring sufficient resources and accommodating
     to their environments,
2.   the problem of setting and implementing goals,
3.   the problem of maintaining solidarity within the school, and

4.   the problem of creating and preserving a unique value system.

In brief, healthy schools effectively meet the instrumental needs of adaptation and goal achievement as well as the expressive needs of social and normative integration. Parsons (1967) also notes that schools have three distinct levels of control over these needs—the technical, managerial, and institutional.

The technical level of the school is concerned with the teaching-learning process. The primary function of the school is to produce educated students. Moreover, teachers and supervisors have primary responsibility for solving the problems associated with effective learning and teaching.

The managerial level controls the internal administrative function of the organization. Principals are the prime administrative officers of the school. They allocate resources and coordinate the work effort. They must find ways to develop teacher loyalty, trust, and commitment as well as to motivate teachers and to influence their own superiors.

The institutional level connects the school with its environment. Schools need legitimacy and support in the community. Both administrators and teachers need backing if they are to perform their respective functions in a harmonious fashion without undue pressure from individuals and groups from outside the school.

Table 3.1.   Characteristics of Healthy Organizations

TASK NEEDS
1. Goal Focus-goals are clear to members, acceptable, and achievable.
2. Communication Adequacy-distortion-free communication produces good and prompt sensing of internal strain.
3. Optimal Power Equalization-the distribution of influence is relatively equitable; subordinates can exert influence upward, and they perceive their boss can do likewise.

MAINTENANCE NEEDS
4. Resource Utilization-personnel is used effectively—neither overloaded nor idling. The fit between needs and demands is good.
5. Cohesiveness-members are attracted to the organization, want to stay, and are influenced by it.
6. Morale-the organization displays a general sense of well being and group satisfaction.

GROWTH AND DEVELOPMENT NEEDS
7. Innovativeness-the organization invents new procedures and moves toward new goals.
8. Autonomy-the organization does not respond passively to the environment; it demonstrates some independence from the environment.
9. Adaptation-the organization has the ability to bring about corrective changes to grow and develop.
10. Problem-Solving Adequacy-problems are solved with minimal energy and the problem-solving mechanism is not weakened.

This broad Parsonian perspective provided the theoretical underpinnings for defining and operationalizing school health. Specifically, a healthy school is one in which the technical, managerial, and institutional levels are in harmony; and the school is meeting both its instrumental and expressive needs as it successfully copes with disruptive external forces and directs its energies toward its mission.

ORGANIZATIONAL HEALTH INVENTORY

The development of the measure of organizational health, the Organizational Health Inventory (OHI), will be described in some detail. First, the items were generated and evaluated. Next, a pilot study was performed to refine and reduce the number of items and to identify the factor structure of the OHI. Finally, the final version of the OHI was tested and the stability of its factor structure and its validity were evaluated.

Item Generation

Items were written to tap the technical, managerial, and institutional levels of organization. At the technical level, attention focused on such issues as morale, cohesiveness, trust, enthusiasm, support, academic press, order, and achievement. The managerial level was described in terms of the behavior of the principal. In particular, interest centered on task- and achievement-oriented behavior, collegial and supportive behavior, ability to influence superiors, and ability to provide adequate resources for teachers. Institutional concern focused on the school's ability to cope successfully with outside forces.

Some items were written by the researchers independently and others jointly, but no item was included unless there was consensus on the following criteria:

1. the statement reflected a property of the school;
2. the statement was clear and concise;
3. the statement had content validity; and
4. the statement had discriminatory potential.

In all 95 items were selected for testing in the pilot.

All items were simple descriptive statements. Respondents were asked to indicate the extent to which each statement characterized their school along a four-point Likert scale as rarely occurs, sometimes occurs, often occurs, or very frequently occurs. Examples of items include the following: "Teachers are protected from unreasonable community and parental demands;" "The principal gets what he or she asks for from superiors;" "The principal looks out for the professional welfare of faculty members;" "The principal lets faculty members know what is expected of them;" "Extra materials are available if requested," "There is a feeling of trust and confidence among the staff;" and "The school sets high standards for academic performance."

Pilot Study

This preliminary version of the OHI contained 95 potential, mostly untested items. Thus, an initial task was to reduce the number of items as the factor structure of the instrument was explored. A sample of 72 secondary schools was identified, which included urban, suburban, and rural schools and represented a diverse subset of secondary schools. Data were collected from a random sample of teachers in each school. Since the unit of analysis was the school, however, the individual data were aggregated at the school level for each item, and the exploratory procedures were performed to reduce the number of items and determine the factor structure of the instrument.

Three criteria were used to refine the OHI. First, the criterion of simple structure was employed in all factor analyses; only items that loaded high on one factor and weak on all the others were retained. Next, in addition to their mathematical contribution to the factor (high factor loadings), items were evaluated for conceptual clarity and fit; that is, items were retained only if they were clearly related to the concept being measured. Finally, items were eliminated if they reduced substantially the internal consistency of the subtest as measured by Cronbach's coefficient alpha. School mean scores were generated for each item and the item-correlation matrices were factored.

Using the criteria specified above, a series of exploratory factor analyses of the pilot data was performed and the number of items was reduced by one half. Ultimately, a seven-factor solution was selected as the best solution. Forty-four items remained in the refined OHI, which defined seven dimensions of school health (see Table 3.2).

Dimensions of Organizational Health

The pilot study led to the specification and measure of seven dimensions of organizational health—institutional integrity, principal influence,

Table 3.2.   Sample Items From the OHI

INSTITUTIONAL INTEGRITY
— Teachers are protected from unreasonable community and parental demands.
— The school is vulnerable to outside pressures.*
— A few vocal parents can change school policy.*

PRINCIPAL INFLUENCE
— The principal gets what he or she wants from superiors.
— The principal is able to work well with the superintendent
— The principal is impeded by superiors.*

CONSIDERATION
— The principal is friendly and approachable.
— The principal treats all faculty members as his or her equal.
— The principal puts suggestions made by the faculty into operation.

INITIATING STRUCTURE
— The principal makes his or her attitudes clear to the school.
— The principal lets faculty members know what is expected of them.
— The principal maintains definite standards of performance.

RESOURCE SUPPORT
— Extra materials are available if requested.
— Teachers have access to needed instructional materials.
— Supplementary materials are available for classroom use,

MORALE
— Teachers in this school like each other.
— Teachers accomplish their jobs with enthusiasm.
— Teachers in this school are cool and aloof from each other.*

ACADEMIC EMPHASIS
— The school sets high standards for academic performance.
— Students respect others who get good grades.
— The learning environment is orderly and serious.
*Reverse score.

consideration, initiating structure, resource support, morale, and academic emphasis. These critical aspects of organizational life meet the instrumental and expressive needs of the school social system, and they fall into Parsons' three levels of responsibility and control within the school.

Institutional integrity is the school's ability to cope with its environment to maintain the educational integrity of its programs. Teachers are protected from unreasonable community and parental demands.

Principal influence is the principal's ability to influence the actions of superiors. Being able to persuade superiors to get additional consideration and to not be impeded by the hierarchy are important aspects of school administration.

Consideration is principal behavior that is friendly, supportive, open, and collegial; it represents a genuine concern on the part of the principal for the welfare of the teachers.

Initiating structure is principal behavior that is both task- and achievement-oriented. Work expectations, standards of performance, and procedures are clearly articulated by the principal.

Resource support refers to a school where adequate classroom supplies and instructional materials are available and extra material is readily supplied if requested.

Morale is a collective sense of friendliness, openness, enthusiasm, and trust among faculty members. Teachers like each other, like their jobs, and help each other; and they are proud of their school and feel a sense of accomplishment in their jobs.

Academic emphasis is the extent to which the school is driven by a quest for academic excellence. High but achievable academic goals are set for students; the learning environment is orderly and serious; teachers believe in their students' ability to achieve; and students work hard and respect those who do well academically.

A Test of the New Instrument (OHI)

Having completed the data reduction and conceptualization of the OHI in the pilot study, the 44-item instrument was ready to be tested with a new data set in order to demonstrate the stability of the factor structure, to confirm the validity and stability of the subtests, and to explore the second-order factor structure.

Sample

Seventy-eight secondary schools in New Jersey agreed to participate in the study. A separate, new random sample of at least five teachers was drawn from each of the 72 pilot schools and from 6 additional schools that were added to the sample. Although the school sample was not a random one, it was a diverse one representing a broad range of districts and spanning the entire range of socio-economic status. Schools that participated came from 17 to 21 counties in the state. If any group of schools was under-represented it was the urban one; only 7.5% of the schools came from urban districts.

Typically, data were collected by a researcher at a regular faculty meeting, but in a few schools, a faculty member collected the anonymous questionnaires. The faculty selected at random responded to the OHI and the others responded to a battery of instruments, which was not part of the instrument development. In total, 1131 teachers and principals in 78 secondary schools participated in the study.

Factor Analysis

School mean scores were calculated for each item, and the item-correlation matrix from the 78 schools was factor analyzed. Seven factors with eigenvalues from 14.28 to 1.35 explaining 74% of the variance were retained. The seven-factor solution, after varimax rotation, is summarized and presented in Table 3.3.

The results strongly support the factor structure discovered in the pilot study. The items loaded on the appropriate subtest, and the reliability scores for each subtest were relatively high; the alpha coefficients were as follows: institutional integrity (.91), principal influence (.87), consideration (.90), initiating structure (.89), resource allocation (.95), morale (.92), and academic influence (.93). A comparison of the pattern of factor loadings with those of the pilot study were remarkably similar; in fact, the factor structures for both data sets were virtually identical.

The stability of the factor structure of the OHI also supports the construct validity of the seven dimensions of school health. Factor analysis enables the researcher to study the constitutive meanings of constructs and thus, their construct validity (Kerlinger, (1976). In the present investigation, seven hypothetical entities, dimensions of organizational health, were constructed. The relations among the items consistently held up as theoretically expected; that is, the items (variables) measuring each dimension were systematically related as predicted.

Second-Order Factor Analysis

Next, attention turned to the underlying structure of the seven dimensions of the OHI. Is there a more general set of factors that defines the health of a school? To answer this question, subtest scores for each school were computed and a correlation matrix among the subtests was derived. Since the correlations were moderate (see Table 3.4), it was appropriate to perform a second-order factor analysis on the subtest correlations.

One strong general factor emerged that accounted for 45 of the variance; in fact, this factor was the only one to meet Kaiser's (1960) criterion of an eigenvalue greater than one. Likewise, a scree test (Rummel, 1970) yielded the same second-order factor. All of the dimensions of organizational health had strong factor loadings on this general factor: institutional integrity (.563), principal influence (.747), consideration (.633), initiating structure (.722), resource support (.607), morale (.707), and aca-

Table 3.3.   Seven-Factor Varimax Solution for the 44 Items of the OHI

Subtest	Item	I	II	III	IV	V	VI	VII
	1	.66	.28	.09	.30	.20	.12	.05
	2	.83	.16	.07	.17	.09	.25	.13
	3	.82	.16	-.07	.06	.12	-.09	.16
Academic Emphasis	4	.75	-.07	.09	.14	.17	-.01	.05
	5	.84	.11	.11	.16	.14	.12	.02
	6	.74	.12	-.14	.01	.08	.32	.02
	7	.85	.17	-.01	.06	.03	.11	.11
	8	.68	.29	-.22	.32	.07	.32	.10
	9	.08	.52	-.27	.26	.42	.23	.17
	10	.15	.69	-.26	-.02	.42	.09	.19
	11	.07	.80	-.03	.20	.02	.07	-.07
	12	.20	.87	-.12	-.01	-.02	.03	.03
Morale	13	.46	.61	-.11	.16	.09	.07	.17
	14	-.12	-.79	.17	.09	.07	-.08	.07
	15	.26	.66	-.28	.29	.24	.15	-.09
	16	.16	.83	-.16	.09	.03	-.02	.07
	17	.04	-.72	.15	-.08	-.10	-.04	.04
	18	.20	.21	-.70	.23	.12	.23	.20
	19	-.12	-.10	.85	.06	-.01	-.05	-.19
Institutional Integrity	20	.00	-.14	.81	-.12	-.11	-.17	.06
	21	.28	-.19	.78	-.04	.01	.09	.04
	22	.09	-.24	.70	.02	.22	.11	-.20
	23	-.10	-.09	.75	-.08	-.18	-.24	.07
	24	-.04	-.18	.82	-.01	-.15	-.13	-.16
	25	.07	.04	-.06	.86	.20	.01	.15
Resource Support	26	.23	.14	-.05	.88	.04	.11	.04
	27	.17	.17	.08	.88	.05	.12	.14
	28	.16	.15	.03	.88	.02	-.01	.10
	29	.17	.21	-.21	.84	.10	.04	.19
	30	.08	.07	-.14	-.01	.91	-.02	.03
	31	.08	.22	-.18	-.07	.80	-.06	.10
Consideration	32	.10	.07	-.08	.12	.77	.25	.04
	33	.27	.04	-.11	.27	.74	.18	-.01
	34	.25	.13	-.09	.18	.74	.30	-.02
	35	-.02	.13	-.07	.03	-.10	.79	-.02
Initiating Structure	36	.27	.10	-.17	.03	.24	.78	.16
	37	.23	.13	-.17	.01	.23	.80	.18
	38	.43	.09	-.23	-.02	.28	.64	.26
	39	.10	-.06	.04	.15	.15	.70	.25
	40	.31	.02	-.30	.21	.04	.27	.66

Table continues on next page.

**Table 3.3.   Seven-Factor Varimax Solution for
the 44 Items of the OHI Continued**

Subtest	Item	I	II	III	IV	V	VI	VII
Principal Influence	41	.30	.11	-.16	.36	.16	.42	.55
	42	.26	.12	-.19	.23	.12	.50	.55
	43	.10	-.02	-.04	.10	.09	.13	.83
	44	-.01	-.07	.22	-.39	.08	-.15	-.60

demic emphasis (.703). The factor identified schools that were relatively strong on all seven dimensions. Accordingly, the factor was called school health. An index of the health of a school can be determined by simply adding the standard scores on the seven subtests; the higher the score, the healthier the school dynamics. It is possible to sketch a description of the prototype for each of the poles of the continuum—that is, for very healthy and unhealthy schools.

Healthy School

A healthy school is protected from unreasonable community and parental pressures. The board successfully resists all narrow efforts of vested interest groups to influence policy (high institutional integrity). The principal of a healthy school is a dynamic leader, integrating both task-oriented and relations-oriented leader behavior. Such behavior is supportive of teachers and yet provides high standards for performance (high consideration and initiating structure). Moreover, the principal has influence with her or his superiors, which is demonstrated by the ability to get what is needed for the effective operation of the school (high influence). Teachers in a healthy school are committed to teaching and learning. They set high but achievable goals for students, maintain high standards of performance, and promote a serious and orderly learning environment. Furthermore, students work hard on their school work, are

Table 3.4.   Correlations Among the Seven Subtexts of the OHI

Subtest	AE	M	II	RA	C	IS	PI
Academic Emphasis (AE)	1.00						
Morale (M)	.45	1.00					
Institutional Integrity (II)	.11	.46	1.00				
Resource Support (RA)	.40	.37	.18	1.00			
Consideration (C)	.36	.42	.32	.25	1.00		
Initiating Structure (IS)	.47	.34	.31	.23	.39	1.00	
Principal Influence (PI)	.44	.30	.37	.47	.28	.58	1.00

highly motivated and respect other students who achieve academically (high academic emphasis). Classroom supplies, instructional materials, and supplementary materials are always available (high resource support). Finally, in healthy schools, teachers like each other, trust each other, are enthusiastic about their work, and identify positively with the school. They are proud of their school (high morale).

Unhealthy School

The unhealthy school is vulnerable to destructive outside forces. Teachers and administrators are bombarded by unreasonable parental demands, and the school is buffeted by the whims of the public (low institutional integrity). The school is without an effective principal. The principal provides little direction or structure (low initiating structure), exhibits little encouragement and support for teachers (low consideration), and has little clout with superiors (low influence). Teachers feel neither good about their colleagues nor their jobs. They act aloof, suspicious, and defensive (low morale). Instructional materials, supplies, and supplementary materials are not available when needed (low resource support). Finally, there is little press for academic excellence. Neither teachers nor students take academic life seriously; in fact, academically-oriented students are ridiculed by their peers and viewed by their teachers as threats (low academic emphasis).

Summary and Discussion

The Organizational Health Inventory OHI, is a new 44-item instrument that maps the organizational health of secondary schools along seven dimensions. At the technical level, the faculty morale and the academic press of the school are seen as critical ingredients of good school health. At the managerial level, the leadership and support of the principal in terms of considerations, initiating structure, influence with superiors, and resource support are key elements. Finally, healthy schools have institutional integrity; they cope with disruptive external forces and direct their energies toward their educational missions.

The seven subtests developed to measure these critical dimensions of school life are highly reliable scales that have reasonable construct validity. Moreover, the seven aspects of health fit together to form a general indicator of health. Simply by summing the standard scores of all the subtests a health index is computed—the higher the score, the healthier the organizational dynamics in the school. In the present study, the schools did array themselves along a continuum from healthy to unhealthy. A copy of the OHI is available at www.coe.ohio-state.edu/whoy.

The OHI has considerable research as well as practical potential. Our preliminary research findings are encouraging and provide further support for the validity of the instrument. As one would expect, the healthier the organizational dynamics of a school, the greater the degree of faculty trust in the principal, trust in colleagues, and trust in the organization itself. Indeed, trust has been identified as a basic characteristic of effective organizational cultures (Ouchi, 1981; Peters & Waterman, 1982). As Ouchi (1981) notes, "productivity and trust go hand in hand." Healthy school climates also have more open organizational climates; teacher interactions with each other and the principal are open and authentic. Likewise, trust and authenticity go together (Hoy & Kupersmith, 1984). In brief, healthy school climates are characterized by many of the same attributes stressed in the effective school literature: an orderly and serious environment, visible rewards for academic achievement, influential principals who blend their behavior to fit the situation, openness in behavior, and a cohesive work unit based upon mutual trust.

Much remains to be demonstrated by subsequent study, but we suspect that a school's health is likely to be related to less student alienation, lower dropout rates, greater student and faculty motivation, and higher student achievement. Clearly, their are a host of other important school variables that are likely related to school health, including absenteeism, the number of merit scholars, and the comprehensiveness of extra curricular and athletic programs. Healthy schools should also have principals who are more resourceful, confident, secure, and change-oriented than those found in less healthy schools. Moreover, principals of healthy schools should have more dedicated, loyal, and satisfied teachers who are resourceful, secure, and innovative. Healthy organizational climates also provide atmospheres conducive to the improvement of instruction through cooperative and diagnostic supervision; in fact, healthy organizational dynamics are necessary conditions for an effective program of supervision (Hoy & Forsyth, 1986).

Implications

What implications does this research have for students of administration? The OHI is a parsimonious and reliable research tool ready for further testing. The instrument is one of the few measures that has been designed for use in secondary schools. The health inventory provides measures of seven important attributes of student-teacher, teacher-teacher, teacher-principal, and principal-superior relationships, which fit together in a way that yields a global index of the state of organizational health.

The instrument and its conceptual underpinnings provide a framework for the study of leadership, motivation, decision making, structure, communication, and school effectiveness, as well as perspective for evaluating school improvement programs. Although the OHI was developed for use in secondary schools, the framework seems sound for work in elementary schools, but it should be tested and evaluated in a variety of other samples, including elementary ones. Clearly the OHI is a heuristic instrument for both researchers and practitioners. Recent research as provided similar health (OHI) measures for middle and high schools (see www.coe.ohio-state.edu/whoy/).

What implications does this research have for administrators? For those administrators who are seriously interested in change and improving school effectiveness, the OHI offers a simple diagnostic tool. Improvement of instruction, curriculum development, and critical inquiry of the teaching-learning process are likely only in schools with a healthy organizational climate. Enlightened and secure administrators who are willing to systematically evaluate the state of health of their schools can facilitate healthy climates. The OHI can be used to provide base-line data on seven critical dimensions as well as a general index of organizational health. Principals and superintendents can not only determine the health of their schools, they can compare their own perceptions of the working atmosphere with the perceptions of their teachers. Discrepancies in such perceptions are often at the heart of many school problems.

The position taken here is that improvement in the state of organizational health should the prime target of change efforts in schools because only when the systems' dynamics are open and healthy will more specific change strategies be effective. Successful innovation requires self-study, security, and commitment of the professional staff of a school. Change is a systemic process that requires not only modifying individual attitudes but also developing new relationships among members in group settings. Focusing efforts on groups and relationships, and increasing the flow of information about the organization to participants often alters existing norms that regulate interpersonal transactions in groups.

We agree with Miles (1969) that the state of organizational health will likely tell us more than anything else about the probable success of most change efforts:

> Economy of effort would suggest that we should look at the state of an organization's health as such, and try to improve it—in preference to struggling

with a series of more or less inspired short-run change efforts as ends-in-themselves. (p. 388).

This is not to say that schools must be in a perfect state of organizational health before any meaningful change can occur, but rather that the basic innovation should be one of organizational development itself.

REFERENCES

Brookover, W. B., Switzer, J. H., Schneider, J. M., Brady, C. H., Flood, P K., & Wisenbaker, J. M. (1978). Elementary school climate and school achievement. *American Education Research Journal, 75*, 301-318.

Etzioni, E. (1975). *A comparative analysis of complex organizations* (2nd ed.). New York: Free Press.

Hoy, W. K., & Forsyth, P. A. (1986). *Effective supervision: Theory into practice.* New York: Random House.

Hoy, W. K., & Kupersmith, W (1984). Principal authenticity and faculty trust: Key elements in organizational behavior. *Planning and Changing, 15*, 80-88.

Kaiser, H. F. (1960). The application of electronic computers to factor analysis. *Educational and Psychological Measurement, 20*, 141-151.

Kerlinger, F. N. (1976). *Foundations of behavioral research* (2nd ed.). New York: Holt, Rhineholt & Winston.

Kimpston, R. D., & Sonnabend, L. C. (1978). Public schools: The interrelationships between organizational health and innovativeness and between organizational health and staff characteristics. *Urban Education, 10*, 27-48.

Miles M. B. (1969). Planned change and organizational health: Figure and ground. In F. D. Carver & T. J. Sergiovanni (Eds.), *Organizations and human behavior: Focus on schools* (pp. 375-391). New York: McGraw Hill.

Ouchi, W. (1981). *Theory Z.* Reading, MA: Addison-Wesley.

Parsons, T., Bales, R. F., & Shils, E. A. (1953). *Working papers in the theory of action.* New York: Free Press.

Parsons, T. (1967). Some ingredients of a general theory of organization. In A. W. Halpin (Eds.), *Administrative theory in education.* New York: Macmillan.

Peters, T. J., & Waterman, R. H. (1982). *In search of excellence.* New York: Harper & Row.

Rummel, R. J. (1970). *Applied factor analysis.* Evanston: Northwestern University Press.

CHAPTER 4

ACADEMIC EMPHASIS OF URBAN ELEMENTARY SCHOOLS AND STUDENT ACHIEVEMENT IN READING AND MATHEMATICS

A Multilevel Analysis

Roger D. Goddard, Scott R. Sweetland, and Wayne K. Hoy

This research examines the importance of a school climate characterized by high levels of academic emphasis. Effective schools research is reviewed to develop a conceptual model undergirding the measurement of academic emphasis. In addition, social cognitive theory is employed as a theoretical framework explaining the development and effect of academic emphasis on student achievement. With the use of hierarchical linear modeling, the authors show that academic emphasis is important to differences among urban elementary schools in student mathematics and reading achieve-

Reprinted by permission from the *Educational Administration Quarterly*, Vol. 36, pp. 683-703. Copyright © 2000. All rights reserved.

Essential Ideas for the Reform of American Schools, pp. 63–83
Copyright © 2007 by Information Age Publishing
All rights of reproduction in any form reserved.

ment. The relationship between current academic achievement and students' prior achievement and demographic characteristics is also modeled in this study.

A major challenge for those who study schools and school administration is to learn how organizations contribute to students' academic success. Whereas teachers are directly responsible for teaching and learning in the classroom, school administrators are charged with the development of organizations that facilitate teaching and learning (Murphy & Louis, 1999; Rowan, 1995). As states move toward models that embrace systems of student assessment and minimum standards for advancement, public awareness of differences between schools in student achievement is heightening. Indeed, as educators look for means to improve school performance in response to this policy development, the time is ripe for consideration of school organizational features that facilitate teaching and learning and improve student achievement.

One school property that educational administration researchers have found to be consistently related to student achievement is the academic emphasis of a school—a general perspective of the importance of academics in a school held by administrators, teachers, and students themselves. We are interested in the academic emphasis of schools as a facet of school climate for several reasons. First, research suggests that successful schools maintain a focus on academics. For example, Smylie and his colleagues (Smylie, Lazarus, & Brownlee-Conyers, 1996) found that schools that improved instruction through participative decision making maintained a core focus on student learning. In addition, Beck and Murphy (1996) refer to such a school focus as the "learning imperative." We agree that school effectiveness requires a focus on student learning and a rigorous instructional program. Thus, we believe that academic emphasis, or the extent to which a drive for academic excellence contributes to the behavioral and environmental press of the school, is important to school success. In response, the purpose of our research is to examine the theoretical underpinnings of academic emphasis and to provide evidence that explains how academic emphasis is related to differences between schools in student achievement.

Although the construct of academic emphasis has received some research attention, our study is intended to advance knowledge in several ways. For example, Hoy and his colleagues (Hoy & Sabo, 1998; Hoy, Tarter, & Kottkamp, 1991) have demonstrated the impact of academic emphasis on student achievement in high schools and middle schools, but they have not analyzed the relationship in elementary schools. This study will add to that line of inquiry by examining the relationship between the academic emphasis of urban elementary schools and student achievement in reading and mathematics. Furthermore, it is important to observe that Hoy and colleagues' analyses of academic emphasis in middle and high schools omitted measures of students' prior academic achievement. Hence, little is known about the relative effects on student achievement of academic emphasis and prior student achievement. We address this issue by modeling the effects of both prior student achievement and academic emphasis in an analysis of differences among schools in student achievement. To accomplish the goal of examining both student and school attributes, we employ hierarchical linear modeling (HLM). As we discuss more fully later, HLM permits the simultaneous analysis of student-and school-level variables while avoiding the traditional problems of aggregation bias and heterogeneity of regression that may compromise the results of studies in which student characteristics are aggregated to the school level (Bryk & Raudenbush, 1992).

To summarize, our work here is intended to investigate how school effectiveness may be enhanced by a school climate characterized by high levels of academic emphasis. To this end, we provide a detailed consideration of the theoretical foundations of the academic emphasis construct and then test its effect on differences among urban schools in elementary student achievement.

CONCEPTUAL FRAMEWORK

Early research on effective schools suggested a number of characteristics that were important to facilitate student achievement. For example, Edmonds (1979) and Stedman (1987) suggested a five-factor effective schools formula, which included strong principal leadership, high teacher expectations for student achievement, an emphasis on basic skills, an orderly environment, and frequent, systematic evaluations of students. Others have suggested similar lists (Astuto & Clark 1985; Bossert, 1988; Purkey & Smith, 1983). Most early school effectiveness research that linked school properties to student achievement came from comparisons of "effective" and "ineffective" schools. After a small number of effective and ineffective schools were identified, researchers cataloged school characteristics, attempting to find consistent differences between the two groups of schools; most were post hoc comparisons.

The comparative approach has since been extended to include larger numbers of schools in mixed-model school effectiveness studies that simultaneously take advantage of quantitative methods and qualitative case analysis (Stringfield & Herman, 1996; Stringfield & Teddlie, 1991; Teddlie & Stringfield, 1993). Stringfield and Teddlie (1991) found that effective schools were focused on academic plans, academic tasks, and a state of academic push. Teddlie and Stringfield's (1993) study was supported by a quantitative reanalysis using HLM. Stringfield and Herman (1996), however, argued that the development of effective schools theories is sorely needed. Moreover, studies that make a priori predictions about what organizational attributes are related to student achievement and then test and confirm them are rare. This is unfortunate, as Raudenbush (1994) critically asserted in debate with Aitkin and Zuzovsky (1994) about the need for a priori specifications in multilevel school effectiveness studies. The current study develops an a priori theoretical argument and then tests a hypothesis about the climate variable of academic emphasis in a sample of urban elementary schools located in the Midwest.

Academic Emphasis of Schools

One construct that captures a number of the aspects highlighted by early effective schools research is the academic emphasis of schools. Edmonds (1979) was the first of the effective schools researchers to offer evidence that school factors other than socioeconomic status (SES) were related student achievement. He found five school properties that enhanced and were predictive of student achievement: strong principal leadership, high expectations for students, emphasis on basic skills, an orderly school environment, and frequent evaluation of students. Other school effectiveness researchers (Astuto & Clark, 1985; Bossert, 1988; Purkey & Smith, 1983; Stedman, 1987; Wimpelberg, Teddlie, & Stringfield, 1989) subsequently supported Edmonds's findings. Later, Hoy and his colleagues captured many of these effectiveness characteristics in a construct they labeled *academic emphasis*, a single factor of school climate identified in three separate factor analytic studies (Hoy & Sabo, 1998; Hoy & Tarter, 1997; Hoy, Tarter, & Kottkamp, 1991).

Academic emphasis is the extent to which the school is driven by a quest for academic excellence (Hoy & Sabo, 1998; Hoy & Tarter, 1997; Hoy, Tarter, & Kottkamp, 1991). In such schools, teachers set high but achievable goals, they believe in the capability of their students to achieve, the school environment is orderly and serious, and students, as well as teachers and principals, pursue and respect academic success. (The scale and the specific items that measure academic emphasis are presented in the appendix.) Academic emphasis is a way of conceptualizing the normative and behavioral environment of a school, and we postulate that it influences both personal and organizational behavior. For example, teachers' beliefs about students' capabilities to successfully learn and the importance of academic performance constitute norms that influence the actions and achievements of schools.

At the collective level, views about academic emphasis are social perceptions that support teaching and learning in the school. As with other facets of school climate, perceptions about academic emphasis begin with group members who consider various sources of information to form their perceptions of the group's focus on academic matters. Thus, the assessment of academic emphasis necessarily involves the combination of individual-level perceptual measures. Typically, researchers interested in collective measures have addressed the nested nature of group perceptual data by aggregating individual perceptions to the group level (e.g., Bandura, 1993, 1997; Goddard, Hoy, & Woolfolk Hoy, in press; Sampson, Raudenbush, & Earls, 1997). In relation to the growth of standardized testing and school accountability, we argue that our collective measure of academic emphasis is a particularly potent way of characterizing how schools differ so markedly in their "feel."

We conceive of academic emphasis as an important feature of school climate that fosters academic success. It is important that Putnam (1993) refers to such beneficial social features as moral resources—ones that are strengthened rather than depleted through their use. The potential for academic emphasis to grow rather than deplete through use is also indicated by the cyclical nature implied by the reciprocal causality involved in social perception (Bandura, 1997). That is, if academic emphasis enhances organizational performance, reciprocal causality suggests that resulting performance improvements may in turn strengthen academic emphasis in the school. Thus, to the extent that a strong academic emphasis is positively associated with student achievement, there is important reason to lead schools in a direction that will systematically develop more emphasis on academics. Such efforts may indeed be rewarded with continuous growth not only in academic emphasis but also in student achievement. Individual perceptions of academic emphasis are inextricably bound to a collective sense of academic emphasis, and this collective sense serves as a value-added component of the school climate (Teddlie & Reynolds, 2000) that reinforces academic matters for individuals and in turn is itself reinforced.

Organizational Agency, Organizational Learning, and Social Cognition

We derive our notion of a school's academic emphasis from the perceptions of individual teachers about the collective. The aggregation of individual perceptions to the collective level in the analysis of organizations occurs frequently (see, e.g, Bandura, 1993, 1997; Bryk & Raudenbush, 1992). Indeed, the extension of individual capabilities to the organizational level is a key aspect of organizational analysis. For example, we assume that organizations learn (Cohen & Sproull, 1996; Senge, 1990), and we base our notion of organizational learning on the cognitive activity of individual learning; that is, organizations use learning processes akin to those of individuals (Cook & Yanon, 1996). Hence, we consider the emphasis organizational members place on students' academic success as a key characteristic shaping the climate of schools. The greater the academic emphasis of a school, the more capable is the school of facilitating student learning. Framed this way, a school's academic emphasis addresses an important end of school organization. It is important to note that schools alone do not act; it is the members of schools who act. At the same time, however, it is collective activity that makes possible outcomes individuals alone could not accomplish (Bolman & Deal, 1997). Thus, we consider individual perception as key to our understanding of collective influence.

An essential question about collective perceptions that influence school effectiveness involves how they are formed and changed. To this end, Goddard, Hoy, and Woolfolk Hoy (in press) applied social cognitive theory to explain the development of a faculty's collective perception of efficacy. We take a similar approach, holding that social cognitive theory provides a useful framework that explains both individual and collective behavior. We theorize that the mechanisms of social cognitive theory, as with collective efficacy (Bandura, 1997), act to develop both individual and school-level perceptions of academic emphasis. Accordingly, we review the key assumptions of social cognitive theory to provide a framework that explains how a school's academic emphasis develops and may be enhanced.

A fundamental element of social cognitive theory is human agency (Bandura, 1997, pp. 164-168). Extended to the school level, the parallel concept is organizational agency. Because *agency* refers to the intentional pursuit of a course of action, we may begin to understand school behavior as agentive when we consider that schools act purposefully in pursuit of their educational goals. For example, one school may be working to improve the postsecondary attendance rate of its graduates while another works to increase the rate and quality of community involvement in school activities. If we consider that such differences are purposeful, we may view them as evidence of organizational agency. The purposive actions schools take as they strive to meet their goals thus reflect organizational intentionality or agency. Of course, organizational agency results from the agentive actions of individuals. The principle of organizational agency suggests that schools may choose, through a number of individual and collective efforts, to value student achievement, and likewise they may act purposefully to strengthen member perceptions of the import of student academic success.

Given that individuals and schools exercise choice when they choose the endeavors they will pursue, an important question concerns how perceptions of academic emphasis might be developed to influence those choices positively. That is, How can schools be led in a direction that builds academic emphasis? To answer this question, we turn to the other assumptions of social cognitive theory. In addition to agency, social cognitive theory addresses the influence of knowledge, self-reflection, and self-regulation (Maddux, 1995). Furthermore, mastery experiences, vicarious experiences, social persuasion, and affective states convey information that influences teacher perceptions about school academic emphasis (Bandura, 1993, 1997; Pajares, 1997). For example, a school that responds to an increasing drop-out rate by implementing a program for at-risk students that was effective in another school is engaged in a self-regulatory process that is informed by the vicarious learning of its members and, perhaps, the social persuasion of leaders of the successful program. Such examples demonstrate that social cognitive theory helps to explain how changes in social perception influence the courses of action organizations choose to pursue. Collective perceptions about academic emphasis that shape a school's normative environment, therefore, may be developed through experiences (mastery, vicarious, etc.) that convey the importance of valuing academics. Such experiences influence perceptions and provide feedback that aids school members in the regulation of their actions.

Theoretical Rationale and Hypothesis

Given that academic emphasis shapes the normative and behavioral environment of a school, understanding how it influences student achievement requires that we consider the influence of social norms on the behavior of group members. Because social cognitive theory specifies that teachers' perceptions of self-and group capability influence their actions, it follows that these actions will be judged by the group relative to group norms such as those set by strong beliefs about the importance of academic pursuits in schools (Bandura, 1986, 1997). According to Coleman (1985, 1987), norms develop to permit group members some control over the actions of others when those actions have consequences for the group. When a school member's actions are incongruent with the shared beliefs of the group, group members will sanction the member's actions. For example, in a school with a high degree of academic emphasis, it is reasonable to expect some form of redirection for a student who ridicules a peer's academic success. Indeed, Coleman argues that the severity of the social sanctions delivered to those who break norms will be proportional in magnitude to the effect of norm breaking on the collective. Thus, if most members of the school are highly committed to academic performance, the normative and behavioral environment will pressure school members to persist in their educational efforts so that students excel. Moreover, the press to perform will be accompanied by social sanctions for those who do not. The greater the academic emphasis of the school, the stronger the normative press for students to achieve academically. Certainly, there will be exceptions, but generally, if such norms of academic success exist, their influence will too.

Academic emphasis, which helps shape the normative environment of a school, will have a strong influence over teacher behavior and, consequently, student achievement. Such emphasis creates a school climate in which both teachers and students are more likely to persist in their academic efforts. Students are motivated by the respect they get from other students and teachers when they succeed, and teachers accept responsibility for student achievement and do not let temporary setbacks unduly frustrate them. Thus, a strong climate of academic emphasis not only enhances individual student and teacher performance but also influences the pattern of shared beliefs held by organizational members. For example, given the influence of group norms, a teacher with a moderate set of academic expectations and beliefs may tend to exert greater effort on joining a school with a high press for academic success. Such behavioral changes reflect the normative effect of a school's climate on its individual members. Again, although there will be exceptions, we believe that organizational dynamics will tend to press members to perform when there are high expectations for academic success.

There are extant empirical studies that support the theoretical assumptions we have just sketched. First, academic emphasis has been positively related to student achievement in middle schools (Hoy & Sabo, 1998) and high schools (Hoy & Tarter, 1997; Hoy, Tarter, & Kottkamp, 1991). Both high schools and middle schools with orderly and serious learning environments, teachers who set high but achievable goals, and students who work hard and respect others who excel academically have higher levels of student achievement, even controlling for socioeconomic level. Using a similar theoretical rationale for linking collective efficacy to student achievement, Goddard, Hoy, and Woolfolk Hoy (in press) demonstrated that collective teacher efficacy was positively associated with differences between schools in student-level achievement. A few other studies have also linked academic emphasis and student achievement in high schools (Bryk, Lee, & Holland, 1993; Lee, 1995; Shouse & Brinson, 1995).

Academic emphasis is conceived as an emergent characteristic of school climate, one that gains its meaning from collective perceptions and is, therefore, not reducible to the individual measures from which group level aggregates are constructed. Yet, academic emphasis, along with many organizational features such as school size and collective efficacy, is experienced individually by each organizational member. From a methodological perspective, this is a multilevel phenomenon. And, although the occasional teacher may resist school influence, we believe this influence generally has a far-reaching effect. In other words, we believe that group members are aware of the norms and expectations associated with their job performance. For instance, although an individual teacher may be very academically oriented, that teacher might perform differently depending on whether the school climate is such that others place high value on academic success. In other words, the effect of an individual teacher's academic emphasis may be either attenuated or enhanced depending on the collective or school-level academic emphasis. Thus, the academic emphasis of a school may positively affect numerous teacher behaviors that tend to increase student achievement.

Accordingly, we hypothesize that the academic emphasis of a school is positively associated with differences between schools in student-level achievement in both reading and mathematics.

METHOD

To test the general hypothesis of this study, data from urban elementary schools were collected and analyzed. The sample, data collection procedures, measures, and method are described below.

Sample

The population for this study was the elementary schools within one large urban Midwestern school district. An urban district was selected to hold constant differences in academic emphasis that might occur between urban and nonurban districts. In addition, because this study focused on schools in just one district, there was no possibility for uncontrolled between-district effects. Furthermore, limiting this study to elementary schools controls for the organizational structure (i.e., elementary, middle, secondary) of the schools, thus allowing for a constant approach to the measurement of academic emphasis in elementary schools. A power analysis (Cohen, 1977; Keppel, 1991) was performed to determine the size of the sample, which yielded a minimum sample size of 44. Thus, the principals of each of the 50 randomly selected schools were solicited via telephone by a researcher to schedule the administration of surveys to school faculty. One principal declined to participate. Of the 49 participating schools, there were 4 in which too few faculty members were available to complete the questionnaires. Our decision rule for including a school in the data analysis was that it had at least 5 respondents (Halpin, 1959); thus, these 4 schools were dropped from the sample, leaving 45 schools, or 90% of the 50 schools randomly selected for inclusion. Because this number exceeded the minimally acceptable sample size for this study, the sample was deemed sufficient to test the hypothesis. A total of 442 teachers completed surveys, and more than 99% of the forms returned were usable.

Data Collection

Data were obtained from both teachers and students in the 45 elementary schools. Student achievement and demographic data for all schools in the sample were obtained from the central administrative office of the district. Teacher surveys, on the other hand, were researcher administered. To the greatest extent possible, the researcher controlled the location, time, and conditions under which these surveys were administered to teachers. Surveys were administered to faculty groups in the afternoon during regularly scheduled meetings. During these meetings, other data beyond the scope of the present study were also collected from teachers. For this reason, only half of the teachers in the room, selected at random, received a survey containing questions assessing academic emphasis. Elementary school faculties in the selected district ranged in size from approximately 10 to 40. Thus, for any given school, faculty perceptions were represented by the responses of half the faculty (approximately 5 to 20 teachers, depending on school size).

Student Measures

The school district provided us with data on student achievement in mathematics and reading at two time points. As dependent variables, we used the mathematics and reading achievement scores of students who were in the fourth grade at the time our surveys were administered. Prior achievement was represented by the mathematics and reading achievement scores for the same students obtained 1 year earlier. Hence, our dependent measures were the mathematics and reading achievement scores of fourth grade students, and as a statistical control, we used scores in the same subjects obtained from the same students 1 year earlier, when they were in the third grade. Thus, our study incorporated two waves of student achievement data.

The dependent variables for this study were measured by student scores in mathematics and reading (equal interval, item response theory scaled) on a state-mandated achievement test administered to fourth grade students in our sampled schools approximately 1 month after the faculties were surveyed. It is important that, although the state achievement tests did include traditional multiple-choice items, their authenticity (Newmann, 1996) was considerably enhanced by the inclusion of items requiring students to compose short and extended responses. Reliability and validity evidence for the state-mandated achievement tests was obtained from the state department of education. Cronbach's alpha suggested that our dependent measures were acceptably reliable (.88 for mathematics and .86 for reading). In addition, test documentation suggested strong content validity resulting from the extensive involvement of expert educators in the development and selection of test items. Furthermore, the school district from which our sample was drawn followed the state model curriculum for which the mandatory assessments were developed.

Students' prior achievement was measured by the seventh edition of the Metropolitan Achievement Test (MAT7), administered to slightly more than 86% of the sampled students who were enrolled in the district 1 year before teacher surveys were administered. In a review of MAT7, Finley (1995) reported that Kruder-Richardson-20, Kruder-Richardson-21, and alternate-forms correlations indicate adequate reliability for the test. In addition, separate reviews indicate that although adequate concurrent and construct validity evidence exists for the MAT, its content validity is specific to a school district's own curricular objectives (Hambleton, 1995; Nitko, 1994; Rogers, 1994). Conversation with the director of testing and assessment for the district sampled indicated that the district administers the MAT7 to elementary school students specifically because of the congruence between the content of the MAT7 and the district's curriculum. For these reasons, the MAT7 was judged to be a valid and reliable measure of prior achievement for students in the district sampled.

Data on gender, race and ethnicity, free and reduced-price lunch status (a proxy for SES), and school size were also provided by the school district. Our final sample included 2,429 students and 444 teachers in the 45 sampled elementary schools from one large urban school district.

Academic Emphasis Measure

Teacher responses to the academic emphasis instrument were aggregated to the school level because it was a measure of an organizational property. The 8-item scale is part of the Organizational Health Inventory for Elementary Schools (Hoy & Tarter, 1997; Hoy, Tarter, & Kottkamp, 1991), which has been expanded to improve its reliability. In the current sample, the alpha coefficient of reliability for the scale was .92. Moreover, there is evidence of strong construct and predictive validity for scores on the academic emphasis scale in three separate factor analytic studies (Hoy & Sabo, 1998; Hoy & Tarter, 1997; Hoy, Tarter, & Kottkamp, 1991). In all studies, the items theoretically constructed to measure academic emphasis form an independent factor of academic emphasis; furthermore, the measure consistently has high reliability and is an integral part of the broader construct of organizational health. Teachers were asked to respond along a 6-point Likert scale ranging from *strongly disagree* to *strongly agree*. Examples of the items include "Students respect others who get good grades," "Students try hard to improve on previous work," "The learning environment is orderly and serious," and "Teachers in this school believe that their students have the ability to achieve academically." All items are found in the Appendix.

It is important to note that some of our scale items required teachers to make informed judgments about student behavior. A limit of this approach to measurement is that we did not ask students these questions directly. Yet, although we recognize this as a limit, we believe that schools are characterized by a certain feel, as well as daily events that inform teachers' judgments about the academic emphasis of the schools (Halpin, 1966; Hoy, Tarter, & Kottkamp, 1991).

Data Analysis

We were interested in how a school's academic emphasis effects the achievement of students within the school. However, because student achievement occurs at the individual level, whereas the academic emphasis facet of school climate exists at the school level, we encountered an enduring methodological dilemma in school effects research; namely, the unit of analysis problem (Teddlie & Reynolds, 2000). Typically, researchers have addressed the unit of analysis problem by aggregating individual-level variables to the group level. Although aggregation has the advantage of enabling an ordinary least squares regression analysis (OLS), this analytic strategy is often compromised by aggregation bias, misestimated standard errors, and heterogeneity of regression among groups (Bryk & Raudenbush, 1992).

To avoid these problems and to allow for precise estimation of the effect of academic emphasis on between-school differences in student achievement, we addressed the unit of analysis problem through the use of HLM. HLM is a multilevel modeling technique intended for nested data (e.g., students nested in schools). Unlike OLS regression, HLM accounts for the interdependence of individual measures collected within the same organizational unit (e.g., students within the same school). A distinct advantage of HLM is that it partitions the variance in a dependent variable into its within-and between-school components. Thus, we were able to model the effect of academic emphasis on only the portion of variance in student achievement occurring between schools while modeling the influence of students' prior academic achievement, race and ethnicity, gender, and SES without aggregating these variables to the school level.

RESULTS

The first step in our HLM analysis was to examine the results of fully unconditional models for mathematics and reading to determine the extent of variation between schools in student achievement. Without significant variation, the main hypothesis of this study would have no potential for support. In addition to determining the degree to which student achievement varies between schools, these estimates also provide a basis for later assessing the proportion of variance explained by academic emphasis in the full multilevel model. As expected, the proportion of variance between schools in students' mathematics (25.2%) and reading (19.1%) achievement was statistically significant, so we proceeded with multilevel tests of our research hypothesis.

Our within-school model included measures of students' prior mathematics and reading achievement and demographic variables for race and ethnicity, gender, and SES. We created dummy variables for the demographic variables and analyzed the MAT7 prior achievement scores in the normal curve equivalent metric. SES was operationalized as a dichotomous variable reflecting a student's free or reduced-price lunch status. Students receiving a free or reduced-price lunch were coded 1, and all others were coded 0 for the SES variable. Similarly, African American students were coded 1 for the African American variable, and female students were coded 1 for the female variable. Descriptive statistics for the student-and school-level variables are reported in Table 4.1, and correlations among student variables are reported in Table 4.2.

The main question motivating our research pertained to differences between schools in student achievement identified in the unconditional

Table 4.1.   Descriptive Statistics

	M	SD	Minimum	Maximum
Student Level (n = 2,429)				
Mathematics[a]	199.91	23.63	106.00	323.00
Reading[a]	207.77	18.09	137.00	279.00
MAT7 mathematics[b]	44.35	22.48	1.00	99.00
MAT7 reading[b]	45.66	20.80	1.00	99.00
Socioeconomic status	0.67	0.47	0.00	1.00
African American	0.57	0.49	0.00	1.00
Female	0.48	0.50	0.00	1.00
School Level (n = 45)				
Academic emphasis	3.79	0.53	2.85	4.93
School size	399.91	109.28	229.00	710.00
Faculty size	21.24	5.51	13.00	37.00
Faculty members surveyed	9.71	2.60	5.00	15.00
Proportion of students with disadvantaged socioeconomic status	0.62	0.21	0.10	0.89
Proportion of African American students	0.56	0.28	0.08	1.00
Proportion of female students	0.46	0.08	0.27	0.64

Note: MAT7 = Metropolitan Achievement Test, seventh edition.
a. Dependent variables in the multilevel analysis.
b. Prior achievement control variables in the multilevel analysis.

analysis. Thus, our multilevel hypothesis frames between-school variability in the Level 1 intercepts (B_{j0}s) as the school-level dependent variable. The intercepts for each of the 45 sampled schools are the operational measure of between-school differences in student achievement. Our within-school variables are group mean centered; thus, their respective beta coefficients represent the average deviation from the school mean associated with a 1-unit increase for each variable. Hence, the intercept for school *j* reflects the mean achievement score for students in school *j*. At the school level, these intercepts are the dependent variables, and academic emphasis is the independent variable. Our full model allows us to predict between-school variability in mathematics and reading achievement with academic emphasis.

The corresponding structural equations employed in the full HLM for both mathematics and reading achievement are given below.

Table 4.2.   Correlations Among Student-Level Variables

Variable	Mathemat-ics	Read-ing	MAT7 Mathemat-ics	MAT7 Read-ing	Socioeco-nomic Status	African Ameri-can	Female
Mathematics	1.0						
Reading	.73**	1.0					
MAT7 mathematics	.73**	.67**	1.0				
MAT7 reading	.63**	.69**	.72**	1.0			
Socio-economic status	−.31**	−.29**	−.33**	−.34**	1.0		
African American	−.31**	−.22**	−.29**	−.26**	.27**	1.0	
Female	.01	.10**	−.05*	.07**	.01	.01	1.0

Note: MAT7 = Metropolitan Achievement Test, seventh edition.
* Significant at the .05 level. ** Significant at the .01 level.

Level 1: $Y_{ij} = B_{j0} + B_{jMAT7\ Mathematics}\ X_{ijMAT7\ Mathematics} + B_{jMAT7\ Reading}\ X_{ijMAT7\ Reading}$
$+ B_{jSocioeconomic\ status}\ X_{ijSocioeconomic\ status} + B_{jAfrican\ Am.}\ X_{ijAfrican\ Am.}$
$+ B_{jFemale}\ X_{ijFemale} + r_{ij}$

Level 2: $B_{j0} = \gamma_{00} + \gamma_{0Academic\ Emphasis}\ W_{jAcademic\ Emphasis} + \mu_{0j}$

Table 4.3.   Academic Emphasis as a Predictor of Between-School Variability in Mathematics Achievement

Coefficient		Standard Error	T Ratio	p Value
Intercept	200.94	1.33	150.90	< .001
Academic emphasis[a]	16.53	2.22	7.45	< .001
MAT7 mathematics[b]	0.46	0.03	16.24	< .001
MAT7 reading[b]	0.18	0.02	8.11	< .001
Socioeconomic status[b]	−2.89	0.85	−3.41	< .001
African American[b]	−5.37	0.86	−6.24	< .001
Female[b]	0.31	0.57	0.54	ns

Note: MAT7 = Metropolitan Achievement Test, seventh edition.
a. Academic emphasis was modeled as the school-level independent variable.
b. These variables were included as student-level predictors.

**Table 4.4.   Academic Emphasis as a Predictor of
Between-School Variability in Reading Achievement**

Coefficient		Standard Error	T Ratio	p Value
Intercept	51.91	0.71	72.65	< .001
Academic emphasis[a]	11.39	1.70	6.71	< .001
MAT7 mathematics[b]	0.23	0.02	12.87	< .001
MAT7 reading[b]	0.29	0.02	16.51	< .001
Socioeconomic status[b]	−2.41	0.70	−3.43	< .001
African American[b]	−3.51	0.61	−5.77	< .001
Female[b]	2.11	0.46	4.54	< .001

Note: MAT7 = Metropolitan Achievement Test, seventh edition.
a. Academic emphasis was modeled as the school-level independent variable.
b. These variables were included as student-level predictors.

The coefficient $\gamma_{0Academic\ Emphasis}$ thus provides an estimate of the relation between academic emphasis and differences between schools in student achievement. The results of the hypothesis tests for mathematics and reading achievement are shown in Tables 4.3 and 4.4.

As predicted, academic emphasis was a significant predictor of between-school differences in student achievement in both mathematics and reading. In our full model, academic emphasis explained 47.4% and 50.4% of the between-school variability in mathematics and reading, respectively. This suggests that academic emphasis explained about half of the variance between schools in student achievement. With the effects of academic emphasis controlled, the remaining between-school variance was statistically nonzero. Hence, in addition to academic emphasis, other school characteristics may also be systematically associated with between-school differences in student achievement.

DISCUSSION

The results of our research support the theoretical foundations of the study. The operational measure of academic emphasis was a collective one that emphasized a school atmosphere in which teachers set reasonable goals and believe in their students' abilities to achieve, students work hard to succeed and respect those who do the same, and the learning environment is orderly and serious. It should be no surprise that such a school climate has a positive impact on student achievement in both mathematics and reading. Norms that reinforce such student and teacher behaviors are functional for teaching and learning because they encourage both teachers and students to plan more, persist longer, accept responsibility for achievement, and overcome temporary setbacks. A school climate with a strong academic emphasis influences not only individual teacher and student behavior but also reinforces a pattern of collective beliefs that are good for the school.

As predicted, academic emphasis is positively associated with the differences in student achievement that occur between schools. The results confirm those of other studies on different student and school populations. Our multilevel analysis demonstrates that a 1-unit increase in a school's academic emphasis score is associated with a 16.53-point average gain in student mathematics achievement and an 11.39-point average gain in reading achievement. In other words, an increase in academic emphasis of 1 standard deviation is associated with a gain of nearly 40% of a standard deviation in student achievement in mathematics and more than one third of a standard deviation in reading achievement. The magnitude of the effect of academic emphasis in comparison with that of the within-school student-level variables is also noteworthy. For example, although students receiving a free or reduced-price lunch scored on average 2.41 points below their schools' mean reading scores (see Table 4.4), the school means averaged 11.39 points higher where there was a strong academic emphasis.

The results offer evidence that the academic emphasis of the school is systematically related to student achievement in urban elementary schools. Indeed, given that more than two thirds of the students in our sample received a free or reduced-price lunch and that nearly 60% were African American, our results suggest that schools with strong academic emphases positively effect achievement for poor and minority students. Moreover, the findings confirm that perceptions about the importance of student academic success and the effort required to attain it do matter to differences between schools in student achievement. Similar results have been found in middle and high schools (Hoy & Sabo, 1998; Hoy, Tarter, & Kottkamp, 1991; Shouse, 1998).

Finally, the results are consistent with the theoretical argument that academic emphasis in schools is a unified construct that promotes student achievement. Our theoretical analysis suggests that the assumptions of social cognitive theory (e.g., agency, vicarious learning, and self-regulation) can be applied at the organizational level to explain the influence of a climate of academic emphasis on between-school differences in student achievement. In a school with a high level of academic emphasis, school members are more likely to act purposefully to enhance student learning. Such purposeful actions result from organizational agency that influences a school to intentionally pursue its goals. Those interested in reforming schools for improved student achievement would do well to note that mastery and vicarious experiences, social persuasion, and affective states influence the activities that individuals choose to pursue (Bandura, 1997; Pajares, 1997). To the extent that the value of academic emphasis can be communicated to school members through such experiences, enhanced student learning is a likely outcome, at least in the urban elementary schools we sampled.

CONCLUSIONS

We have identified a collective measure of school climate, a variable that seems to influence student achievement in urban elementary schools. Academic emphasis refers to a climate in which teachers believe that their students have the capabilities to achieve, students work hard to succeed and are respected for their academic accomplishments, and the learning atmosphere is orderly and serious. Student achievement in mathematics and reading is facilitated by such a climate.

This research is a modest beginning for theorists, researchers, and school administrators who are interested in developing organizational climates in urban areas that enhance student achievement in reading and mathematics. Our findings confirm that in the urban elementary schools we sampled, academic emphasis matters to student achievement. The results provide initial support for Bandura's (1986, 1997) suggestion that the concepts and assumptions of social cognitive theory can be extended to organizations and are useful in examining school outcomes. We hasten to add that further testing of social cognitive theory in the schools is needed, but the current results are encouraging because our hypothesis was driven by this theory. We hope that the identification of the theoretical underpinnings of academic emphasis illuminates pathways to future research on school improvement and that school leaders can apply these ideas to make their schools better places for student to learn.

Appendix: Academic Emphasis Scale Items

Students respect others who get good grades
Students try hard to improve on previous work
The learning environment is orderly and serious
Teachers in this school believe that their students have the ability to achieve academically
Students neglect to complete homework[a]
Students make provisions to acquire extra help from teachers
Students seek extra work so they can get good grades
Academically oriented students are not ridiculed by their peers

Note: Each item coded from 1 *(strongly disagree)* to 6 *(strongly agree)*.
a. Item reversed.

REFERENCES

Aitkin, M., & Zuzovsky, R. (1994). A response to Raudenbush's comment. *School Effectiveness and School Improvement, 5*, 199-201.

Astuto, T. A., & Clark, D. L. (1985). Strength of organizational coupling in the instructionally effective school. *Urban Education, 19*, 331-356.

Bandura, A. (1986). *Social foundations of thought and action: A social cognitive theory.* Englewood Cliffs, NJ: Prentice Hall.

Bandura, A. (1993). Perceived self-efficacy in cognitive development and functioning. *Educational Psychologist, 28*(2), 117-148.

Bandura, A. (1997). *Self-efficacy: The exercise of control.* New York: Freeman.

Beck, L., & Murphy, J. (1996). *The four imperatives of a successful school.* Thousand Oaks, CA: Corwin Press.

Bolman, L. G., & Deal, T. E. (1997). *Reframing organizations: Artistry, choice, and leadership* (2nd ed.). San Francisco: Jossey-Bass.

Bossert, S. T. (1988). School effects. In N. J. Boyan (Ed.), *Handbook of research on educational administration* (pp. 341-352). New York: Longman.

Bryk, A. S., Lee, V. E., & Holland, P. (1993). *Catholic schools and the common good.* Cambridge, MA: Harvard University Press.

Bryk, A. S., & Raudenbush, S. W. (1992). *Hierarchical linear models: Applications and data analysis methods.* Newbury Park, CA: Sage.

Cohen, J. (1977). *Statistical power analysis for the behavioral sciences.* New York: Academic Press.

Cohen, M. D., & Sproull, L. S. (Eds.). (1996). *Organizational learning.* Thousand Oaks, CA: Sage.

Coleman, J. S. (1985). Schools and the communities they serve. *Phi Delta Kappan, 66*(8), 527-532.

Coleman, J. S. (1987). Norms as social capital. In G. Radnitzky & P. Bernholz (Eds.), *Economic imperialism: The economic approach applied outside the field of economics.* New York: Paragon House.

Cook, S. D. N., & Yanon, D. (1996). Culture and organizational learning. In M. D. Cohen & L. S. Sproull (Eds.), *Organizational learning* (pp. 430-459). Thousand Oaks, CA: Sage.

Edmonds, R. (1979). Some schools work and more can. *Social Policy, 9*, 28-32.

Finley, C. J. (1995). Review of the Metropolitan Achievement Test (7th ed). In J. C. Conoley & J. C. Impara (Eds.), *The twelfth mental measurements yearbook* (pp. 603-606). Lincoln: The University of Nebraska Press.

Goddard, R. D., Hoy, W. K., & Woolfolk Hoy, A. (in press). Collective efficacy: Its meaning, measure, and impact on student achievement. *American Journal of Educational Research.*

Halpin, A. W. (1959). *The leader behavior of school superintendents.* Chicago: Midwest Administrative Center.

Halpin, A. W. (1966). *Theory and research in administration.* New York: Macmillan.

Hambleton, R. K. (1995). Review of the Metropolitan Achievement Test, seventh edition. In J. C. Conoley & J. C. Impara (Eds.), *The twelfth mental measurements yearbook* (pp. 606-610). Lincoln: The University of Nebraska Press.

Hoy, W. K., & Sabo, D. J. (1998). *Quality middle schools: Open and healthy.* Thousand Oaks, CA: Corwin Press.

Hoy, W. K., & Tarter, C. J. (1997). *The road to open and healthy schools: A handbook for change* (Elementary and secondary school ed.). Thousand Oaks, CA: Corwin Press.

Hoy, W. K., Tarter, C. J., & Kottkamp, R. (1991). *Open schools/healthy schools: Measuring organizational climate.* Newbury Park, CA: Sage.

Keppel, G. (1991). *Design and analysis: A researcher's handbook.* Englewood Cliffs, NJ: Prentice Hall.

Lee, V. (1995). Another look at high school restructuring: More evidence that it improves student achievement and more insight into why. *Issues in Restructuring Schools, 9,* 1-10.

Maddux, J. E. (1995). Self-efficacy theory: An introduction. In J. E. Maddux (Ed.), *Self-efficacy, adaptation, and adjustment: Theory, research, and application* (pp. 3-33). New York: Plenum.

Murphy, J., & Louis, K. S. (1999). Handbook editor's introduction: Notes from the handbook. *Educational Administration Quarterly, 35*(4), 472-476.

Newmann, F. (1996). *Authentic achievement: Restructuring schools for intellectual quality.* San Francisco: Jossey-Bass.

Nitko, A. J. (1994). Review of the Metropolitan Achievement Test (6th ed.) In J. C. Impara & L. L. Murphy (Eds.), *Buros desk reference: Psychological assessment in the schools* (pp. 31-35). Lincoln: The University of Nebraska Press.

Pajares, F. (1997). Current directions in self-efficacy research. In M. L. Maehr & P. R. Pintrich (Eds.), *Advances in motivation and achievement* (pp. 1-49). Greenwich, CT: JAI.

Purkey, S. C., & Smith, M. S. (1983). Effective schools: A review. *Elementary School Journal, 83,* 427-452.

Putnam, R. D. (1993). *Making democracy work: Civic traditions in modern Italy.* Princeton, NJ: Princeton University Press.

Raudenbush, S. (1994). Searching for balance between a priori and post hoc model specification: Is a "general approach" desirable? *School Effectiveness and School Improvement, 5,* 196-198.

Rogers, B. G. (1994). Review of the Metropolitan Achievement Test (6th ed.). In J. C. Impara & L. L. Murphy (Eds.), *Buros desk reference: Psychological assessment in the schools* (pp. 35-40). Lincoln: The University of Nebraska Press.

Rowan, B. (1995). Learning, teaching and educational administration: Toward a research agenda. *Educational Administration Quarterly, 31,* 344-354.

Sampson, R. J., Raudenbush, S. W., & Earls, F. (1997). Neighborhoods and violent crime: A multilevel study of collective efficacy. *Science, 277,* 918-924.

Senge, P. M. (1990). *The fifth discipline: The art and practice of the learning organization.* New York: Doubleday.

Shouse, R. C. (1998). Restructuring's impact on student achievement: Contrasts by school urbanicity. *Educational Administration Quarterly, 34,* 677-699.

Shouse, R. C., & Brinson, K. (1995, October). *Sense of community and academic effectiveness in American high schools: Some cautionary, yet promising evidence from NELS:88.* Paper presented at the annual meeting of the University Council for Educational Administration, Salt Lake City, UT.

Smylie, M. A., Lazarus, V., & Brownlee-Conyers, J. (1996). Instructional outcomes of school-based participative decision making. *Educational Evaluation and Policy Analysis, 18*(3), 181-198.

Stedman, L. C. (1987). It's time we changed the effective schools formula. *Phi Delta Kappan, 69,* 214-224.

Stringfield, S., & Herman, R. (1996). Assessment of the state of school effectiveness research in the United States of America. *School Effectiveness and School Improvement, 7,* 159-180.

Stringfield, S., & Teddlie, C. (1991). Observers as predictors of schools' multi-year outlier status. *Elementary School Journal, 91,* 357-376.

Teddlie, C., & Reynolds, D. (2000). *The international handbook of school effectiveness research.* New York: Falmer.

Teddlie, C., & Stringfield, S. (1993). *Schools make a difference: Lessons learned from a 10-year study of school effects.* New York: Teachers College Press.

Wimpelberg, R. K., Teddlie, C., & Stringfield, S. (1989). Sensitivity to context: The past and future of effective schools research. *Educational Administration Quarterly, 25,* 82-107.

PART V

ON ORGANIZATIONAL TRUST

CHAPTER 5

THE CONCEPTUALIZATION AND MEASUREMENT OF FACULTY TRUST IN SCHOOLS

The Omnibus T-Scale[1]

Wayne K. Hoy and Megan Tschannen-Moran

Trust has long been a subject of philosophers and politicians, but the systematic study of the construct is of more recent vintage. Trust means many things; in fact, most people intuitively know what it is, but it is quite a different matter to articulate a definition of trust because it is a complex, multifaceted concept. The purpose of this inquiry is threefold: first, to conceptualize the many facets of trust and develop a working definition; second, to explore empirically four referents of trust in schools—faculty trust in students, in teachers, in the principal, and in parents; and finally, to develop a short, valid and reliable measure of faculty trust for use in both elementary and secondary schools—The Omnibus T-Scale.

Essential Ideas for the Reform of American Schools, pp. 87–114
Copyright © 2007 by Information Age Publishing
All rights of reproduction in any form reserved.

Most of us notice a given form of trust most easily after its sudden demise or severe injury. We inhabit a climate of trust as we inhabit an atmosphere and notice it as we notice air, only when it becomes scarce or polluted.

—(Baier, 1994, p. 98)

Trust is a critical ingredient of all human learning (Rotter, 1967), one that is especially important in schools where learning is the central mission. Moreover, trust is crucial in facilitating cooperation (Deutsch, 1958; Tschannen-Moran, 2001), in developing open school cultures (Hoffman, Sabo, Bliss, & Hoy, 1994), in promoting group cohesiveness (Zand, 1971, 1997), in school leadership (Sergiovanni, 1992), in student achievement (Goddard, Tschannen-Moran, & Hoy, 2001; Hoy, in press), and in increasing the quality of schooling (Hoy & Sabo, 1998).

Although trust has long been the subject of philosophers and politicians, the systematic investigation of trust by social scientists is of more recent vintage. In the late 1950s, the impetus for the empirical study of trust came from the escalating suspicion of the Cold War and optimism that science could provide answers to the dangerous and costly arms race (Deutsch, 1958). In the late 1960s, in response to a generation of young people who had become disillusioned with established institutions and authority, the study of trust shifted to individual personality traits (Rotter, 1967). In the 1980s, with soaring divorce rates and radical changes in the American family, research on trust next turned to interpersonal relationships (Johnson-George & Swap, 1982; Larzelere & Huston, 1980; Rempel, Holmes, & Zanna, 1985). In the 1990s, with shifts in technology and society, trust continues as a subject of study in sociology (Coleman, 1990), in economics (Fukuyama, 1995) and in organizational science (Gambetta, 1988; Kramer & Tyler, 1996; Shaw, 1997). Thus, it should not be surprising that the nature and meaning of trust in schools has recently taken on added importance.

Trust is good. Everyone wants to trust and be trusted. But trust means many things. Everyone knows intuitively what it is to trust, yet articulating a precise definition is no simple matter. Trust is difficult to define because it is so complex; in fact, Hosmer (1995) has observed, "There appears to be widespread agreement on the importance of trust in human conduct, but unfortunately there also appears to be an equally widespread lack of agreement on a suitable definition of the construct" (p. 380).

Trust is a multi-faceted construct, which may have different bases and phases depending on the context. It is also a dynamic construct that can change over the course of a relationship. The purpose of this inquiry, which builds on earlier work (Hoy & Tschannen-Moran, 1999; Tschannen-Moran & Hoy, 1998), is to examine the meaning, and measure of faculty trust in schools. The current analysis has three goals:

- First, to conceptualize the many facets of faulty trust in schools and then to provide a working definition of faculty trust;
- Second, to explore empirically four referents of faculty trust—in students, in teachers, in the principal, and in parents; and
- Third, to develop reliable and valid measures of faculty trust for use in both elementary and secondary schools.

TRUST

A review of the extant literature on trust (Tschannen-Moran & Hoy, 2000) led to the identification of a host of different definitions. With one exception (Frost, Stimpson, & Maughan, 1978), all were multi-faceted definitions. Most were based on common beliefs that individuals or groups would act in ways that were in the best interest of the concerned party. The literature on trust is diverse and yet it has some common threads running through it regardless of whether the focus is on the individual, organization, or society itself.

Trust relationships are based upon interdependence; that is, the interests of one party cannot be achieved without reliance upon another (Rousseau, Sitkin, Burt, & Camerer, 1998). If there is no interdependence, there is no need for trust. Interdependence in a relationship typically creates vulnerability, and vulnerability is a common feature of most definitions of trust (Baier, 1986; Bigley & Pearce, 1998; Coleman, 1990; Mayer, Davis, & Schoorman, 1995; Mishra, 1996). Trust involves taking risk and making oneself vulnerable to another with confidence that the other will act in ways that are not detrimental to the trusting party.

Facets of Trust

There are at least five facets of trust that can be gleaned from the literature on trust (Hoy & Tschannen-Moran, 1999; Tschannen-Moran & Hoy, 2000). Benevolence, reliability, competence, honesty, and openness are all elements of trust.

Benevolence
Perhaps the most common facet of trust is a sense of benevolence—confidence that one's well being or something one cares about will be protected and not harmed by the trusted party (Baier, 1986; Butler & Cantrell, 1984; Cummings & Bromily, 1996; Deutsch, 1958; Frost, Stimpson, & aughan, 1978; Gambetta, 1988; Hosmer, 1995; Hoy & Kupersmith, 1985; Mishra, 1996). Trust is the assurance that others will not

exploit one's vulnerability or take advantage even when the opportunity is available (Cummings & Bromily, 1996). Benevolence is the "accepted vulnerability to another's possible but not expected ill will" (Baier, 1986, p. 236).

In situations of interdependence, faith in the altruism of the other is especially important. Parents who trust educators to care for their children are confident that teachers will act with the best interests of their child in mind and that their child will be treated not only with fairness but with compassion. When trust in the benevolence of the other is missing, there are costs in productivity because energy is invested in anticipating and in making alternative plans. Teachers who don't trust their students spend much of their time planning for expected or imagined student misbehavior. Benevolence is an important element of trust relationships because a mutual attitude of good will is so important in interpersonal relationships.

Reliability

At its most basic level trust has to do with predictability, that is, consistency of behavior and knowing what to expect from others (Butler & Cantrell, 1984; Hosmer, 1995). In and of itself, however, predictability is insufficient for trust. We can expect a person to be invariably late, consistently malicious, inauthentic, or dishonest. When our well being is diminished or damaged in a predictable way, expectations may be met, but the sense in which we trust the other person or group is weak.

Reliability combines a sense of predictability with benevolence. In a situation of interdependence, when something is required from another person or group, the individual can be relied upon to supply it (Butler & Cantrell; Mishra, 1996; Rotter, 1967). Reliability implies that there is a sense of confidence that one's needs will be met in positive ways. Hence, one need neither invest energy worrying about whether the person will come through nor make alternative mental provisions.

Competence

Good intentions are not always enough. When a person is dependent on another but some level of skill is involved in fulfilling an expectation, an individual who means well may nonetheless not be trusted (Baier, 1986; Butler & Cantrell, 1984; Mishra, 1996). Competence is the ability to perform as expected and according to standards appropriate to task at hand. Many organizational tasks rely on competence. In situations of interdependence, when a team's project depends on the participation of others, trust will depend on an "assured confidence" that deadlines will be met and that the work will be of sufficient quality to meet project goals. In schools, principals and teachers depend upon one another to accomplish the teaching and learning goals of the school. Students are dependent on the competence of their teachers. A student may believe that her teacher is benevolent and wants to help her learn, but if the teacher lacks knowledge of the subject-matter or cannot adequately communicate that knowledge, then the student's trust in her teacher may be limited.

Honesty

Honesty is the person's character, integrity, and authenticity. Rotter (1967) defined trust as "the expectancy that the word, promise, verbal or written statement of another individual or group can be relied upon" (p. 651). Statements are truthful when they conform to "what really happened" from that person's perspective and when commitments made about future actions are kept. A correspondence between a person's statements and deeds demonstrates integrity. Moreover, acceptance of responsibility for one's actions and not distorting the truth in order to shift blame to another exemplifies authenticity (Tschannen-Moran & Hoy, 1998). Many scholars and researchers see honesty as a pivotal feature of trust (Baier, 1986; Butler & Cantrell, 1984; Cummings & Bromily, 1996). Indeed, honesty is assumed when we think of what is entailed in trust.

Openness

Openness is the extent to which relevant information is shared; it is a process by which individuals make themselves vulnerable to others. The information shared may be strictly about organizational matters or it may be personal information, but it is a giving of oneself (Butler & Cantrell, 1984; Mishra, 1996). Such openness signals reciprocal trust, a confidence that neither the information nor the individual will be exploited, and recipients can feel the same confidence in return.

Just as trust breeds trust, so too does distrust breed distrust. People who are guarded in the information they share provoke suspicion; people wonder what is being hidden and why. Individuals who are unwilling to extend trust through openness end up isolated (Kramer, Brewer, & Hanna, 1996). For example, principals in closed school climates engender distrust by withholding information and spinning the truth in order to make their view of reality the accepted standard (Sweetland & Hoy, 2001); most teachers are not fooled by such behavior and the principal's future actions become even more suspect.

Definition

The review of the extant literature on trust identified a myriad of definitions of trust. Most were multi-faceted definitions and were based upon expectations or common beliefs that individuals or groups would act in ways that were in the best interest of the concerned party. The analysis led to the following definition of trust: *Trust is an individual's or group's willingness to be vulnerable to another party based on the confidence that the latter party is benevolent, reliable, competent, honest, and open.*

Faculty trust is a collective property—the extent to which the faculty as a group is willing to risk vulnerability. Notice that this definition includes multiple facets—

- *Benevolence*— confidence that one's well being will be protected by trusted party.
- *Reliability*—the extent to which one can count on another person or group.
- *Competency*—the extent to which the trusted party has knowledge and skill.
- *Honesty*—the character, integrity, and authenticity of the trusted party.
- *Openness*—the extent to which there is no withholding of information from others.

Trust is embedded in relationships, and the referent of trust influences the meaning. In the current analysis four referents of faculty trust are of interest:

- Faculty trust in students
- Faculty trust in colleagues
- Faculty trust in the principal
- Faculty trust in parents

DEVELOPING MEASURES OF FACULTY TRUST—THE TRUST SCALE

Using the conceptual formulation of trust developed above, items were written by a team of researchers. For each trust referent (student, colleagues, principal, parent), items were written to include all five facets of trust. Although there were no extant measures for trust that fitted the proposed conceptual framework, Hoy and Kupersmith (1985) had developed scales to measure faculty trust in colleagues and in principals. Their work was a starting point for this research. An analysis of their items, however, revealed that none of them tapped competency or openness; hence, new items were added to the existing ones to measure the missing facets of trust. In addition, sets of items were written for faculty trust in students and in parents, making sure that each facet of trust was represented for each referent group.

The format of the Trust Scales was a 6-point Likert response set from strongly agree to strongly disagree. Teachers were asked to indicate the extent to which they agreed with the items. Sample items from each of the four levels of trust being measured include:

- Teachers in this school are suspicious of students.
- The principal is unresponsive to teachers' concerns.
- Teachers in this school are reliable.
- Teachers can count on parents in this school to support them.

Items were developed that tapped each proposed facet of trust. The development of the instrument went through a number of phases:

1.   The researchers created a pool of items.
2.   A panel of experts reacted to the items.
3.   A preliminary version was field tested with teachers.
4.   A pilot study as done with a small group of schools to test the factor structure, reliability, and validity of the instrument.
5.   Two large-scale studies were conducted to assess psychometric properties of the measures.

Developing Items

Using the conceptual framework developed above, the researchers created a pool of items to measure the facets and referents of faculty trust. Specifically, willingness to risk vulnerability and five facets of trust were considered—benevolence, reliability, competency, honesty, and openness—as the items were written, and four referents of faculty trust—student, teacher, principal, and parent—guided the creation of the four separate sets of trust items.

Panel of Experts

To check the content validity of the items, the Trust Scale was submitted to a panel of experts, all professors at The Ohio State University from the College of Education and the Fisher Business School. The panel was asked to judge which facet of trust each item measured. There was strong agreement among the judges, and in those few cases where the panelists disagreed, the items were retained and the question of the appropriate category was left to an empirical test using factor analysis. There was consensus that the items measured all the facets of trust for each referent group.

Field Test

A field test was conducted to test the clarity of instructions, appropriateness of the response set, and face validity of the items. Six experienced teachers were asked to examine, respond to the items, and to give some feedback. Again there was general agreement that the items were clear, reasonable, and had face validity. In a few instances, specific comments led to minor modification of an item.

Pilot Study

After the panel review and field test, 48 items remained and were used in a pilot study to explore the factor structure, reliability, and validity of the measure.

Sample

A sample of 50 teachers from 50 different schools in five states was selected to test the psychometric properties of the Trust Scales. Half of the schools selected were schools with reputations of relatively high conflict and the other half had relatively low conflict among the faculty.

Instruments

In addition to the 48-item Trust Scales survey, teachers were asked to respond a self-estrangement scale (Forsyth & Hoy, 1978), a sense of powerlessness scale (Zielinski & Hoy, 1983), a teacher sense of efficacy scale (Bandura, n.d.), and one item measuring the perception of conflict in the school. These additional measures were used to check the validity of the trust measure. It was predicted that each aspect of trust would be positively related to sense of teacher efficacy and negatively related to self-estrangement, sense of powerlessness, and degree of conflict.

Data Collection

Data were collected from 50 different schools through two procedures. University professors identified about a third of the schools as coming from either low trust or high trust schools, and the other two-thirds were sent the questionnaire by mail. Ninety-one percent of those contacted agreed to participate and returned usable questionnaires.

Results

The items were submitted to a factor analysis to test whether they loaded strongly and as expected. Although we anticipated four factors, only three strong factors emerged. The three-factor solution was supported by a scree test and made conceptual sense. Surprisingly, trust in students and trust in parents items loaded together on a single factor. Teachers did not distinguish between trusting students and trusting parents. Thus, the two sets of items combined into a single factor, which was called "Trust in Clients." The clients in this case are students and parents; both are recipients of the services offered by schools. The other two factors, as predicted, were Trust in the Principal and Trust in Colleagues. On the whole, factor loadings were strong and loaded together with other items from the same subtest. Results are reported in Table 5.1.

Decisions of whether to retain, eliminate, or modify each of the items were based on theoretical (conceptual fit) and empirical (factor loadings) grounds. When an item loaded at .40 or above on more than one factor, it typically was removed. In a few cases, however, such items were retained because either the conceptual fit was strong or the item could be modified to enhance the conceptual fit. For example, the item, "Teachers in this school trust their students," loaded strongly on Trust in Clients at .75 but also loaded on Trust in Colleagues at .43. This item was retained because of its strong conceptual fit with trust in clients. Any item that failed the empirical test of loading .40 or higher on at least one factor was eliminated. Likewise, regardless of the factor loading, any item that loaded on the wrong factor conceptually was eliminated. Finally, a few redundant items were also eliminated when another item measured the same property of trust and had an even stronger loading.

As a result of the factor analysis, four items from Trust in the Principal, five from Trust in Colleagues and four in the Trust in Clients factor were eliminated. Some of the eliminated items revealed interesting patterns. Whether teachers shared information about their lives outside of school with their colleagues was not strongly related to trust factors. And when teachers were asked whether they would feel comfortable putting their own child in their school, judgments of their colleagues' competence were confounded with trust for clients. Teachers were apparently as concerned about their level of trust in students as in their trust in colleagues in determining how comfortable they would be in enrolling their own child in the school. In brief, the pilot study produced a 35-item survey that reliably measured three kinds of trust: Trust in the Principal (alpha = .95), Trust in Colleagues (alpha = .94) and Trust in Clients (alpha = .92).

Table 5.1.   Factor Analysis of Trust Items (Pilot Study, *n* = 50)

	F1	*F2*	*F3*
1. The principal is unresponsive to teachers' concerns	-.93	-.12	.06
2. Teachers in this school can rely on the principal.	-.92	.10	.14
3. Teachers in this school trust the principal	.88	.10	.28
4. The principal in this school typically acts with the best interests of teachers in mind.	.84	.21	.15
5. The principal of this school does not show concern for teachers.	-.79	-.10	-.12
6. The principal doesn't really tell teachers what is going on.	-.78	-.27	-.12
7. The principal in this school keeps his or her word.	.77	.20	.23
8. The principal takes unfair advantage of the teachers in this school.	-.74	-.21	-.06
9. The teachers in this school have faith in the integrity of the principal.	.73	.11	.46
10. The teachers in this school are suspicious of most of the principal's action.	-.71	-.03	-.23
11. Teachers in this school often question the motives of the principal.	-.70	.09	-.42
12. The principal openly shares personal information with teachers.	.63	-.01	.26
13. When the principal commits to something teachers can be sure it will get done.	.61	.26	.19
14. The principal in this school is competent in doing his or her job.	.60	.33	-.02
15. Teachers feel comfortable admitting to the principal they have made a mistake.	.51	.02	.35
16. Teachers in this school believe in each other.	.27	.20	.86
17. Even in difficult situations, teachers in this school can depend on each other	.19	.15	.86
18. Teachers in this school are open with each other.	.28	.10	.82
19. When teachers in this school tell you something you can believe it.	.19	.06	.82
20. Teachers in this school typically look out for each other.	.29	.19	.80
21. Teachers in this school trust each other.	.29	.25	.79
22. Teachers in this school have faith in the integrity of their colleagues.	.16	.37	.76
23. Teachers here only trust teachers in their clique.	-.31	-.30	-.64
24. If I had a school-aged child, I would feel comfortable putting my own child in most anyone's classroom in this school.	.11	.54	.61
25. Teachers take unfair advantage of each other in this school.	-.11	-.41	-.59
26. Teachers in this school are suspicious of each other.	−.31	−.39	−.58
27. Teachers in this school are reliable.	.30	.55	.50
28. Teachers in this school do their jobs well.	.31	.59	.40

Table continues on next page.

Table 5.1.   Factor Analysis of Trust Items
(Pilot Study, *n* = 50) Continued

	F1	*F2*	*F3*
29. Teachers in this school don't share much about their lives outside of school.	-.36	-.23	-.20
30. Students in this school are reliable.	.10	.81	.18
31. Students in this school can be counted on.	.05	.80	.12
32. Teachers think that most of the parents do a good job.	.07	.79	.24
33. The students in this school have to be closely supervised.	-.16	-.78	.02
34. Parents in this school are reliable in their commitments.	.06	.75	.44
35. Teachers in this school trust their students.	.06	.75	.43
36. Students in this school care about each other.	-.08	.72	.29
37. Teachers can count on the parental support.	.06	.71	.19
38. Students here are secretive.	-.17	-.70	-.10
39. Students in this school cheat if they have a chance.	-.09	-.65	-.06
40. Students in this school can be counted on to do their work.	.16	.66	.21
41. Teachers in this school are suspicious of students.	-.32	-.61	-.20
42. Teachers avoid making contact with parents.	-.24	-.60	-.22
44. Teachers are suspicious of parents' motives.	-.21	-.49	-.31
45. Teachers in this school believe what students say.	.11	.47	.65
46. Teachers in this school trust parents.	.04	.45	.56
47. The students in this school talk freely about their lives outside of school.	.07	.04	.40
48. Teachers are guarded in what they say to parents.	-.36	-.27	-.22
Eigenvalue	19.00	6.20	3.79
Cumulative Variance explained	39.60	52.50	60.40
New items:			
49. Teachers here believe that students are competent learners.			
50. Teachers can believe what parents tell them.			

Bold items composed the next version of the instrument.

Next, a content analysis was performed. That is, each level of trust was examined to make sure that all the facets of trust (benevolence, reliability, competence, honesty, and openness) were represented in each scale, and indeed that was the case. The factor structure also supported the construct validity of the trust measures; items generally loaded correctly for each referent of trust. Moreover, all the facets of trust covaried together to for a coherent pattern of trust for each referent group—principal, colleagues, and clients. Nevertheless, two items were added for the next iterations of the trust scale, one to tap the competence of students (Teachers here believe that students are competent learners) and one to measure the honesty of parents (Teachers can believe what parents tell them), which yielded a 37-item instrument for further analysis.

We examined the validity of the measures and their ability to distinguish trust from other related constructs. Discriminant validity of the measures of trust was strong. As predicted, self-estrangement, powerlessness, and conflict were all negatively related to dimensions of trust, and teacher sense of efficacy was positively related to the subscales of trust. The results of the correlational analyses are summarized in Table 5.2.

A TEST OF THE REVISED TRUST SCALE

Having developed a measure of trust in field and pilot studies, the next step was to evaluate the Trust Scale in a more comprehensive sample. In particular, the goal was to refine the scales and check their reliability and validity. To that end, we tested the 37-item Trust Scale (which included two new items along with 35 original items) along with a measure of parent collaboration in a sample of elementary schools (Hoy & Tschannen-Moran, 1999).

The Elementary Sample

The population for this phase of the study was the elementary schools within one large urban midwestern school district. Permission to conduct research was requested following school district procedures. Schools were selected at random. Ninety percent of the schools contacted agreed to participate, resulting in a sample of 50 elementary schools.

Table 5.2.   Some Validity Evidence:
Correlations Between Trust and Criterion Variables

Subscale	1	2	3	4	5	6	7
1. Trust in Principal	(.95)	.54**	.40**	-.47**	-.22**	-.28**	.46**
2. Trust in Colleagues		(.94)	.62**	-.32**	-.31**	-.76**	.30*
3. Trust in Clients			(.92)	-.51**	-.31*	-.56**	.47**
4. Powerlessness				(.83)	.42**	.38**	-.55**
5. Self-estrangement					-(.88)	.36**	-.61**
6. School Conflict						—	-.28*
7. Teacher Efficacy							-(.87)

$*p < .05$, $**p < .01$
Alpha coefficients of reliability are on the diagonal.

Halpin (1956) has provided strong evidence that average scores on descriptive questionnaire items such as the LBDQ computed on the basis of 5-7 respondents per school yield reasonably stable scores (p. 28); thus, schools with fewer than five teachers responding to the instruments were not used. Of the 50 schools surveyed, 45 returned a sufficient number of each of the two surveys to be included in the sample. A total of 898 teachers completed surveys and over 99% of forms returned were useable.

Data Collection

Data were collected from the urban elementary schools at a regularly scheduled faculty meeting. A member of the research team explained the purpose of the study, assured the confidentiality of all participants, and requested that the teachers complete the surveys. The instruments, which had been printed on scannable forms, were distributed along with pencils. Half the teachers present responded to the trust questionnaire and half completed the questionnaire on collaboration. The separation was to assure methodological independence of the responses. No attempt was made to gather data from faculty who were not present at the meetings.

Factor Analysis and Reliability of the Trust Scale

A factor analysis was conducted to check the stability of the factor structure of trust, to refine the measure, to insure that all items loaded on the appropriate scale, and to assess the construct validity. Varimax orthogonal rotation was guided by simple structure; items were expected to load high on one factor and low or near zero on the other factors. Moreover, it was anticipated that all faces of trust—benevolence, reliability, competence, honesty, and openness—would be represented in each scale and form a coherent pattern of trust for each of the three referent groups—principal, colleagues, and clients.

A factor analysis of the 37-item trust measure resulted in the elimination of three items due to poor factor loadings. On the Trust in Colleagues subscale one item, "Teachers in this school do their jobs well," was eliminated because it loaded on more than one factor—it loaded on Trust in Colleagues (.72) but also on Trust in Clients (.46). "Teachers avoid making contact with parents" loaded almost equally with Trust in Clients and Trust in Colleagues (.49 and .50, respectively), and "Teachers in this school show concern for their students" loaded as expected on Trust in

Colleagues (.58) but was confounded by the level of trust in the principal (.66); hence, both items were eliminated, reducing the number of items on the Trust Scale to 34.[2]

Factor loadings of the items for Trust in the Principal subscale ranged from .44 to .94 with a subscale reliability of .98 using Cronbach's alpha. Loadings for the Trust in Colleagues ranged from .84 to .93 and the reliability for the subscale was also .98. Loadings for Trust in Clients ranged from .62 to .91 and the alpha for subscale was .97. The results of the factor analysis are found in Table 5.3.

The factor structure for the Trust Scale was very similar to that found in the pilot study and demonstrated a stable factor structure. In addition, reliabilities for the three subscales were even higher than those found in the pilot study. Kerlinger (1973) argues that factor analysis is perhaps the most powerful method of construct validation, and the findings of this study support the construct validity of faculty trust. The proposed faces or facets of trust—benevolence, reliability, competence, honesty, and openness—vary together and belong to an overall conception of trust that is coherent. Moreover, the facets of trust are present for each referent of trust. In brief, the Trust Scale provides reasonably valid and reliable measures of faculty trust in principals, colleagues and clients.

Not surprisingly, the three measures of faculty trust were moderately related to each other. Faculty trust in the principal was related to faculty trust in colleagues ($r = .37, p < .01$) and in clients ($r = .42, p < .01$), and faculty trust in colleagues was correlated with faculty trust in clients ($r = .35, p < .01$).

Another Validity Check

The extent to which parents are included and have influence in school decision making varies from school to school. Teachers sometimes resist the intrusion of parents into school affairs; life is simpler for teachers without interference from outsiders, especially parents (Hoy, Tarter, & Kottkamp, 1991; Hoy & Sabo, 1998). Yet there has been increasing demand to get parents involved in school decision making. In this study, we measured parent collaboration with a collaboration index (Tschannen-Moran, 2001), which was constructed by asking teachers how much influence parents had over the outcomes of the following important school activities: "planning school activities," "determining school rules," "resolving problems with community groups," "fostering community relations," "determining curriculum priorities," "determining areas in need

Table 5.3. Factor Analysis of Trust Items (Pilot Study, $n = 45$)

	F1	F2	F3
1. The principal is unresponsive to teachers' concerns	-.22	-.93	.01
2. Teachers in this school can rely on the principal.	.19	.94	.17
3. Teachers in this school trust the principal	.21	.88	.16
4. The principal in this school typically acts in the best interests of teachers.	.14	.94	.19
5. The principal of this school does not show concern for teachers.	-.21	-.19	-.07
6. The principal doesn't really tell teachers what is going on.	-.16	-.89	-.19
7. The principal in this school keeps his or her word.	.19	.85	.10
8. The teachers in this school have faith in the integrity of the principal.	.17	.92	.28
9. The teachers in this school are suspicious of most of the principal's actions.	-.20	-.86	-.29
10. The principal in this school is competent in doing his or her job.	-.20	.92	.12
11. The principal openly shares personal information with teachers.	-.90	.44	.15
1. Teachers in this school believe in each other.	.16	.18	.92
2. Even in difficult situations, teachers in this school can depend on each other.	.10	.20	.93
3. Teachers in this school are open with each other.	.14	.11	.91
4. When teachers in this school tell you something you can believe it.	.27	.19	.84
5. Teachers in this school typically look out for each other.	.09	.19	.91
6. Teachers in this school trust each other.	.05	.19	.91
7. Teachers in this school have faith in the integrity of their colleagues.	.28	.09	.92
8. Teachers in this school are suspicious of each other.	-.02	-.14	-.89
9.* Teachers in this school do their jobs well.	.45	.20	.12
1. Students in this school are reliable.	.91	.25	.79
2. Students in this school can be counted on to do their work.	.90	.18	.22
3. Teachers think that most of the parents do a good job.	.90	.11	.18
4. The students in this school have to be closely supervised.	-.89	.03	-.15
5. Parents in this school are reliable in their commitments.	-.91	.11	.07
6. Teachers in this school trust their students.	-.79	.24	.32
7. Students in this school care about each other.	.89	.23	.23
8. Teachers can count on parental support.	.91	.12	.14
9. Students here are secretive.	-.75	-.26	-.04
10. Students in this school cheat if they have a chance.	-.72	-.25	-.31
11. Teachers can believe what parents tell them.	.84	.23	.09
12. Teachers in this school believe what students say.	.80	.32	.14

Table continues on next page.

**Table 5.3.   Factor Analysis of Trust Items
(Pilot Study, _n_ = 45) Continued**

	F1	F2	F3
13.Teachers in this school trust parents (to support them).	.89	.16	.15
14. The students in this school talk freely about their lives outside of school.	.62	.05	.11
15. Teachers here believe that students are competent learners.	.75	.19	.38
16.* Teachers avoid making contact with parents.	-.49	-.26	-.50
17.* Teachers in this school show concern for their students	.57	.18	.65
Eigenvalue	18.32	6.08	5.44
Cumulative Variance explained	49.50	65.90	80.60
Items deleted			

of improvement," "determining how to comply with mandates and legislation," "approving extracurricular activities," and "determining how to allocate school resources (the school budget)." These items formed a parent collaboration index that had reliability in this sample of .94.

It was theorized that parent collaboration would be more likely in schools in which the faculty was trusting. For example, it seems unlikely that teachers will want to engage in any authentic collaboration with parents if they do not trust them. Thus, we expected that faculty trust in clients would be strongly related to collaboration with parents. The general hypothesis was supported—the greater the degree of faculty trust, the stronger the degree of parental collaboration in decision making as perceived by teachers. The correlations for all three dimensions of trust were statistically significant with parental collaboration, for faculty trust in the principal (r = .45, p < .01), for faculty trust in colleagues (r = .37, p <. 01), and for faculty trust in clients (r = .79, p < .01).

The multiple relationships between the dimensions of faculty trust and parental collaboration was also examined. Parental collaboration was regressed on the three dimensions of faculty trust. Although the simple correlations indicated that all three aspects of trust were related to parental collaboration, the multiple regression analysis demonstrated that trust in clients overwhelmingly explains the degree of parental collaboration in school decision making: in fact, only faculty trust in clients had a significant independent relationship with parental collaboration in decision making (b =. 72, p <. 01). Not surprisingly, when the faculty trusts the parents and students, parental collaboration is greatest. The multiple R^2 of .64 (p <. 01) indicates that almost two thirds of the variance in parental collaboration in decision making is explained by faculty trust. The results of this analysis also support the predictive validity of the items that measure trust.

FACULTY TRUST IN SECONDARY SCHOOLS

To this point, the analysis of trust focused on elementary schools. Would the same structure of trust emerge in secondary schools? Would faculty trust in students and parents combine into a unitary measure of trust or would it separate into two aspects of trust? Would the trust scales used at the elementary level work as well at the secondary level? Next, attention turned to these questions.

Secondary Sample

The secondary sample consisted of 97 high schools in Ohio. Although procedures were not used to ensure a random sample from the population of high schools, care was taken to select urban, suburban, and rural schools from diverse geographic areas of the state, and the sample proved to be fairly representative of secondary schools in Ohio. Only schools with 15 or more faculty members were considered candidates for the study. One hundred fifty high schools were contacted and invited to participate, but for a variety of reasons only 97 agreed to participate (65%). High schools were defined by grade span levels that included grades 9-12 and grades 10-12. Schools in the sample represented the entire range of socioeconomic status (SES); in fact, data from the Ohio Department of Education support the representativness of the sample in terms of size, SES, and urban-rural balance.

Data Collection

Data were collected from the high schools at a regularly scheduled faculty meeting. After the purpose of the study was explained and the confidentiality of all participants was guaranteed, teachers were asked to complete the surveys. In this study, we were interested in a number of other variables; hence, the Trust Scale was given to one group of teachers selected at random while those in another random group responded to an organizational climate index. The separation was to assure methodological independence of the responses. No attempt was made to gather data from faculty who were not present at the meetings.

Factor Analysis and Reliability of the Trust Scale

The trust scale that was developed at the elementary level had 34 items. To use this scale for the secondary schools, we added the item, "Teachers in this school do their jobs well," (which had been eliminated from the elementary scale) because we needed a competency item for the Trust in Colleagues subscale. The following four items: "The principal is unresponsive to teachers' concerns," "Teachers in this school believe in each other," The students in this school have to be closely supervised," and "The students in this school talk freely about their lives outside of school" were eliminated because another item tapped the same facet of trust for each group. Hence, a 31-item scale was used in the analysis of secondary schools.

Would trust in students and trust in parents merge into one aspect of client trust as they did in elementary schools or remain separate aspects of trust? In fact, the results were the same in both kinds of schools. Regardless of level, elementary or secondary, trust in students and trust in parents combined to form one unitary construct of trust—faculty trust in clients. Once again, the three-factor solution was best and explained about 70% of the variance. Indeed the factor analytic results of the two samples were remarkably similar. The factor structure remained stable; all items loaded as predicted and defined three dimensions of trust—faculty trust in the principal, in colleagues, and in clients (students and teachers). The results of the factor analysis for secondary schools are summarized in Table 5.4. Alpha coefficients of reliabilities for the three scales were also high for this sample—faculty trust in principal (.98), faculty trust in colleagues (.93), and faculty trust in clients (.93).

OMNIBUS TRUST SCALE

At this point in the instrument development, there were two slightly different versions of the trust scale—one for elementary schools and one for secondary schools. To simplify things, it was decided to develop a single scale that could be used for either elementary or secondary schools. The goal was to create a scale, such that:

1. each of the three referents of faculty trust was measured by a subscale,

Table 5.4.   Factor Analysis of Trust Items (*n* = 97 Secondary Schools)

	F1	F2	F3
1. Teachers in this school trust the principal	.97	.05	.12
2. The teachers in this school are suspicious of most of the principal's actions.	-.90	-.07	-.07
3. The principal in this school typically acts in the best interests of teachers.	.94	.08	.16
4. The principal of this school does not show concern for teachers	-.83	-.06	-.14
5. Teachers in this school can rely on the principal.	.97	.04	.06
6. The principal in this school is competent in doing his or her job.	.91	.03	.15
7. The principal in this school keeps his or her word.	.85	.02	.13
8. The teachers in this school have faith in the integrity of the principal.	.92	.02	.17
9. The principal doesn't really tell teachers what is going on.	-.83	-.10	-.09
10. The principal openly shares personal information with teachers.	.88	.08	.17
1. Teachers in this school trust each other.	.19	.24	.85
2. Teachers in this school are suspicious of each other.	-.06	-.31	-.65
3. Teachers in this school typically look out for each other.	.13	.21	.83
4. Even in difficult situations, teachers in this school can depend on each other.	.25	.31	.78
5. Teachers in this school do their jobs well	.04	.65	.42
6. When teachers in this school tell you something you can believe it.	.24	.41	.64
7. Teachers in this school have faith in the integrity of their colleagues.	.10	.40	.74
8. Teachers in this school are open with each other.	.32	.08	.75
1. Teachers in this school trust their students.	.07	.73	.32
2. Teachers in this school trust parents (to support them).	.06	.89	.23
3. Students in this school care about each other.	.03	.79	.24
4. Teachers can count on parental support.	.14	.82	.16
5. Students in this school are reliable	.05	.89	.18
6. Students in this school can be counted on to do their work.	.01	.83	.10
7. Parents in this school are reliable in their commitments.	.18	.80	.22
8. Teachers here believe that students are competent learners.	.13	.82	.16
9. Teachers think that most of the parents do a good job.	-.02	.90	.11
10. Students in this school cheat if they have a chance.	-.02	-.28	-.09
11. Teachers can believe what parents tell them.	.13	.72	.30
12. Teachers in this school believe what students say.	.12	.61	.17
13. Students here are secretive.	-.07	-.27	-.05
Eigenvalue	12.19	7.12	2.35
Cumulative Variance explained	39.3	62.3	69.87

2.   each trust subscale contained all facets of trust,

3.   each subscale had high reliability,

4.   each subscale was relatively parsimonious, and

5.   each subscale correlated strongly with the original elementary and secondary subscales.

The analysis started with the 31-item secondary version of the trust scale. All the facets of trust were represented on of each subscales (see Table 5.5).

Next, a comparison was made on the factor loadings on the items for elementary and secondary samples. The factor loadings were quite high for all the items. Even the competency item that we added had reasonably high loadings (see Table 5.6). In fact, only two items had low loadings. The item, "The students in this school cheat if they get a chance," loaded high on the elementary sample but low on the secondary sample. Because we had another honesty items with high loading for both samples, we deleted this item from the omnibus measure. The other item with a low loading in the secondary sample was an openness item, "Students here are secretive," which loaded only at −.30; however, because it was the only openness item on the trust in clients subscale, we retained it for conceptual reasons. Next, we eliminated some of the redundant items on the other subscales, making sure that all facets of trust were measured for each subscale. The result was an omnibus trust scale of 26 items that measured three aspects of faculty trust—faculty trust in colleagues, in the principal, and in clients. The alpha coefficients of reliability were high in both samples—Trust in principal (.98), trust in colleagues (.93), and trust in clients (.94). Moreover, the omnibus subscales correlated very highly with the longer subscale versions for both samples—none were lower than .96.

SUMMARY

Trust was conceptualized as a concept with multiple facets; the willingness to risk or be vulnerable is inherent in all trust relations as are the facets of benevolence, reliability, competence, honesty, and openness. Thus our constitutive definition of trust was *an individual's or group's willingness to be vulnerable to another party based on the confidence that the latter party is benevolent, reliable, competent, honest, and open.*

This conceptual perspective of trust proved useful and was supported. All the conditions of trust were found empirically; in fact, factor analytic techniques demonstrated all facets of trust for each of three referents—

Table 5.5.   Common Items for Trust Scale
(Elementary and Secondary)

Faculty Trust in Principal	*Facet of Trust*
1. Teachers in this school can rely on the principal.	Reliability
2. Teachers in this school trust the principal.	Vulnerability
3. The principal in this school typically acts in the best interests of teachers.	Reliability
4. The principal of this school does not show concern for teachers.	Benevolence
5. The principal doesn't really tell teachers what is going on.	Openness
6. The principal in this school keeps his or her word.	Honesty
7. The teachers in this school have faith in the integrity of the principal.	Honesty
8. The teachers in this school are suspicious of most of the principal's action.	Vulnerability
9. The principal in this school is competent in doing his or her job.	Competence
10. The principal openly shares personal information with teachers.	Openness

Faculty Trust in Colleagues	
1. Teachers in this school do their jobs well.	Competence
2. Even in difficult situations, teachers in this school can depend on each other.	Reliability
3. Teachers in this school are open with each other.	Openness
4. When teachers in this school tell you something you can believe it.	Honesty
5. Teachers in this school typically look out for each other.	Benevolence
6. Teachers in this school trust each other.	Vulnerability
7. Teachers in this school have faith in the integrity of their colleagues.	Honesty
8. Teachers in this school are suspicious of each other.	Vulnerability

Faculty Trust in Clients (students and parents)	
1. Students in this school are reliable.	Reliability
2. Students in this school can be counted on to do their work.	Reliability
3. Teachers think that most of the parents do a good job.	Competence
4. Parents in this school are reliable in their commitments.	Reliability
5. Teachers in this school trust their students.	Vulnerability
6. Students in this school care about each other.	Benevolence
7. Teachers can count on parental support.	Reliability
8. Students here are secretive.	Openness
9. Students in this school cheat if they have a chance.	Honesty
10. Teachers can believe what parents tell them.	Honesty
11. Teachers in this school believe what students say.	Honesty
12. Teachers in this school trust parents.	Vulnerability
13. Teachers here believe that students are competent learners.	Competence

Table 5.6.   Items and Factor Loadings for the
Omnibus Trust Scale (T-Scale)

		Factor Loadings	
	Subscales and Items	*Elementary*	*Secondary*
Trust in Principal			
1H	Teachers in this school typically look out for each other.	.92	.92
2R	The principal in this school typically acts in the best interests of the teachers	.94	.94
3O	The principal doesn't tell teachers what is really going on.*	-.89	-.84
4V	Teachers in this school trust the principal.	.88	.97
5B	The principal of this school does not show concern for teachers.*	-.91	-.84
6V	The teachers in this school are suspicious of most of the principal's actions.*	-.86	-.91
7R	Teachers in this school can rely on the principal.	.94	.97
8C	The principal in this school is competent in doing his or her job.	.92	.91
Trust in Colleagues		.91	.83
1B	Teachers in this school typically look out for each other.	.91	.74
2V	Teachers in this school trust each other.	.93	.79
3R	Even in difficult situations, teachers in this school can depend on each other.	.92	.73
4H	Teachers in this school have faith in the integrity of their colleagues.	.89	-.66
5V	Teachers in this school are suspicious of each other.*	.71	.43
6C	Teachers in this school do their jobs well.	.84	.63
7H	When teachers in this school tell you something you can believe it.		
8O	Teachers in this school are open with each other.	.91	.74
Trust in Clients (students and parents)			
1V	Teachers in this school trust their students.	.79	.72
2R	Students in this school can be counted on to do their work.	.90	.83
3B	Students in this school care about each other.	.89	.80
4O	Students here are secretive.*	-.75	-.30
5C	Teachers here believe that students are competent learners.	.75	.81
6R	Teachers can count on parental support.	.91	.82
7H	Teachers in this school believe what parents tell them.	.84	.72
8C	Teachers think that most of the parents do a good job.	.90	.90
9R	Parents in this school are reliable in their commitments.	.91	.81
10V	Teachers in this school trust the parents.	.89	.89

H=Honesty; B=Benevolence; C=Competence; O=Openness; V=Risk of Vulnerability; R=Reliability.
*Reverse the scoring

principals, colleagues, and clients. Moreover, the trust subscales yielded reliable and valid measures for faculty trust in principals, in colleagues, and in clients. As predicted, faculty trust in each of these three groups were moderately related to each other. Faculty trust in schools tends to be pervasive. When teachers trust their principal, for example, they are also more likely to trust each other and their clients. Conversely, distrust also tends to breed distrust. Broken trust is likely to ripple through the system.

The analyses of referents of faculty trust indicated that they were related to other school variables in predictable ways. On the one hand, teachers' sense of powerlessness and estrangement were negatively related to trust. On the other hand, trust was positively related to teacher sense of efficacy; the greater the degree of perceived trust in a school, the stronger the belief in teachers' ability to organize and execute courses of action that lead to success. Also, not unexpectedly, the greater the degree of faculty trust in a school, the less the degree of conflict. All of the aspects of trust measured by the trust scales were related to other school variables as predicted.

The research also tested the hypothesis that faculty trust was related to the degree of schools' collaboration with parents on important aspects of school decision making. The assumption that trust was a key element in collaboration with parents on school decision making was supported by the results. Although all aspects of faculty trust were correlated with parental collaboration and explained about two-thirds of the variance in collaboration, it was faculty trust in clients that proved the strongest predictor of collaboration; in fact, it was the only dimension of trust that was independently related to parental collaboration in decision making. The greater the faculty trust in clients, the more influence teachers say parents have in making important decisions.

Another intriguing finding of the study was that for both elementary and secondary samples, faculty trust in students and parents converged. The relationship was so strong that the trust for the two groups was indistinguishable. Faculty trust for the two referents merged to form a single factor, which we called faculty trust in clients. When teachers trust the students, they also trust their parents, and vice versa.

In sum, a multi-faceted definition of trust was developed based on an extensive review of the literature. That definition was operationalized and confirmed with Trust Scales for elementary and secondary schools. Each scale had three reliable and valid subscales of faculty trust. Finally, a measure of faculty trust, the Omnibus T-Scale, was constructed and tested for use in both elementary and secondary schools. The omnibus measure is short and has the added general advantage of being useful regardless of the school level—elementary or secondary. A chronology of the develop-

Table 5.7.   Chronology of Omnibus T-Scale Development

Number of Items	48	37	34	31	26
Iterations	1	2	3	4	5
1. The principal is unresponsive to teachers' concerns.	x	x	x		
2. Teachers in this school can rely on the principal.	x	x	x	x	x
3. Teachers in this school trust the principal	x	x	x	x	x
4. The principal in this school typically acts in the best interests of teachers.	x	x	x	x	x
5. The principal of this school does not show concern for teachers	x	x	x	x	x
6. The principal doesn't really tell teachers what is going on.	x	x	x	x	x
7. The principal in this school keeps his or her word.	x	x	x	x	
8. The principal takes unfair advantage of the teachers in this school.	x				
9. The teachers in this school have faith in the integrity of the principal.	x	x	x	x	x
10. The teachers in this school are suspicious of most of the principal's actions.	x	x	x	x	x
11. Teachers in this school often question the motives of the principal.	x				
12. The principal openly shares personal information with teachers.	x	x	x	x	
13. When the principal commits to something teachers can be sure it will get done.	x				
14. The principal in this school is competent in doing his or her job.	x	x	x	x	x
15. Teachers feel comfortable admitting to the principal they have made a mistake.	x				
16. Teachers in this school believe in each other.	x	x	x		
17. Even in difficult situations, teachers in this school on depend on each other.	x	x	x	x	x
18. Teachers in this school are open with each other.	x	x	x	x	x
19. When teachers in this school tell you something you can believe it.	x	x	x	x	x
20. Teachers in this school typically look out for each other.	x	x	x	x	x
21. Teachers in this school trust each other.	x	x	x	x	x
22. Teachers in this school have faith in the integrity of their colleagues.	x	x	x	x	x
23. Teachers here only trust teachers in their clique.	x				

Table continues on next page.

Table 5.7.   Chronology of Omnibus T-Scale Development Continued

Number of Items	48	37	34	31	26
Iterations	1	2	3	4	5
24. If I had a school-aged child, I would feel comfortable putting my own child in most anyone's classroom in this school.	x				
25. Teachers take unfair advantage of each other in this school.	x				
26. Teachers in this school are suspicious of each other.	x	x	x	x	x
27. Teachers in this school are reliable.	x				
28. Teachers in this school do their jobs well.	x	x		x	x
29. Teachers in this school don't share much about their lives outside of school.	x				
30. Students in this school are reliable.	x	x	x	x	
31. Students in this school can be counted on.	x				
32. The students in this school have to be closely supervised.	x	x	x		
33. Teachers think that most of the parents do a good job.	x	x	x	x	x
34. Parents in this school are reliable in their commitments.	x	x	x	x	x
35. Teachers in this school trust their students.	x	x	x	x	x
36. Students in this school care about each other.	x	x	x	x	x
37. Teachers can count on the parental support.	x	x	x	x	x
38. Students here are secretive.	x	x	x	x	x
39. Students in this school cheat if they have a chance.	x	x	x	x	
40. Students in this school can be counted on to do their work.	x	x	x	x	x
41. Teachers in this school are suspicious of students.	x				
42. Teachers avoid making contact with parents.	x	x			
43. Teachers in this school show concern for their students.	x	x			
44. Teachers are suspicious of parents' motives.	x				
45. Teachers in this school believe what students say.	x	x	x	x	
46. Teachers in this school trust parents.	x	x	x	x	x
47. The students in this school talk freely about their lives outside of school.	x	x	x		

Table continues on next page.

Table 5.7.   Chronology of Omnibus T-Scale Development Continued

Number of Items	48	37	34	31	26
Iterations	1	2	3	4	5
48. Teachers are guarded in what they say to parents	x				
—Teachers here believe that students are competent learners.		x	x	x	x
—Teachers can believe what parents tell them.		x	x	x	x

Iterations 1-5:
1 = All pilot items (see Table 5.1); 2 = Surviving pilot items plus new items (see Table 5.1);
3 = Final elementary items (See Table 5.3); 4 = Final secondary items (see Table 5.4);
5 = Final omnibus items (see Table 5.5, 5.6).

ment of the Omnibus Trust Scale and the resulting items in the various iterations are found in the gird in Table 5.7.

The final Omnibus T-Scale can be found on line at www.coe.ohio-state.edu/whoy; under research instruments. Students and professors are invited to use the scale for research purposes and administrators for professional and organizational development. Just download the scale, copy it, and use it.

NOTES

1. Page A. Smith of the University of Texas at San Antonio was part of the research team at various points in the research, and we are grateful for his help. This research builds on our previous work (Hoy & Tschannen-Moran, 1999).
2. We (Hoy & Tschannen-Moran, 1999) suggested adding another item, but subsequent analysis proved that unnecessary.

REFERENCES

Baier, A. C. (1994). *Moral prejudices: Essays on ethics.* Cambridge, MA: Harvard University Press.

Baier, A. C. (1986). Trust and antitrust. *Ethics, 96,* 231-260.

Bandura, A. (n.d.). *Teacher self-efficacy scale.* Unpublished manuscript.

Bigley, G. A., & Pearce, J. L. (1998). Straining for shared meaning in organization science: Problems of trust and distrust. *The Academy of Management Review, 23,* 405-421.

Butler, J. K., & Cantrell, R. S. (1984). A behavioral decision theory approach to modeling dyadic trust in superiors and subordinates. *Psychological Reports, 55,* 81-105.

Deutsch, M. (1958). Trust and suspicion. *Journal of Conflict Resolution, 2*, 265-279.

Coleman, J. S. (1990), *Foundations of social theory*. Cambridge, MA: The Belknap Press of Harvard University Press.

Cummings, L. L., & Bromily, P. (1996). The organizational trust inventory (OTI): Development and validation. In R. Kramer & T. Tyler (Eds.), *Trust in Organizations*. Thousand Oaks, CA: Sage.

Forsyth, P. B., & Hoy, W. K. (1978). Isolation and alienation in educational organizations. *Educational Administration Quarterly, 14*, 80-96.

Frost, T., Stimpson, D. V., & Maughan, M. R. (1978). Some correlates of trust. *The Journal of Psychology, 99*, 103-108.

Fukuyama, F. (1995). *Trust: The social virtues and the creation of prosperity*. New York: Simon & Schuster.

Gambetta, D. (1988). Can we trust? In D. Gambetta (Ed.), *Trust: Making and breaking cooperative relations* (pp. 213-238). Cambridge, MA: Basil Blackwell.

Goddard, R. D., Tschannen-Moran, M., & Hoy, W. K. (2001). A multilevel examination of the distribution and effects of trust in students and parents in urban elementary schools. *The Elementary School Journal, 102*, 3-17.

Halpin, A. W. (1956). *The leader behavior of school superintendents*. Columbus: College of Education, The Ohio State University.

Hoffman, J., Sabo, D., Bliss, J., & Hoy, W. K. (1994). Building a culture of trust. *Journal of School Leadership, 4*, 484-501.

Hoy, W. K. (in press). Faculty trust: A key to student achievement. *Journal of School Public Relations*.

Hoy, W. K., & Kupersmith, W. J. (1985). The meaning and measure of faulty trust. *Educational and Psychological Research, 5*, 1-10.

Hoy, W. K., & Sabo, D. J. (1998). *Quality middle schools: Open and healthy*. Thousand Oaks, CA: Corwin.

Hoy, W. K., & Tschannen-Moran, M. (1999). Five faces of trust: An empirical confirmation in urban elementary schools. *Journal of School Leadership, 9*, 184-208.

Hoy, W. K., Tarter, C. J., & Kottkamp, R. B. (1991). Open schools, healthy schools: Measuring organizational climate. Newbury Park, CA: Sage.

Hosmer, L. T. (1995). Trust: The connecting link between organizational theory and philosophical ethics. *Academy of Management Review, 20*(2), 379-403.

Johnson-George, C. E., & Swap, W.C. (1982). Measurement of specific interpersonal trust: Construction and validation of a scale to assess trust in a specific other. *Journal of Personality and Social Psychology, 43*, 1306-1317.

Kerlinger, F. N. (1973). *Foundations of behavioral research* (2nd ed.). New York: Holt, Rinehart, and Winston.

Kramer, R. M., & Tyler, T. (Eds.). (1996). *Trust in Organizations*. Thousand Oaks, CA: Sage.

Kramer, R. M., Brewer, M. B., & Hanna, B. A. (1996). Collective trust and collective action: The decision to trust as a social decision. In R. Kramer & T. Tyler (Eds.), *Trust in organizations*. Thousand Oaks, CA: Sage.

Larzelere, R. E., & Huston, T. L. (1980). The dyadic trust scale: Toward understanding interpersonal trust in close relationships. *Journal of Marriage and the Family, 42*, 595-604.

Mayer, R. C., Davis, J. H., & Schoorman, F. D. (1995). An integrative model of organizational trust. *Academy of Management Review, 20,* 709-734.

Mishra, A. K. (1996). Organizational responses to crisis: The centrality of trust. In R. Kramer & T. Tyler (Eds.), *Trust in organizations.* Thousand Oaks, CA: Sage.

Rempel, J. K., Holmes, J. G., & Zanna, M. D. (1985). Trust in close relationships. *Journal of Personality and Social Psychology, 49,* 95-112.

Rousseau, D., Sitkin, S. B., Burt, R., & Camerer, C. (1998). Not so different after all: A cross-discipline view of trust. *The Academy of Management Review, 23*(3), 393-404.

Shaw, R. B. (1997). *Trust in the balance: Building successful organizations on results, integrity and concern.* San Francisco: Jossey-Bass.

Solomon, R. C., & Flores, F. (2001). Building trust in business, politics, relationships, and life. New York: Oxford University Press.

Sweetland, S. R., & Hoy, W. K. (2001). Varnishing the truth: Principals and teachers spinning reality. *Journal of Educational Administration, 39,* 282-293.

Rotter, J. B. (1967). A new scale for the measurement of interpersonal trust. *Journal of Personality, 35,* 651-665.

Sergiovanni, T. J. (1992). *Moral leadership: Getting to the heart of school improvement.* San Francisco: Jossey Bass.

Tschannen-Moran, M. (2001). Collaboration and the need for trust. *Journal of Educational Administration, 39,* 308-331.

Tschannen-Moran, M., & Hoy, W. K. (1998). A conceptual and empirical analysis of trust in schools. *Journal of Educational Administration, 36,* 334-352.

Tschannen-Moran, M., & Hoy, W. K. (2000). A multidisciplinary analysis of the nature, meaning, and measurement of trust. *Review of Educational Research, 70,* 547-593.

Zand, D. E. (1997). *The leadership triad: Knowledge, trust, and power.* New York: Oxford University Press.

Zand, D. E. (1971). Trust and managerial problem solving. *Administrative Science Quarterly, 17,* 229-239.

Zielinski, A. E., & Hoy, W. K. (1983). Isolation and alienation in elementary schools. *Educational Administration Quarterly, 19,* 27-45.

CHAPTER 6

A MULTILEVEL EXAMINATION OF THE DISTRIBUTION AND EFFECTS OF TEACHER TRUST IN STUDENTS AND PARENTS IN URBAN ELEMENTARY SCHOOLS

Roger D. Goddard, Megan Tschannen-Moran, and Wayne K. Hoy

In this article we develop the theoretical argument that teacher trust in students and parents is critical to school success. Next, using data collected on 452 teachers and 2,536 students in 47 urban elementary schools, we show that trust varies greatly among the elementary schools and that this variation is strongly related to differences among schools in socioeconomic status. Finally, results of the study showed that even after accounting for variation among schools in student demographic characteristics, prior achievement, and school socioeconomic status, trust was a significant positive predictor of differences among schools in student achievement. We dis-

Reprinted by permission from the *Elementary School Journal*, Vol. 102, pp. 3-17.
Copyright © 2001. All rights reserved.

Essential Ideas for the Reform of American Schools, pp. 115–136
Copyright © 2007 by Information Age Publishing
All rights of reproduction in any form reserved.

cuss the implications of these findings for improving academic achievement in elementary schools and for future research.

Researchers have increasingly recognized the importance of relationships that connect families and schools. Indeed, several studies have suggested that strong school-family relationships matter to student achievement (Bank & Slavings, 1990; Garnier & Raudenbush, 1991; Jones & Maloy, 1988; Lareau, 1987; Lee & Croninger, 1994; Sui-Chu & Douglas, 1996). Relationships between families and schools are also the focus of federal and state educational policy. For example, the National Education Goals Panel (1995) stated, "if the National Education Goals are to be achieved, families, schools, and communities must work collaboratively to form strong family-school-community partnerships" (p. 63). Thus, strong relationships are the focus of both research and policy. But what is it that makes relationships *strong*? In large part, we believe the answer is trust. We believe that trust is at the heart of strong relationships that help children learn, particularly disadvantaged children. The purpose of this study was to investigate trust as a critical element of the relational networks that facilitate success in urban elementary schools.

For several reasons, we focused on teacher trust as key to the relationships that connect students and their families to schools. To be sure, other individuals have social influence that affects students, families, and schools. For example, principals, guidance counselors, extended family, and student peers each uniquely influence the decisions children make and the success they experience in school. But teachers are in daily contact with students, and they are the first line of communication between the school and the family. Moreover, as we discuss more fully later, for disadvantaged children whose families lack the cultural capital to prepare their children to take advantage of the opportunities schools can present (Bourdieu & Passeron, 1977; Lareau, 1987), teachers are the primary institutional agents responsible for guiding these students to academic success (Stanton-Salazar, 1997). Thus, we examined teacher trust in students and parents.

We believe that the extent to which teacher-student and teacher-parent interactions are productive is affected by the trust that holds these relationships together. Our interest in teacher trust as a social feature that is important to the success of students in urban elementary schools led us to consider two research questions. First, we were curious to learn more about how teacher trust is associated with school membership. Therefore, one research question investigated asked how trust is distributed among and within urban elementary schools. We also wanted to know more about how trust relates to the unequal distribution of school success. That is, we were interested in the extent to which trust predicted differences between schools in student achievement. Thus, we investigated how teacher trust in students and parents affects student academic success.

Both of our research questions involve the distribution of characteristics (trust and achievement) across and within organizational units. For this reason, and because we designed our study to provide access to nested data (students in schools), we chose multilevel modeling to address our research questions. The primary analytic technique employed was hierarchical linear modeling (HLM) (Bryk & Raudenbush, 1992). The HLM technique has the capability to partition variance in a dependent variable into its within- and between-group components. This feature enabled us to examine the extent to which teachers' perceptions of trust varied both across and within schools. In addition, HLM has the advantage of avoiding the problems of aggregation bias, misestimated standard errors, and heterogeneity of regression that sometimes compromise the results of ordinary least squares regression.

In sum, this article serves several purposes. First, we review literature on trust to develop a theoretical model guiding our measurement of teacher trust. Next, we employ multilevel modeling to offer new knowledge about the distribution of trust across and within schools. Finally, we examine the relation between trust and student achievement among schools after controlling for achievement variance related to student demographic characteristics and prior achievement. The findings of this study offer insight into teacher trust as a social feature that matters to the success of urban elementary schools.

TRUST AND SCHOOLS

Baier (1986) defined trust as the reliance on others' competence and their willingness to look after rather than harm what is entrusted to their care. Because what people typically care about and value often includes things that they cannot single-handedly either create or sustain, people allow others to get into positions where they can help, if people choose. Trust is thus a fundamental concern for school organizations positioned to help students learn. Yet, because trust requires vulnerability to further good causes, it creates opportunities for those one trusts to injure what one cares about (Baier, 1986, p. 236). What one cares about may be tangible things, such as one's possessions or money, or intangible things such as democracy, or norms of respect and tolerance. Schools look after all of these for society and consequently, the issue of trust is critical to an understanding of how schools educate students. Indeed, the in loco parentis responsibility conferred on schools by American society requires trust.

Schools are also vested with the responsibility for realizing the increasing vision of social justice (Vinovskis, 1999). This has created new roles and expectations for schools. Goodlad (1984) observed that society used to be content with schools that functioned to sort and rank students for various strata of society. That goal is being supplanted by a newer goal of fostering equality of opportunity for all students, even those with disabilities (Yell, 1995) or who come from lower socioeconomic strata. For example, a fundamental goal of state and federal education finance policy is to redress inequity by providing adequate opportunity for all students to achieve to high standards (Odden & Busch, 1998; Odden & Picus, 2000). Yet, schools struggle to realize these aspirations. Almost a half-century after the Brown decision to desegregate the schools, the dream of schools eliminating class distinctions and providing equal opportunities to learn seems far from becoming reality (Kozol, 1991). Further, the professional knowledge teachers possess is held suspect as much-touted innovations (e.g., open classrooms or new math) have failed to bring the dramatic results they promised (Tyack & Cuban, 1995). Values schools promote may be at odds with the conflicting values of a diverse society. All these dynamics contribute to greater public distrust of schools. Indeed, growing distrust of schools is evidenced in the exploding population of people unwilling to entrust their children to schools at all. From a phenomenon that was virtually unheard of in the early 1980s, in 1997 an estimated 1.23 million American children were taught at home (Ray, 1997).

Trust and Educational Governance Reform: School and Classroom Perspectives

Lack of trust is a serious impediment to many of the reforms taking shape in American schools. Traditional management practices have tended to emphasize social distance and divergent interests among competing parties, and so they have engendered distrust or a low expectation of responsiveness on the part of other parties. But new forms of governance are taking shape, with greater expectations of shared interests and goals, greater effectiveness, and increased flexibility to changing demands and environmental pressures (Powell, 1990, 1996). These more inclusive forms of governance increasingly require an atmosphere of trust. For example, moves to site-based management and shared decision making require school leaders to trust those who are granted decision-making discretion (Hoy & Tarter, 1995). Moreover, as school reformers ask teachers to change their beliefs and instructional techniques, teachers need to have a community of support in which to challenge and debate new practices (Putnam & Borko, 1997); such a community requires trust among teachers.

A number of initiatives call for the inclusion of parents in school governance. Indeed, not only in America but also in other English-speaking countries such as England and Australia, calls for parental involvement in educational decision making are key policy objectives (Odden & Busch, 1998). Such forms of governance espouse the devolution of control to schools and their stakeholders. Yet, decentralization alone will not necessarily produce meaningful improvements; parents and other stakeholders must cultivate productive relationships with those working in schools (Glickman, 1990). The productive involvement of parents in educational decision making thus requires that teachers trust parents.

Not only is school-based reform frequently influenced by trust in parents, contemporary teaching methods require teacher trust in students. For example, collaborative learning may reduce students' alienation by giving them a greater voice in their lives at school, but the change to more active styles of learning implicitly requires teachers to trust that students will participate in meaningful ways (Johnson & Johnson, 1999). In sum, decades of school reform have led to calls for devolution of decision making, power, and authority to students and their parents. For schools to realize the kinds of positive transformation envisioned by these reform efforts, attention must be paid to teacher trust in both students and parents.

Teachers and Institutional Access: The Importance of Trust

Another way in which the importance of teacher trust to students' educational success has received attention is through the work of social capital theorists. Within this theory, trust strengthens the productive norms and relational networks that facilitate group and individual accomplishment (Coleman, 1985, 1987, 1990; Driscoll & Kerchner, 1999; Putnam, 1993; Smylie & Hart, 1999). Some scholars contend, however, that minority children are often excluded from productive relationships because they are not members of the dominant culture. According to Stanton-Salazar (1997)

> the structural features of middle class networks are analogous to social freeways that allow people to move about the complex mainstream landscape quickly and efficiently ... a fundamental dimension of social inequality is that some are able to use these freeways, while others are not. (p. 4)

From this perspective, disadvantaged children are not prepared to take advantage of the opportunities schools present because they lack the ability to successfully navigate the mainstream. Such students are therefore dependent on relationships with school institutional agents to help them decode the dominant culture and gain access to the "social freeway." Trusting relationships between students and teachers thus can create social capital that fosters academic success for disadvantaged children.

Trust and Human Learning

Trusting that others can be believed is an important element in human learning. Rotter (1967) asserted that,

> Much of the formal and informal learning that human beings acquire is based on the verbal and written statements of others, and what they learn must be significantly affected by the degree to which they believe their informants without independent evidence. (p. 651)

Webb (1992) echoed this proposition, observing that much of what is known in the fields of history, geography, science, and many others can only be learned by relying on the words of other people. He proposed,

> One is justified in believing what other people say, provided only that there is no positive reason to doubt them.... After all, if I am not justified in believing others, then I don't know that there is such a place as Australia, that electrons have plus or minus one-half spin, that Pluto has a moon, or even that I am thirty-four years old; I can't know so much as the time of day. (p. 390)

Webb explained that trust is even fundamental to learning a common language. Learning a language would be impossible if those who know the language were not consistent in their references to objects and did not correct the misuse of words or syntax in a reliable way. Speaking a common language forms a linguistic community. Webb asserted that people are justified in trusting others within their own community because people in a community have a stake in one another being generally reliable (pp. 396-397). The theoretical implication for schools is that teachers, parents, and students have a vested interest in developing high levels of trust.

Trust, then, is vital to human survival, learning, and functioning in a complex society. Trust can keep participants in a community or collective in line. It can be costly to earn the distrust of others one must interact with in an ongoing relationship. Such distrust would make it difficult for people to cooperate in accomplishing common goals. Teachers must trust students and parents in order to cooperate with them in accomplishing common goals. Schools play a special role in society and as such the relationships of trust in schools are vital.

The Facets of Trust

Trust is a complex concept with a variety of facets. However, a number of common conditions characterize most definitions of trust. What is common across virtually all definitions of trust is a willingness to risk in the face of vulnerability. Where there is no vulnerability, there is no need for trust. Along with vulnerability, other facets drawn from the theoretical and empirical work on trust in a variety of contexts include: benevolence, reliability, competency, honesty, and openness (Tschannen-Moran & Hoy, 1998). All these facets of trust have been shown to be important features of school social interaction (Hoy & Tschannen-Moran, 1999).

Perhaps the most familiar facet of trust is a sense of benevolence, conceived as confidence in the good will of those who are trusted, or an attitude of mutual concern. Reliability is also important in social relations because behavior occurs over time. Trust is usually not a one-time affair. Trusted individuals are expected to behave both positively and consistently. Good intentions, however, are not enough. Competence is also critical in trust relations; individuals are not trusted if they do not have the skills to perform the task at hand. Teachers are likely not to trust an incompetent administrator, just as they are suspicious of parents who do not demonstrate appropriate care for their children. Honesty speaks to the integrity and authenticity of behavior and is another facet of trust. One must be able to rely on the word and action of another in order to trust the other. Finally, openness is the extent to which relevant information is shared and not withheld; it is a process by which people make themselves vulnerable by sharing information with others. Openness breeds trust, whereas withholding behavior provokes suspicion and distrust. Hence, we define trust as "an individual's or group's willingness to be vulnerable to another party based on the confidence that the latter party is benevolent, reliable, competent, honest, and open" (Hoy & Tschannen-Moran, 1999, p. 189). Teachers' trust in students and parents contains all of the facets of trust that we have outlined.

Research Questions

Little is known about the distribution of trust across and within groups in schools. Indeed, although several studies have suggested that trust is important to schools (Hoffman, Sabo, Bliss, & Hoy, 1994; Hoy, Sabo, & Barnes, 1996; Hoy, Tarter, & Witkoskie, 1992; Hoy & Tschannen-Moran,

1999; Tarter, Bliss, & Hoy, 1989; Tarter, Sabo, & Hoy, 1995; Tschannen-Moran, 2001; Tschannen-Moran & Hoy, 1998; Tschannen-Moran & Hoy, 2000), none has considered its distribution among schools. In response, our first research question investigated the extent to which trust varied within and among schools. We also examined the extent to which school demographics and size explained variation in trust.

The relative effectiveness of urban elementary schools is a pressing issue for concerned parents and educators. Our review suggested that teacher trust in students and parents is critical to the effectiveness of parental and student involvement in inclusive forms of school governance. The extant literature also indicated that trust is a social feature that enables group members to achieve common goals. Trust is also important to the success of disadvantaged youth. Accordingly, we hypothesized that the trust teachers have in students and parents would be positively and significantly related to differences between urban elementary schools in student academic achievement.

METHODOLOGY

Sample

Our study focused on trust in urban elementary schools. The population for this study was 47 elementary schools in one large urban school district in the Midwest. We selected an urban district for this research because we believed that trust is important to confronting the challenges these districts face. A benefit of this design feature is that our sample included only one type of district, thereby holding constant differences in trust that might occur between urban and non-urban districts. Further, because we focused on schools in one district, there was no possibility for uncontrolled between-district effects. Finally, because we limited this study to elementary schools, our design controlled for the organizational structure of schools as it varies between elementary, middle, secondary schools.

Based on the results of a power analysis (Cohen, 1977; Keppel, 1991) that indicated a minimum required sample size of 44, we randomly selected 52 schools for inclusion in our study. After obtaining permission from the district office, a researcher contacted the principal from each school by phone to request an opportunity to administer surveys to school faculty. Three principals declined to participate. Of the 49 participating schools, two provided fewer than five faculty respondents on the trust measure. Following Halpin (1959), our decision rule for inclusion of a school in the data analysis was having a minimum of five faculty respondents. Therefore, these two schools were dropped from the sample, leaving 47 schools or 90% of the 52 schools randomly selected for inclusion.

Data Collection

We obtained data on teacher trust by surveying the faculty in each of the 47 schools; student data were obtained from the central administrative office of the district. Below we describe our data collection procedures in detail.

Student Variables

We selected student achievement in mathematics and reading as the dependent variables for our study. We were interested in both of these variables not only because each is important to student literacy but also because each involves different student capabilities. In addition, as statistical controls for prior student achievement, we used measures of students' achievement in the same subjects collected 1 year earlier by the school district. Because we sought to include prior achievement in our analyses, we needed two waves of data. The district provided us with student achievement data, measured by a mandatory state achievement test for fourth-grade students, administered approximately 1 month after we surveyed faculties. Prior achievement scores were also provided by the school district for those fourth-grade students who had attended the district the previous year when the seventh edition of the Metropolitan Achievement Test was administered to third graders.

The state department of education provided data indicating adequate KR-20 reliability scores (.88 mathematics, .86 reading) for the state assessment administered to the fourth-grade students in this study. Turning to student scores on the Metropolitan Test, Finley (1995) reported that KR-20 reliability scores are adequate. In addition, separate reviews indicated that although concurrent and construct validity evidence for the Metropolitan Test are adequate, content validity is specific to schools' curricular objectives (Hambleton, 1995; Nitko, 1994; Rogers, 1994). In the sampled district, administrators indicated that the Metropolitan Test was used because it was an appropriate assessment that matched the district's third-grade curriculum. Also, the district followed the state's model fourth-grade curriculum. In sum, we judged student achievement scores on both the third- and fourth-grade assessments to be sufficiently valid and reliable.

In addition to student achievement data, the school district also provided gender, race/ethnicity, and free and reduced-price lunch status (a proxy for SES) data for the fourth-grade students in the schools we sampled. We dummy-coded each of these variables so that a value of "1" respectively denoted female and African American as well as the receipt of a free or reduced-price lunch.

Teacher Trust

Teacher surveys were administered by a researcher during regularly scheduled faculty meetings. Because other data not reported in this article were also collected from teachers during these meetings, half of the teachers in the room received a survey containing questions assessing teacher trust and other social processes in schools. The other half received another survey with different questions. Distribution of surveys to teachers at the meetings was randomized.

Our measure of teacher trust in students and parents consisted of 15 items (see Appendix). The items measured all the facets of trust described earlier. For example, honesty was measured with items such as, "Students in this school cheat if they have the chance," and "Teachers believe what parents tell them." "Students are caring toward one another," was an example of benevolence. Reliability was tapped by, "Parents in this school are reliable in their commitments," and openness was measured by, "The students in this school talk freely about their lives outside of school." Finally, items such as "Teachers in this school trust the parents," and "Teachers in this school trust the students," were general measures of the willingness to risk vulnerability. Response options for these questions ranged along a six-point Likert-type scale from "Strongly Disagree" to "Strongly Agree." The construct and predictive validity of scores on the trust scale have been supported in earlier research; as was expected, trust was negatively related to alienation and conflict and positively related to teacher efficacy. These validity findings and the factor analytic study of the instrument are reported in Hoy and Tschannen-Moran (1999). In the present sample, the alpha coefficient of reliability was .97.

Data Analysis

One reason for the lack of knowledge about the distribution of trust may be that conventional methods of analysis (e.g., correlation and regression) do not permit the partitioning of variance in a dependent variable between and within organizational units. Therefore, to examine the distribution of teacher trust across and within schools, we employed hierarchical linear modeling (HLM). This enabled us to model teacher trust as a feature of school organization that varied both within and among schools. In addition, our second research question was multilevel, focusing on differences among schools in student achievement. Therefore, we also applied HLM to model the effect of trust on this variable. In the multilevel analyses, both student- and school-level variables were grand-mean-centered. In addition, we set the intercept and slopes to vary among schools.

RESULTS

Our final student sample included 2,536 fourth-grade students and 452 teachers in 47 schools. Because we conducted longitudinal research in an urban district with high student mobility, some missing data were an inevitable consequence of our efforts to include prior student achievement in our models. Of the fourth-grade students attending the schools we sampled, slightly over 86% had taken both the mathematics and reading Metropolitan Achievement Tests in the district 1 year earlier as third-grade students. Descriptive statistics for both the student- and school level variables appear in Table 6.1.

The mean size of the elementary school faculties surveyed was just over 21. By design we intended to measure teacher trust by obtaining responses from approximately half of the faculty. However, because there were uncontrollable events (e.g., teacher absences and schedule conflicts), not every teacher attended the meetings in which surveys were administered. Our research team did not attempt to collect data from those who were absent. On average across the schools in the study, we obtained responses from approximately 45% of the teachers in the school. As

Table 6.1. Descriptive Statistics for Student and School Variables

Student level (n = 2,536)	Mean	Std Dev.	Min.	Max.
Female	.48	.50	0	1
African American	.57	.49	0	1
Socioeconomic status	.67	.47	0	1
Mathematics achievement	199.85	23.47	106.00	323.00
Reading achievement	207.73	18.04	137.00	279.00
Prior mathematics achievement	44.31	22.34	1.00	99.00
Prior reading achievement	45.51	20.68	1.00	99.00
School level (n = 47)				
Teacher trust in students and parents	3.70	0.58	2.76	4.88
School size	401.40	107.26	229	710
Faculty size	21.24	5.51	13	37
Faculty members surveyed	9.62	2.58	5	15
Proportion of students with disadvantaged SES	0.62	.20	.10	.89
Proportion of African American students	.56	.28	.08	1.00
Proportion of female students	.46	.08	.27	.64

shown in Table 6.1, the mean number of responses per school was about 10. In no case did teachers present at the faculty meetings we attended refuse to complete the surveys. Over 99% of the teacher surveys returned were usable. The elementary schools we sampled were K-5, and teachers from all grades attended the meetings in which we collected our data. Because we were interested in the collective level of trust and because our surveys were anonymous, we did not attempt to track the grade level that teachers taught.

Teacher responses to the separate trust items were aggregated to the school level. This procedure resulted in a mean score for each school on each of the 15 items. At the school level, the items were submitted to a principal axis factor analysis. We were surprised that items assessing trust in parents and trust in students united to form a single measure of trust. Apparently, teachers did not differentiate their trust between parents and students in these elementary schools. Trust in both parents and students was measured by one scale that represented all of the facets of trust. In this analysis, one factor was extracted with an eigenvalue of 11.11 explaining over 74% of the variance. Factor loadings are reported in the appendix. The factor loadings ranged from .95 to .60, with all but one at .76 or higher. The single-factor structure, combined with the strong factor loadings, suggested that the variables in our scale captured the underlying factor of school trust. The measure of trust for each school was then constructed as the mean of the 15 mean item scores for each school.

Distribution of Teacher Trust

Our first research question addressed the extent to which trust varied among schools. To answer this question we conducted an unconditional multilevel analysis with teacher trust as the dependent variable. The unconditional analysis in HLM is a model with no predictors serving to partition the variance in a dependent variable into its within- and between-school components. Results of this analysis are displayed in Table 2. The HLM estimate of reliability for the school means (i.e., intercepts) was strong (lambda = .902). The results indicated that trust in the sampled urban elementary schools varied slightly more between schools than within (proportion of variance in trust between schools = 50.5%). In other words, half the variation in teachers' perceptions of trust was associated with school membership.

Given the substantial differences among schools in teacher trust, we sought to identify school characteristics that might explain this variation. In particular, we were interested in the extent to which the demographic composition and size of the student body were predictive of differences

**Table 6.2.   HLM Unconditional Model Characteristics:
Variation Between Schools in
Teacher Trust (*n* = 452 Teachers in 47 Schools)**

Intercept (school average)	3.69
Parameter variance:	
Between school	.30045
Within school	.902
HLM reliability estimate	.902
Proportion of variance between schools	.50589[a]

a. Chi-square = 491.93, *df* = 46, *p* < .001

among schools in trust. In Table 6.3 we display the results of several means as outcomes HLM models. In the first three models we independently tested the relation between trust and (1) the proportion of the student body that was African American, (2) the proportion of the student body that received a free or reduced-price lunch, and (3) school size. In Model 4, we show the results of an analysis that combined the statistically significant predictors identified in Models 1 through 3.

The results of Model 1 demonstrated that, with no other predictors in the model, the proportion of African-American students in the student body was associated with 33% of the variance between schools in trust. Importantly, Model 2 showed that SES explained twice as much between-school variance in trust. Model 3 showed that although the gamma coefficient for school size was negative, the effect was not statistically significant. Model 4 combined SES and race/ethnicity to explain variation in trust. Notably, though SES alone explained 66% (Model 2) of the variance in trust, the addition of race/ethnicity in the Model 4 added little (about

**Table 6.3.   Prediction of Variation in
Teacher Trust Among School Means With
Selected School Characteristics (*n* = 452 Teachers in 47 Schools)**

	Model 1	Model 2	Model 3	Model 4
Intercept	3.69	3.69	3.70	3.69
Proportion African American	-1.15*			-.43
Proportion low SES		-2.22*		-1.90*
Number of students			-.0013	
Proportion of between-school variability explained by model[a]	.33	.66*	.04	.69

p < .001
a. Calculated as the reduction in between-school parameter variance reported in Table 6.2.

3%) to its explanatory power. Thus, Model 4 indicated that when they were considered together, student social class, not race/ethnicity, explained the majority of the variability between schools in teacher trust in the urban elementary schools we studied.

Effects of Trust

After identifying trust as a social feature that varied considerably among schools, we used HLM analyses to test our main hypothesis that trust is related to differences among schools in student achievement. We began the multilevel tests with a set of unconditional models, one for each dependent variable (mathematics and reading achievement). Our purpose was to estimate the extent to which student achievement varied between schools. The results of the unconditional models for mathematics and reading achievement are displayed in Table 6.4. The HLM estimates of reliability were strong for both mathematics (lambda = .952) and reading (lambda =.933). The chi-square tests of significance indicated that the proportion of variance between schools for both mathematics (26.8%) and reading (20.4%) was statistically non-zero. Hence, we continued our multilevel modeling to test the hypothesis that teacher trust in students and teachers was significantly and positively related to the achievement differences among the schools in our sample.

Next, we adjusted school means for student demographics (race, gender, and SES) and prior achievement by grand-mean-centering these variables and allowing all level-2 error terms to vary between schools. With school means adjusted for student characteristics, we entered teacher trust in students and parents as a level-2 predictor of differ-

**Table 6.4.   HLM Unconditional Model Characteristics:
Variation Between Schools in
Mathematics and Reading Achievement
(n = 2,536 Students in 47 Schools)**

	Mathematics	Reading
Intercept (school average)	200.57	208.05
Between-school parameter variance	149.03	65.34
Within-school parameter variance	406.77	254.52
HLM reliability estimate for intercepts	.952	.933
Proportion of variance between schools	.26814[a]	.20428[b]

a. Chi-square = 900.40, df = 46, p < .001
b. Chi-square = 635.49, df = 46, p < .001

ences between schools in student achievement. The results of this analysis are reported in Table 6.5. The findings showed that student achievement was significantly and negatively associated with both minority status and disadvantaged socioeconomic status while prior achievement has a significant positive effect. Interestingly, gender was not significantly associated with mathematics achievement but was positively and significantly related to reading achievement. The most important finding in this analysis, however, was that even with school means adjusted for student characteristics, trust was a significant positive predictor of the differences between schools in student achievement. Notably, this model explained 81% of the between-school variation in both mathematics and reading achievement.

Although the results in Table 6.5 were encouraging, we were concerned that other school-level characteristics were not adequately controlled in our level-2 model, which in Table 6.5 contained only trust as a school-level predictor. Because our earlier analysis of the variation in teacher trust (Table 6.3) suggested the school-level SES was the largest predictor of variation between schools in teacher trust, we decided to add school-level SES to our model. For this final test of the effects of trust, we aggregated student SES to the school level for each school to produce a mean score that represented the proportion of students in a school receiving a

Table 6.5. HLM Analysis of the Effect of Student Characteristics and Teacher Trust on Mathematics and Reading Achievement (n = 2,536 Students in 47 Schools)

	Mathematics	*Reading*
Intercept (school average)	200.00	207.89
Teacher Trust[a] (average effect of trust)	6.89*	5.15*
Socioeconomic status	-3.09*	-2.65*
Female	1.01	1.27**
African American	-4.35*	-3.90*
Prior mathematics achievement	.54*	—
Prior reading achievement		.42*
HLM Variance Parameters		
Between-school parameter variance	28.00	12.38
Proportion of between-school variability explained by model	.81	.81

*p < .001
**p < .01
a. Teacher trust is a level-2 predictor of between-school variability in student achievement, adjusted for student demographics and prior achievement.

free or reduced-price lunch. This variable was then entered in our final HLM model together with trust and the student-level control variables.

The results of the final HLM model are displayed in Table 6.6. Because the size of the effects of student-level predictors changed little from those reported in Table 6.5, and in the interest of parsimonious presentation, Table 6.6 includes only the level-2 coefficients for the effect of trust and of school SES. Notably, the addition of SES at the school level did not improve the explanatory power of the model. Moreover, school-level SES was a non-significant predictor, whereas trust continued to be a positive predictor of differences between schools in student mathematics and reading achievement.

DISCUSSION

The results of our study provide important insight into the distribution and effects of teacher trust among urban elementary schools. First, more than half of the variance in teacher trust is associated with school membership. Teachers in different schools, even in schools within the same district, vary considerably in the collective level of trust they hold for students and parents. When we examined this variability, we found that teacher trust is not affected much by the size of the schools. Instead, teacher trust is systematically associated with student socioeconomic sta-

Table 6.6.   Full HLM Analysis: The Effect of Teacher Trust and School SES on Differences Between Schools in Student Achievement (n = 2,536 Students in 47 Schools)

	Mathematics	Reading
Intercept[a] (school average)	200.01	207.88
Teacher trust	6.39*	3.61**
Proportion of students receiving free or reduced-price lunch	-2.06[b]	-5.95[c]
HLM reliability estimate for intercepts	2.73	.65
HLM Variance Parameters:		
Between-school parameter variance	28.71	12.30
Proportion of between-school variability explained by full model	.81	.81

*$p < .001$
**$p < .01$
a. Intercepts are adjusted for all level-1 variables appearing Table 6.5.
b. $p = .747$
c. $p = .203$

tus—the larger the proportion of poor students in the school, the lower teachers' perceptions of trust. Indeed, the proportion of students receiving a free or reduced-price lunch in a given school explains about two-thirds of the differences in trust between schools. Although this finding is distressing, it is important to realize that SES—not race—explained the majority of the variance in teacher trust. This distinction suggests that poverty has a large negative influence on the social relationships between students and parents, and the teachers who serve them. Cultural differences that arise from differences in economic class seem to be harder to overcome in the establishment of trusting relationships.

Trusting relationships make an important contribution to students' academic achievement. Our results showed that after accounting for the effects of student characteristics, including race, gender, SES, and past achievement, trust is a positive predictor of the variance in student achievement among schools. Further, even after controlling for the effects of the proportion of low-income students in a school as a whole, trust still plays an important role in student achievement. In fact, the amount of trust teachers have in students and in parents outweighs the effects of poverty because school SES is not a significant predictor of differences between schools in student achievement when the effect of trust is considered. Trust seems to foster a context that supports student achievement, even in the face of poverty.

Given the continuous calls for reform and accountability in public education, particularly in large urban districts such as the one studied here, we suggest that the critical need to build supportive social features such as trust deserves more attention. Our findings indicate that teacher trust in students and parents is an important social feature that is distributed inequitably among the schools we studied. The need to build trust is signaled by the strength of the effect of trust on student achievement. Students have higher achievement in schools where teachers report greater trust. Our findings also suggest that teachers in schools with more low-income students seem to find trust harder to cultivate. These are the places with the most critical need to learn more about building trust.

This study is only a beginning. Although intriguing, the findings stem from one study of one district, at one level of schooling, in one context. Although the narrowness of the sample helped to control for unexplained variance, it also limits the generalizability of the results. Future research should examine the link between trust and achievement in other contexts and at other levels of schooling. The negative relation between trust and poverty should be confirmed in other settings. In addition, because of the small size of most elementary schools and the design of the study, findings are based on the perceptions of an average of ten teachers per school. Larger schools with larger faculties might provide a finer-grained picture of trust.

CONCLUSION

This study offers new insight into the importance of teacher trust to student learning. To our knowledge, this is the first study that links faculty trust in students and parents with student achievement. Our findings suggest that trust makes schools better places for students to learn, perhaps by enabling and empowering productive connections between families and schools. There seems to be a collective effect of trust; in schools where there was greater trust, student achievement was generally higher.

In some ways, the findings are not surprising. Rotter (1967) asserted that trust is a fundamental component of human learning. When teachers believe their students are competent and reliable, they create learning environments that facilitate student academic success. When students trust their teachers, they are more likely to take the risks that new learning entails.

Trust is a reciprocal, not a one-way process. All members of a school community, not just teachers, need to act to build trust. Attention must be paid to the various facets of trust. Parents and teachers alike need to be explicit in demonstrating their concern for the well being of students. Schools can assist overwhelmed parents in finding constructive ways to care for and discipline their children. Teachers need to persuade parents not only of their caring, but also of their competence to foster student learning. They should discuss their teaching methods so that parents can become partners in the educational process. School personnel need to be not only reliable but open and scrupulously honest in their dealings with families. When families fail to respond in kind, they need to be confronted with kindness and understanding rather than judgment and disdain in order to foster norms that support mutual respect and trustworthiness.

If teachers are to help students make maximum use of the opportunities that schooling can provide (Stanton-Salazar, 1997), the results of this study signal the need to build trust. Without trust, students lose a valuable form of social support. When teachers, students, and parents trust each other and work together cooperatively, a climate of success is likely. In contrast, when these groups do not trust one another, they seek to minimize their vulnerability. The result is disengagement from the educational process that comes at the expense of student achievement. Because of the tendency of trust to build on itself, higher student achievement is likely to produce even greater trust, whereas low student achievement could be expected to lead to a self-reinforcing spiral of blame and suspicion on the part of teachers, parents, and students that would further impair student achievement (Tschannen-Moran & Hoy, 2000).

The development of trusting relationships seems a critical vehicle for improving urban elementary schools and overcoming some of the disadvantages of poverty. We found that poverty more than ethnicity seems to be the culprit in hindering the trust that could lead to achievement for many students in urban schools. This suggests that schools with high concentrations of poor students, not just urban schools, may need to focus on the development of trust. Future research on trust in rural and suburban schools could respond to this conjecture.

Educators and researchers need to understand more about the mechanisms that link trust and achievement. Our findings should encourage further exploration not only of how trust relationships among teachers, parents, and students relate to risk taking but also of how they influence persistence and effort. Teachers' efficacy beliefs may be hampered in a climate of distrust. Teachers' level of trust and their attitudes about student control also seem promising avenues to explore in understanding the link between trust and achievement. With the compelling evidence presented in this article of the important link between trust and student achievement, and especially the importance of that link in explaining the learning outcomes of low-income students, researchers need to work vigorously to unlock the secrets of trust in school settings.

Appendix: Items on the Measure of Teacher Trust[a] and Their Factor Loadings

Item	Factor Loading
1. Students in this school are reliable.	.947
2. Students are caring toward one another.	.945
3. Students in this school can be counted on to do their work.	.944
4. Teachers can count on the parents in this school.	.925
5. Teachers think most of the parents do a good job.	.910
6. Teachers in this school trust the parents to support them.	.909
7. Parents in this school are reliable in their commitments.	.909
8. Teachers in this school believe what students say.	.857
9. Teachers in this school trust their students.	.855
10. Teachers can believe what parents tell them.	.855
11. The students in this school have to be closely supervised.	.819
12. Teachers here believe students are competent learners.	.814

Appendix continues on next page

Appendix: Items on the Measure of Teacher Trust[a] and Their Factor Loadings Continued

Item	Factor Loading
13. Students in this school cheat if they have the chance.	.789
14. Students here are secretive.	.760
15. The students in this school talk freely about their lives outside of school.	.600

a. Alpha coefficient of reliability = .97.

REFERENCES

Baier, A. (1986). Trust and antitrust. *Ethics, 96,* 231-260.

Bank, B. J., & Slavings, R.L. (1990). Effects of peer, faculty, and parental influence on students' persistence. *Sociology of Education, 63,* 208-225.

Bourdieu, P., & Passeron, J.C. (1977). *Reproduction in education, society, and culture.* Beverly Hills, CA: Sage.

Bryk, A. S., & Raudenbush, S. W. (1992). *Hierarchical linear models: Applications and data analysis methods.* Newbury Park, CA: Sage.

Cohen, J. (1977). *Statistical power analysis for the behavioral sciences.* New York: Academic Press.

Coleman, J. S. (1985). Schools and the communities they serve. *Phi Delta Kappan, 66*(8), 527-532.

Coleman, J. S. (1987). Norms as social capital. In G. Radnitzky & P. Bernholz (Eds.), *Economic imperialism: The economic approach applied outside the field of economics* (pp. 135-155), New York: Paragon House.

Driscoll, M. E., & Kerchner, C. T. (1999). The implications of social capital for school, communities, and cities: Educational administration as if a sense of place mattered. In J. Murphy & K. S. Louis (Eds.), *Handbook of research on educational administration* (2d ed., pp. 385-404), San Francisco: Jossey Bass.

Finley, C. J. (1995). Review of the Metropolitan Achievement Test (7th ed.). In J. C. Conoley & J. C. Impara (Eds.), *Twelfth mental measurements yearbook* (pp. 603-606). Lincoln: University of Nebraska Press.

Garnier, C. L., & Raudenbush, S. W. (1991). Neighborhood effects on educational attainment: A multilevel analysis. *Sociology of Education, 64,* 251-262.

Glickman, C. D. (1990, September). Pushing school reform to a new edge: The seven ironies of school empowerment. *Phi Delta Kappan, 72*(1), 68-75.

Goodlad, J. I. (1984). *A place called school: Prospects for the future.* New York: McGraw-Hill.

Halpin, A. W. (1959). *The leader behavior of school superintendents.* Chicago: Midwest Administrative Center.

Hambleton, R. K. (1995). Review of the Metropolitan Achievement Test (7th ed.). In J. C. Conoley & J. C. Impara (Eds.), *Twelfth mental measurements yearbook* (pp. 606-610). Lincoln: University of Nebraska Press.

Hoffman, J., Sabo, D., Bliss, J., & Hoy, W. K. (1994). Building a culture of trust. *Journal of School Leadership, 4,* 484-501.

Hoy, W. K., Sabo, D., & Barnes, K. (1996). Organizational health and faculty trust: A view from the middle level. *Research in Middle Level Education Quarterly, 19*(3), 21-39.

Hoy, W. K., & Tarter, J. C. (1995). *Administrators solving the problems of practice: Decision making concepts, consequences, and cases.* Boston: Allyn and Bacon.

Hoy, W. K., Tarter, C. J., & Witkoskie, L. (1992). Faculty trust in colleagues: Linking the principal with school effectiveness. *Journal of Research and Development in Education, 26*(1), 38-45.

Hoy, W. K., & Tschannen-Moran, M. (1999). Five faces of trust: An empirical confirmation in urban elementary schools. *Journal of School Leadership, 9*(3), 184-208.

Johnson. D. W., & Johnson, R. T. (1999). *Learning together and alone: Cooperative, competitive, and individualistic learning.* Boston: Allyn & Bacon.

Jones, B. L., & Maloy, R. W. (1988). *Partnerships for improving schools.* New York: Glenwood.

Keppel, G. (1991). *Design and analysis: A researcher's handbook.* Englewood Cliffs, NJ: Prentice Hall.

Kozol, J. (1991). *Savage inequalities: Children in America's schools.* New York: Crown.

Lareau, A. (1987). Social class differences in family-school relationships: The importance of cultural capital. *Sociology of Education, 60,* 73-85.

Lee, V., & Croninger, R.G. (1994). The relative importance of home and school in the development of literacy skills for middle-grade students. *American Journal of Education, 102,* 286-329.

National Education Goals Panel. (1995). *The national education goals report: Building a nation of learners.* Washington, DC: U.S. Government Printing Office.

Nitko, A. J. (1994). Review of the Metropolitan Achievement Test (6th ed.). In J. C. Impara & L. L. Murphy (Eds.), *Buros desk reference: Psychological assessment in the schools* (pp. 31-35). Lincoln: University of Nebraska Press.

Odden, A., & Busch, C. (1998). *Financing schools for high performance: Strategies for improving the use of educational resources.* San Francisco: Jossey-Bass.

Odden, A., & Picus, L. (2000). *School finance: A policy perspective* (2d ed.). New York: McGraw-Hill.

Powell, W. W. (1990). Neither market nor hierarchy: Network forms of organization. In B. M. Staw & L. L. Cummings (Eds.), *Research in organizational behavior* (Vol. 12, pp. 295-336). Greenwich, CT: JAI.

Powell, W. W. (1996). Trust-based forms of governance. In R. Kramer & T. Tyler (Eds.), *Trust in organizations: Frontiers of theory and research* (pp. 51-67). Thousand Oaks, CA: Sage.

Putnam, R. D. (1993). *Making democracy work: Civic traditions in modern Italy.* Princeton, NJ: Princeton University Press.

Putnam, R. T., & Borko, H. (1997). Teacher learning: Implications of new views of cognition. In B. J. Biddle, T. L. Good, & I. F. Goodson (Eds.), *International handbook of teachers and teaching* (pp. 1223-1296). Dordrecht, The Netherlands: Kluwer.

Ray, B. (1997). *Home education across the United States*. Purcellville, VA: Home School Legal Defense Association.

Rogers, B. G., (1994). Review of the Metropolitan Achievement Test (6th ed.). In J. C. Impara & L. L. Murphy (Eds.), *Buros desk reference: Psychological assessment in the schools* (pp. 35-40). Lincoln: University of Nebraska Press.

Rotter, J. B. (1967). A new scale for the measurement of interpersonal trust. *Journal of Personality, 35,* 651-665.

Smylie, M. A., & Hart, A. W. (1999). School leadership and teacher learning and change: A human and social capital development perspective. In J. Murphy, & K.S. Louis (Eds.), *Handbook of research on educational administration* (2d ed., pp. 421-442), San Francisco: Jossey Bass.

Stanton-Salazar, R. (1997). A social capital framework for understanding the socialization of racial minority children and youths. *Harvard Educational Review, 67*(1), 1-40.

Sui-Chu, E. H., & Douglas, W. J. (1996). Effects of parental involvement on grade achievement. *Sociology of Education, 69,* 126-141.

Tarter, C. J., Bliss, J. R., & Hoy, W. K. (1989). School characteristics and faculty trust in secondary schools. *Educational Administration Quarterly, 25*(3), 294-308.

Tarter, C. J., Sabo, D., & Hoy, W. K. (1995). Middle school climate, faculty trust and effectiveness: A path analysis. *Journal of Research and Development in Education, 29*(1), 41-49.

Tschannen-Moran, M., & Hoy, W. K. (1998). A conceptual and empirical analysis of trust in schools. *Journal of Educational Administration, 36,* 334-352.

Tschannen-Moran, M., & Hoy, W. K. (2000). *A multidisciplinary analysis of the nature, meaning, and measurement of trust.* Manuscript submitted for publication.

Tschannen-Moran, M. (2001). Collaboration and the need for trust. *Journal of Educational Administration, 39,* 308-331.

Tyack, D., & Cuban, L. (1995). *Tinkering toward utopia: A century of public school reform.* Cambridge, MA: Harvard University Press.

Vinovskis, M. A. (1999). *History and educational policymaking* (Ch. 7, pp. 171-202). New Haven: Yale University Press.

Webb, M. O. (1992). The epistemology of trust and the politics of suspicion. *Pacific Philosophical Quarterly, 73,* 390-400.

Yell, M. L. (1995). Least restrictive environment, inclusion, and students with disabilities: A legal analysis. *Journal of Special Education, 28,* 389-404.

PART VI

ON COLLECTIVE EFFICACY

CHAPTER 7

COLLECTIVE TEACHER EFFICACY

Its Meaning, Measure, and Impact on Student Achievement

Roger D. Goddard, Wayne K. Hoy, and Anita Woolfolk Hoy

One of the great challenges for those who study schools is to learn how school organizations contribute to students' academic success. Schools affect students and their achievement differentially. Identification of school characteristics associated with differences in student achievement is important to the development of effective schools. Bandura (1993, 1997) argues that one powerful construct that varies greatly among schools and that is systematically associated with student achievement is the collective efficacy of teachers within a school.

Collective teacher efficacy, *the perceptions of teachers in a school that the efforts of the faculty as a whole will have a positive effect on students*, is based on Bandura's (1977, 1986, 1997) social cognitive theory, a unified theory of

Reprinted by permission from the *American Educational Research Journal*, Vol. 37, pp. 479-508. Copyright © 2000. All rights reserved.

Essential Ideas for the Reform of American Schools, pp. 139–170
Copyright © 2007 by Information Age Publishing
All rights of reproduction in any form reserved.

behavior change. Social cognitive theory is concerned with human agency, or the ways that people exercise some level of control over their own lives. Central to the exercise of control is sense of self-efficacy or "beliefs in one's capabilities to organize and execute a course of action required to produce a given attainment" (Bandura, 1997, p. 3). But social cognitive theory acknowledges that "personal agency operates within a broad network of sociostructural influences" (p. 6) and thus the theory "extends the analysis of mechanisms of human agency to the exercise of collective agency" (p. 7)—people's shared beliefs that they can work together to produce effects.

As a self-referent perception of capability to execute specific behaviors, individual efficacy beliefs are excellent predictors of individual behavior. In fact, over the last 20 years, researchers have established strong connections between teacher efficacy and teacher behaviors that foster student achievement (Allinder, 1994; Ashton & Webb, 1986; Gibson & Dembo, 1984; Meijer & Foster, 1988; Woolfolk & Hoy, 1990). Although such research has identified links between teachers' perceptions of their own efficacy and student achievement, collective teacher efficacy has received relatively little research attention (Bandura, 1993, 1997; Esselman & Moore, 1992; Newmann, Rutter, & Smith, 1989). Pajares (1997) suggests that studies of collective teacher efficacy are scant because of limits imposed by the intensive data collection required in the study of multiple schools. The purposes of this research are to extend the concept of teacher efficacy to the organizational level, to explore the theoretical nature of collective teacher efficacy, to develop a reliable and valid measure, and to examine the effects of collective teacher efficacy on student achievement. To better understand the concept of collective teacher efficacy, it is useful to examine what is known about individual teacher efficacy.

TEACHER EFFICACY

Over the last 20 years, the construct of teacher efficacy has evolved from J. B. Rotter's (1966) locus of control theory and Albert Bandura's (1977, 1986, 1997) social cognitive theory. However, the meaning and measure of teacher efficacy has been the subject of considerable debate among scholars and researchers (Ashton, Olejnik, Crocker, & McAuliffe, 1982; Gibson & Dembo, 1984; Guskey, 1987; Guskey & Passaro, 1994; Pajares 1996a, 1996b, 1997; Tschannen-Moran, Woolfolk Hoy, & Hoy, 1998).

Historical Perspectives

With the work of J. B. Rotter (1966) as a theoretical base, the researchers at the Rand Corporation studying the effectiveness of reading instruction first conceived of teacher efficacy as the extent to which teachers believed that they could control the reinforcement of their actions. The critical question was whether control of reinforcement lay within the teachers themselves or in the environment. Student motivation and performance were assumed to major sources of reinforcement for teachers. Hence, teachers who believed that they could influence student achievement and motivation were seen as assuming that they could control the reinforcement of their actions and thus having a high level of efficacy. A second conceptual strand of theory and research grew out of the work of Bandura (1977), who identified teacher efficacy as a type of self-efficacy—the outcome of a cognitive process in which people construct beliefs about their capacity to perform at a given level of competence. These beliefs affect how much effort people expend, how long they will persist in the face of difficulties, their resilience in dealing with failures, and the stress they experience in coping with demanding situations (Bandura, 1997).

The existence of the two separate but intertwined conceptual strands growing from two theoretical perspectives has contributed to some confusion about the nature of teacher efficacy. Some educators have assumed that Rotter's internal locus of control and Bandura's perceived self-efficacy are the roughly the same. Bandura (1997) clarifies the difference between these two concepts in his latest work. Beliefs about one's capability to produce certain actions (perceived self-efficacy) are not the same as beliefs about whether actions affect outcomes (locus of control). Indeed, perceived self-efficacy and locus of control bear little or no empirical relationship with each other. Further, perceived self-efficacy is a much stronger predictor of behavior than locus of control. Rotter's scheme of internal-external locus of control is concerned primarily with causal beliefs about the relationship between actions and outcomes, not with personal efficacy. One may believe that a particular outcome is internally controllable, that is, caused by the actions of the individual, but still have little confidence that he or she can accomplish the desired actions.

An Integrated Model of Teacher Efficacy

In response to the conceptual confusion surrounding teacher efficacy and in keeping with the substantial body of research, Tschannen-Moran, Woolfolk Hoy, and Hoy (1998) proposed an integrated model of teacher efficacy. Consistent with social cognitive theory, the major influences on efficacy beliefs are assumed to be the attributional analysis and interpretation of the four sources of information about efficacy described by Bandura (1986, 1997)—mastery experience, physiological arousal, vicarious experience, and verbal persuasion. However, teachers do not feel equally efficacious for all teaching situations. Teacher efficacy is context-specific. Teachers feel efficacious for teaching particular subjects to certain students in specific settings, and they can be expected to feel more or less efficacious under different circumstances. Even from one class period to another, teachers' level of efficacy may change (Ross et al., 1996). Therefore, in making an efficacy judgment, consideration of the teaching task and its context are required. In addition, it is necessary to assess one's strengths and weaknesses *in relation to* the requirements of the task at hand.

In analyzing the *teaching task and its context*, the relative importance of factors that make teaching difficult or act as constraints are weighed against an assessment of the resources available that facilitate learning. In assessing *self-perceptions of teaching competence*, the teacher judges personal capabilities such as skills, knowledge, strategies, or personality traits balanced against personal weaknesses or liabilities in this particular teaching context. The interaction of these two components leads to judgments about self-efficacy for the teaching task at hand. These same four sources of efficacy and the two dimensions of task analysis and teaching competence are included in our model of collective efficacy, as described in the following section.

A MODEL OF COLLECTIVE EFFICACY

Our formulation of collective teacher efficacy builds on the self-efficacy formulation of Bandura (1997) and the model of teacher efficacy described above developed by Tschannen-Moran, Woolfolk Hoy, and Hoy (1998). Collective teacher efficacy is an emergent group-level attribute—the product of the interactive dynamics of the group members. As such, this emergent property is more than the sum of the individual attributes. It is "the groups' shared belief in its conjoint capabilities to organize and execute courses of action required to produce given levels of attainments" (Bandura, 1997, p. 477).

From Individual to Collective Efficacy: Conceptual Underpinnings

Teachers are members of school organizations. Their shared beliefs influence the social milieu of schools (Hoy & Miskel, 1996). Within an organization, perceived collective efficacy represents the shared perceptions of group members concerning "the performance capability of a social system as a whole" (Bandura, 1997, p. 469). Analogous to self-efficacy, collective efficacy is associated with the tasks, level of effort, persistence, shared thoughts, stress levels, and achievement of groups.

Collective Efficacy as a Property of Schools

According to Bandura (1993, 1997), collective teacher efficacy is an important school property. One reason for this conclusion is the link between teacher efficacy and student achievement (Anderson, Greene, & Loewen, 1988; Armor et al., 1976; Ashton & Webb, 1986; Ross, 1992, 1994). Just as individual teacher efficacy may partially explain the effect of teachers on student achievement, from an organizational perspective, collective teacher efficacy may help to explain the differential effect that schools have on student achievement. Collective teacher efficacy, therefore, has the potential to contribute to our understanding of how schools differ in the attainment of their most important objective – the education of students.

Bandura (1997) observes that because schools present teachers with a host of unique challenges involving such things as public accountability, shared responsibility for student outcomes, and minimal control over work environments, the task of developing high levels of collective teacher efficacy is difficult but not impossible. Moreover, there is reason to believe that collective teacher efficacy, once developed, will thrive. At the collective level, efficacy beliefs are social perceptions. Putnam (1993) refers to such social features as moral resources—ones that are strengthened rather than depleted through their use. The potential for efficacy to grow rather than deplete through use is also indicated by the cyclic nature of efficacy implied by reciprocal causality (Bandura, 1997). That is, if collective efficacy gains enhance organizational performance, reciprocal causality suggests that resulting performance improvements may, in turn, strengthen collective organizational efficacy. Thus, to the extent collective teacher efficacy is positively associated with student achievement, there is strong reason to lead schools in a direction that will systematically develop teacher efficacy; such efforts may indeed be rewarded with continuous growth in not only collective teacher efficacy but also student achievement.

Organizational Agency and Organizational Learning

We assume that organizations learn (Cohen & Sproull, 1996; Senge, 1990) and base our notion of organizational learning on the cognitive activity of individual learning; that is, organizations use processes akin to learning in individuals (Cook & Yanon, 1996). One way to extend self-efficacy theory to the collective level is to apply the assumptions of social cognitive theory to the organizational level. A fundamental element of social cognitive theory is human agency. Extended to the school level, the parallel concept is organizational agency. Since agency refers to the intentional pursuit of a course of action, we may begin to understand school organizations as agentive when we consider that schools act purposefully in pursuit of their educational goals. For example, one school may be working to raise student achievement scores while another works to increase the rate and quality of parental involvement. If we consider that such differences are purposeful, we may view them as evidence of organizational agency. The purposive actions schools take as they strive to meet their goals thus reflect organizational intentionality, or agency. Of course, organizational agency results from the agentive actions of individuals.

In addition to human agency, organizational functioning also depends on the knowledge, vicarious learning, self-reflection and self-regulation of individual members. For example, a school that responds to declining achievement scores by implementing a curricular reform that was effective in a neighboring district is engaged in a self-regulatory process that is informed by the vicarious learning of its members. Such examples make clear that the assumptions of social cognitive theory about the importance of vicarious learning and self-regulation also apply to organizations, though we must recognize that it is through individuals that organizations act. In addition, the sources of efficacy information identified for individuals in social cognitive theory can be seen as sources of collective efficacy information.

Sources of Collective Efficacy Information

Bandura (1986, 1997) postulates four sources of self-efficacy information: mastery experience, vicarious experience, social persuasion, and emotional arousal. Just as these sources are critical for individuals, they are also fundamental in the development of collective teacher efficacy.

Mastery Experience

Mastery experiences are important for organizations. Teachers as a group experience successes and failures. Successes build a robust belief in the faculty's sense of collective efficacy, while failures undermine it. If success, however, is frequent and too easy, failure is likely to produce discouragement. A resilient sense of collective efficacy probably requires experience in overcoming difficulties through persistent effort. Indeed, organizations learn by experience whether they are likely to succeed in attaining their goals (Huber, 1996; Levitt & March, 1996).

Vicarious Experience

Teachers do not rely on direct experience as the only source of information about their collective efficacy. They listen to stories told to them about achievements of their colleagues as well as success stories of other schools. Similarly, the effective schools research enumerates the characteristics of exemplary schools. So just as vicarious experience and modeling serve as effective ways to develop personal teacher efficacy, so too do they promote collective teacher efficacy. Organizations learn by observing other organizations (Huber, 1996).

Social Persuasion

Social persuasion is another means of strengthening a faculty's conviction that they have the capabilities to achieve what they seek. Talks, workshops, professional development opportunities, and feedback about achievement can move teachers. The more cohesive the faculty, the more likely the group as a whole can be persuaded by sound argument. Verbal persuasion alone is not likely to be a powerful change agent, but coupled with models of success and positive direct experience, it can influence the collective efficacy of a faculty. Persuasion can also encourage a faculty to give the extra effort that leads to success; thus, persuasion can support persistence and persistence can lead to the solution of problems.

Affective States

Organizations have affective states. Just as individuals react to stress, so do organizations. Efficacious organizations can tolerate pressure and crises and continue to function without severe negative consequences; in fact, they learn how to adapt and cope with disruptive forces. Less efficacious organizations when confronted by such forces, react in dysfunctional ways, which reinforce their basic dispositions of failure. They misinterpret stimuli, sometimes overreacting and other times underreacting or not reacting at all. The affective state of an organization has much to do with how challenges are interpreted by the organizations.

Elements of Collective Efficacy

Although all four of these sources of information are pivotal in the creation of collective teacher efficacy, it is the cognitive processing and interpretation of this information that is critical. Consistent with the Tschannen-Moran et al. (1998) model of teacher efficacy described earlier, we postulate two key elements in the development of collective teaching efficacy: analysis of the teaching task and the assessment of teaching competence. Further, we postulate that perceptions of a group capability to successfully educate students result when teachers consider the level of difficulty of the teaching task *in relation* to their perceptions of group competence. Thus, while we may discuss analysis of the teaching task and perceptions of group competence separately, perceptions of collective efficacy are formed only after teachers weigh these elements in relation to one another.

Analysis of the Teaching Task

Teachers assess what will be required as they engage in teaching; we call this process the analysis of the teaching task. Such analysis occurs at two levels—the individual and the school. At the school level, the analysis produces inferences about the challenges of teaching in that school, that is, what it would take for teachers in the school to be successful. Factors that characterize the task include the abilities and motivations of students, the availability of instructional materials, the presence of community resources and constraints, and the appropriateness of the school's physical facilities. To summarize, teachers analyze what constitutes successful teaching in their school, what barriers or limitations must be overcome, and what resources are available to achieve success.

Assessment of Teaching Competence

Teachers analyze the teaching task in conjunction with their assessment of the teaching competency of the faculty; in fact, teachers make explicit judgments of the teaching competence of their colleagues in light of an analysis of the teaching task in their specific school. At the school level, the analysis of teaching competence produces inferences about the faculty's teaching skills, methods, training, and expertise. Judgments of teaching competence might also include positive faculty beliefs in the ability of all children in their school to succeed. Because the analyses of task and competence occur simultaneously, it is difficult to separate these two domains of collective teacher efficacy. They interact with each other as collective teacher efficacy emerges. In sum, the major influences on collective teacher efficacy are assumed to be the attributional analysis and interpretation of the four sources of information—mastery experience, vicarious experience, social persuasion, and affective state (Gist & Mitchell, 1992). In these processes, the organization focuses its attention on two related domains: the teaching task and teaching competence. Both domains are assessed in terms of whether the organization has the capacities to succeed in teaching students. The interactions of these assessments lead to the shaping of collective teacher efficacy in a school.

We theorize that the consequences of high collective teacher efficacy will be the acceptance of challenging goals, strong organizational effort, and a persistence that leads to better performance. Of course, the opposite is also true. Lower collective efficacy leads to less effort, the propensity to give up, and a lower level of performance. The development and components of collective teacher efficacy are summarized in Figure 7.1. As shown in Figure 7.1, the proficiency of performance provides feedback to the organization, which provides new information that will further shape the collective teacher efficacy of the school. Beliefs about both the task of teaching and the teaching competence, however, are likely to remain unchanged unless compelling evidence intrudes and causes them to be reevaluated (Bandura, 1997). Thus, once established, the collective efficacy of a school is a relatively stable property that requires substantial effort to change.

We sought to develop a measure of collective teacher efficacy guided by the theoretical model developed above. Collective teacher efficacy is a construct measuring teachers' beliefs about the collective (not individual) capability of a faculty to influence student achievement; it refers to the perceptions of teachers that the efforts of the faculty of a school will have a positive effect on student achievement. One must consider, however, whether an assessment of collective teacher efficacy should ask teachers about perceptions of themselves, or ask about perceptions of the faculty as

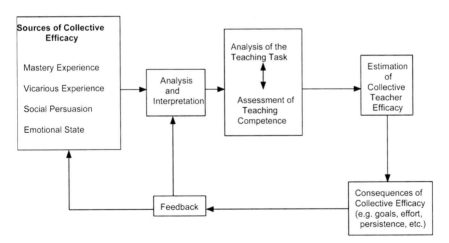

Figure 7.1.   A Simplified Model of Collective Teacher Efficacy.

a whole. The difference between these two alternatives is represented in the following sample items about teacher competence:

- Individual orientation: "I am able to get through to the most difficult students."
- Group orientation: "Teachers in this school can get through to the most difficult students."

Our decision to choose a group orientation for the items in our collective efficacy scale was influenced by two factors. First, Bandura (1993, 1997) stated that when a researcher is attempting to measure collective efficacy, it is important that the orientation (individual or group) reflect the degree of coupling (loose to tight) present in an organization. According to Bandura, the more loosely coupled an organization, the more appropriate it is to measure collective efficacy as the aggregate of each individual's perceptions of his or her efficaciousness. However, for more tightly coupled systems with higher levels of interdependence among jobs, it is more appropriate to assess collective efficacy as the average of perceptions individuals hold of the collective. Because of the shared goals (e.g., to educate all children) and similarity of responsibilities across teaching positions, elementary schools are generally considered to be more tightly coupled than loosely coupled (Bandura, 1993; Clarke, Ellett, Bateman, & Rugutt, 1996; Hoy & Miskel, 1996). Thus, Bandura's strategy suggests that questions about collective teacher efficacy in elementary schools should be written to reflect a group orientation. If we accept that elementary schools are more tightly than loosely coupled, Bandura's reasoning suggests that questions about collective teacher efficacy be written to reflect a group orientation. However, a second perspective suggests that, independent of the degree of coupling, group orientated items reflect the collective experience of group members better than individually-oriented items. Porter (1992) notes that when organizational-level aggregates are constructed from individual-level responses, the individual responses are not independent, but rather they are subject to the influences of group membership. Porter therefore suggests that if questions reflect a group orientation (as in example 2 above), group level influences are more accurately reflected in the group mean. Because we intended our scale to operationalize a group level construct—collective teacher efficacy—and, because we find schools to be more tightly structured than loosely structured, we chose a group orientation for the items in our collective teacher efficacy scale.

Researchers examining teacher efficacy scales have cautioned that the wording of items may influence respondents. In particular, teachers may express different efficacy beliefs depending on whether the outcomes described are positive or negative (Guskey, 1982, 1987; Woolfolk & Hoy, 1990). Thus we made certain to include both positively-worded (+) and negatively-worded (-) items in our scale. Finally, following the model of collective teacher efficacy developed in this paper, items were worded so that teachers would consider both group competence (GC) and task analysis (TA) in their efficacy assessments. This approach led to the identification of four types of items to assess collective efficacy beliefs: group competence/positive (GC+), group competence/negative (GC-), task analysis/positive (TA+), and task analysis/negative (TA-).

One of the most commonly used and well-researched instruments for assessing teacher efficacy is the Likert-type scale developed by Gibson and Dembo (1984). Although the original scale contains 30 items, researchers often use a 16-item version that contains the most reliable and factorially pure items. We used the 16-item version of the Gibson and Dembo instrument as a beginning point in developing our scale, adapting the items to adhere to the four categories described above (GC+, GC-, TA+, TA-). One obvious difference between the Gibson and Dembo teacher efficacy instrument and the collective teacher efficacy instrument developed here is that Gibson and Dembo's measure used individually-oriented items whereas our items are group-oriented. For example, a Gibson and Dembo item such as "I can reach a difficult student," was restated to assess collective efficacy as follows, "Teachers in this school can reach a difficult student." Using our four categories to analyze the 16-item Gibson and Dembo instrument, we found that only two categories were represented—positively worded items about competence and negatively worded items about the task. Thus, in order to represent all four types in our model, we had to create negatively-worded items addressing competence and positively worded items addressing task. The sample items below are examples of the four types of collective efficacy:

- Teachers in this school are well-prepared to teach the subjects they are assigned to teach (GC+).
- Teachers here don't have the skills needed to produce meaningful student learning (GC-).
- The opportunities in this community help ensure that these students will learn (TA+).
- The lack of instructional materials and supplies in this school makes teaching very difficult (TA-).

The response format of our scale is the same 6-point Likert ("strongly agree" to "strongly disagree") format used by Gibson and Dembo.

Preliminary Review

To insure that the items selected for inclusion in the survey adequately represented the content of collective teacher efficacy, a panel of three experts from The Ohio State University (a professor of educational psychology, a professor of educational administration, and a teacher efficacy researcher) reviewed the questionnaire. Each member received copies of the collective teacher efficacy instrument and was asked to judge whether the items adequately represented the four response categories of collective teacher efficacy outlined above (GC+, GC-, TA+, TA-). The experts noted that in addition to influences from outside the school such as home support and student readiness, the teaching task also included influences from within the school such as the availability of a wide range of materials and supplies used in teaching. In response, items reflecting the availability of teaching materials and supplies were added to the collective teacher efficacy instrument in an attempt reflect the teaching task faced by elementary school teachers. One panel member also made several helpful comments on the wording of the items. Changes in response to the panel concerns were made.

Field Test

Next, the revised instrument was submitted to a field test. Six teachers were asked to give feedback regarding the clarity of instructions, length of the instrument, appropriateness of the questions, and any other responses they had to the instrument. The feedback of these teachers was intended to provide another opportunity to revise the survey instrument before conducting a pilot study, but the teachers who participated in the field test noted no difficulties or concerns with the instrument.

Pilot Study

Sample

A sample of 70 teachers, one from each of 70 different schools in five states, was selected to test the psychometric properties of the Collective Teacher Efficacy Scale using the method of known groups (Rokeach, 1960). Half of the schools selected had reputations of relatively high conflict and the other half had relatively low conflict among the faculty.

School reputations for conflict were ascertained from educators, administrators, and professors of education familiar with the school. Because our sample was a convenience sample consisting of schools recommended as high or low in conflict, we did not confront the problem of persons' inability to classify the schools. Sampled schools were those identified as falling into one category or the other; by design, this approach facilitated our application of the method of known groups. The 46 teachers in 46 schools who returned useable responses represented 66% of the schools sampled. Of these 46 schools, 24 were low conflict and 22 were high conflict schools.

Instruments

In addition to the collective teacher efficacy items, teachers were asked to respond to a sense of powerless scale (Zielinski & Hoy, 1983), an individual teacher efficacy scale (Bandura, unpublished), and a measure of teacher trust in colleagues (Hoy & Kupersmith, 1985; Hoy & Sabo, 1998). These additional measures were included to provide a validity check on the efficacy measure. We predicted that collective teacher efficacy would be positively related to teacher efficacy and trust in colleagues and negatively related sense of powerlessness and degree of conflict.

Results

Teacher responses were submitted to a principal axis factor analysis with a varimax rotation. Two factors emerged from the collective efficacy items (eigenvalues of 7.53 and 1.96) that explained a total of 63.2 percent of the variance in the collective teacher efficacy items. Close inspection of the factor loadings revealed that, with one exception, the items loading on factors one and two reflected the group competence and task analysis dimensions of collective efficacy respectively.

The only item that did not load higher on the expected factor was written to assess teachers' perceptions of group competence, "Teachers here don't have the skills needed to reach all of the students." The skills needed to reach all of the students certainly depend on the characteristics of the students as well as other relevant dimensions of the teaching task. This item loaded slightly higher on the task analysis factor. Although the item is the only one that did not load higher on the factor expected, there were five other items loading .40 or higher on both factors. These dual loadings indicated that teachers had difficulty separating their perceptions of the collective capabilities of a faculty from their perceptions of the teaching task. This finding was consistent with our theoretical model that indicates collective efficacy, rather than being comprised of two separate and unique dimensions, results from cognitive processing that integrates teachers' perceptions of group competence and their assessment of the task; in other words, collective efficacy reflects perceptions of group competence judged relative to the task at hand. We further examined the independence of the factors by correlating them. The correlation coefficient indicated a strong relation (r = .71, p < .001) between the factors. Given the theoretical connection between perceptions of competence and the task in defining collective efficacy as well as the dual loading of many of the items in the initial factor analysis and the high correlation between the factors, we performed a second factor analysis, calling for a one-factor solution. The single factor explained 50.5 percent of the variance in the collective efficacy items. The loadings for the items ranged from .47 to .87 with all but four items loading .71 or above.

These results provided evidence that collective teacher efficacy in elementary schools is a single construct uniting the concepts of group competence and task analysis. Accordingly, a single collective teacher efficacy score was constructed for each of the pilot study schools. The scale was calculated as the mean score of all items in the collective teacher efficacy survey.

To check for criterion-related validity of the collective teacher efficacy scale, we examined the relationships between collective teacher efficacy and conflict, sense of powerlessness, trust in colleagues, and individual efficacy. As predicted, conflict was negatively related to collective efficacy. The mean collective teacher efficacy score for low conflict schools (4.27) was significantly higher (t = 5.08, p < .001) than the mean score for high conflict schools (3.17).

Teacher powerlessness (Zielinski & Hoy, 1983) served as a criterion expected to be negatively related to collective teacher efficacy. In a school where teachers feel powerless, it is likely that organizational agency, a key mechanism of collective teacher efficacy, would be weakened. As predicted, the correlation between collective teacher efficacy and teacher powerlessness was significant and negative (r = -.51, p < .001).

Trust in colleagues (Hoy & Kupersmith, 1985; Hoy & Sabo, 1998) served as a criterion expected to be positively related to collective teacher efficacy. Schools with highly trusting teachers offer enhanced levels of collegiality and, therefore, more opportunities for vicarious learning than are found in schools where teachers perceive less trust. Increased exposure to efficacy-building, vicarious learning likely leads to higher collective efficacy. As expected, the correlation between collective efficacy and trust among colleagues was positive and significant (r = .67, p < .001).

Finally, the validity of the collective teacher efficacy scale was also tested using a 10-item measure of teacher efficacy developed by Bandura (Bandura, unpublished). As expected, collective teacher efficacy and aggregated individual teacher efficacy were moderately and positively related ($r = .41$, $p < .001$). The results of the correlational analyses along with reliability information are summarized in Table 7.1.

The results of the pilot study supported the validity and reliability of our collective efficacy measure, but several minor weaknesses were revealed. One was item redundancy. In particular, two items were similar in the way that they united perceptions of task and competence ("Teachers here need more training to know how to deal with these students" and "Teachers here don't have the skills needed to reach all of the students"). In the interest of parsimony, we decided to delete the latter item based on its lower factor loading. Of the 14 remaining items, four related to task analysis. Of these four task analysis items, two referred to materials and supplies and again we decided to delete the item with the lower loading.

The pilot analysis also led to the development of new items about perceptions of group competence and task analysis. After deleting the items above, we re-examined our scale to determine whether additional items could be generated that would strengthen our measure of collective efficacy. Three additional group competence items reflecting teachers' perceptions of the subject matter knowledge (CTE17), pedagogical skills (CTE18), and classroom management skills (CTE21) of their colleagues were written in consultation with the panel of experts. To provide a more comprehensive assessment of the difficulties and resources inherent to the task of teaching in a given school, the task analysis dimension was enhanced with additional items reflecting the influence of student safety concerns (CTE19), drug and alcohol abuse (CTE20), school facilities (CTE15), student motivation (CTE14), and community support (CTE16). All of the items in the final collective teacher efficacy instrument are summarized in Table 7.2.

Table 7.1.   Reliabilities and Correlations for Pilot Study Variables

Variable	CTE	TP	TT	TE
Collective teacher efficacy CTE	.92[a]			
Teacher powerlessness (TP)	-.51**	.83[a]		
Trust in teachers (TT)	.67**	-.33*	.95[a*]	
Teacher efficacy (TE)	.41**	-.55**	.30*	.87[a]

** Correlation significant at the 0.01 level.

a. Scale reliabilities along diagonal

Table 7.2.   Revised Collective Teacher Efficacy Instrument

Study No.	Pilot No.	Item	GC+	GC-	TA+	TA-
CTE1	1	Teachers in this school have what it takes to get the children to learn.	X			
CTE2	2	Teachers in this school are able to get through to difficult students.	X			
CTE3	3	If a child doesn't learn something the first time teachers will try another way.	X			
CTE4	4	Teachers here are confident they will be able to motivate their students.	X			
CTE5	5	Teachers in this school really believe every child can learn.	X			
CTE6	6	If a child doesn't want to learn teachers here give up.		X		
CTE7	7	Teachers here need more training to know how to deal with these students.		X		
CTE8	8	Teachers in this school think there are some students that no one can reach.		X		
CTE9	9	Teachers here don't have the skills needed to produce meaningful student learning.		X		
CTE10	11	Teachers here fail to reach some students because of poor teaching methods.		X		
CTE11	12	These students come to school ready to learn.			X	
CTE12	13	Homelife provides so many advantages they are bound to learn.			X	
CTE13	14	The lack of instructional materials and supplies makes teaching very difficult.				X
CTE14	new	Students here just aren't motivated to learn.				X
CTE15	new	The quality of school facilities here really facilitates the teaching and learning process.			X	
CTE16	new	The opportunities in this community help ensure that these students will learn.			X	
CTE17	new	Teachers here are well-prepared to teach the subjects they are assigned to teach.	X			
CTE18	new	Teachers in this school are skilled in various methods of teaching.	X			
CTE19	new	Learning is more difficult at this school because students are worried about their safety.				X
CTE20	new	Drug and alcohol abuse in the community make learning difficult for students here.				X
CET21	new	Teachers in this school do not have the skills to deal with student disciplinary problems.		X		

A FURTHER TEST OF THE COLLECTIVE EFFICACY SCALE

Having developed a measure of collective teacher efficacy in our field and pilot studies, we were ready to test the scale in a more comprehensive sample. In particular, we were interested in checking its psychometric properties and using the scale to test some predictions about collective teacher efficacy and student achievement in urban elementary schools.

Sample

The population for this study was the elementary schools within one large urban midwestern school district. An urban district was selected to hold constant differences in teacher efficacy that might occur between urban and non-urban districts. Additionally, because this study focused on schools in just one district, there is no possibility for uncontrolled between-district effects. Further, limiting this study to elementary schools controls for the organizational structure (i.e., elementary, middle, secondary) of the schools, thus allowing for a constant approach to the measurement of collective efficacy. The principal from each of 50 randomly selected schools was solicited via phone by a researcher to schedule a time for the administration of surveys to school faculty (no schools from the pilot study were included in this group). One principal declined to participate. Of the 49 participating schools, two provided fewer than five faculty respondents. Our decision rule for including a school in the data analysis was having at least five respondents (Halpin, 1959), thus these two schools were dropped from the sample, leaving 47 schools or 94% of the 50 schools randomly selected for inclusion. A total of 452 teachers completed surveys and over 99% of the forms returned were useable.

Data Collection

Data were obtained from both teachers and students in the 47 elementary schools. Student achievement and demographic data for all schools in the final sample were obtained from the central administrative office of the district. Teacher surveys, on the other hand, were researcher-administered. To the greatest extent possible, the researcher controlled the location, time, and conditions under which these surveys were administered to teachers. Surveys were administered to faculty groups in the afternoon, during regularly-scheduled faculty meetings. During these meetings, other data beyond the scope of the present study were also collected from teachers. For this reason, half of the teachers in the room received a survey containing questions assessing collective efficacy and other social processes in school—personal teaching efficacy (Woolfolk & Hoy, 1993) and faculty trust in colleagues (Hoy & Kupersmith, 1985). The other half received another survey with different questions, including a measure of institutional integrity (Hoy & Sabo, 1998). Distribution occurred so that every other teacher received a collective efficacy survey; teachers sitting next to one another had different surveys. Elementary school faculties in the selected district ranged in size from approximately 10 to 40. Thus, for any given school, faculty perceptions are represented by the responses of half the faculty (approximately 5 to 20 teachers, depending on school size).

Because this study was guided by Bandura's work and because there is evidence to support the conjecture that efficacy perceptions are associated with student achievement in mathematics and reading, both subjects were selected as the dependent variables for the present study. The achievement variables were measured by the seventh edition of the Metropolitan Achievement Test. Student test scores, gender, race/ethnicity, free and reduced-price lunch status (a proxy for SES) and school size were provided by the school district. The Metropolitan tests are given in the 2nd, 3rd, and 5th grades; there were 2520 students in grade two, 2438 in grade three, and 2058 in grade five, for a total of 7016 students in the final sample.

Collective Teacher Efficacy Scale

Teacher responses to the 21-item collective teacher efficacy instrument were aggregated to the school level and submitted to a factor analysis. The aggregation procedure produced a mean school score for each of the 21 items. Given our model for collective teacher efficacy and the results from the pilot, we expected one strong factor to be extracted. Inspection of the loadings in Table 7.3 reveals that, in fact, all items loaded strongly on a single factor and explained 57.89 percent of the variance. As a test of factor independence we constructed the two factors indicated by the factor loadings. The strength of the correlation between these factors ($r =$ .75, $p <$ .001) provided further evidence that collective teacher efficacy is the common unobserved factor operationalized by our revised collective efficacy scale (See Appendix).

Validity and Reliability

The collective teacher efficacy data were gathered along with data measuring other social processes in schools. These additional data provided the opportunity to perform further tests of criterion-related validity for

Table 7.3.   Factor Loadings for a One-Factor Solution

Item No.	Items	Factor Loadings
CTE4	Teachers here are confident they will be able to motivate their students.	.93
CTE1	Teachers in this school have what it takes to get the children to learn.	.84
CTE5	Teachers in this school really believe every child can learn.	.84
CTE2	Teachers in this school are able to get through to difficult students.	.83
CTE11	These students come to school ready to learn.	.82
CTE19	Learning is more difficult at this school because students are worried about their safety.	.80
CTE9	Teachers here don't have the skills needed to produce meaningful student learning.	.79
CTE14	Students here just aren't motivated to learn.	.79
CTE21	Teachers in this school do not have the skills to deal with student disciplinary problems.	.77
CTE6	If a child doesn't want to learn teachers here give up.	.77
CTE10	Teachers here fail to reach some students because of poor teaching methods.	.76
CTE7	Teachers here need more training to know how to deal with these students.	.74
CTE16	The opportunities in this community help ensure that these students will learn.	.73
CTE17	Teachers here are well-prepared to teach the subjects they are assigned to teach.	.72
CTE20	Drug and alcohol abuse in the community make learning difficult for students here.	.72
CTE3	If a child doesn't learn something the first time teachers will try another way.	.72
CTE8	Teachers in this school think there are some students that no one can reach.	.69
CTE12	Homelife provides so many advantages they are bound to learn.	.65
CTE18	Teachers in this school are skilled in various methods of teaching.	.64
CTE13	The lack of instructional materials and supplies makes teaching very difficult.	.62
CTE15	The quality of school facilities here really facilitates the teaching and learning process.	.61

the collective teacher efficacy scale. The criterion variables examined were personal teaching efficacy (Hoy & Woolfolk, 1993), faculty trust in colleagues (Hoy & Kupersmith, 1985), and environmental press (Hoy & Sabo, 1998). Personal teaching efficacy is a measure of a teacher's self-perceptions of capability to educate students. It was predicted that when aggregated to the school level, teachers' perceptions of personal efficacy would be moderately and positively related to collective teacher efficacy; a high correlation was not expected because personal and collective teacher efficacy have different referents (self versus group). Moreover, the collective teacher efficacy measure directly assesses perceptions of both perceived competence and task whereas the personal teacher efficacy measure includes only items about competence. As predicted, there was a moderate and positive ($r = .54$, $p < .01$) correlation between personal teacher efficacy aggregated at the school level and collective teacher efficacy.

A positive relationship between faculty trust in colleagues and collective teacher efficacy was predicted, and similar to the pilot results, trust in colleagues was positively and significantly related to collective teacher efficacy ($r = .62$, $p < .01$).

Finally, we predicted no relationship between collective teacher efficacy and environmental press or the extent to which teachers experience "unreasonable community demands" (Hoy & Sabo, 1998). There is no a priori reason to expect that teachers' assessments of group capabilities would be associated with their perceptions of external demands. In other words, a demanding task and external pressures do not necessarily make people feel more or less capable. It is how they handle the pressure that determines capability. As predicted, the observed relationship between collective teacher efficacy and environmental press was not statistically significant ($r = .05$, n.s.). See Table 7.4 for a summary of the correlational results.

According to Kerlinger (1986), the construct validity of an operational measure may be established with correlational evidence that shows a given construct is positively related, negatively related, and not related to other constructs as expected. Taken together the results from both the pilot and full study show that, as predicted, our measure of collective teacher efficacy was *positively* related to: (a) aggregated teacher efficacy as assessed by Bandura's (unpublished) measure, (b) aggregated personal teacher efficacy assessed using Hoy and Woolfolk (1993) adaptation of a set of Gibson and Dembo (1984) items, (c) and faculty trust in colleagues.

Table 7.4. Reliabilities and Correlations for Collective Teacher Efficacy Scale

Variable	CTE	PTE	TC	II
Collective teacher efficacy (CTE)	.96[a]			
Personal teaching efficacy (PTE)	.54**	.79[a]		
Trust in colleagues (TC)	.62**	.23	.92[a]	
Institutional Integrity (II)	.05	-.01	-.05	.66[a]

** Correlation significant at the 0.01 level.
a. Scale reliabilities along diagonal.

In addition, collective efficacy was *negatively* related to teacher powerlessness and *unrelated* to environmental press. These results provide evidence that the collective teacher efficacy scale employed in this study is valid. In addition, the measure has high internal reliability (alpha = .96).

COLLECTIVE TEACHER EFFICACY AND STUDENT ACHIEVEMENT

Collective teacher efficacy is a way of conceptualizing the normative environment of a school and its influence on both personal and organizational behavior. That is, teachers' beliefs about the faculty's capability to successfully educate students constitute a norm that influences the actions and achievements of schools. Given that collective teacher efficacy shapes the normative environment of a school, understanding how collective teacher efficacy influences student achievement requires that we consider the influence of social norms on the behavior of group members.

Rationale and Hypothesis

Because social cognitive theory specifies that teachers' perceptions of self and group capability influence their actions, it follows that these actions will be judged by the group relative to group norms such as those set by collective efficacy beliefs. According to Coleman (1985, 1987), norms develop to permit group members some control over the actions of others when those actions have consequences for the group. When a teacher's actions are incongruent with the shared beliefs of the group, the teacher's actions will be sanctioned by group members; in fact, Coleman argues that the severity of the social sanctions delivered to those who break norms will be equal in magnitude to the effect of norm-breaking on the collective. Thus, if most teachers in a school are highly efficacious, the normative environment will press teachers to persist in their educational efforts. Moreover, the press to perform will be accompanied by social sanctions for those who do not.

It is because collective teacher efficacy beliefs shape the normative environment of a school that they have a strong influence over teacher behavior and, consequently, student achievement. Based on self-efficacy theory we suggest that when collective efficacy is high, teachers in a school believe they can reach their students and that they can overcome negative external influences. Given these beliefs, teachers are more persistent in their efforts; they plan more; they accept responsibility for student achievement; and temporary setbacks or failures do not discourage them. Thus, strong collective efficacy perceptions not only enhance individual teacher performance, but also influence the pattern of shared beliefs held by organizational members. Given the influence of group norms, a teacher with average personal efficacy beliefs may tend to exert even more effort upon joining a faculty with high levels of collective teacher efficacy. Such behavioral changes reflect the normative effect of a school's collective efficacy on its individual members.

Several school-level studies indicate that aggregated teacher efficacy is associated with increased rates of parental involvement (Hoover-Demp-sey, Bassler, & Brissie, 1987), students' prior ability, school orderliness, teacher innovation, and teacher knowledge of other teachers' courses (Newmann, Rutter, & Smith, 1989), and suspensions and dropout rates (Esselman & Moore, 1992). Although these studies suggest that the organizational characteristic measured by aggregated individual *teacher* efficacy has desirable effects, these studies did not examine *collective* teacher efficacy. Indeed, if we search for studies of collective teacher efficacy that focus on student achievement, we find only one, published by Bandura (1993). In this groundbreaking study of collective teacher efficacy and student achievement, Bandura reached two important conclusions: (a) student achievement (aggregated to the school level) is significantly and positively related to collective efficacy, and (b) collective efficacy has a greater effect on student achievement than does student socioeconomic status (aggregated to the school level).

Bandura's conclusions are powerful ones that offer great hope to schools struggling to increase student achievement and overcome the association between socioeconomic status and achievement. Our study is influenced by Bandura's (1993) research; however, it is not a replication. While our study does consider the variables investigated by Bandura, there is an important methodological difference. Unlike Bandura and the authors of prior studies of aggregated teacher efficacy (Esselman & Moore, 1992; Newmann, Rutter, & Smith, 1989), we did not aggregate student achievement or socioeconomic status to the school level. This analytic decision preserves the considerable variance in student characteristics that occurs within schools and avoids the bias that results when student characteristics are aggregated to the school level. Instead of aggregating student characteristics to the school level, this study of collective teacher efficacy was conducted using multilevel modeling thereby allowing us to analyze only the portion of variance in student characteristics that occurs between schools. Hierarchical linear modeling (HLM) was employed to avoid the aggregation bias, misestimated standard errors, and heterogeneity of regression that may compromise the results of studies in which student characteristics are aggregated to the school level (Bryk & Raudenbush, 1992).

Collective teacher efficacy is conceived as an emergent characteristic of schools, one that gains its meaning from collective perceptions and is, therefore, not reducible to the individual measures from which group level aggregates are constructed. Yet, collective teacher efficacy, along with many organizational features such as school size and climate, is experienced individually by each organizational member. From a methodological perspective, this reality is a multilevel phenomenon. For example, while an individual teacher may be highly inefficacious, that teacher might perform differently depending on whether the majority of teacher colleagues in a school share strong perceptions of collective efficacy. In other words, the effect of an individual teacher's efficaciousness may be either attenuated or enhanced depending on the level of collective efficacy in a school. Collective teacher efficacy may, thus, positively affect numerous teacher behaviors that tend to increase student achievement. Accordingly, we hypothesize that *collective teacher efficacy is positively associated with differences between schools in student-level achievement.*

Results

The dependent variables for this study were student achievement in mathematics and reading. The decision to investigate the relationship between these dependent variables and collective teacher efficacy was made in light of the relationships observed between teacher efficacy and student achievement in prior studies and the theoretical rationale described above. The dependent variables in previous studies of teacher efficacy include reasoning in language as measured by the New Jersey Test of Reasoning Skills (Anderson, Greene, & Loewen, 1988), reading achievement (Armor et al., 1976), and mathematics, language, and reading as measured by the Metropolitan Achievement Test (Ashton & Webb, 1986). Additionally, in his study of collective efficacy, Bandura (1993) observed a relationship between collective efficacy and mathematics and reading achievement. Because our study is guided by Bandura's work and because there is additional evidence to support the conjecture that efficacy perceptions are associated with student achievement in mathematics and reading, these were selected as the dependent variables for the present study. Furthermore, consistent with the reasoning of Lee and Smith (1997), we chose math and reading achievement because these subjects are important to students' future and different from one another.

Within each school, we modeled the variance in student mathematics and reading achievement associated with student-level demographic variables representing socioeconomic status, African-American status, and gender. Socioeconomic status was operationalized as a dichotomous variable reflecting a student's free or reduced price lunch status. Students receiving a free or reduced price lunch were coded "1" while all others were coded "0" for the variable SES. Similarly, African-American students were coded "1" for AFAM and, female students were coded "1" for FEMALE. Thus African-American status, socioeconomic status, and gender were used as control variables as we examined the relation between collective efficacy and student achievement. Descriptive statistics for the student level variables are reported in Table 7.5 and correlations among these variables are reported in Table 7.6.

Our multilevel analyses began with an estimation of the proportion of variance in the dependent variables that occurs between schools. These estimates provided a basis for later assessing the proportion of variance explained by collective teacher efficacy in the full multilevel model. As expected, the proportion of variance between schools in both students' mathematics (19%) and reading (15%) achievement was statistically significant so we proceeded with multilevel tests of our research hypothesis.

Our multilevel hypothesis frames between-school variance in the level-1 intercepts ($B_{j}0$s) as the school-level dependent variable. At level 1, the intercepts for each of the 47 sampled schools are the operational measure of between-school differences in student achievement. At the school level, these intercepts are the dependent variable and collective teacher efficacy is the independent variable. The corresponding structural equations employed for both mathematics and reading achievement were as given below.

Level 1: $Y_{ij} = B_{j0} + B_{jSES}X_{ijSES} + B_{jAFAM}X_{ijAFAM} + B_{jFEMALE}X_{ijFEMALE} + r_{ij}$

Level 2: $B_{j0} = \gamma_{00} + \gamma_{0CE}W_{jCE} + \mu_{0j}$

The results of the hypothesis tests for mathematics and reading achievement are shown in Tables 7.7 and 7.8.

As predicted, collective teacher efficacy is a significant predictor of student achievement in both mathematics and reading achievement. Indeed,

Table 7.5.   Descriptive Statistics for Student-Level Variables

Variable	Mean	Standard Deviation	Minimum	Maximum
Mathematics	44.90	20.42	6.70	99.00
Reading	46.23	19.86	6.70	99.00
SES	.66	.47	0.00	1.00
AFAM	.57	.50	0.00	1.00
FEMALE	.50	.50	0.00	1.00

Table 7.6.   Correlations Among Student-level Variables

Variable	MATH	READING	SES	AFAM	FEMALE
MATH	1.0				
READING	.66**	1.0			
SES	-.27**	-.29**	1.0		
AFAM	-.23**	-.22**	.26**	1.0	
FEMALE	.00*	.10**	.01	.01	1.0

** Significant at the 0.01 level.

Table 7.7.   Collective Efficacy as a Predictor of Variation in Slopes and Intercepts for Mathematics Achievement

Variable	Coefficient	Std Error	T-Ratio	P-Value
Intercept	52.78	1.04	50.67	<.001
CE	8.62	1.96	4.40	<.001
SES Slope	-5.49	.52	-10.56	<.001
AFAM Slope	-7.00	.53	-13.32	<.001
FEMALE Slope	-.03	.44	-.08	n.s

Table 7.8.   Collective Efficacy as a Predictor of Variation in Slopes and Intercepts for Reading Achievement

Variable	Coefficient	Std Error	T-Ratio	P-Value
Intercept	51.99	.81	64.11	<.001
CE	8.49	1.42	9.58	<.001
SES Slope	-6.62	.51	-12.98	<.001
AFAM Slope	-5.74	.51	-11.20	<.001
FEMALE Slope	4.12	.43	9.59	<.001

the effect of collective teacher efficacy is greater in magnitude than that of any one of the demographic controls for both achievement variables. This is consistent with Bandura's (1993) assertion that collective teacher efficacy has a greater effect on student achievement than does student socioeconomic status. That is, the negative association between SES and achievement is more than offset by the positive association between collective teacher efficacy and student achievement.

The proportion of between-school variance in student achievement explained by collective teacher efficacy was calculated as the reduction in the unconditional between-school variance reported earlier. In our full model, collective teacher efficacy explained 53.27% and 69.64% of the between-school variance in mathematics and reading, respectively. This suggests that collective teacher efficacy explains roughly between half and two-thirds of the variance between schools in student achievement. With the effects of collective teacher efficacy controlled, the remaining half of the between-school variance is statistically non-zero. This suggests that, in addition to collective teacher efficacy, other school characteristics are systematically associated with between-school differences in student achievement.

DISCUSSION

Our study of collective teacher efficacy led to several important findings. First, the theoretical elements of collective teacher efficacy – group competence and task analysis—are highly related in schools. The empirical results are consistent with our model of collective efficacy (Figure 7.1), which suggests that both analysis of the task and assessment of group competencies interact to orchestrate a conception of collective teacher efficacy in a school. Factor analyses of both pilot study and final study data support a single measure of collective teacher efficacy consisting of items that assess both analysis of the task and group competency.

Next, as predicted, collective teacher efficacy is positively associated with the differences in student achievement that occur between schools. The multilevel analysis demonstrates that a one unit increase in a school's collective teacher efficacy scale score is associated with a 8.62 point average gain in student mathematics achievement and a 8.49 point average gain in reading achievement. In other words, a one unit increase in collective teacher efficacy is associated with an increase of more than 40% of a standard deviation in student achievement. These results are consistent with Bandura's (1993) study which indicates that collective efficacy was significantly and positively associated with school level student achievement. Collective teacher efficacy perceptions are predictive of student achievement.

Our study offers initial evidence that collective efficacy perceptions are systematically related to student achievement. Although our hypothesis was supported by data drawn from a population of urban elementary schools, social cognitive theory does not predict that the impact of collective teacher efficacy would be limited to the urban schools we sampled. Accordingly, an open research question concerns whether there is also a positive relation between student performance and the collective efficacy of faculties in non-urban settings.

Finally, the theoretical conceptualization of teacher efficacy, grounded in social cognitive theory, can be extended to the organizational level to explain collective teacher efficacy. The empirical findings are consistent with the theoretical argument that collective teacher efficacy is a unified construct that promotes student achievement. Our theoretical analysis suggests that the assumptions of social cognitive theory (e.g., agency, vicarious learning, and self-regulation) can be applied at the organizational level to explain the influence of collective teacher efficacy on between-school differences in student achievement. In a school with a high level of collective teacher efficacy, teachers are more likely to act purposefully to enhance student learning. Such purposeful actions result from organizational agency that influences a school to intentionally pursue its goals. Schools are capable of self-regulation and self-regulation helps in the identification, selection, and monitoring of educational efforts that are likely to meet the unique needs of students.

To understand the influence of collective teacher efficacy in schools, it is necessary to understand that teachers' shared beliefs shape the normative environment of schools. These shared beliefs are an important aspect of the culture of a school. Collective teacher efficacy is a way of conceptualizing the normative environment of a school and its influence on both personal and organizational behavior. That is, teachers' beliefs about their faculty's capability to educate students constitute a norm that influences the actions and achievements of schools.

At the heart of the theoretical rationale explaining the relationship observed between collective teacher efficacy and student achievement is Bandura's (1997) theory of triadic reciprocal causation. Triadic reciprocal causation indicates that collective teacher efficacy beliefs influence the level of effort and persistence that individual teachers put forth in their daily work. Therefore, one way for school administrators to improve student achievement is by working to raise the collective efficacy beliefs of their faculties. While mastery experiences are the most powerful efficacy changing forces, they may be the most difficult to deliver to a faculty with low collective efficacy. Thoughtfully designed staff development activities and action research projects, however, are ways school administrators might provide efficacy-building mastery experiences.

School administrators should also take opportunities to provide vicarious learning experiences and social persuasion to build the collective efficacy of their faculty. Visits to model schools and videos of effective schools may be useful in this regard, especially when the models are similar in population and resources to the teachers' own school. Additionally, administrators should be attentive to both the competence and task dimensions of efficacy. It is not enough to hire and retain the brightest teachers – they must also believe they can successfully meet the challenges of the task at hand. When teachers believe they are members of a faculty that is both competent and able to overcome the detrimental effects of the environment, the students in their building have higher achievement scores than students in buildings with lower levels of collective teacher efficacy. Collective teacher efficacy is, however, not a panacea. There are other reasons that schools have different effects on student achievement. This study offers only initial evidence supporting a strong relationship between collective teacher efficacy and student achievement.

CONCLUSIONS

We have elaborated a theoretical model (Figure 7.1) that maps key elements of collective efficacy as well as its antecedents and consequences. The model suggests that collective teacher efficacy is an extension of individual teacher efficacy (Tschannen-Moran, Woolfolk Hoy, & Hoy, 1998) to the organizational level. The attributional analysis and interpretation of mastery experiences, vicarious experiences, social persuasion, and affective states constitute processes through which the organization assesses the teaching task and faculty competence. Both domains are evaluated to determine whether the organization has the capacities to succeed in teaching students. Simply put, collective teacher efficacy is the perception of teachers in a school that the efforts of the faculty as a whole will have a positive effect on students.

Using the model, we developed and tested an instrument to measure collective teacher efficacy. This efficacy scale proved to be reliable and valid in two independent samples, and it was useful in predicting student achievement in mathematics and reading. In both samples, assessments

Appendix: Collective Teacher Efficacy Scale: A Two-Factor Rotated Solution

Item No.	Item	Factor One	Factor Two
CTE3	If a child doesn't learn something the first time teachers will try another way.	.83	.16
CTE18	Teachers in this school are skilled in various methods of teaching.	.83	.06
CTE17	Teachers here are well-prepared to teach the subjects they are assigned to teach.	.83	.18
CTE5	Teachers in this school really believe every child can learn.	.82	.34
CTE6	If a child doesn't want to learn teachers here give up.	.78	.30

Appendix continues on next page.

Appendix: Collective Teacher Efficacy Scale:
A Two-Factor Rotated Solution Continued

Item No.	Item	Factor One	Factor Two
CTE10	Teachers here fail to reach some students because of poor teaching methods.	.74	.33
CTE9	Teachers here don't have the skills needed to produce meaningful student learning.	.70	.41
CTE1	Teachers in this school have what it takes to get the children to learn.	.68	.51
CTE2	Teachers in this school are able to get through to difficult students.	.67	.50
CTE4	Teachers here are confident they will be able to motivate their students.	.67	.64
CTE13	The lack of instructional materials and supplies makes teaching very difficult.	.66	.22
CTE21	Teachers in this school do not have the skills to deal with student disciplinary problems.	.63	.48
CTE8	Teachers in this school think there are some students that no one can reach.	.61	.39
CTE15	The quality of school facilities here really facilitates the teaching and learning process.	.58	.29
CTE12	Homelife provides so many advantages they are bound to learn.	.07	.93
CTE11	These students come to school ready to learn.	.33	.89
CTE20	Drugs and alcohol abuse in the community make learning difficult for students here.	.22	.87
CTE16	The opportunities in this community help ensure that these students will learn.	.26	.82
CTE14	Students here just aren't motivated to learn.	.36	.80
CTE19	Learning is more difficult at this school because students are worried about their safety.	.47	.74
CTE7	Teachers here need more training to know how to deal with these students.	.46	.62

of the teaching task and teaching competence were strongly interrelated and formed a single, strong factor of collective efficacy.

This research constitutes a useful beginning for theorists, researchers, and school administrators alike who are interested in teacher efficacy, schools, and student achievement. The extant literature contains few investigations of collective teacher efficacy and fewer yet examine the relation between collective efficacy and student achievement. The results support Bandura's (1993) study by providing additional evidence that teacher beliefs about the capabilities of their faculty are systematically related to student achievement. Moreover, the findings confirm that the concepts and assumptions of social cognitive theory may be used to examine organizational behavior.

REFERENCES

Allinder, R. M. (1994). The relationship between efficacy and the instructional-practices of special education teachers and consultants. *Teacher Education and-Special Education, 17,* 86-95.

Anderson, R., Greene, M., & Loewen, P. (1988). Relationships among teachers'and students' thinking skills, sense of efficacy, and student achievement. *Alberta Journal of Educational Research, 34*(2), 148-165.

Armor, D., Conroy-Oseguera, P., Cox, M., King, N., McDonnell, L., Pascal, A., Pauly, E., & Zellman, G. (1976). *Analysis of the school preferred reading program in selected Los Angeles minority schools* [Report No. R-2007-LAUSD; ERIC Document Reproduction No. 130 243]. Santa Monica, CA: Rand Corporation.

Ashton, P. T., Olejnik, S., Crocker, L., & McAuliffe, M. (1982, April). *Measurement problems in the study of teachers' sense of efficacy.* Paper presented at the annual meeting of the American Educational Research Association, New York.

Ashton, P. T., & Webb, R. B., (1986). *Making a difference: Teachers' sense of efficacy and student achievement.* New York: Longman.

Bandura, A. (1977). Self-efficacy: Toward a unifying theory of behavioral change. *Psychological Review, 84,* 191-215.

Bandura, A. (1986). *Social foundations of thought and action: A social cognitive theory.* Englewood Cliffs, NJ: Prentice-Hall.

Bandura, A. (1993). Perceived self-efficacy in cognitive development andfunctioning. *Educational Psychologist, 28*(2), 117-148.

Bandura, A. (1997). *Self-efficacy: The exercise of control.* New York: W. H. Freeman and Company.

Clarke, J. S. Ellet, C. D., Bateman, J. M., & Rugutt, J. K. (1996, October). *Faculty receptivity/resistance to change, personal and organizational efficacy, decision deprivation and effectiveness in research I universities.* Paper presented at the annual meeting of the Association for the Study of Higher Education, Memphis, TN.

Cohen, M. D., & Sproull L. S. (Eds.). (1996). *Organizational learning.* Thousand Oaks, CA: Sage.

Coleman, J. S. (1985). Schools and the communities they serve. *Phi Delta Kappan, 66*(8), 527-532.

Coleman, J. S. (1987). Norms as social capital. In G. Radnitzky & P. Bernholz (Eds.), *Economic Imperialism: the economic approach applied outside the field of economics.* New York: Paragon House Publishers.

Coleman, J. S. (1990). *Foundations of social theory.* Cambridge, MA: Harvard University Press.

Cook S. D. N., & Yanon, D. (1996). Culture and organizational learning. In Cohen, M. D., & Sproull L. S. (Eds.), *Organizational learning* (pp. 430-459). Thousand Oaks, CA: Sage.

Esselman, M. E., & Moore, W. P. (1992, April). *In search of organizational variables which can be altered to promote an increased sense of teacher efficacy.* Paper presented at the annual meeting of the American EducationalResearch Association, San Francisco.

Forsyth, P. B., & Hoy, W. K. (1978). Isolation and alienation in educational organizations. *Educational Administration Quarterly, 14*(1), 80-96.

Gist, M. E., & Mitchell, T. R. (1992). Self-efficacy: A theoretical analysis of its determinants and malleability. *Academy of Management Review, 17*(2), 183-211.

Gibson, S., & Dembo, M. (1984). Teacher efficacy: A construct validation. *Journal of Educational Psychology, 76*(4), 569-582.

Guskey, T. R. (1982). Differences in teachers' perceptions of personal control of positive and negative student learning outcomes. *Contemporary Educational Psychology, 7,* 70-80.

Guskey, T. R. (1987). Context variables that affect measures of teacher efficacy. *Journal of Educational Research, 81*(1), 41-47.

Guskey, T. R., & Passaro, P. (1994). Teacher efficacy: A study of construct dimensions. *American Educational Research Journal, 31,* 627-643.

Halpin, A. W. (1959). *The leader behavior of school superintendents.* Chicago: Midwest Administrative Center.

Hoover-Dempsey, K., Bassler, O. C., & Brissie, J. S., (1987). Parent involvement: contributions of teacher efficacy, school socioeconomic status, and other school characteristics. *American Educational Research Journal, 24,* 417-4 35.

Hoy, W. K., & Miskel, C., G. (1996). *Educational administration: Theory, research, and practice.* New York: McGraw-Hill.

Huber, G. P. (1996). Organizational learning: The contributing processes and literatures. In Cohen, M. D., & Sproull L. S. (Eds.), *Organizational learning* (pp. 124-162). Thousand Oaks, CA: Sage.

Levitt, B. L., & March, J. G. (1996). In M. D. Cohen & L. S. Sproull (Eds.), *Organizational learning* (pp. 516-540). Thousand Oaks, CA: Sage.

Meijer, C., & Foster, S. (1988). The effect of teacher self-efficacy on referralchance. *Journal of Special Education, 22,* 378-385.

Newmann, F. M., Rutter, R. A., & Smith, M. S. (1989). Organizational factors thataffect school sense of efficacy, community and expectations. *Sociology of Education, 62,* 221-238.

Pajares, F. (1996a, April). *Current directions in self research: Self-efficacy.* Paper presented at the annual meeting of the American Educational Research Association, New York.

Pajares, F. (1996b, April). *Assessing self-efficacy beliefs and academic outcomes: The case for specificity and correspondence.* Paper presented at the annual meeting of the American Educational Research Association, New York.

Pajares, F. (1997). Current directions in self-efficacy research. In M. L. Maehr & P. R. Pintrich (Eds.), *Advances in motivation and achievement* (pp. 1-49). Greenwich, CT: JAI Press.

Porter, G. (1992). *Collective efficacy and esteem: Measurement and study of "self" attributes at a group level.* Unpublished doctoral dissertation, The Ohio State University.

Putnam, R. D. (1993). *Making democracy work: Civic traditions in modern Italy.* Princeton, NJ: Princeton University Press.

Ross, J. A. (1992). Teacher efficacy and the effect of coaching on studentachievement. *Canadian Journal of Education, 17*(1), 51-65.

Ross, J. A. (1994, June). *Beliefs that make a difference: The origins and impacts of teacher efficacy.* Paper presented at the annual meeting of the Canadian Association for Curriculum Studies.

Rotter, J. B. (1966). Generalized expectancies for internal versus external control of reinforcement. *Psychological Monographs, 80,* 1-28.

Senge, P. M. (1990). *The fifth discipline: The art and practice of the learning organization.* New York: Doubleday.

Tschannen-Moran, M., Woolfolk Hoy, A., & Hoy, W. K. (1998). Teacher efficacy: Its meaning and measure. *Review of Educational Research, 68,* 202-248.

Woolfolk, A., & Hoy, W., K. (1990). Prospective teachers' sense of efficacy and beliefs about control. *Journal of Educational Psychology, 82,* 81-91.

Zielinski, A. W., & Hoy, W. K. (1983). Isolation and alienation in elementary schools. *Educational Administration Quarterly, 19,* 27-45.

CHAPTER 8

COLLECTIVE EFFICACY BELIEFS

Theoretical Developments, Empirical Evidence, and Future Directions

Roger D. Goddard, Wayne K. Hoy, and Anita Woolfolk Hoy

This analysis synthesizes existing research to discuss how teachers' practice and student learning are affected by perceptions of collective efficacy. Social cognitive theory is employed to explain that the choices teachers make—the ways in which they exercise personal agency—are strongly influenced by collective efficacy beliefs. Although empirically related, teacher and collective efficacy perceptions are theoretically distinct constructs, each having unique effects on educational decisions and student achievement. Our purpose is to advance awareness about perceived collective efficacy and develop a conceptual model to explain the formation and influence of perceived collective efficacy in schools. We also examine the relevance of efficacy beliefs to teachers' professional work and outline future research possibilities.

Reprinted by permission from the *Educational Researcher,* Vol. 33, pp. 3-13.
Copyright © 2004. All rights reserved.

Essential Ideas for the Reform of American Schools, pp. 171–196
Copyright © 2007 by Information Age Publishing
All rights of reproduction in any form reserved.

Over a quarter century ago, Albert Bandura (1977) introduced the concept of self-efficacy perceptions or "beliefs in one's capacity to organize and execute the courses of action required to produce given attainments" (Bandura, 1997, p. 3). Since that time, research in many arenas has demonstrated the power of efficacy judgments in human learning, performance, and motivation. For example, efficacy beliefs are related to smoking cessation, adherence to exercise and diet programs, performance in sports, political participation, and academic achievement (Bandura, 1997).

The last arena is of particular importance to educators. In the past two decades, researchers have found links between student achievement and three kinds of efficacy beliefs—the self-efficacy judgments of students (cf. Pajares, 1994, 1997), teachers' beliefs in their own instructional efficacy (cf. Tschannen-Moran, Woolfolk Hoy, & Hoy, 1998), and teachers' beliefs about the collective efficacy of their school (Goddard, Hoy, & Woolfolk Hoy, 2000). Of the three, perceived collective efficacy is the most recent construct developed and has received the least attention from educational researchers. The purpose of this inquiry is to advance awareness about collective efficacy beliefs and develop a conceptual model to explain the formation and influence of perceived collective efficacy in schools. We also explore the relevance of efficacy beliefs to teachers' professional work and outline future research possibilities.

The connections between collective efficacy beliefs and student outcomes depend in part on the reciprocal relationships among these collective efficacy beliefs, teachers' personal sense of efficacy, teachers' professional practice, and teacher's influence over instructionally relevant school decisions. Although we argue that perceived collective efficacy is emerging as an important concern for educational researchers, we do not confine our review of the literature to the field of education. Indeed, our case is strengthened by the striking similarity of findings in other fields, such as business/management and sociology, which demonstrate that collective efficacy beliefs are strongly related to other important group outcomes such as work group effectiveness and neighborhood safety. In the course of developing our case, we examine the social cognitive underpinnings of efficacy belief theory. Specifically, we address the nature of efficacy beliefs, their formation and change, and we focus on the extension of social cognitive theory to thinking about group capabilities. We begin with a look at efficacy constructs in general.

EFFICACY CONSTRUCTS: DISTINCTIONS AND CLARICATIONS

As defined in social cognitive theory, all efficacy belief constructs—student, teacher, and collective—are future-oriented judgments about capabilities to organize and execute the courses of action required to produce given attainments in specific situations or contexts (Bandura, 1997). The question is, Can I (the student or the teacher) or we (the faculty) orchestrate the thoughts and actions necessary to perform the task?

Efficacy judgments are beliefs about individual or group capability, not necessarily accurate assessments of those capabilities. This is an important distinction because people regularly over or underestimate their actual abilities, and these estimations may have consequences for the courses of action they choose to pursue and the effort they exert in those pursuits. Over- or underestimating capabilities also may influence how well they use the skills they possess. As Bandura (1997) observes, "A capability is only as good as its execution. The self-assurance with which people approach and manage difficult tasks determines whether they make good or poor use of their capabilities. Insidious self-doubts can easily overrule the best of skills" (p. 35). For example, Bouffard-Bouchard, Parent, and Larivee (1991) found that children with the same level of skill development in mathematics differed significantly in their math problem-solving success, depending on the strength of their efficacy beliefs. Children with a higher sense of self-efficacy more consistently and effectively applied what they knew; they were more persistent and less likely to reject correct solutions prematurely. In most cases, slightly overestimating one's actual capabilities has the most positive effect on performance.

In order to set the stage for an examination of perceived collective efficacy, we first consider the more well-researched efficacy belief constructs related to self and teaching.

Self-Efficacy Beliefs

Perceived self-efficacy is distinct from other conceptions of self, such as self-concept, self-worth, and self-esteem, in that it is *specific to a particular task*. "Self-esteem usually is considered to be a trait reflecting an individual's characteristic affective evaluation of self (e.g., feelings of self-worth or self-liking). By contrast, ... [perceived] efficacy is a judgment about task capability that is not inherently evaluative" (Gist & Mitchell, 1992, p. 185). On the one hand, a person may possess a low sense of efficacy for a particular activity, such as figure drawing or downhill skiing, and suffer no diminishment of self-esteem because that person has not invested self-worth in doing that activity well. On the other hand, high achievers may display a great deal of skill, and yet evaluate themselves negatively because they have set personal standards that are very difficult to meet. Persons may question their self-worth, despite being very competent, if important others do not value their accomplishments, if their skills cause harm to others, or if they are members of groups that are not valued by society (Bandura, 1997). As self-referent perception of capability to execute specific behaviors, individual efficacy beliefs are better predictors of individual behavior than self-concept and self-esteem (Pajares & Miller, 1994). In fact, Bandura (1986) suggests that other self-referent constructs, such as self-concept, are related to outcomes mostly through their influence on self-efficacy beliefs; that is, one's sense of self-efficacy mediates the effects of self-concept on task success.

Teachers' Sense of Efficacy

The distinction between perception of competence and actual competence or performance is particularly important when considering teachers' sense of efficacy. The shorthand term often used is "teacher efficacy." Using this term, however, can be misleading because readers may make the logical mistake of assuming that "teacher efficacy" is the same as "teacher effectiveness" or successful teaching. Thus, it is important to avoid the term "teacher efficacy," talking instead about teachers' perceptions of efficacy, efficacy judgments, sense of efficacy, perceived efficacy, or efficacy beliefs. All these terms connote judgments about capabilities to accomplish a task.

The meaning and measure of teachers' sense of efficacy have been the subjects of considerable debate among scholars and researchers (Ashton, Olejnik, Crocker, & McAuliffe, 1982; Gibson & Dembo, 1984; Guskey, 1987; Guskey & Passaro, 1994; Pajares 1996a, 1996b, 1997; Tschannen-Moran et al., 1998). We know, for example, that teachers' sense of efficacy is a significant predictor of productive teaching practices. Compared to teachers with lower self-efficacy beliefs, teachers with strong perceptions of self-capability tend to employ classroom strategies that are more organized and better planned (Allinder, 1994), student centered (Czerniak & Schriver, 1994; Enochs, Scharmann, & Riggs, 1995), and humanistic (Woolfolk & Hoy, 1990). Teachers' efficacy judgments are also strongly related to trust (Da Costa & Riordan, 1996), openness (DeForest & Hughes, 1992), and job satisfaction (Lee, Dedrick, & Smith, 1991). These studies provide considerable explanation for the positive link between teachers' sense of efficacy and student achievement (e.g., Anderson, Greene, & Loewen, 1988; Armor, Conroy-Oseguera, Cox, King, McDonnell, Pascal, et al., 1976; Ashton & Webb, 1986; Gibson & Dembo, 1984; Ross, 1992, 1994) because such approaches and attitudes are widely accepted as educationally productive.

Collective Efficacy Beliefs

In light of the promising findings about teachers' sense of efficacy, recent research has added an organizational dimension to inquiry about efficacy beliefs in schools. This section of the article considers the social cognitive underpinnings of efficacy belief theory and recent advances in research on collective efficacy beliefs.

Inquiry into collective efficacy beliefs emphasizes that teachers have not only self-referent efficacy perceptions but also beliefs about the conjoint capability of a school faculty. Such group-referent perceptions reflect an emergent organizational property known as *perceived collective efficacy* (see, e.g., Bandura, 1997; Goddard, Hoy, & Woolfolk Hoy, 2000; Hoy, Sweetland, & Smith, 2002). Within an organization, perceived collective efficacy represents the beliefs of group members concerning "the performance capability of a social system as a whole" (Bandura, 1997, p. 469). For schools, perceived collective efficacy refers to the judgment of teachers in a school that the faculty as a whole can organize and execute the courses of action required to have a positive effect on students.

If perceived collective efficacy is to be a useful construct for educational researchers, then the theoretical foundations of scholarship on efficacy beliefs should be thoroughly understood. We turn to that task next.

A SOCIAL COGNITIVE PERSPECTIVE ON THE FORMATION AND CHANGE OF EFFICACY BELIEFS

Although conceptually distinct, the constructs of perceived self and collective efficacy are both derived from social cognitive theory. The most fundamental assumption of social cognitive theory involves the choices that individuals and collectives make through the exercise of agency. According to social cognitive theory, the choices that individuals and organizations (through the actions of individuals) make are influenced by the strength of their efficacy beliefs.

Human and Organizational Agency

Agency concerns the ways that people exercise some level of control over their own lives. People are more likely to purposefully pursue goals that seem challenging, rewarding, and attainable (Bandura, 1997). When applied to teaching, social cognitive theory predicts that the decisions teachers make about their classroom practices are directly influenced by their sense of efficacy for teaching. The higher teachers' sense of efficacy, the more likely they are to tenaciously overcome obstacles and persist in the face of failure. Such resiliency, in turn, tends to foster innovative teaching and student learning.

Human agency is also critical to our understanding of group functioning. Indeed, social cognitive theory acknowledges that "personal agency operates within a broad network of sociostructural influences" (Bandura, 1997, p. 6) and, thus, the theory "extends the analysis of mechanisms of human agency to the exercise of collective agency" (p. 7)—people's combined beliefs that they can work together to produce desired effects. When individuals and collectives choose to work in pursuit of certain attainments, their actions reflect the exercise of agency. Because agency refers to the intentional pursuit of a course of action, we see school organizations as agentive when they act purposefully in pursuit of educational goals. For example, one school may work to close achievement gaps by race while another acts to increase the quality of teacher professional development. When such differences are purposeful, they reflect the exercise of organizational agency. Of course, organizational agency results from the agentive actions of individuals directed at the attainment of desired goals.

Sources of Efficacy-Shaping Information for Groups

Bandura (1986, 1997) postulates four sources of efficacy-shaping information: mastery experience, vicarious experience, social persuasion, and affective state. Just as these sources are critical for individuals, they are also important to the development of collective efficacy beliefs. According to Bandura (1997), "[p]erceived personal and collective efficacy differ in the unit of agency, but in both forms efficacy beliefs have similar sources, serve similar functions, and operate through similar processes" (p. 478). In theory, on the one hand, all sources of personal efficacy-shaping information may indeed hold at the group level. On the other hand, it may be that some sources—affective states, for example— are less germane, or at least less well understood, as explanations for how collective efficacy perceptions form and change. With this caveat, we proceed with a discussion of the theoretical rationales and related evidence for assuming that each of the four sources of efficacy belief-shaping information specified in social cognitive theory operates at the group level.

Mastery Experience

A mastery experience is the most powerful source of efficacy information. The perception that a performance has been successful tends to raise efficacy beliefs, contributing to the expectation that performance will be proficient in the future. The perception that one's performance has been a failure tends to lower efficacy beliefs, contributing to the expectation that future performances will also be inept. Attributions play a role as well. If the success is attributed to internal or controllable causes, such as ability or effort, self-efficacy beliefs are enhanced. But if success is attributed to luck or the intervention of others, self-efficacy beliefs may not be strengthened (Bandura, 1993; Pintrich & Schunk, 2002).

Mastery experiences are important for organizations; in fact, a substantial body of research is emerging on organizational learning (Huber, 1996; March, 1996; Simon, 1996). Consistent with Huber's analysis of learning organizations, schools, like individuals, "tend to learn well what they do, and tend to do what they learn well" (p. 152). Of course, it is through the learning of group members that organizational learning occurs. Teachers as a group experience successes and failures. Past school successes build teachers' beliefs in the capability of the faculty, whereas failures tend to undermine a sense of collective efficacy. If success is frequent and too easy, however, failure is likely to produce discouragement. A resilient sense of collective efficacy requires experience in overcoming difficulties through persistent effort.

Goddard (2001) recently tested the hypothesis that mastery experience significantly influences collective efficacy beliefs. He found that mastery experience (operationalized as prior school reading achievement) is a significant positive predictor of differences among schools in perceived collective efficacy. Indeed, not only was past school achievement a significant predictor of differences among schools in teachers' perceptions of collective efficacy, but past school achievement was also a stronger predictor of perceived collective efficacy than aggregate measures of school race (i.e., proportion minority) and SES (operationalized as the proportion of students in a school who received a subsidized lunch). This finding supports the sociocognitive assumption that collective efficacy perceptions are strongly informed by mastery experience. Also, although mastery experience explained the majority of the variation among schools in collective efficacy beliefs, more than a third of this variation was unexplained. In other words, in addition to mastery experience, there are other factors systematically associated with organizations that may explain variation among groups in collective efficacy beliefs. These factors may include the other sources of efficacy belief-shaping information postulated by social cognitive theory and described next.

Vicarious Experience

A vicarious experience is one in which the skill in question is modeled by someone else. When a model with whom the observer identifies performs well, the efficacy beliefs of the observer are most likely enhanced. When the model performs poorly, the efficacy beliefs of the observer tend to decrease.

Just as teachers' sense of efficacy is enhanced by observing successful models with similar characteristics (Gorrell & Capron, 1988; Schunk, 1981, 1983, 1987; Schunk & Zimmerman, 1997), perceived collective efficacy may also be enhanced by observing successful organizations, especially those that attain similar goals in the face of familiar opportunities and constraints. Organizations may also learn from somewhat dissimilar counterparts provided they have attained highly valued outcomes. Replication of successful educational programs across a wide variety of settings by schools aspiring to achieve similar success is a familiar example. Indeed, in the current high-stakes system of state-mandated testing and accountability, schools wanting improved educational outcomes may experience gains in perceived collective efficacy by observing successful educational programs offered by higher achieving schools. Borrowing from other organizations is a form of vicarious organizational learning, which is sometimes as effective as firsthand learning (Dutton & Freedman, 1985). These examples suggest that social cognitive theory may extend to the group level to explain that organizations do indeed learn vicariously about their capabilities (Argote, Beckman, & Epple, 1990; Huber, 1996; Levitt & March, 1988). We hasten to add, however, that the research on organizational learning is not nearly as developed as the work on individual learning, and, thus, more research is needed to understand better how observational learning affects perceived collective efficacy in organizations.

Social Persuasion

Social persuasion may entail encouragement or specific performance feedback from a supervisor or a colleague or it may involve discussions in the teachers' lounge, community, or media about the ability of teachers to influence students. Although social persuasion alone may be limited in its power to create enduring changes in efficacy beliefs, it may counter occasional setbacks that might have instilled enough self-doubt to interrupt persistence. The potency of persuasion depends on the credibility, trustworthiness, and expertise of the persuader (Bandura, 1986).

Social persuasion is another means of strengthening a faculty's conviction that it has the capabilities to set and achieve goals. Talks, workshops, professional development opportunities, and feedback about achievement can inspire action. Although verbal persuasion alone is not likely to compel profound organizational change, when coupled with models of success and positive direct experience, it can influence the collective efficacy beliefs of a faculty. Persuasion can encourage group members to innovate and overcome difficult challenges.

At the group level, social persuasion is a way of conceiving the ongoing socialization that organizational participants interdependently create and experience. Collective efficacy perceptions serve as normative expectations for goal attainment. A robust sense of group capability establishes a strong press for collective performance. Teachers new to a given school are socialized by the organization (Hoy & Woolfolk, 1990) and quickly learn about this aspect of their school's culture in interactions with other teachers and administrators. In schools possessed by a high degree of perceived collective efficacy, new teachers learn that extra effort and educational success are the norm. In turn, these high expectations for action create a normative press that encourages all teachers to do what it takes to excel and discourages them from giving up when faced with difficult obstacles.

Although the expectations of peer groups do not always win the day, organizational life is nevertheless filled with social exchanges that communicate expectations, sanctions, and rewards to members. Part of the organizational learning process deals with the acquisition of requisite orientations for satisfactorily functioning in a role (Parsons, 1951). Hence, expectations for action set by collective efficacy beliefs do not go unnoticed; rather, these expectations are an important part of organizational socialization and fundamental aspects of an organization's culture and its influence on group member performance.

Affective States

The level of arousal, either of anxiety or excitement, adds to individual's perceptions of self-capability or incompetence. We postulate that, just as individuals react to stress, so do organizations. For example, immediate past performance on state-mandated tests, which is typically widely publicized, plays a key role in influencing the mood of local schools. Organizations with strong beliefs in group capability can tolerate pressure and crises and continue to function without debilitating consequences; indeed, such organizations learn to rise to the challenge when confronted with disruptive forces. Less efficacious organizations, however, are more likely to react dysfunctionally, which, in turn, increases the likelihood of failure. Thus, affective states may influence how organizations interpret and react to the myriad challenges they face.

Admittedly, however, there is little research on the impact of the affective states of organizations on the collective efficacy beliefs and performance of participants; but, the theory is plausible and merits attention in future research.

The Pivotal Role of Cognition in the Interpretation of Efficacy Belief-Shaping Information

Ultimately, the exercise of agency depends upon how individuals and groups interpret efficacy beliefs shaping information and experiences. Raudenbush, Rowan, and Cheong (1992) interpret Bandura's (1986) work by characterizing perceived self-efficacy as "a cognition that mediates between knowledge and action" (p. 150). Indeed, Bandura (1997) more recently emphasized that the impact of mastery experience on efficacy beliefs does not depend entirely on the actual events of the performance; rather, efficacy beliefs are created when individuals weigh and interpret their performance relative to other information. According to Bandura, "changes in perceived efficacy result from cognitive processing of the diagnostic information that performances convey about capability rather than the performances per se" (1997, p. 81). The same is true for all four sources of efficacy information—the role of cognition is critical. That is, perceptions of efficacy for various individual and collective pursuits arise from cognitive and metacognitive processing of the sources of efficacy belief-shaping information described here.

We now describe several approaches to the conceptualization and measurement of perceived collective efficacy that serve to ground the meaning of the construct and inform those interested in its measure.

MEASUREMENT ISSUES

There are several approaches to the measurement of collective efficacy perceptions. One approach is to aggregate measures of individual (self-) efficacy beliefs. Such an aggregate measure of self-efficacy beliefs would be a group mean of self-referent perceptions. For example, a teacher efficacy belief survey item might read, "I have what it takes to get my students to learn." Responses to this and other "I-" referent statements would be averaged to assess the collective sense of efficacy of the school.

Another possibility is to aggregate measures of individuals' perceptions of *group-referent* capability. The difference here refers to the object of the efficacy perception—"we" instead of "I." A group-referent collective efficacy belief item might read, "Teachers in this school have what it takes to educate students here." Responses to this and other "we-" referent statements would be averaged to assess the collective sense of efficacy in a school.

A third approach is to ask group members to discuss their group capabilities together and come to a consensus about their sense of collective efficacy. One problem with the group consensus approach is that it is susceptible to social desirability bias that can undermine the validity of the assessment (Bandura, 1997). Another concern is that seeking a group consensus masks within-group variability in collective efficacy perceptions (Bandura, 1997).

A fourth approach is to focus on the extent to which there is agreement among group members across their individual perceptions. Before discussing this option, however, we elaborate on the second approach above (i.e., group-referent perceptions of capability), because we believe creating aggregate measures of group-referent perceptions is an effective means of assessing perceived collective efficacy.

Bandura (1997) observed that "perceived collective efficacy is an emergent group-level attribute rather than simply the sum of members' perceived *personal* efficacies" (emphasis added, p. 478). Conceptually, we agree. Aggregating individual perceptions of *group* (as opposed to *self*) capability serves to assess perceived collective efficacy as an emergent organizational property by combining individual group members' interdependent perspectives on group capability. Questions about group capability elicit perspectives on the obstacles, constraints, and opportunities of a given social system more readily than do items asking individuals about their self-capability, which varies more as a function of *individual* (as opposed to *group*) differences. Importantly, in a study of teachers' beliefs, Goddard (2003) showed that individual perceptions of self-capability varied less than 5% between groups. In drastic contrast, individual perceptions of group capability varied more than 40% among groups. Empirically, this finding is consistent with Bandura's (1997) assertion that perceived collective efficacy varies greatly among groups. Thus, we argue that to better capture the emergent properties created by group interdependence, even in somewhat loosely coupled systems such as schools, it is usually appropriate to conceive and assess perceived collective efficacy as the aggregate of individual perceptions of group capability.

This leaves one final question about the measure of perceived collective efficacy. In addition to using group mean scores, should researchers also consider the amount of agreement among teachers in the assessment of collective efficacy beliefs? Fortunately, this question has been addressed in empirical work on collective efficacy beliefs. Goddard (2001) measured a school's sense of collective efficacy as an aggregate of teachers' group-referent efficacy perceptions and also as the degree of agreement around the mean (variance measures were employed to estimate the amount of within-school variability among faculty perceptions of collective efficacy). The results showed that although the level of agreement did vary across schools, this variability was a non-significant predictor of differences among schools in student achievement; in contrast, the aggregate (school mean) measure of perceived collective efficacy was a strong positive predictor of student achievement differences among schools even after accounting for the variance in achievement explained by students' socio-demographic backgrounds.

Goddard offered as a theoretical possibility that the non-findings for agreement were consistent with the median voter model from economic theory (Hyman, 1995), which explains that political election outcomes so often represent the preferences of median voters because these preferences are the ones most likely to gain majority support in a given social system. The parallel for a normative theory of social organization is that aggregate scores representing the mean of organizational members' group-referent efficacy perceptions appear to effectively tap expectations for group performance that, in fact, do influence the outcomes of organized activity. This conclusion, however, is tentative because no other studies comparing the effects of agreement among group members and mean perceived collective efficacy scores are currently available.

Further research is needed to more fully understand what role agreement may play in our conception of perceived collective efficacy and its effects. The preponderance of evidence to date, however, suggests that aggregates of individual perceptions of group capability do indeed tap the perceived collective efficacy of organizations. Therefore, for the remainder of this article, when we refer to collective efficacy beliefs, we are referring to the *aggregate of individual group members' perceptions of group capability*. To avoid repeating this important but awkward detail, we imply this conceptual understanding when we define collective efficacy beliefs as the perceptions of teachers in a school that the faculty as a whole can organize and execute the courses of action required to have a positive effect on students. Also important to note is that the research on perceived collective efficacy to date has been concerned with teachers' beliefs about the capability of a faculty to promote student achievement. Future researchers may nd it useful to conceive of collective efficacy beliefs relative to other important aspects of schooling such as students' emotional growth and development or community involvement. In this article, however, our consideration of collective efficacy perceptions involves teachers' judgments of group capability to promote student achievement.

With this understanding of the conceptualization and measurement of perceived collective efficacy, we turn next to a discussion of evidence relating collective efficacy beliefs to the attainments of organized activity.

COLLECTIVE EFFICACY BELIEFS AND GROUP GOAL ATTAINMENT

Perhaps the most compelling reason for the recent development of interest in perceived collective efficacy is the probable link between collective efficacy beliefs and group goal attainment. Within education, several studies have documented a strong link between perceived collective efficacy and differences in student achievement among schools (Bandura, 1993; Goddard, 2001; Goddard et al., 2000). Bandura demonstrated that the effect of perceived collective efficacy on student achievement was stronger than the direct link between SES and student achievement. Similarly, Goddard and his colleagues have shown that, even after controlling for students' prior achievement, race/ethnicity, SES, and gender, collective efficacy beliefs have stronger effects on student achievement than student race or SES. Teachers' beliefs about the collective capability of their faculty vary greatly among schools and are strongly linked to student achievement.

In addition to its strong relationship with student academic outcomes, recent research in other fields also suggests the importance of collective efficacy beliefs to goal attainment. For example, Sampson, Raudenbush, and Earls (1997) showed that the more robust the sense of collective efficacy in city neighborhoods, the less likely was the occurrence of neighborhood violence. Neighborhoods in which residents reported a strong sense of collective efficacy were also ones in which citizens felt an expectation for action that predisposed them to intervene to decrease violent activity. Such social sanctions serve as deterrents to those who might otherwise violate group expectations. In addition, Little and Madigan (1997) have shown that perceived collective efficacy is a strong positive predictor of work group effectiveness. They observe that a group's sense of collective efficacy has "a mediating, or facilitating effect on team performance" (p. 518). As these examples demonstrate, the conceptualization of perceived collective efficacy is robust; across settings, perceptions of group capability tend to be strongly and positively related to group processes and outcomes.

The power of collective efficacy perceptions to influence organizational life and outcomes lies in the expectations for action that are socially transmitted by collective efficacy perceptions (Sampson, Morenoff, & Earls, 2000). Indeed, Sampson et al. (2000) argue that collective efficacy beliefs are important to group functioning because they explain *how organized capacity for action is tapped to produce results.* For example, dense and trusting relational networks might reflect high levels of social capital in a group; however, the potential for such social resources to influence outcomes is reached only when a group's sense of collective efficacy is sufficiently robust to compel members to action in pursuit of desired organized attainments (Sampson et al., 2000). Perceptions of collective efficacy directly affect the diligence and resolve with which groups choose to pursue their goals. Hence, perceived collective efficacy is a potent way of characterizing the strong normative and behavioral influence of an organization's culture. Knowledge about collective efficacy beliefs is, therefore, critical to understanding the influence of school culture on teachers' professional work and, in turn, student achievement.

As educators look for approaches to school improvement that can help all students reach high levels of achievement, it is timely and important to examine how schools can be empowered to exert control over their circumstances. The strong link between group performance and perceived collective efficacy can be explained by the resiliency with which the efficacious pursue given goals. Analogous to self-efficacy judgments, perceived collective efficacy is associated with the tasks, level of effort, persistence, shared thoughts, stress levels, and achievement of groups. Thus, just as teachers' sense of efficacy partially explains the effect of teachers on student achievement, from an organizational perspective, a faculty's sense of collective efficacy helps to explain the differential effect that school cultures have on teachers and students. Hence, it is reasonable (and correct) to expect that some schools have a positive influence on teachers whereas the impact of other schools is much less productive. For example, some teachers will nd themselves in schools with low morale and a depressed sense of collective efficacy whereas other teachers will work in schools possessed by a high degree of mutuality, shared responsibility, and confidence in the conjoint capability of the faculty. As the possibilities sketched here suggest, the sense of collective efficacy in a school can affect teachers' self-referent thoughts and, hence, their teaching performance and student learning.

Having discussed the social cognitive underpinnings of perceived collective efficacy and its relation to group goal attainment, we turn now to a discussion of how collective efficacy beliefs are related to two important dimensions of schooling. Specifically, this section of the article examines the theoretical and empirical linkages among perceived collective efficacy, teachers' sense of efficacy and, teachers' influence over instructionally relevant school decisions.

COLLECTIVE EFFICACY BELIEFS IN SCHOOLS: CONNECTIONS TO TEACHERS' SENSE OF EFFICACY AND INFLUENCE

Research suggests that perceived collective efficacy is strongly related to student achievement in schools (e.g., Bandura, 1993; Goddard, Hoy, & Woolfolk Hoy, 2000). The link between collective efficacy beliefs and student achievement occurs, from a theoretical perspective, because a robust sense of group capability establishes expectations (cultural norms) for success that encourages organizational members to work resiliently toward desired ends. The purpose of this section of the article is to expand our knowledge about this relationship by examining recent research on the linkages between perceived collective efficacy and teachers' sense of efficacy for instruction and, between perceived collective efficacy and teachers' influence over instructionally relevant decisions in schools. These recent findings contribute to our understanding of both how collective efficacy beliefs are related to student achievement, and also to how collective efficacy beliefs may be developed in organizations.

Linking Collective Efficacy Beliefs to Teachers' Sense of Efficacy in Schools

We know that teachers' efficacy judgments vary among schools (Goddard & Goddard, 2001; Raudenbush et al., 1992). Moreover, evidence suggests that teachers' sense of efficacy is positively related to aspects of organizational context such as positive school climate, lack of impediments to effective instruction, and teacher empowerment (Moore & Esselman, 1992) as well as principal influence with superiors and the academic press of a school (Hoy & Woolfolk, 1993). Together, these studies suggest that emergent school contextual factors influence teachers' perceptions of self-efficacy for educating students successfully.

The research suggests that a school's culture of perceived collective efficacy may exert a strong influence on teachers' sense of efficacy for instruction. Given, however, that teachers work almost exclusively in the isolation of their classrooms, one might reasonably ask how perceived collective efficacy could make a meaningful difference to their perceptions of self-efficacy for teaching and, in turn, their teaching practice. Indeed, many argue that educational processes and outcomes are loosely coupled (e.g., Meyer & Rowan, 1977, 1978); such loose coupling, in turn, makes the work of teaching complex and shelters it from influence situated beyond the classroom. However, even if we accept that within a broad set of constraints teachers have a great deal of pedagogical freedom, this alone does not prevent the social influence of organizational culture from reaching classrooms through its influence on teachers' thoughts and beliefs. According to Bandura (1997),

> People working independently within a group structure do not function as social isolates totally immune to the influence of those around them ... the resources, impediments, and opportunities provided by a given system partly determine how efficacious individuals can be, even though their work may be only loosely coupled. (p. 469)

Bandura's (1997) argument suggests that it is quite reasonable to expect a positive relationship between teachers' sense of efficacy and the emergent school property, perceived collective efficacy. To explain this link more fully, we draw upon Coleman's social theory of normative influence and Bandura's social cognitive theory.

Social Theory Of Normative Influence

Given the general agreement among scholars and researchers that beliefs about group capability influence the actions of organizational members (Bandura, 1986; Raudenbush, Rowan, & Cheong, 1992; Sampson, Morenoff, & Earls, 2000), it is useful to consider the influence of social norms on individual behavior. According to Coleman (1985, 1987, 1990), norms develop in order to provide members of a community with some influence over the actions of others, particularly when those actions have consequences for the group. Thus, in a school characterized by a high level of perceived collective efficacy, a teacher whose actions are inconsistent with group expectations for academic achievement is likely to be sanctioned by the faculty. A good example of this phenomenon was documented recently by Skrla and Goddard (2002) who studied collective efficacy beliefs in schools serving a student population characterized by a majority of Hispanic students living in poverty. According to one teacher in a focus group interview,

> [W]e're told it so many times, it's just a part of life, we know that to work here you have to do whatever it takes to get [the students to succeed]. To reach our goal. And, you know, I believe there are enough teachers who have bought into that belief to where if you hear a teacher that may not be quite there, I believe that by the time they hang around, either they will be there, or they'll be out the door. (pp. 17–18)

Such language suggests that collective expectations for action are indeed a powerful aspect of a school's operative culture and its influence on individual teachers. From a sociocognitive perspective, the power of this normative press lies in the social persuasion it exerts on teachers. In other words, collective efficacy beliefs serve to encourage certain actions and constrain others.

Mastery Experience

Consideration of the impact of mastery experiences on teacher beliefs about self and group capability also helps explain why teacher and collective efficacy perceptions should positively covary. In schools, collective mastery experiences usually result from the actual successes of individual teachers. A school with high scores on state-mandated achievement tests, for example, has one or more teachers who were directly successful with the students in their classrooms. Mastery experience, thus, can act in concert at both the individual and organizational level. Given this, teacher and collective efficacy beliefs will likely covary positively in response to group successes.

Together these rationales suggest that individuals are aware of and influenced by the social processes and collective beliefs that characterize an organization's culture. Applied to schools, such reasoning suggests that teachers' thoughts about their own capabilities will be influenced by beliefs about group capability that characterize the culture of their schools. It is also important to note that this influenced relationship is mutual, not unidirectional. That is, an organization in which most participants are individually quite confident about their own capabilities will also likely be one in which collective efficacy perceptions are relatively strong and expectations for success are high. Such mutual influence relationships reflect what Bandura (1997) has termed *reciprocal causality*.

Notably, Goddard and Goddard (2001) recently tested the multilevel relationship between teacher and collective efficacy beliefs. Specifically, they employed data collected from elementary teachers in a large Midwestern school district to test the hypothesis that perceived collective efficacy was positively related to differences among schools in teachers' sense of efficacy. In addition to perceived collective efficacy, school SES, proportion minority, and school size were employed as covariate measures of school context. In their analyses, perceived collective efficacy emerged as the strongest predictor of variation among schools in teachers' sense of efficacy. Indeed, before accounting for the effects of SES and past math achievement, a one standard deviation increase in perceived collective efficacy was associated with a .191 standard deviation increase in teachers' sense of efficacy. Moreover, after adjusting for differences related to school SES and past achievement, the increase in teachers' sense of efficacy associated with a one standard deviation increase in perceived collective efficacy was .25 standard deviations.

To understand the strength of this multilevel relationship between teacher and collective efficacy beliefs, it is essential to review the variance decomposition statistics reported in the study. Specifically, when school SES, proportion minority, size, and past achievement were tested as stand-alone predictors, each explained less than 25% of the variance among schools in teachers' sense of efficacy. When perceived collective efficacy was tested as a standalone predictor, it explained nearly 75% of the between-school variation in teachers' sense of efficacy. In combination (combined model), SES, past achievement, and perceived collective efficacy explained slightly more than 80% of the between-school variability in teachers' sense of efficacy. It is important to note that in the combined model only perceived collective efficacy was a statistically significant predictor. Hence, when compared with the impact of several powerful and commonly employed school contextual controls (SES, proportion minority, school size, and past achievement), perceived collective efficacy is the aspect of school cultural context most strongly related to teachers' sense of personal efficacy. Notably, the reason for the stand-alone analyses was that the combined model likely suffers from multi-colinearity because of the positive association between perceived collective efficacy, past achievement, and SES. Still, these finding support the theoretical explanations sketched earlier to explain that perceived collective efficacy has a strong influence on the normative environment of schools and makes a difference to teachers' self-referent perceptions of capability.

These findings indicate that perceived collective efficacy is a potent way of characterizing school culture. Indeed, collective efficacy beliefs are far more strongly related to teachers' perceptions of self-capability than many more common measures of school context. Moreover, these findings also suggest that collective efficacy beliefs may influence student achievement indirectly through their relationship with teachers' sense of efficacy. As postulated by social cognitive theory, social influence shapes self-efficacy beliefs. That is, where teachers tend to think highly of the collective capability of the faculty, they sense an expectation for successful teaching and hence are increasingly likely to put forth the effort required to help students learn. Conversely, where perceived collective efficacy is lower, it is less likely that teachers will be pressed by their colleagues to persist in the face of failure or that they will change their teaching when students do not learn.

Having reviewed evidence that perceived collective efficacy is systematically related to teachers' sense of efficacy and student achievement differences among schools, we turn now to an important question that has received relatively little research attention. Specifically, what do we know about strengthening perceived collective efficacy in schools?

Organizing Schools to Foster Collective Agency

We know that schools high in perceived collective efficacy usually have relatively high levels of student achievement (e.g., Bandura, 1993). To make such knowledge useful, however, it is important to understand how schools can be organized to foster positive collective efficacy beliefs. Given the social cognitive assumption that the agentive choices of individuals and organizations are strongly influenced by efficacy beliefs, we report the findings of recent research that offers a strong link between opportunities to exercise collective agency and levels of perceived collective efficacy.

When teachers have the opportunity to influence *instruction-ally relevant* school decisions, collective conditions encourage teachers to exercise organizational agency. The more teachers have the opportunity to influence instructionally relevant school decisions, the more likely a school is to be characterized by a robust sense of collective efficacy. To learn more about this possibility, Goddard (2002a) examined perceived collective efficacy as a predictor of differences among schools in the level of influence teachers have over instructionally relevant school decisions. Scale items employed to tap teacher influence over instruction-ally relevant decisions reflect teachers' reported level of control over curriculum, instructional materials and activities, professional development, communication with parents, student placement, and disciplinary policy. Findings from this study indicate that, after adjusting for school context, a .41 standard deviation increase in the extent to which teachers reported exerting influence over instructionally relevant school decisions was positively associated with a one standard deviation increase in perceived collective efficacy. That is, where teachers have the opportunity to influence important school decisions, they also tend to have stronger beliefs in the conjoint capability of their faculty.

From the perspective of social cognitive theory, the results highlight the important role of structures and actions that enable groups to exercise collective agency. When group influence is stifled, people are more likely to see the events around them as outside their control. This is the case, for example, in many traditional schools where principals retain power over nearly all decisions. The results of Goddard's (2002a) study, however, suggest the need for practices that enable group members to exert influence and exercise organizational agency. Bandura (1997) refers to such efforts as "group enablement." He observes that "... collective enablement programs take many different forms, but the shared assumption is that they work in part by enhancing people's sense of efficacy to bring about change in their lives" (p. 503). Schools that formally turn over instructionally relevant school decisions to teachers tend to have higher levels of perceived collective efficacy. Collective efficacy beliefs, in turn, foster commitment to school goals and gains in student achievement.

CONCLUSIONS AND A FRAMEWORK FOR FUTURE RESEARCH

There seems to be little doubt that collective efficacy beliefs are an important aspect of an organization's operative culture. The strong relationship between teachers' sense of efficacy and perceived collective efficacy provides evidence that organizational socialization involves the communication of influential normative expectations for achievement. Indeed, the research analyzed here suggests that a strong sense of collective efficacy enhances teachers' self-efficacy beliefs while weak collective efficacy beliefs undermine teachers' sense of efficacy, and vice versa. This mutual influence relationship helps explain the consistent finding that perceived collective efficacy is a significant factor in the attainment of organizational goals. Moreover, the research evidence suggests that, when teachers are empowered to influence instructionally relevant school decisions, they are likely to report more confidence in the capability of their faculty to educate students than would be the case if teachers were given less control over decisions that affect their professional work. Indeed, enabling faculty members to exert some control over school decisions may be one approach to strengthening collective efficacy beliefs in schools. Still, the question of how perceptions of group capability might be changed to strengthen organizational culture is an understudied area in collective efficacy belief research.

Thus, much remains to be known about perceived collective efficacy and the group-level extensions of its social cognitive underpinnings. Toward the end of providing a framework for future research into the meaning, effects, and change of collective efficacy perceptions, Figure 8.1 summarizes a preliminary conceptual model that depicts the hypothesized formation and influence of collective efficacy beliefs in organizations. This model reflects the social cognitive underpinnings of collective efficacy belief research and also suggests several areas for future research. For example, as we have noted, more research is needed to understand whether all sources of efficacy belief-shaping information depicted in the model (e.g., affective state) hold at the group level. In addition, the model notes a number of plausible outcomes of collective efficacy perceptions. Cultural change might be evidenced, for example, by changes in the outcomes suggested in Figure 8.1, such as student achievement and teacher commitment. A better understanding of the outcomes of perceived collec-

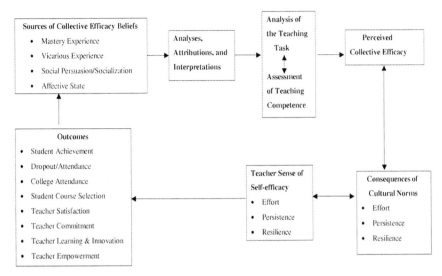

Figure 8.1.   Proposed model of the formation, influence, and change of perceived collective efficacy in schools.

tive efficacy holds a potential to deepen our understanding of how to improve organizational culture.

In sum, we believe that, while complex, questions regarding teachers' collective efficacy beliefs are important to our understanding of organizational transformation and, in particular, the success of public schools in educating our youth for effective participation in a democratic society. The recently passed No Child Left Behind Act calls for elevated levels of student achievement and the closing of achievement gaps by race and ethnicity. Such changes to the landscape of U.S. public education are unparalleled. We believe that the study of collective efficacy beliefs provides an opportunity to understand organizational culture and its influence on participants and group outcomes in new ways that hold promise for deeper theoretical understanding and practical knowledge concerning the improved function of organized activity, particularly schooling.

ACKNOWLEDGMENTS

The authors wish to dedicate this article to the memory of their friend and colleague Dr. Paul Pintrich of the University of Michigan. The authors also wish to acknowledge generous funding provided by the

National Academy of Education and the Spencer Foundation that helped make this research possible. The views expressed in this article are solely the responsibility of the authors.

REFERENCES

Allinder, R. M. (1994). The relationship between efficacy and the instructional practices of special education teachers and consultants. *Teacher Education and Special Education, 17*, 86–95.

Anderson, R., Greene, M., & Loewen, P. (1988). Relationships among teachers' and students' thinking skills, sense of efficacy, and student achievement. *Alberta Journal of Educational Research, 34*(2), 148–165.

Argote, L., Beckman, S. L., & Epple, D. (1990). The persistence and transfer of learning in industrial settings. *Management Science, 36*, 140–154.

Armor, D., Conroy-Oseguera, P., Cox, M., King, N., McDonnell, L., Pascal, A., et al. (1976). *Analysis of the school preferred reading program in selected Los Angeles minority schools* (Report No. R2007LAUSD; ERIC Document Reproduction No. 130 243). Santa Monica, CA: Rand Corporation.

Ashton, P. T., & Webb, R. B. (1986). *Making a difference: Teachers' sense of efficacy and student achievement.* New York: Longman.

Ashton, P. T., Olejnik, S., Crocker, L., & McAuliffe, M. (1982, April). *Measurement problems in the study of teachers' sense of efficacy.* Paper presented at the annual meeting of the American Educational Research Association, New York.

Bandura, A. (1977). Self-efficacy: Toward a unifying theory of behavioral change. *Psychological Review, 84*, 191–215.

Bandura, A. (1986). *Social foundations of thought and action: A social cognitive theory.* Englewood Cliffs, NJ: PrenticeHall.

Bandura, A. (1993). Perceived self-efficacy in cognitive development and functioning. *Educational Psychologist, 28*(2), 117–148.

Bandura, A. (1997). *Selfefficacy: The exercise of control.* New York: W. H. Freeman and Company.

Bouffard-Bouchard, T., Parent, S., & Larivee, S. (1991). Influence of self-efficacy on self-regulation and performance among junior and senior high-school students. *International Journal of Behavioral Development, 14*, 153–164.

Coleman, J. S. (1985). Schools and the communities they serve. *Phi Delta Kappan, 66*, 527–532.

Coleman, J. S. (1987). Norms as social capital. In G. Radnitzky & P. Bernholz (Eds.), *Economic imperialism: The economic approach applied outside the field of economics.* New York: Paragon House Publishers.

Coleman, J. S. (1990). *Foundations of social theory.* Cambridge, MA: Harvard University Press.

Czerniak, C. M., & Schriver, M. L. (1994). An examination of preservice science teachers' beliefs and behaviors as related to self-efficacy. *Journal of Science Teacher Education, 5*(3), 77–86.

Da Costa, J. L., & Riordan, G. (1996, April). *Teacher efficacy and the capacity to trust.* Paper presented at the annual meeting of the American Educational Research Association, New York.

DeForest, P. A., & Hughes, J. N. (1992). Effect of teacher involvement and teacher self-efficacy on ratings of consultant effectiveness and intervention acceptability. *Journal of Educational and Psychological Consultation, 3,* 301–316.

Dutton, J. M., & Freedman, R. D. (1985). External environment and internal strategies: Calculating, and experimenting, and initiating organizations. In R. Lamb & P. Shrivastava (Eds.), *Advances in strategic management* (pp. 39–67). Greenwich, CT: JAI.

Enochs, L. G., Scharmann, L. C., & Riggs, I. M. (1995). The relationship of pupil control to preservice elementary science teacher self-efficacy and outcome expectancy. *Science Education, 79*(1), 63–75.

Gibson, S., & Dembo, M. (1984). Teacher efficacy: A construct validation. *Journal of Educational Psychology, 76*(4), 569–582.

Gist, M. E., & Mitchell, T. R. (1992). Self-efficacy: A theoretical analysis of its determinants and malleability. *Academy of Management Review, 17,* 183–211.

Goddard, R. D. (2001). Collective efficacy: A neglected construct in the study of schools and student achievement. *Journal of Educational Psychology, 93*(3), 467–476.

Goddard, R. D. (2002a). Collective efficacy and school organization: A multilevel analysis of teacher influence in schools. *Theory and Research in Educational Administration, 1,* 169–184.

Goddard, R. D. (2003). The impact of schools on teacher beliefs, influence, and student achievement: The role of collective efficacy. In J. Raths & A. McAninch (Eds.), *Advances in teacher education (Vol. 6),* pp. 183–204. Westport, CT: Information Age Publishing.

Goddard, R. D., & Goddard, Y. L. (2001). A multilevel analysis of teacher and collective efficacy. *Teaching and Teacher Education, 17,* 807–818.

Goddard, R. D., Hoy, W. K., & Woolfolk Hoy, A. (2000). Collective teacher efficacy: Its meaning, measure, and effect on student achievement. *American Education Research Journal, 37*(2), 479–507.

Gorrell, J., & Capron, E. W. (1988). Effects of instrumental type and feedback on prospective teachers' self-efficacy beliefs. *The Journal of Experimental Education, 56*(3), 120–123.

Guskey, T. R. (1987). Context variables that affect measures of teacher efficacy. *Journal of Educational Research, 81*(1), 41–47.

Guskey, T. R., & Passaro, P. (1994). Teacher efficacy: A study of construct dimensions. *American Educational Research Journal, 31,* 627–643.

Hoy, W. K., Sweetland, S. R., & Smith, P. A. (2002). *Toward an organizational model of achievement in high schools: The significance of collective efficacy. Educational Administration Quarterly, 38*(1), 77–93.

Hoy, W. K., & Woolfolk, A. E. (1990). Socialization of student teachers. *American Educational Research Journal, 27,* 279–300.

Hoy, W. K., & Woolfolk, A. E. (1993). Teachers' sense of efficacy and the organizational health of schools. *The Elementary School Journal, 93*(4), 355–372.

Huber, G. P. (1996). Organizational learning: The contributing processes and literatures. In M. D. Cohen & L. S. Sproull (Eds.), *Organizational learning* (pp. 124–162). Thousand Oaks, CA: Sage.

Hyman, D. N. (1995). Public finance: A contemporary application of theory to policy. New York: Harcourt Brace.

Lee, V. E., Dedrick, R., & Smith, J. (1991). The effect of the social organization of schools on teachers' efficacy and satisfaction. *Sociology of Education*, *64*,190–208.

Levitt, B., & March, J. G. (1998). Organizational learning. *Annual Review of Sociology*, *14*, 319–340.

Little, B. L., & Madigan, R. M. (1997). The relationship between collective efficacy and performance in manufacturing work teams. *Small Group Research*, *28*(4), 517–534.

March, J. G. (1996). Exploration and exploitation in organizational learning. In M. D. Cohen & L. S. Sproull (Eds.), *Organizational learning* (pp. 101–123). Thousand Oaks, CA: Sage.

Meyer, J. W., & Rowan, B. (1977). Institutionalized organizations: Formal structure as myth and ceremony. *American Journal of Sociology*, *83*, 340–363.

Meyer, J. W., & Rowan, B. (1978). The structure of educational organizations. In M. W. Meyer (Ed.), *Environments and organizations* (pp. 78–109). San Francisco: Jossey-Bass.

Moore, W., & Esselman, M. (1992, April). *Teacher efficacy, power, school climate and achievement: A desegregating district's experience*. Paper presented at the annual meeting of the American Educational Research Association, San Francisco.

Pajares, F. (1994). Role of self-efficacy and self-concept beliefs in mathematical problem solving: A path analysis. *Journal of Educational Pyschology*, *86*, 193–203.

Pajares, F. (1997). Current directions in self-efficacy research. In M. L. Maehr & P. R. Pintrich (Eds.), *Advances in motivation and achievement* (pp. 1–49). Greenwich, CT: JAI Press.

Pajares, F., & Miller, D. (1994). Role of self-efficacy and self-concept beliefs in mathematical problem solving: A path analysis. *Journal of Educational Psychology*, *86*(2), 193–203.

Pajares, F. (1996a, April). *Current directions in self-research: Self-efficacy*. Paper presented at the annual meeting of the American Educational Research Association, New York.

Pajares, F. (1996b, April). *Assessing self-efficacy beliefs and academic outcomes: The case for specificity and correspondence*. Paper presented at the annual meeting of the American Educational Research Association, New York.

Parsons, T. (1951). *The social system*. Glencoe, IL: Free Press.

Pintrich, P. R., & Schunk, D. H. (2002). *Motivation in education: Theory, research, and applications* (2nd ed.). Columbus, OH: Merrill Prentice-Hall.

Raudenbush, S. W., Rowan, B., & Cheong, Y. F. (1992). Contextual effects on the self-perceived efficacy of high school teachers. *Sociology of Education*, *65*, 150–167.

Ross, J. A. (1992). Teacher efficacy and the effect of coaching on student achievement. *Canadian Journal of Education*, *17*(1), 51–65.

Ross, J. A. (1994, June). *Beliefs that make a difference: The origins and impacts of teacher efficacy.* Paper presented at the annual meeting of the Canadian Association for Curriculum Studies.

Sampson, R. J., Morenoff, J. D., & Earls, F. (2000). Beyond social capital: Spatial dynamics of collective efficacy for children. *American Sociological Review, 64,* 633–660.

Sampson, R. J., Raudenbush, S. W., & Earls, F. (1997). Neighborhoods and violent crime: A multilevel study of collective efficacy. *Science, 277,* 918–924.

Schunk, D. H. (1981). Modeling and attributional effects on children's achievement: A self-efficacy analysis. *Journal of Educational Psychology, 73,* 93–105.

Schunk, D. H. (1983). Developing children's self-efficacy and skills: The roles of social comparative information and goal setting. *Educational Psychology, 8,* 76–86.

Schunk, D. H. (1987). Peer models and children's behavioral change. *Review of Educational Research, 57,* 149–174.

Schunk, D. H., & Zimmerman, B. J. (1997). Social origins of self-regulatory competence. *Educational Psychologist, 32*(4), 195–208.

Simon, H. A. (1996). Bounded rationality and organizational learning. In M. D. Cohen & L. S. Sproull (Eds.), *Organizational learning* (pp. 175–187). Thousand Oaks, CA: Sage.

Skrla, L., & Goddard, R. D. (2002, November). *Accountability, equity, and collective efficacy in an urban school district: A mixed methods study.* Paper presented at the annual conference of the University Council for Educational Administration, Pittsburgh, PA.

Tschannen-Moran, M., Woolfolk Hoy, A. W., & Hoy, W. K. (1998). Teacher efficacy: Its meaning and measure. *Review of Educational Research, 68,* 202–248.

Woolfolk, A., & Hoy, W., K. (1990). Prospective teachers' sense of efficacy and beliefs about control. *Journal of Educational Psychology, 82,* 81–91.

Roger D. Goddard *is Assistant Professor of Education, University of Michigan-Ann Arbor, 610 East University Avenue, Room 216A, Ann Arbor, MI 48109-1259; rgoddard@mich.edu. His areas of specialization include educational administration, the social psychology of organization, and the measurement, sources, and effects of collective efficacy beliefs.*

Wayne K. Hoy *is the Novice Fawcett Chair in Educational Administration at The Ohio State University, 116 Ramseyer Hall, Columbus, OH 43210; whoy@mac.com. His areas of specialization include the edge, teachers' sense of efficacy, and educational psychology in teacher school as a social system, social psychology of administration, and or-education.ganizational theory.*

Anita Woolfolk Hoy *is a Professor of Educational Psychology at Manuscript received February 25, 2003 The Ohio State University, 159 Ramseyer Hall, Columbus, OH 43210; Revision received September 3, 2003 anitahoy@mac.com.*

Her areas of specialization include teacher knowledge, teacher's sense of efficacy, and educational psychology in teacher education.

PART VII

ON ACADEMIC OPTIMISM

CHAPTER 9

ACADEMIC OPTIMISM
OF SCHOOLS

A Force for Student Achievement

Wayne K. Hoy, C. John Tarter, and Anita Woolfolk Hoy

Researchers have been challenged to go beyond socioeconomic status in the search for school-level characteristics that make a difference in student achievement. The purpose of the present study was to identify a new construct, academic optimism, and then use it to explain student achievement while controlling for socioeconomic status, previous achievement, and urbanicity. The study focused on a diverse sample of 96 high schools. A random sample of teachers from each school provided data on the school's academic optimism, and student achievement scores and demographic characteristics were obtained from the state department of education. A confirmatory factor analysis and hypothesis tests were conducted simultaneously via structural equation modeling. As predicted, academic optimism made a significant contribution to student achievement after controlling for demographic variables and previous achievement. The findings support the critical nature of academic optimism.

Reprinted by permission from the *American Educational Research Journal*, Vol. 43, pp. 425-446. Copyright © 2006. All rights reserved.

Essential Ideas for the Reform of American Schools, pp. 199–224

Coleman startled educators with his finding that the characteristics of a school mattered little in explaining student achievement (Coleman et al., 1966). He argued that schools had only a negligible effect on student performance and that most of the variation in student learning was a product of differences in family background. Edmonds (1979) was one of the first to dispute Coleman's conclusions. His familiar list of effective school characteristics—strong principal leadership, high expectations for student achievement, an emphasis on basic skills, an orderly environment, and frequent and systematic evaluation of students—seemed to refute Coleman. Good schools were the product of good administrators. As simple as the connection seems, empirical demonstrations of direct administrative influences on student achievement have been elusive.

It is one thing to identify high-performing schools in neighborhoods of low socioeconomic status (SES) and attribute their performance to leadership characteristics or climate or an orderly environment, any of which may be present at those schools. It is quite another matter to demonstrate a priori that school leadership or other school properties will be directly and systematically related to student success in a controlled study involving a large sample. Although administrators do not perceive this to be the case, the weight of the evidence suggests that little or no direct relationship exists between principal leadership and student achievement (Hallinger & Heck, 1996).[1] In fact, it is difficult to find school properties that are consistently related to student achievement when controlling for the socioeconomic level of the school (for a notable exception in private high schools, see Bryk, Lee, & Holland, 1993). Nevertheless, educational leaders and policymakers alike have been reluctant to conclude that schools have little or no effect on student achievement. Instead, the quest has turned to identifying school characteristics that make a difference in achievement, in spite of student SES.

Coleman was not wrong; socioeconomic factors are powerful shapers of student performance. In fact, in large-scale studies such as those of Coleman et al. (1966) and Jencks (1972), SES overwhelms the association between school properties and achievement; the influence of school factors vanishes after social factors have been controlled. But Coleman was not entirely right; there are a few school characteristics that consistently predict student achievement, even after controlling for socioeconomic factors. Three organizational properties seem to make a difference in student achievement: the academic emphasis of the school, the collective efficacy of the faculty, and the faculty's trust in parents and students. We suspect that there are other such school properties, but they have not been readily revealed despite continuing research.

Academic emphasis, collective efficacy, and faculty trust are tightly woven together and seem to reinforce each other as they positively constrain student performance. We first examine the research on each of these three school properties, and then we explore the theory and research that link the three together as a single powerful force explaining school performance. We call this force academic optimism, which has been demonstrated to be a general latent construct (Hoy, Tarter, & Woolfolk Hoy, 2006). In this inquiry, we attempt to show that academic optimism is a general latent concept related to student achievement even after controlling for SES, previous performance, and other demographic variables.

Academic Emphasis of Schools

Academic emphasis is the extent to which a school is driven by a quest for academic excellence—a press for academic achievement. High but achievable academic goals are set for students; the learning environment is orderly and serious; students are motivated to work hard; and students respect academic achievement (Hoy & Miskel, 2005; Hoy, Tarter, & Kottkamp, 1991).

Lee and Bryk (1989) were two early researchers who underscored the importance of academic emphasis and student achievement. Hoy and his colleagues (Hoy et al., 1991) also demonstrated that academic emphasis as a collective property was positively and directly related to student achievement in high schools after controlling for SES. Whether school effectiveness was conceived as the commitment of teachers to the school, teachers' judgments of the effectiveness of the school, or actual student test scores, academic emphasis remained a potent force. Academic emphasis and achievement were positively related at both the middle school and high school levels, even after controlling for socioeconomic factors (Hoy & Hannum, 1997; Hoy & Sabo, 1998; Hoy, Tarter, & Bliss, 1990).

The findings are the same for elementary schools. Using hierarchical linear modeling and controlling for SES, school size, student race, and gender, Goddard, Sweetland, and Hoy (2000) found that academic emphasis was an important element in explaining achievement in both mathematics and reading. They concluded that "elementary schools with strong academic emphases positively affect achievement for poor and minority students" (p. 698).

Alig-Mielcarek and Hoy (2005) considered the influence of the instructional leadership of the principal and the academic emphasis of the school. They also found that academic emphasis was significant in explaining student achievement, even after controlling for SES. Using structural equation modeling, they found that the academic emphasis of the school, rather than instructional leadership, was the critical variable explaining achievement. In fact, instructional leadership worked indirectly, not directly, through academic emphasis to influence student achievement.

Notwithstanding different methodological approaches and school levels, the results are consistent. Whether the type of analysis used is multiple regression, structural equation modeling, or hierarchical linear modeling, and whether the level is elementary, middle, or secondary, academic emphasis is a key variable in explaining student achievement, even after controlling for SES, previous achievement, and other demographic variables.

COLLECTIVE EFFICACY

Social cognitive theory (Bandura, 1986, 1997) is a general framework for understanding human learning and motivation. Self-efficacy, a critical component of the theory, is an individual's belief about her or his capacity to organize and execute the actions required to produce a given level of attainment (Bandura, 1997). efficacy beliefs are central mechanisms in human agency, the intentional pursuit of a course of action. Individuals and groups are unlikely to initiate action without a positive sense of efficacy. The strength of efficacy beliefs affects the choices individuals and schools make about future plans and actions.

Student achievement and sense of efficacy are related. Researchers have found positive associations between student achievement and three kinds of efficacy beliefs: self-efficacy beliefs of students (Pajares, 1994, 1997), self-efficacy beliefs of teachers (Tschannen-Moran, Woolfolk Hoy, & Hoy, 1998), and teachers' collective efficacy beliefs about the school (Goddard, Hoy, & Woolfolk Hoy, 2000). We focus on the collective efficacy of schools and student achievement because collective efficacy is a school property amenable to change.

Within schools, perceived collective efficacy represents judgments about the performance capability of the social system as a whole (Bandura, 1997). Teachers have efficacy beliefs about themselves as well as the entire faculty. Simply put, perceived collective efficacy is the judgment of teachers that the faculty as a whole can organize and execute the actions required to have positive effects on students (Goddard, Hoy, & Woolfolk Hoy, 2004).

Bandura (1993) was the first to show the relationship between a sense of collective efficacy and academic school performance, a relationship that existed in spite of low SES. Schools in which the faculty had a strong sense of collective efficacy flourished, whereas those in which faculty members had serious doubts about their collective efficacy declined in academic performance or showed little academic progress. Continuing research has provided support for the importance of collective efficacy in explaining student achievement.

Goddard, Hoy, and Woolfolk Hoy (2000) supported the role of collective efficacy in promoting school achievement in urban elementary schools. They hypothesized that perceived collective efficacy would enhance student achievement in mathematics and reading. After controlling for SES and using hierarchical linear modeling, they found that collective efficacy was significantly related to student achievement in urban elementary schools.

Hoy, Sweetland, and Smith (2002), continuing this line of inquiry, predicted school achievement in high schools using collective efficacy as the central variable. They found that collective efficacy was the key variable in explaining student achievement; in fact, it was more important than either SES or academic emphasis. Hoy and his colleagues concluded that the school norms supporting academic achievement and collective efficacy are especially important in motivating achievement among both teachers and students, but academic emphasis is most forceful when collective efficacy is strong. That is, academic emphasis works through collective efficacy. They further theorized that when collective efficacy is strong, an emphasis on academic pursuits directs teachers' behaviors, helps them persist, and reinforces social norms of collective efficacy.

In a similar vein, Goddard, LoGerfo, and Hoy (2004) tested a more comprehensive model of perceived collective efficacy and student achievement. Using structural equation modeling, they also found that collective efficacy explained student achievement in reading, writing, and social studies regardless of minority student enrollment, urbanicity, SES, school size, or earlier achievement.

Research has consistently demonstrated the power of positive efficacy judgments in human learning, motivation, and achievement in such diverse areas as dieting, smoking cessation, sports performance, political participation, and academic achievement (Bandura, 1997; Goddard, Hoy, & Woolfolk Hoy, 2004). Similarly, the results of the school studies just reported underscore the importance of collective efficacy.

FACULTY TRUST IN PARENTS AND STUDENTS

Faculty trust in parents and students is the third school property that is related to student achievement. Faculty trust in parents and students is a collective school property in the same fashion as collective efficacy and academic emphasis. Although one might think that trust in parents and trust in students are separate concepts, several factor analyses have demonstrated they are not (Goddard, Tschannen-Moran, & Hoy, 2001; Hoy & Tschannen-Moran, 1999). Furthermore, Bryk and Schneider (2002) made the theoretical argument that teacher-student trust in elementary schools operates primarily through teacher-parent trust.

Trust is one's vulnerability to another in terms of the belief that the other will act in one's best interests. Tschannen-Moran and Hoy (2000), after an extensive review of the literature, concluded that trust is a general concept with at least five facets: benevolence, reliability, competence, honesty, and openness. Although it is theoretically possible that these facets do not vary together, research on schools shows that all five facets of trust in schools do indeed vary together to form an integrated construct of faculty trust in schools, whether the schools are elementary (Hoy & Tschannen-Moran, 1999, 2003) or secondary (Smith, Hoy, & Sweetland, 2001). Thus, we defined faculty trust as a willingness to be vulnerable to another party based on the confidence that that party is benevolent, reliable, competent, honest, and open (Hoy & Tschannen-Moran, 2003).

Cooperation and trust should set the stage for effective student learning, but only a few studies have examined this relationship. Goddard et al. (2001) examined the role of faculty trust in promoting achievement in urban elementary schools. Using a multilevel model, they demonstrated a significant direct, relationship between faculty trust in clients (students and parents) and higher student achievement, even after controlling for SES. Similar to collective efficacy, faculty trust was a key property enabling schools to overcome some of the disadvantages of low SES.

Hoy (2002) examined the trust-achievement hypothesis in high schools and again found that faculty trust in parents and students was positively related to student achievement after controlling for socioeconomic factors. He theorized that trusting others is a fundamental aspect of human learning because learning is typically a cooperative process, and distrust makes cooperation virtually impossible. When students, teachers, and parents have common learning goals, trust and cooperation are likely ingredients that improve teaching and learning.

Finally, Bryk and Schneider (2002) performed a 3-year longitudinal study in 12 Chicago elementary schools. Using hierarchical linear modeling, survey and achievement data, and in-depth interviews, they concluded that relational trust was a prime source of school improvement. Trust and cooperation among students, teachers, and parents influenced regular student attendance, persistent learning, and faculty experimentation with new practices. In brief, trust among teachers, parents, and students produced schools that showed marked gains in student learning, whereas schools with weak trust relationships exhibited virtually no improvement. The research of Bryk and Schneider and that of Hoy and his colleagues reinforce each other in the common conclusion that faculty trust of students and parents enhances student achievement.

COMMON THEMES AND A NEW CONSTRUCT: ACADEMIC OPTIMISM

Why are academic emphasis, collective efficacy, and trust consistently related to student achievement when SES is controlled, whereas other school-level properties are not? Is there a latent construct that undergirds these three properties? Are there common theoretical bases for these properties?

Academic emphasis, collective efficacy, and faculty trust were the collective properties analyzed in this inquiry. These perceived properties are assessed as emergent organizational attributes in aggregated individual perceptions of the *group*, as opposed to the *individual;* that is, these variables are emergent group-level attributes rather than simply the sum of teachers' perceived personal attributes (Bandura, 1986, 1997).

The research just reviewed suggests that academic emphasis, collective efficacy beliefs, and faculty trust shape school norms and behavioral expectations. Coleman (1985, 1987) explained that group norms give organizational members some degree of control over the actions of others because individual actions have consequences for the group. When teachers behave in ways that conflict with group norms, the group sanctions their behavior; in fact, Coleman argued that such social sanctions are proportionate to the importance of the norms. For example, when a faculty is highly committed to academic performance, the organization will sanction teachers who do not persist in their efforts to help students achieve.

Likewise, a strong sense of collective efficacy in a school creates a powerful set of norms and behavioral expectations that reinforce the self-efficacy beliefs of teachers. The push for efficacious teacher behaviors will be accompanied by social sanctions for those who lack self-efficacy. Similar cases can be made for trust in parents and students and academic emphasis. When the faculty has strong norms that support teachers' trusting and working with parents, the group will strive for cooperation and collaboration. The power of the school culture and its values and norms rests in large part on the social persuasion exerted on teachers to constrain certain actions and encourage others.

Academic emphasis, efficacy, and trust are similar not only in their nature and function but also in their potent and positive influence on student achievement. The three concepts have much in common; in fact, Hoy and his colleagues (Hoy et al., 2006) demonstrated that these three collective properties work together in a unified fashion to create a positive academic environment characterized by the label *academic optimism.*

In many conceptions of optimism, it is treated as a cognitive characteristic—a goal or expectancy based on knowledge and thinking (Peterson, 2000; Snyder et al., 2002). Our conception of academic optimism includes both cognitive and affective (emotional) dimensions and adds a behavioral element. Collective efficacy is a group belief or expectation; it is *cognitive.* Faculty trust in parents and students is an *affective* response. Academic emphasis is the push for particular *behaviors* in the school workplace (Hoy et al., 2006). Hoy and his colleagues concluded that "collective efficacy reflects the thoughts and beliefs of the group; faculty trust adds an affective dimension, and academic emphasis captures the behavioral enactment of efficacy and trust" (p. 14). Academic optimism paints a rich picture of human agency that explains collective behavior in terms of cognitive, affective, and behavioral dimensions.

The relationships among the three major dimensions of academic optimism can be seen as a triadic set of interactions with each element functionally dependent on the others. Faculty trust in parents and students encourages a sense of collective efficacy, and collective efficacy reinforces and enhances trust. Similarly, when the faculty trusts parents, teachers can insist on higher academic standards with confidence that they will not be determined by parents, and high academic standards in turn reinforce faculty trust. Finally, when the faculty believes it has the capability to organize and execute actions that will have positive effects on student achievement, academic achievement is emphasized, and academic emphasis in turn reinforces a strong sense of collective efficacy. In summary, all of the elements of academic optimism have transactional relationships with each other and interact to create a culture of academic optimism in schools. This postulated reciprocal causality between each pair of elements is shown in Figure 9.1.

Hoy and his colleagues (2006) chose the term academic optimism to reflect beliefs about agency in schools. They explained:

> Optimism is an appropriate overarching construct to unite efficacy, trust, and academic emphasis because each concept contains a sense of the possible. Efficacy is the belief that the faculty can make a positive difference in student learning; teachers believe in themselves. Faculty trust in students and parents is the belief that teachers, parents, and students can cooperate to improve learning, that is, the faculty believes in its students. Academic emphasis is the enacted behavior prompted by these beliefs, that is, the focus is student success. Thus, a school with high academic optimism is a collectivity in which the faculty believes that *it can* make a difference, that *students can* learn, and academic performance *can be* achieved. (p. 145)

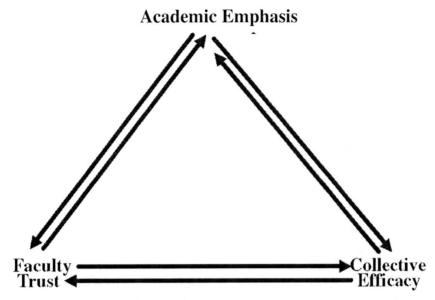

Figure 9.1.   Reciprocal causal relationships among the three dimensions of academic optimism.

Another attraction to the term academic optimism is the idea that it can be learned; a pessimistic school can become optimistic. Academic optimism gains its name from the conviction that its composite properties all express optimism and are malleable. Administrators and teachers have reason to be optimistic. They can be empowered; neither they nor their students are irretrievably trapped by socioeconomic factors.

HYPOTHESES

In the empirical phase of this investigation, we tested two hypotheses. The first involved the original finding that the collective properties of academic emphasis, efficacy, and faculty trust are the composite elements of academic optimism (Hoy et al., 2006). Therefore, our first hypothesis was that academic emphasis, collective efficacy, and faculty trust in parents and students would form a general latent construct labeled academic optimism. Our second hypothesis went beyond the original work done by Hoy and his colleagues (2006). To extend previous work, we proposed a test of the relationship between academic optimism and achievement, hypothesizing student academic achievement would be a function of academic optimism after control for SES, urbanicity (population density), and previous student achievement.

Finally, we expected that SES and previous achievement would be directly related to both academic optimism and student achievement and that both would make indirect contributions to achievement through academic optimism. Hence, our third hypothesis was that SES and previous student achievement would make direct contributions to student achievement, as well as indirect contributions through academic optimism. The three hypotheses are illustrated in the path model in Figure 9.2.

METHOD

Sample

The sample consisted of 96 high schools (comprising both Grades 9–12 and 10–12) located in a midwestern state. Although the sample was not a random one, care was taken to select urban, suburban, and rural schools to represent a diverse set of schools from the state. Only schools with 15 or more faculty members were considered for selection into the sample. We contacted 149 schools and invited them to take part in the study; however, only 97 (65%) agreed to participate, and we later excluded one of these schools because we were unable to obtain the

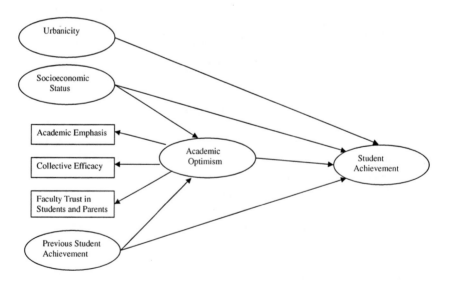

Figure 9.2.   Theoretical model of academic optimism and school achievement.

required achievement data. The participating schools represented a large range in terms of SES. Data from the state department of education suggested that the sample was representative of the population in regard to both SES and urban-suburban-rural balance.

Data Collection

Data were collected from faculty members attending one regularly scheduled faculty meeting at each school. A random set of teachers in each school (ranging from 10 to 40 depending on faculty size) were selected to respond to measures focusing on academic emphasis, collective efficacy, and faculty trust in parents and students.[2] Participants were guaranteed anonymity and confidentially, and no attempt was made to collect data from the few teachers who missed the faculty meeting.

Also, data for 2001 on school SES and student achievement in mathematics, science, reading, social studies, and writing were collected from the state department of education. Because our analysis was conducted at the school level, achievement in each content area was measured as the proportion of students in each school who passed mandatory content assessments; these data, which represented school-level variables, were available from the state. In addition, we were able to obtain data on previous average achievement in these same content areas for ninth-grade students.

Measures

Each of the three main study variables—academic emphasis of schools, collective efficacy, and faculty trust in students and parents—was assessed with a valid and reliable measure.

Academic Emphasis

The academic emphasis of a school refers to the extent to which the school focuses on intellectual activity and student achievement. The faculty stresses high achievement, and students work hard, are cooperative, and respect others who achieve high grades. The academic emphasis subscale of the Organizational Health Inventory (Hoy & Miskel, 2005; Hoy & Tarter, 1997; Hoy et al., 1991) was used to tap the academic emphasis of the school. Previous research has demonstrated the reliability and construct validity of this subscale. The measure is composed of eight Likert items scored on a 4-point scale ranging from *rarely occurs* (1) to *very frequently occurs* (4). Sample items include "Students respect others who get good grades," "Students in this school can achieve the goals that have been set for them," "The school sets high standards for academic performance," and "Academic achievement is recognized and acknowledged by the school." The reliability of the scale in this study was supported, with an alpha coefficient of .83. The construct and predictive validities of the scale also have been supported (Hoy & Tarter, 1997).

Collective Efficacy

The perceived collective efficacy of a school refers to the judgment of the teachers that the faculty as a whole can organize and execute the actions required to have positive effects on students (Goddard, Hoy, & Woolfolk Hoy, 2000, 2004). The construct was measured via the short version of the 12-item Collective efficacy Scale (Goddard, Hoy, & Woolfolk Hoy, 2000). Items were scored on a 6-point Likert scale ranging from *strongly disagree* (1) to *strongly agree* (6). Sample items include "Teachers here are confident they will be able to motivate their students," "Drug and alcohol abuse in the community make learning difficult for students here" (reverse scored), "These students come to school ready to learn," and "Students here just aren't motivated to learn" (reverse scored). Previous research has demonstrated the construct validity and reliability of the scale (Goddard, Hoy, & Woolfolk Hoy, 2000, 2004). The alpha coefficient in the present study was .91.

Faculty Trust in Students and Parents

Faculty trust in students and parents was measured with the Omnibus Trust Scale (Hoy & Tschannen-Moran, 2003). Items were scored on a 6-point Likert scale ranging from *strongly disagree* (1) to *strongly agree* (6). Sample items include "Teachers in this school can trust their students," "Parents in this school are reliable in their commitment," "Students in this school can be counted on to do their work," and "Teachers can count on parental support." The reliability and construct validity of the scale have been supported in several factor-analytic studies (Hoy & Tschannen-Moran, 2003). The alpha coefficient in this study was .94.

Socioeconomic Status

SES, a standardized measure ($M = 0$, $SD = 1$) maintained by the state, was a composite variable including common indicators such as income, educational level, and neighborhood residential stability.

Urbanicity

Urbanicity was a standardized variable (created by the state) in which population density was used to distinguish urban schools, which had higher scores.

Achievement

Measures of the proportions of students passing the state-mandated 12th-grade mathematics, science, reading, social studies, and writing tests were obtained from the state department of education. These measures served as the outcome variables in our structural equation models. Students completed the 12th-grade assessments approximately 1 to 2 months after the faculties completed our survey.

Previous Achievement

To control for prior school achievement levels, we were able to obtain average ninth-grade assessment scores 2 years before the current study. Although students were not tracked longitudinally, prior achievement scores provided reasonable estimates of their previous achievement.

Analysis

First, we calculated descriptive statistics for each of the variables assessed in the study (see Table 9.1). Although many studies of school effectiveness employ hierarchical methods to account for the nested nature of students in classrooms within schools, neither student- nor teacher-level outcome data could be obtained here. For this reason, and because our hypothesized model involved several complicated structural relations, we selected structural equation modeling as our primary analytic tool. As we describe next, however, we did use hierarchical linear modeling to demonstrate that our aggregated measures of faculty trust in parents and students, academic emphasis, and collective efficacy were collective properties and not merely averages of individual measures. Two points are relevant in this regard. first, the items were written to refer to school properties and not to individual characteristics (e.g., "Teachers in this school can trust their students"). Second, intraclass correlation coefficients for the measures showed that there was a substantial group effect for each of the three variables.

Intraclass Correlations

To demonstrate this latter point, we analyzed the data using a fully unconditional analysis of variance (via HLM 5.4 software; Raudenbush & Bryk, 2002) for the three variables that defined academic optimism. The intraclass correlation coefficients were .23 for collective efficacy, .21 for trust in parents and students, and .24 for academic emphasis. In other words, of the variance in perceived collective efficacy, 23% existed between schools; of the variance for trust in parents and students, 21% existed between schools; and of the variance for academic emphasis, 24%

existed between schools. Thus, in all cases, according to standards adopted by other researchers (Caprara, Barbaranelli, Borgogni, & Steca, 2003; Hox, 2002; Stevens, 1990), the intraclass correlation coefficients were sufficiently strong to suggest a relatively high grouping effect. Furthermore, this relatively high percentage of between-school variance suggests that academic optimism can be conceived as an important latent school property that can be attributed to the school (see Table 9.1).

Structural Equation Model

We tested our hypotheses using structural equation modeling. The first hypothesis—that academic emphasis, collective efficacy, and faculty trust in parents and students would form a general latent construct called academic optimism—was tested with the measurement part of our model.

Because our objective was to test the underlying theory of a new construct (academic optimism), we assessed our theory by conducting a first-order factor analysis using LISREL 8.5. The theoretical analysis discussed earlier led us to hypothesize that the three concepts of collective efficacy, faculty trust in students and parents, and academic emphasis would identify the first-order factor labeled academic optimism.

The structural model was used to test the next two hypotheses: that student academic achievement would be a function of academic optimism

Table 9.1.   Description of Variables (N = 96 Schools)

Variable	M	SD	Minimum	Maximum
Academic emphasis	2.75	0.26	2.21	3.38
Collective efcacy	3.96	0.33	3.23	4.85
Trust in clients	3.65	0.39	2.79	4.72
Socioeconomic status	0.04	0.88	1.21	3.59
Urbanicity	0.04	0.96	2.07	2.09
9th-grade reading achievement	90.19	8.17	50.00	100.00
9th-grade social studies achievement	81.39	13.42	12.50	100.00
9th-grade writing achievement	90.59	9.86	25.00	100.00
9th-grade math achievement	71.35	15.83	22.20	98.70
9th-grade science achievement	75.31	5.83	11.10	100.00
12th-grade reading achievement	64.45	11.07	26.40	85.30
12th-grade social studies achievement	66.64	13.07	23.80	88.90
12th-grade writing achievement	82.37	10.06	53.60	100.00
12th-grade math achievement	57.47	15.07	20.80	90.40
12th-grade science achievement	59.97	13.82	15.10	87.70

Note: Achievement scores represent the proportion of students who passed the assessment.

after controlling for SES, urbanicity, and previous student achievement and that SES and previous student achievement would make direct contributions, and indirect contributions through academic optimism, to student achievement. Thus, using the structural equation model, we estimated direct and indirect effects simultaneously. Furthermore, each path coefficient was estimated after the effects of all of the other paths had been taken into account.

Both the measurement and structural models are shown in the path model of Figure 9.2. We used LISREL 8.5 to create the latent variable of academic optimism using confirmatory factor analysis and then generated estimates of the relationships among the theoretical variables using path analysis.

Many goodness of t statistics are used to determine the acceptance or rejection of a theoretical model. first, we conducted a chi-square test; a nonsignificant chi-square value means that the hypothesized model is not rejected but, in fact, is supported. The chi-square statistic, however, is strongly influenced by sample size (Bentler & Bonnett, 1980; Thompson, 2004). To complement the chi-square test, we also computed the norm-fit index (NFI), the comparative-fit index (CFI), and the mean root square error of approximation (RMSEA).

RESULTS

The analyses were computed from the raw data collected as described earlier. The data were used as input to LISREL 8.5 (Joreskog & Sorbom, 1993). We tested the model twice. Initially, student achievement was considered as a latent dependent variable composed of mathematics and science achievement, and then it was considered as a latent dependent variable composed of social studies, reading, and writing. Our model was supported in both analyses.

The test of the model for mathematics and science achievement indicated an excellent fit to the data: $\chi^2 = 26.15$, $p = .16$, NFI = .97, CFI = .99, RMSEA = 3.05. The standardized solution is depicted in Figure 9.3. Overall, the predictor variables accounted for 67% of the variance in student achievement. As hypothesized, SES was related to student achievement directly (.20) as well as indirectly through academic optimism (.19). Likewise, prior achievement was related to student achievement directly (.60) and indirectly through academic optimism (.61). Finally, as predicted, academic optimism was directly related to achievement (.21).

The test of the model for reading, social studies, and writing achievement also indicated a strong fit to the data: $\chi^2 = 47.71$, $p = .11$, NFI = .96, CFI = .99, RMSEA = .04. The standardized solution is depicted in Figure 9.4. Overall, the predictor variables accounted for 54% of the variance in student achievement. Obviously, other factors, such as individual ability, extra help or tutoring, motivation, and teaching and learning styles, contribute to student achievement. As hypothesized, SES was related to student achievement directly (.23) as well as indirectly through academic optimism (.23). Likewise, prior achievement was related to student achievement directly (.44) and indirectly through academic optimism (.52). Finally, as predicted, academic optimism was directly related to achievement (.27). In brief, the proposed theoretical model was supported in both tests.

DISCUSSION AND CONCLUSIONS

We turn to a discussion of our results, implications for practice, and ideas for future research.

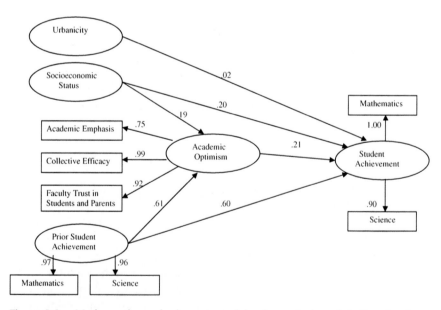

Figure 9.3.   Mathematics and science test of the theoretical model of academic optimism and school achievement. All path coefficients are standardized and, with the exception of urbanicity, are statistically significant.

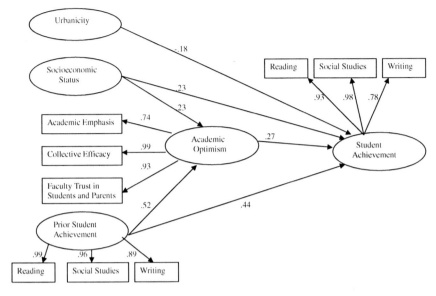

Figure 9.4.   Reading, social studies, and writing test of the theoretical model of academic optimism and school achievement. All path coefficients are standardized and, with the exception of urbanicity, are statistically significant.

Academic Optimism and School Achievement

The results of our measurement model support our theory that the properties of academic emphasis, collective efficacy, and faculty trust in students and parents work together in a unifying fashion to form a general latent construct that can be labeled academic optimism. This finding is consistent with our earlier work in elementary schools (Hoy et al., 2006). Recall that collective efficacy is the cognitive aspect of academic optimism, the thinking and believing side; faculty trust in students and parents is the affective and emotional side of the latent construct; and academic emphasis is the behavioral side, that is, enactment of the cognitive and affective into action.

The traditional view of achievement in schools is that success is a function of talent and motivation; the talented and motivated are high achievers (Seligman, 1998). Seligman offered a third factor in success: optimism. He argued that optimism matters as much as talent or motivation in achievement. Furthermore, optimism can be learned and developed. Clearly, learned optimism is an individual variable (Seligman, 1998), and academic optimism is a collective property. Nonetheless, we anticipate that many conclusions about individual learned optimism can be applied to the collective.

Seligman argued that learned optimism moves people over the wall of learned pessimism, not just as individuals but also as organizational members. In the same way that individuals can develop learned helplessness, organizations can be seduced by pervasive pessimism. According to the pessimistic view, voiced with a tired resignation, "These kids can't learn, and there is nothing I can do about it, so why worry about academic achievement?" This view is reinforcing, self-fullling, and defeating. Academic optimism, in stark contrast, views teachers as capable, students as willing, parents as supportive, and the task as achievable.

The results of our structural model support Seligman's argument that optimism is a strong force for achievement even at the organizational level. In our conception of academic optimism, the three underlying elements suggest why it is effective in enhancing learning. Collective efficacy provides teachers with confidence that they can be effective working with students regardless of the difficulties involved. It motivates teachers to act to achieve challenging goals and persist until they are successful (Goddard, Hoy, & Woolfolk Hoy, 2000; Hoy, Smith, & Sweetland, 2002). Trust in parents and teachers liberates teachers to innovate without fear of retribution if things do not go as planned, and it encourages cooperation and support between parents and teachers (Bryk & Schneider, 2002; Goddard et al., 2001). A focus on academics is enacted in behavior because students and parents trust the teachers. Both accept the means to realize academic performance. Not only do teachers and parents push for academic success, but students also come to value working hard, getting good grades, and achieving. In the defined, efficacy, trust, and academic emphasis produce a powerful synergism that motivates, creates optimism, and channels behavior toward the accomplishment of high academic goals.

In summary, we have demonstrated that academic emphasis, faculty trust, and collective efficacy form a general latent construct that we call academic optimism. The construct draws on three different theories. Collective efficacy comes from Bandura's work (1997) in social cognitive theory; trust emerges as an important concept in Coleman's (1990) analysis of social interaction; and academic emphasis evolves from Hoy and his colleagues' research on the organizational health of schools, with its theoretical underpinnings from Parsons and his colleagues (Parsons, Bales, & Shils, 1953). Bringing these three streams of theory and research together provides a richer and yet more direct explanation of how schools enhance student learning. Furthermore, knowledge of the composite elements of collective academic optimism has the added benefit of providing a wider set of possibilities for improving optimism in schools.

Implications for Practice

How can leaders build academic optimism in their schools? We suspect the general way to enhance the academic optimism of a school is to improve its component parts. Thus, we briefly consider strategies for developing academic emphasis, collective efficacy, and trust and then look to the literature on optimism for additional ideas.

Academic Emphasis

The one goal that virtually everyone shares for schools is the academic achievement of students. The reform and accountability movements have promoted a press toward the academic achievement of all students (No Child Left Behind Act, 2002). The focus of schooling is clear—it is an academic one. A push for academic achievement, however, in an environment where teachers do not feel efficacious is a recipe for frustration and stress. The challenge is to create school conditions in which teachers believe *they are up to the task and so are their students.* How might this be done? Principals move a school by example. They celebrate the achievements of students and faculty, especially the academic ones. Behaviors that foster academics include emphasizing the honor roll, national honor societies, and exemplary student work of all kinds. To be sure, this is an old list, but in conjunction with building efficacy and trust, these activities take on new strength.

Collective Efficacy

Collective efficacy is grounded in Bandura's social cognitive theory (Bandura, 1997); hence, we turn to his sources of efficacy for ideas about how to build collective efficacy in schools. The sources of self-efficacy are mastery experiences, vicarious experiences, social persuasion, and affective states, each of which conveys information that influences teachers' perceptions of the school (Bandura, 1993, 1997; Goddard, Hoy, & Woolfolk Hoy, 2004; Pajares, 1997). For example, consider a school with a poor graduation rate. A neighboring district has implemented a successful program for at-risk students. The principal is in the position to orchestrate the transfer of the neighbor's success to his or her school. In so doing, the school is engaged in a self-regulatory process informed by the vicarious learning of its members and, perhaps, the social persuasion of leaders. Modeling success and persuading teachers to believe in themselves and their capabilities is a reasonable route to improve collective efficacy and enhance academic optimism (Bandura, 1997; Goddard, Hoy, & Woolfolk Hoy, 2004).

Trust in Parents and Students

There is some research on family and community involvement in schools (see Epstein, 1989); however, there is little systematic research on how to build authentic trust. Faculty trust in students and parents can be promoted through useful interchanges, both formal and informal, between parents and teachers. Making the most of vicarious learning, for example, a school can respond to a lack of trust and community participation in school activities by emulating the practices and procedures of magnet schools known for their parental cooperation and involvement. But much more research is needed about what programs and factors support the development of teachers' trust in parents and students. Such examples demonstrate how changes in social perceptions influence the actions organizations choose to pursue. Collective perceptions about efficacy, academic emphasis, and trust shape school norms and can be developed through experiences that convey their value.

A caveat is in order: Interventions should be supportive of all three aspects of optimism. For example, some ways of enhancing academic emphasis, such as more competitive grading and greater punishment for failure, could undermine the development of trust among teachers, students, and parents. Similarly, a focus on developing trust could come as a result of diminishing standards and rewarding students for merely adequate work, that is, providing only positive feedback. Constructive criticism is essential for academic growth.

Optimism

The research on individual optimism suggests some ideas about encouraging a culture of optimism in schools. Peterson (2000) found that optimism is thwarted by stress; thus, decreasing stress should support optimism. Teachers can lower their stress by increasing their agency through appropriate participation in decisions that affect their school lives (Hoy & Tarter, 2004).

People learn from models because observation of the successful performances of others promotes acquisition of their beliefs and actions. The most effective models are those who seem competent, powerful, prestigious, and similar to the observer (Pintrich & Schunk, 2002). Vicarious and observational learning are sources of optimism. Thus, teachers can serve as models for each other. The way in which school problems are discussed should convey the possibilities for resolution rather than defeatism. Novice teachers, for example, should hear optimistic approaches to teaching rather than being exposed to a sense of passive helplessness in teachers' lounges and school hallways.

Snyder and his colleagues (Snyder, Cheavens, & Sympson, 1997; Snyder et al., 2002) have studied *hope*, a concept that combines *pathways think-*

ing (there are multiple ways to reach our goals) with *agentic thinking* (we have the capabilities to reach these goals, changing if necessary). Individuals at high levels on measures of hope often collaborate to achieve shared goals. They enjoy interpersonal interactions: "High-hopers serve to make the group not only more productive but also, perhaps equally important, an interpersonally more enjoyable arena" (Snyder et al., 1997, p. 115). Thus, leaders with high hopes are likely to encourage and build academic optimism in their schools.

Future Research

This inquiry is a modest beginning; much remains to be done. Our analysis is a promising clarification of some of the significant linkages within schools that influence student achievement. Although our data were drawn from high schools, we believe the findings could be applicable to elementary and middle schools because the three elements of academic optimism have explained learning in these settings as well.

One might question whether academic optimism adds any value to the earlier research on effective schools (Purkey & Smith, 1983; Scheerens & Bosker, 1997), which identified such factors as clear goals and high expectations, parental support and involvement, and collaborative planning as being related to student achievement. Clearly, our findings on academic optimism are consistent with this earlier research, but they go further to explain how some of these factors influence teachers' beliefs that lead to student achievement. Parental involvement will not support achievement unless this involvement builds trusts among students, teachers, and parents. Collaborative planning may be effective because it builds a sense of collective efficacy that promotes teacher motivation and persistence. Academic emphasis has consistently been related to achievement, but in the context of pressure and punishment such an emphasis may be deleterious to long-term learning. Students, parents, and teachers will probably be more willing to work toward academically challenging goals if they believe they are capable and the people around them can be trusted to help them. These are all testable propositions in need of further empirical support.

Clearly, more research in a variety of school settings is necessary to build a comprehensive theory of academic optimism in schools. For example, in the tradition of the earlier effective schools research, qualitative investigators could conduct comparative case studies of schools identified as having high and low academic optimism. What would these schools look, sounded, and feel like? Are there curricular differences between such schools? What are the experiences of students, teachers, and parents? How are expectations communicated and enforced? How does teacher trust in parents emerge? What enables and hinders the development of such trust? What is the role of the principal in developing a culture of academic optimism? Are leader optimism and hope necessary conditions for the creation of academic optimism? On the basis of rich descriptions of life in schools, these relationships and other variables could then be identified for further quantitative analyses. It seems obvious that both quantitative and qualitative work are necessary to elaborate a theory of academic optimism in schools.

Academic optimism is especially attractive because it emphasizes the potential of schools to overcome the power of socioeconomic factors that impair student achievement. It is a social psychological construct that is in part related to the positive psychology of Seligman and Csikszentmihalyi (2000), the social cognitive theory of Bandura (1997), Hoy and Tarter's (1997) research on school climates, and the social theory of Coleman (1990). There is real value in focusing on potential, with its strength and resilience, rather than pathology, with its weakness and helplessness. Academic optimism attempts to explain and nurture what is best in schools to facilitate student learning. This simple conclusion should encourage teachers and principals to move forward with confidence, knowing many of the significant linkages within schools that influence student achievement.

ACKNOWLEDGMENTS

The authors are scholars of organizational theory (Hoy & Tarter) and psychology (Woolfolk Hoy). They have conducted studies on educational leadership, organizational culture, motivation, and teachers' sense of collective and personal efficacy in relation to teaching and learning. The current research is a culmination of a decade of investigation searching for school properties that can be altered to improve student achievement, especially in urban schools. Academic optimism is a new concept, grounded in social cognitive theory and positive psychology, that has the potential to disrupt the commonly found linkages between low socioeconomic status and low achievement. Principals and teachers, together with parents and students, can create cultures of optimism that support academic learning and student efficacy.

We thank Xiaodong Liu, Ohio State University, for his excellent advice and guidance in structural equation modeling.

NOTES

1. Hallinger and Heck (1996, p. 39) concluded: "The fact that leadership effects and school achievement appear to be indirect is neither cause for alarm nor dismay." The finding that principal effects are mediated by other in-school variables does not diminish the principal's importance. It is possible that different theoretical models and the application of mixed methods containing qualitative analyses will reveal a more direct path between principals' leadership and student achievement.

2. The current study was part of a larger investigation that required measurement of additional organizational variables. The teachers not randomly selected for participation in this study completed other measures during the faculty meeting.

REFERENCES

Alig-Mielcarek, J., & Hoy, W. K. (2005). Instructional leadership: Its nature, meaning, and influence. In W. K. Hoy & C. Miskel (Eds.), *Educational leadership and reform* (pp. 29–54). Greenwich, CT: Information Age.

Bandura, A. (1977). Self-efficacy: Toward a unifying theory of behavioral change. *Psychological Review, 84,* 191–215.

Bandura, A. (1986). *Social foundations of thought and action.* Englewood Cliffs, NJ: Prentice Hall.

Bandura, A. (1993). Perceived self-efficacy in cognitive development and functioning. *Educational Psychologist, 28,* 117–148.

Bandura, A. (1997). *Self-efficacy: The exercise of control.* New York: Freeman.

Bentler, P. M., & Bonnett, D. G. (1980). Signicance tests and goodness of fit in the analysis of covariance structures. *Psychological Bulletin, 88,* 588–606.

Bryk, A. S., Lee, V., & Holland, P. (1993). *Catholic schools and the common good.* Cambridge, MA: Harvard University Press.

Bryk, A. S., & Schneider, B. (2002). *Trust in schools: A core resource for improvement.* New York: Russell Sage Foundation.

Caprara, G. V., Barbaranelli, C., Borgogni, L., & Steca, P. (2003). efficacy beliefs as determinants of teachers' job satisfaction. *Journal of Educational Psychology, 95,* 821–832.

Coleman, J. S. (1985). Schools and the communities they serve. *Phi Delta Kappan, 66,* 527–532.

Coleman, J. S. (1987). Norms as social capital. In G. Radnitzky & P. Bernholz (Eds.), *Economic imperialism: The economic approach applied outside the field of economics.* New York: Paragon House.

Coleman, J. S. (1990). *Foundations of social theory.* Cambridge, MA: Harvard University Press.

Coleman, J. S., Campbell, E. Q., Hobson, C. J., McPartland, J., Mood, A. M., Weinfeld, F. D., et al. (1966). *Equality of educational opportunity.* Washington, DC: U.S. Government Printing Office.

Edmonds, R. (1979). Some schools work and more can. *Social Policy, 9,* 28–32.

Epstein, J. L. (1989). Family structure and student motivation. In R. E. Ames & C. Ames (Eds.), *Research on motivation in education: Vol. 3. Goals and cognitions* (pp. 259–295). New York: Academic Press.

Goddard, R. G., Hoy, W. K., & Woolfolk Hoy, A. (2000). Collective teacher efficacy: Its meaning, measure, and impact on student achievement. *American Educational Research Journal, 37*, 479–508.

Goddard, R. G., Hoy, W. K., & Woolfolk Hoy, A. (2004). Collective efficacy: Theoretical development, empirical evidence, and future directions. *Educational Researcher, 33*(3), 3–13.

Goddard, R. G., LoGerfo, L., & Hoy, W. K. (2004). High school accountability: The role of collective efficacy. *Educational Policy, 18*, 403–425.

Goddard, R. G., Sweetland, S. R., & Hoy, W. K. (2000). Academic emphasis of urban elementary schools and student achievement: A multi-level analysis. *Educational Administration Quarterly, 36*, 692–701.

Goddard, R. D., Tschannen-Moran, M., & Hoy, W. K. (2001). Teacher trust in students and parents: A multilevel examination of the distribution and effects of teacher trust in urban elementary schools. *Elementary School Journal, 102*, 3–17.

Hallinger, P., & Heck, R. (1996). Reassessing the principal's role in school effectiveness: A review of the empirical research, 1980–1995. *Educational Administration Quarterly, 32*, 5–44.

Hox, J. J. (2002). *Multilevel analysis.* Mahwah, NJ: Erlbaum.

Hoy, W. K. (2002). Faculty trust: A key to student achievement. *Journal of School Public Relations, 23*, 88–103.

Hoy, W. K., & Hannum, J. (1997). Middle school climate: An empirical assessment of organizational health and student achievement. *Educational Administration Quarterly, 33*, 290–311.

Hoy, W. K., & Miskel, C. G. (2005). *Educational administration: Theory, research, and practice* (7th ed). New York: McGraw-Hill.

Hoy, W. K., & Sabo, D. J. (1998). *Quality middle schools: Open and healthy.* Thousand Oaks, CA: Corwin Press.

Hoy, W. K., Smith, P. A., & Sweetland, S. R. (2002). A test of a model of school achievement in rural schools: The significance of collective efficacy. In W. K. Hoy & C. Miskel (Eds.), *Theory and research in educational administration* (pp. 185–202). Greenwich, CT: Information Age.

Hoy, W. K., Sweetland, S. R., & Smith, P. A. (2002). Toward an organizational model of achievement in high schools: The significance of collective efficacy. *Educational Administration Quarterly, 38*, 77–93.

Hoy, W. K., & Tarter, C. J. (1997). *The road to open and healthy schools: A handbook for change* (2nd ed.). Thousand Oaks, CA: Corwin Press.

Hoy, W. K., & Tarter, C. J. (2004). *Administrators solving the problems of practice: Decision-making concepts, cases, and consequences.* Boston: Allyn & Bacon.

Hoy, W. K., Tarter, C. J., & Bliss, J. (1990). Organizational climate, school health, and effectiveness. *Educational Administration Quarterly, 26*, 260–279.

Hoy, W. K., Tarter, C. J., & Kottkamp, R. B. (1991). *Open schools/healthy schools: Measuring organizational climate.* Beverly Hills, CA: Sage.

Hoy, W. K., Tarter, C. J., & Woolfolk Hoy, A. (2006). Academic optimism of schools. In W. K. Hoy & C. Miskel (Eds.), *Contemporary issues in educational policy and school outcomes* (pp. 135–156). Greenwich, CT: Information Age.

Hoy, W. K., & Tschannen-Moran, M. (1999). Five faces of trust: An empirical confirmation in urban elementary schools. *Journal of School Leadership, 9*, 184–208.

Hoy, W. K., & Tschannen-Moran, M. (2003). The conceptualization and measurement of faculty trust in schools. In W. K. Hoy & C. Miskel (Eds.), *Studies in leading and organizing schools* (pp. 181–207). Greenwich, CT: Information Age.

Jencks, C. (1972). *Inequality: A reassessment of the effect of family and schooling in America.* New York: Basic Books.

Joreskog, K. G., & Sorbom, D. (1993). *LISREL 8.* Hillsdale, NJ: Erlbaum.

Lee, V., & Bryk, A. S. (1989). A multilevel model of social distribution of high school achievement. *Sociology of Education, 62*, 172–192.

No Child Left Behind Act, Public Law No. 107-110 (2002).

Pajares, F. (1994). Role of self-efficacy and self-concept beliefs in mathematical problem-solving: A path analysis. *Journal of Educational Psychology, 86*, 193–203.

Pajares, F. (1997). Current directions in self-efficacy research. In M. L. Maehr & P. R. Pintrich (Eds.), *Advances in motivation and achievement* (pp. 1–49). Greenwich, CT: JAI Press.

Parsons, T., Bales, R. F., & Shils, E. A. (1953). *Working papers in the theory of action.* New York: Free Press.

Peterson, C. (2000). The future of optimism. *American Psychologist, 55*, 44–55.

Pintrich, P. R., & Schunk, D. H. (2002). *Motivation in education: Theory, research, and applications* (2defined ed.). Upper Saddle River, NJ: Merrill/Prentice Hall.

Purkey, S. C., & Smith, M. S. (1983). Effective schools: A review. *Elementary School Journal, 83*, 427–452.

Raudenbush, S. W., & Bryk, A. S. (2002). *Hierarchical linear models: Application and data analysis methods* (2defined ed.). Thousands Oaks, CA: Sage.

Scheerens, J., & Bosker, R. (1997). *The foundations of educational effectiveness.* Oxford, England: Pergamon Press.

Seligman, M. E. P. (1998). Positive social science. *APA Monitor, 29*(2), 5.

Seligman, M. E. P., & Csikszentmihalyi, M. (2000). Positive psychology: An introduction. *American Psychologist, 55*, 5–14.

Smith, P. A., Hoy, W. K., & Sweetland, S. R. (2001). Organizational health of high schools and dimensions of faculty trust. *Journal of School Leadership, 11*, 135–151.

Snyder, C. R., Cheavens, J., & Sympson, S. C. (1997). Hope: An individual motive for social commerce. *Group Dynamics, 1*, 107–118.

Snyder, C. R., Shorey, H. S., Cheavens, J., Pulvers, K. M., Adams, V. H., III, & Wiklud, C. (2002). Hope and academic success in college. *Journal of Educational Psychology, 94*, 820–826.

Stevens, J. (1990). *Intermediate statistics: A modern approach.* Hillsdale, NJ: Erlbaum.

Thompson, B. (2004). *Exploratory and confirmatory factor analysis: Understanding concepts and applications.* Washington, DC: American Psychological Association.

Tschannen-Moran, M., & Hoy, W. K. (2000). A multidisciplinary analysis of the nature, meaning, and measurement of trust. *Review of Educational Research, 70*, 547–593.

Tschannen-Moran, M., Woolfolk Hoy, A. W., & Hoy, W. K. (1998). Teacher efficacy: Its meaning and measure. *Review of Educational Research, 68*, 202–248.

Wayne K. Hoy is the Fawcett Chair of Educational Administration, School of Educational Policy and Leadership, 116 Ramseyer Hall, 29 West Woodruff Avenue, Ohio State University, Columbus, OH 43210; e-mail: hoy.16@osu.edu. He specializes in organizational theory and leadership.

C. John Tarter is a Professor of Educational Administration, School of Education MAR-208C, St. John's University, 8000 Utopia Parkway, Jamaica, NY 11439; email: ctarter@aol.com. He specializes in organizational analysis.

Anita Woolfolk Hoy is a Professor of Educational Psychology, School of Educational Policy and Leadership, 159 Ramseyer Hall, 29 West Woodruff Avenue, Ohio State University, Columbus, OH 43210; e-mail: hoy.17@osu.edu. She specializes in teaching and learning.

PART VIII

ON ORGANIZATIONAL CITIZENSHIP

CHAPTER 10

MEASURING ORGANIZATIONAL CITIZENSHIP OF SCHOOLS

The OCB Scale

Michael F. DiPaola, C. John Tarter, and Wayne K. Hoy

Organizational citizenship describes voluntary and discretionary behavior of teachers that exceeds the formal requirements of the job. A review of the literature identified the conceptual underpinnings of organizational citizenship. Then the construct was operationalized for schools. Three theoretical and empirical tests of organizational citizenship behavior were performed in separate samples (elementary, middle, and secondary schools). The results were the same for each sample. The factor structure of the Organizational Citizenship Behavior scale (OCB) was consistent. All analyses identified a single, bipolar construct of high reliability and structural stability. Construct validity was supported, and predictive validity was established in all three samples by linking the citizenship measure to multiple variables. Finally, we presented a research agenda connecting organizational citizenship with other important school properties.

Essential Ideas for the Reform of American Schools, pp. 227–250

INTRODUCTION

Good organizational citizens work hard for their organization and its mission. Bateman and Organ (1983) first used the term "organizational citizenship" to define the beneficial behavior of workers that was not prescribed but occurred freely to help others achieve the task at hand. Research on citizenship behavior has produced some interesting insights in organizational settings (Organ, 1988; Organ & Ryan, 1995), but until recently the concept has been neglected in the study of schools (Cantrell et al., 2001; DiPaola & Hoy, 2004; DiPaola & Tschannen-Moran, 2001; Jurewicz, 2004).

Teachers are professionals in the sense that they study a relatively long time to master the fundamentals of teaching (expertise) and their primary commitment is to their students (service to clients) (Scott, 2003). Teaching is a complex activity that requires professional discretion. Moreover, professional behavior cannot be readily routinized into a set of predetermined activities because complexity is situational and requires judgment (Rowan, Raudenbush, & Cheong, 1993). "Organizational citizenship" is a useful term to describe voluntary teacher behaviors that go the "extra mile" to help students and colleagues succeed; such behavior exceeds the formal or official role requirements of the job.

CONCEPTUALIZING ORGANIZATIONAL CITIZENSHIP

Organizational citizenship behavior, when aggregated over time and across people, influences organizational effectiveness (Bolino & Turnley, 2003; Organ, 1997). Altruism and generalized compliance were the initial dimensions of organizational citizenship (Smith, Organ, & Near, 1983). Altruism is not simply doing good work; rather, it is voluntarily helping people in need of assistance. When individuals have specific problems or seek help, altruistic people go the extra mile in aiding them; they give willingly. Another basic dimension of citizenship behavior is generalized compliance, which is doing the "right thing" to help the organization. Conscientiousness, using time wisely for organizational purposes, is yet another characteristic of organizational citizenship behavior. Citizenship behavior surpasses any enforceable minimum standards; workers willingly go beyond stated expectations in performing their roles.

Organ (1988) elaborates five specific categories of discretionary behavior and the contribution of each to efficiency.

- Altruism is directed toward other individuals, but contributes to group efficiency by enhancing individuals' performance; participants help new colleagues and give freely of their time.

- Conscientiousness is the thoughtful use of time to enhance the efficiency of both individuals and the group; participants give more time to the organization and exert effort beyond the formal requirements.

- Sportsmanship increases the amount of time spent on organizational endeavors; participants decrease time spent on whining, complaining, and carping.

- Courtesy prevents problems and facilitates constructive use of time; participants give advance notice, timely reminders, and appropriate information.

- Civic virtue promotes the interests of the organization broadly; participants voluntarily serve on committees and attend functions.

Empirical analyses of the dimensions of organizational citizenship behaviors have produced conflicting results. Although four categories of organizational citizenship have been identified (Moorman & Blakely, 1995), most factor-analytic evidence suggests a two-factor structure. Williams (1988) developed a two-dimensional definition of organizational citizenship behavior: (1) benefits the organization in general, such as volunteering to serve on committees and (2) benefits directed at individuals within the organization, such as altruism and interpersonal helping. More recently, Skarlicki and Latham (1995) examined university organizational citizenship and also found a two-factor structure (organizational and interpersonal) that underlies the concept.

Organizational citizenship in schools, however, departs from most of the earlier research in that all aspects of citizenship fold into an integrated whole. In two separate factor-analytic studies, DiPaola and Tschannen-Moran (2001) found that there were not five separate dimensions of the construct, or even two for that matter, but rather a single dimension captured all aspects of organizational citizenship in schools. In other words, both benefits to the organization (helping the organization) and benefits to the individual (helping individuals) combined into a single, bipolar construct. See Figure 10.1 for the five elements of organizational citizenship behavior that form a single, integrated concept.

These results in schools are not surprising. First, the evidence suggests that organizational citizenship is context specific, that is, the behaviors inherent in organizational citizenship vary from one type of organization to another (Karambayya, 1989; Organ, 1988). Second, behavior in public schools is different from that found in most private-sector organizations.

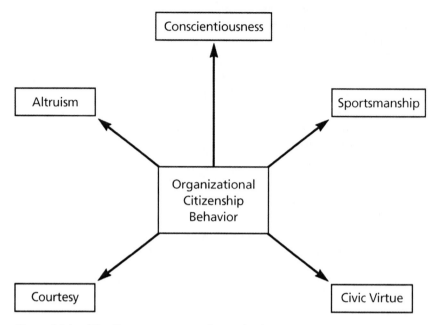

Figure 10.1.   The five components of organizational citizanship behavior.

Schools are service organizations staffed by teacher professionals who are generally committed to doing what is best for their student-clients. The client is the prime beneficiary of the organization (Scott, 2003). Thus, in service organizations like schools, both the professional workers and the organization are committed to the best interests of their clients. Consequently, there is a high degree of congruence between professional goals and organizational goals. The distinction between helping individuals and furthering the organizational mission is blurred because in schools the mission is synonymous with helping student-clients—schools are people-helping organizations.

Most previous studies were performed in private-sector organizations where altruistic behavior toward coworkers was not necessarily intertwined with behaviors that support the organization and its mission. Teachers routinely perform behaviors directed toward helping individuals, both students and colleagues, as part of their professional identity (DiPaola & Tschannen-Moran, 2001).

Teachers who voluntarily go out of their way to help their students, colleagues, and others as they engage in the work of teaching and learning exemplify organizational citizenship. Teachers in schools with high citizenship take it upon themselves to volunteer innovative suggestions, sponsor extracurricular activities, and serve on new committees. Moreover, teachers help students on their own time, stay after school to help if necessary, and resist the temptation to give students busywork. Organizational citizenship in schools provides a serious educational context in which teachers are rarely absent, make efficient use of their time, work collaboratively, and emphasize professional activities rather than personal ones. Teachers use their talents and efforts to benefit all school participants.

In sum, organizational citizenship is discretionary; that is, it is a matter of personal choice and not an enforceable requirement of the role. Organizational citizenship behaviors are manifest without the expectation of recognition or compensation. Moreover, such behavior is not directly rewarded; the rewards are at best indirect and uncertain. Although not every single action contributes to organizational effectiveness, over time the accumulation of organizational citizenship behaviors improves the effectiveness of the organization (Bolino & Turnley, 2003; Organ, 1997).

MEASURING ORGANIZATIONAL CITIZENSHIP

DiPaola and Tschannen-Moran (2001) used the conceptual framework described above as the basis for operationalizing organizational citizenship in schools. After an exploratory factor analysis, they identified 15 items that measured organizational citizenship, which they called the Organizational Citizenship Behaviors in Schools Scale (OCBSS). The scale had reasonable psychometric properties. All the items formed a single, bipolar dimension explaining about 36% of the variance and had an alpha coefficient of reliability of .87. The construct and predictive validity were supported by the factor analyses and the confirmation of a set of hypotheses that predicted positive significant correlations between organizational citizenship behaviors and aspects of organizational climate. In particular, citizenship was significantly and positively related to the collegial leadership of the principal ($r = .23$, $p < .05$), teacher professionalism ($r = .83$, $p < .01$), and academic press ($r = .63$, $p < .01$).

The purposes of the current inquiry were to reexamine the factor structure of the citizenship measure and its psychometric properties; to refine and develop a more parsimonious measure; to extend the measure from high schools to middle and elementary schools; and to test the factor structure, reliability, and validity of the refined scale in middle and elementary schools.

OCBSS in High Schools

First, we replicated and confirmed the factor analysis of DiPaola and Tschannen-Moran (2001) in high schools. The sample of 97 high schools was typical of Ohio high schools in terms of socioeconomic status, size, and type of school (rural, urban, and suburban). Researchers collected data at regularly scheduled faculty meetings with almost all faculty members returning usable responses.

Then in an attempt to find a more parsimonious measure, we refined the OCBSS from 15 items to 12 by dropping all the loadings that were below .45. The shortened scale had psychometric properties that were as good as or better than the longer scale. We called the 12-item shortened scale the Organizational Citizenship Behavior (OCB) scale. The alpha coefficient of reliability was similar. Moreover, the percent of variance explained was greater for the shortened OCB scale (see Table 10.1). The correlation between the OCBSS and the OCB was .97. Clearly, the OCB is a valid and reliable measure of organizational citizenship.

The OCB in Middle Schools

The OCB seemed to work well in high schools, but does it effectively measure citizenship behaviors of middle schools? That is, does it have the same factor structure, high reliability, and validity in middle schools? These were the questions guiding the next phase of the investigation. We expected that the same factor structure that described the OCB in high schools would be found in middle schools. To that end, we identified a typical sample of Ohio middle schools, carried out a factor-analytic analysis of organizational citizenship in middle schools, and assessed the reliability of the OCB in the middle school sample.

METHOD

We turn to a description of the sample, data collection procedures, and the factor analysis of the OCB in middle schools.

Sample

A diverse sample of 75 middle schools was selected to assess the factor structure for the OCB scale. These schools were drawn from 11 counties in Ohio. Although the sample selected was not random, care was taken to

Table 10.1. A Comparison of the Factor Structures for the OCBSS and OCB in High Schools, Middle Schools, and Elementary Schools

Organizational Citizenship Items	High Schools (n=97) OCBSS	High Schools (n=97) OCB	Middle Schools (n=75) OCB	Elementary Schools (n=100) OCB
1. Teacher committees in this school work productively.	.58	.59	.89	.88
2. Teachers begin class promptly and use class time effectively.	.66	.68	.88	.85
3. Teachers make innovative suggestions to improve the overall quality of our school.	.63	.66	.85	.68
4. Teachers volunteer to serve on new committees.	.67	.66	.76	.85
5. Teachers give colleagues advance notice of changes in schedule or routine.	.50	.52	.76	.75
6. Teachers help students on their own time.	.52	.49	.75	.42
7. Teachers voluntarily help new teachers.	.63	.66	.72	.84
8. Teachers arrive to work and meetings on time.	.55	.54	.70	.85
9. Teachers waste a lot of class time.	-.60	-.56	-.68	-.58
10. Teachers volunteer to sponsor extracurricular activities.	.62	.62	.68	.75
11. Teachers give an excessive amount of busywork.	-.48	-.48	-.66	-.64
12. Teachers take the initiative to introduce themselves to substitutes and assist them.	.66	.67	.53	.80
13. Teachers schedule personal appointments at times other than during the school day.	.41			
14. Teachers are rarely absent.	.44			
15. Teachers leave immediately after school is over.	-.42			
Variance Explained	36.21	40.82	58.82	59.48
Alpha Coefficient of Reliability	.87	.86	.93	.93

ensure participation of urban, suburban, and rural schools. The current distribution of middle schools in the state is 39% rural, 34% urban, and 27% suburban, and the study's schools are distributed across 19% rural, 41% urban, and 40% suburban settings. Of the 612 school districts in the state, 43 participated in the study. Staff completed approximately 1,300 usable surveys. The sample was similar to the population of middle schools in the state in terms of student enrollment, average teacher salary, average teacher experience, and the size of the faculty. In brief, the sample of schools was fairly typical of the state's middle schools. See Table 10.2 for a summary of the characteristics of the sample.

Data Collection

Data were collected from the sample of middle schools at regularly scheduled faculty meetings. A member of the research team explained the general purpose of the study, assured the confidentiality of all responses, and asked teachers to complete the questionnaires. Because this project was part of a larger study of organizational properties and because the unit of analysis was the school, a random group of half of the teachers in each school was selected to respond to the measures. No attempt was made to gather data from faculty who were not present at the meeting, but virtually all teachers returned usable questionnaires.

Factor Analysis

To test the stability of the factor structure of the OCB, we performed a principal axis factor analysis specifying a single factor. The results were encouraging. All 12 items loaded strongly on the single factor; the factor loadings ranged from .53 to .89 and the entire factor explained 58.82% of

Table 10.2.   Comparison of Sample and States's Middle Schools

Demographic Indicator	Current Study	State average
Student Enrollment	596	518
Average Teacher Salary	$44,886	$43,016
Average Teacher Experience	12	13
Average Number of Teachers on Staff	39 teachers	35 teachers
Percentage of Teacher Attendance	96%	96%
n/N	75	788

the variance. Furthermore the first factor was the only one with an eigen-value greater than one. A comparison of the factor loadings between the high school sample and the middle school sample revealed the same factor structure. In fact, the factor structure of the middle schools was more robust and provided a stronger theoretical fit with the underlying conceptual framework that predicted the emergence of a single, integrated construct of organizational citizenship. Save for one item, all the factor loadings were stronger in the middle school sample than in the high school sample. In addition, the alpha coefficient of reliability (alpha = .93) for the OCB was stronger in the middle school sample (see Table 10.1). The conclusion seems clear: The OCB scale is reliable and stable and it works well for both high schools and middle schools. Its construct validity was supported by the factor analysis in both samples.

PREDICTIVE VALIDITY OF THE OCB IN MIDDLE SCHOOLS

To test the predictive validity of the OCB, we present a conceptual framework and a series of hypotheses that relate organizational citizenship to a set of theoretically related concepts. The first three hypotheses are replications of the DiPaola and Tschannen-Moran (2001) study. The final two hypotheses are original to this investigation and extend the theory into an explanation of other organizational properties.

Conceptual Framework

The framework for the hypotheses consists of five concepts that will be theoretically linked to organizational citizenship: collegial leadership of the principal, teacher professionalism, academic press, school mindfulness, and perceptions of effectiveness.

Collegial Leadership of the Principal

The principal is the single most important individual in developing the climate of the school (Hoy, Tarter, & Kottkamp, 1991). Effective principals have a leadership style that establishes good interpersonal relations among teachers and initiates actions that lead to the attainment of the goals (Yukl, 2002). Collegial leadership meets the social needs of the faculty and the goal-achieving needs of the school. Principals treat teachers as professionals and are open, egalitarian, and friendly. Moreover, the principal sets clear teacher expectations and standards for performance.

Teacher Professionalism

Schools are service organizations whose focus is helping student-clients. In the classroom, teachers often work alone guided by their knowledge and skills to find effective methods of teaching. They also rely on colleagues for support and help at various times. But, whether alone or in collaboration, working with students has an expert dimension in pedagogy and a social context in which teaching is influenced by colleagues. In that context, professional teachers lend one another support and respect each other's judgments.

Academic Press

Although schools serve a variety of purposes, the primary formal goal of schooling is education; that is, children should be learning and the school should be oriented to that purpose. The academic press of a school refers to a learning environment that is orderly and serious and in which teachers and students alike are committed to intellectual and academic accomplishment. Such schools set high but achievable standards and goals. Students persist, strive to achieve, and are respected by their peers for their academic success. Parents, teachers, and the principal exert pressure for high standards and school improvement.

School Mindfulness

As in any other organization, schools must plan for the unexpected events that hinder their operation. Mindful planning assumes that things may well go wrong, and therefore, complacency works against the successful school. Educators encourage one another to point out the small glitches in the operation of the school rather than ignoring them or assuming that all is well because most things seem to be working properly. Mindful schools (Hoy, Gage, & Tarter, 2004) are always a little on edge because they do not have all the information they need to ensure the successful operation of the school; they constantly monitor. When the unexpected occurs, mindful schools respond; they are not paralyzed with indecision. They seek out the influence of experts, typically those closest to the problem.

Perceived Organizational Effectiveness

The teachers who are in the school every day are situated to assess how well things are done. The notion of asking organizational members to judge performance was developed by Mott (1972), who looked at the effectiveness of agencies that don't produce measurable products. Mott's framework for judging the effectiveness of organizations involves efficiency, flexibilty, adaptability, and innovation, and has been used to assess the effectiveness of schools (Hoy & Ferguson, 1985; Miskel,

Fevurly, & Stewart, 1979; Uline, Miller, Tschannen-Moran, 1998). Effective schools are those that are efficient in the day-to-day operations, are adaptable and flexible as the environment changes, innovate, and produce quality teaching and learning.

Hypotheses

In order to test the predictive validity of the OCB, we developed five hypotheses that should be supported because each links organizational citizenship with a theoretically relevant property. The collegial leadership of the principal should create an atmosphere in which teachers are dedicated to working cooperatively to improve teaching and learning. In such schools, teachers do not simply comply with the bureaucratic requirements of the job; in fact, there is evidence that these teachers are more committed to the school and its students (Hoy & Sabo, 1998; Hoy, Tarter, Kottkamp, 1991). Teachers in schools with collegial principals seem likely to go beyond the official role requirements of their job. Hence, we predict:

H1: Collegial leadership of the principal is positively correlated with organizational citizenship.

Professionalism in teachers manifests itself in at least two ways. First, the practice of teaching shows the influence of expertise. Second, teachers are committed to the success of their students. The purposes of teaching push teachers beyond the minimal requirements specified by classroom tasks. Professionals also exhibit a self-direction based upon their knowledge and their commitment to students. The very nature of professional teacher behavior calls for action beyond that which is officially mandated. Given the nature of professionalism and the character of organizational citizenship, there is an overlap between the two concepts. It is difficult to imagine professional teacher actions without organizational citizenship behavior. Thus, we predict:

H2: Teacher professionalism is positively correlated with organizational citizenship.

Academic press denotes the extent to which the school forces teachers and administrators to push toward academic excellence. The focus of these schools is intellectual, academic, and achievement-oriented. Students respond by valuing academic excellence and respecting the intellectual achievements of their peers. In schools with high academic press, teachers go beyond the minimal requirements to help and encourage students toward excellence. Teachers in these schools voluntarily go out of their way to help their students, colleagues, and others as they engage in the work of teaching and learning. Consequently, we predict:

H3: The academic press of a school is positively correlated with organizational citizenship.

Mindful schools are characterized by their attention to mistakes, reluctance to simplify the complex, and sensitivity to the day-to-day operation of the school. When the unexpected occurs, mindful schools bounce back and attempt to move expertise within the school to the problem at hand. These schools are resilient and quick to move beyond rigid and narrow notions of the job to resolve problems as they arise; and they continue to work toward the purposes of the school. Mindful schools produce a school atmosphere in which administrators and teachers are encouraged to be creative and "do what it takes" to help students achieve. Therefore, we predict:

H4: School mindfulness is positively correlated with organizational citizenship.

Effective schools are efficient, flexible, adaptable, and innovative. Although not every single act of organizational citizenship contributes to effectiveness, together they influence organizational effectiveness (Bolino & Turnley, 2003; Organ, 1997). Overall, using time wisely to help colleagues and students accomplish the goals of instruction, which we call conscientiousness, contributes to the continuing successful operation of the school, that is, to school effectiveness. Thus, we predict:

H5: School effectiveness, as perceived by teachers, is positively correlated to organizational citizenship.

METHOD

Sample

The data to test these hypotheses were collected from a sample of 75 middle schools. Both the sample and the data collection procedures were described above.

Measures

The hypotheses were tested using measures of organizational citizenship, collegial principal behavior, teacher professionalism, academic press, school mindfulness, and teacher perceptions of effectiveness. The operational measures for collegial leadership, teacher professionalism, and academic press are from the Organizational Climate Index (Hoy, Smith, & Sweetland, 2002; see also www.coe.ohio-state.edu/whoy). The psychometric properties of reliability and validity are reported by Hoy and his colleagues (2002).

Organizational citizenship was measured by the OCB scale, the 12-item measure developed in this chapter. The 12 items are found at the end of this chapter in the OCB-Scale. Recall that the factor structure of the scale has been stable for both the high school sample and middle school sample. In this sample of middle schools, the alpha coefficient of reliability was .93.

Collegial leadership of the principal consists of the seven-item subscale of the OCI, which includes the following sample items: "The principal treats all faculty members as his or her equal," "The principal is friendly and approachable," "The principal lets faculty know what is expected of them," "The principal puts suggestions made by the faculty into operation." In the present sample, the reliability coefficient for the leadership subscale was strong (alpha = .96).

Teacher professionalism was measured by the Professional Teacher Behavior subscale of the OCI. The scale includes the following items: "Teachers help and support each other," "Teachers respect the professional competence of their colleagues," "Teachers provide strong social support for colleagues." In the present sample, the reliability coefficient for the leadership subscale was also strong (alpha = .95).

Academic press was measured by the eight-item Achievement Press subscale of the OCI, which includes the following items: "The school sets high standards for academic performance," "Students respect others who get good grades," "Students seek extra work so they can get good grades," "Academic achievement is recognized and acknowledged by the school." In the present sample, the alpha coefficient of reliability for the scale was .95.

School mindfulness was measured by the M-Scale (Hoy et al., 2004). The M-Scale is a 20-item Likert scale. Teachers are asked to respond to each item, which is a description of behavior, along a six-point scale from Strongly Disagree (1) to Strongly Agree (6). The construct and predictive validity of the scale have been supported in a comprehensive factor-analytic study (Hoy et al., 2004). Likewise, reliability coefficients are consistently high, that is, .90 or greater. Similarly, a factor analysis of data for the middle schools in this sample supported the factor structure of the instrument and the high reliabilities; in this study the alpha coefficient of reliability was .92.

School effectiveness was measured by a global subjective measure to gauge the overall effectiveness of each school. The scale, an adaptation of Mott's (1972) measure of the effectiveness of hospitals, was first used in schools by Miskel and his colleagues (1979). The entire measure is found in Hoy and Miskel (2001, p. 307). The instrument is an eight-item Likert scale on which teachers are asked to describe the quality, efficiency, adaptability, and flexibility of the school. For example: "How good a job do the people in your school do in coping with emergencies and disruptions?", "How many of the people in your school readily accept and adjust to the changes?", "How good is the quality of the products or services produced by the people you know in your school?" The higher the score of the faculty, the more effective the school is judged to be. Reliability scores for the scale are typically in the .90 range, and for this study, the alpha coefficient of reliability was .95. Validity of the scale has been supported by numerous studies (Hoy & Ferguson, 1985; Miskel, McDonald, & Bloom, 1983; Mott, 1972; Uline et al., 1998).

RESULTS

The predictive validity of the OCB was supported by the confirmation of the five hypotheses predicting relationships with organizational citizenship. In all cases organizational citizenship was significantly and positively related to the criterion variables of collegial leadership, teacher professionalism, academic press, school mindfulness, and perceived organizational effectiveness, as hypothesized. The first three hypotheses linking citizenship with collegial leadership, teacher professionalism, and academic press were also supported in earlier research in high schools (DiPaola & Tschannen-Moran, 2001) and in a study of middle schools (Jurewicz, 2004).

Collegial leadership of the principal was highly correlated with organizational citizenship ($r = .66, p < .01$); the greater the degree of collegial leadership, the stronger the organizational citizenship behaviors in schools.

Teacher professionalism was also strongly correlated with organizational citizenship ($r = .92, p < .01$); the greater the degree of teacher professional behavior, the stronger the organizational citizenship behaviors in schools.

Academic press of the school was strongly correlated with organizational citizenship ($r = .77$, $p < .01$); the greater the degree of academic press in the school, the greater the organizational citizenship behaviors in schools.

School mindfulness was strongly correlated with organizational citizenship ($r = .60$, $p < .01$); the greater the degree of school mindfulness, the higher the level of organizational citizenship behavior in schools.

Finally, teacher perception of school effectiveness was strongly correlated with organizational citizenship ($r = .88$, $p < .01$); the greater the organizational citizenship behavior in schools, the more did teachers perceive the school to be effective.

In brief, all the predictions supported the validity of our measure of organizational citizenship. See Table 10.3 for a summary of the descriptive and correlational statistics.

THE OCB IN ELEMENTARY SCHOOLS

The OCB worked well in middle and high schools, but does it effectively measure citizenship behaviors of elementary schools? Does the OCB have the same factor structure, high reliability, and validity in elementary schools? Fortunately, our colleague, Page Smith, and his students at the University of Texas in San Antonio, had just completed a study of 109 elementary schools. They agreed to share their data. We expected a similar and stable OCB factor structure in their sample. Using their elementary schools, we performed a factor analysis of the OCB, assessed its reliability, and checked the predictive validity; that is, the same five hypotheses examined in the middle schools were tested again with elementary schools.

Table 10.3. Means, Standard Deviations, Alpha Coefficients, and Intercorrelations of Middle School Variables ($N = 75$)

Variable	Means	SD	Alpha	1	2	3	4	5
1. Citizenship	3.74	.24	.93					
2. Collegial Leadership	3.82	.46	.96	.66[**]				
3. Teacher Professionalism	4.01	.30	.95	.92[**]	.66[**]			
4. Academic Press	3.48	.44	.95	.77[**]	.59[**]	.78[**]		
5. School Mindfulness	4.11	.44	.92	.60[**]	.79[**]	.69[**]	.60[**]	
6. Perceived Effectiveness	3.57	.31	.95	.88[**]	.63[**]	.84[**]	.79[**]	.63[**]

METHOD

We turn to a description of the characteristics of the Texas elementary sample, the factor analysis of the OCB, as well as reliability and validity tests.

Sample

The sample, 109 Texas elementary schools, was not a random one; however, care was taken to select urban, suburban, and rural schools. Only schools with 25 or more faculty members were considered candidates for the study. Schools in the sample represented the entire range of socioeconomic status. All of the elementary schools were identified through their grade configurations and included grades P–6 and grades K–6.

Measures

To further assess the content validity and predictive validity of the OCB, we first replicated the factor analysis of the OCB with the new sample of 109 elementary schools, and then we retested the five hypotheses using the same measures: collegial principal behavior, teacher professionalism, academic press, school mindfulness, and teacher perceptions of effectiveness. The operational measures for these concepts were described earlier; recall that collegial leadership, teacher professionalism, and academic press are from the Organizational Climate Index (Hoy et al., 2002; see also www.coe.ohio-state.edu/whoy).

Data Collection

In each of the 109 elementary schools in the study, data were collected at a regularly scheduled faculty meeting called by the principal. The researcher administered the instruments during faculty meetings held in the mornings before school or in the afternoons after school. Prior to distributing the research measures, the researcher read a statement describing the intent of the study, guaranteeing anonymity and confidentiality, and asking participants for their frank perceptions. The researcher emphasized that faculty members did not need to respond to any item that made them feel uncomfortable. The explanation, distribution, and administration of the instruments took approximately 25 minutes, with virtually all the teachers returning usable questionnaires.

RESULTS

The first step in our analysis was to replicate the factor analysis of the 12 item OCB. To that end, a principal axis factor analysis was performed with the elementary school data. We specified a single factor, and the results were not surprising. All 12 items loaded strongly on the single factor; the factor loadings ranged from .42 to .88, and the single factor explained 59.48% of the variance. A comparison of the factor loadings of these elementary schools with the middle and high school samples revealed the same general pattern of loadings (see Table 10.1). In fact, the factor structure of the elementary schools was remarkably similar to the middle and high schools, and like the other factor analyses, supported a single, integrated construct of organizational citizenship of schools. In addition, the alpha coefficient of reliability (alpha = .93) for the OCB in these elementary schools was strong. In brief, the OCB scale is reliable and stable; it works well for elementary, middle, and high schools; and construct validity was supported by the factor analyses in all three samples. See Table 10.1 for a comparison and summary.

Next, we turn to predictive validity. The findings of the validity hypotheses were replicated; that is, the five theoretically derived hypotheses were again supported, this time with elementary schools. As predicted, organizational citizenship was positively and significantly related to collegial principal behavior, teacher professionalism, academic press, school mindfulness, and perceptions of effectiveness. The results of the tests as well as

Table 10.4.   Means, Standard Deviations, Alpha Coefficients, and Intercorrelations of all Elementary School Variables (N = 109)

Variable	Means	SD	Alpha	1	2	3	4	5
1. Citizenship	3.86	.27	.93					
2. Collegial Leadership	4.00	.47	.96	.61**				
3. Teacher Professionalism	4.17	.33	.95	.92**	.63**			
4. Academic Press	3.65	.22	.91	.72**	.56**	.70**		
5. School Mindfulness	4.35	.44	.94	.66**	.75**	.68**	.61**	
6. Perceived Effectiveness	3.80	.36	.97	.87**	.70**	.88**	.75**	.73**

**p < .01

Table 10.5.   A Comparison of Correlations of Predictor Variables With Organizational Citizenship Behaviors for Middle and Elementary Schools

Predictor Variables	Sample 1 Middle Schools	Sample 2 Elementary Schools
Collegial Principal Behavior	.66[**]	.61[**]
Teacher Professionalism	.92[**]	.92[**]
Academic Press	.77[**]	.72[**]
School Mindfulness	.60[**]	.66[**]
Effectiveness	.88[**]	.87[**]

[**]$p < .01$

a comparison with the findings in the middle school sample are summarized in Tables 10.4 and 10.5. The evidence clearly supports the predictive validity for organizational citizenship of schools.

SUMMARY AND DISCUSSION

The underlying theory of organizational citizenship behavior was sustained by the study. First, the factor structure supported the construct validity of organizational citizenship behavior. All of the items loaded strongly and predictably on a single first-order factor. The factor structure was essentially the same and stable in all three samples. Second, the hypothesis results reinforced the predictive validity of the construct of organizational citizenship. Finally, the reliability coefficients of the OCB were strong; in fact, in the elementary and middle school samples they were the same, a robust .93, and in the high school sample the reliability was still a healthy .86.

We assumed that the collegial leadership of the principal would cultivate a climate that would encourage organizational citizenship behaviors (Organ, 1997). That assumption was borne out in the results of the correlational analysis. We hasten to add that although we expected that leadership of the principal created a climate of citizenship, we also believe that organizational citizenship behaviors enable collegial leadership.

Professional teacher and organizational citizenship behaviors seem inextricably related. Organizational citizenship behavior is professional behavior. Good school citizens go out of their way to help their colleagues and students. Moreover, they carry out their tasks in a conscientious manner, they make wise use of school time, and they are willing to give of their own time for the sake of the organization. Organizational citizenship is discretionary; such behavior is its own reward. We suspect that all organizational citizenship behavior is professional, but not all professional behavior is good citizenship. The emphasis of organizational citizenship behavior is that it is voluntary and discretionary. In the final analysis, it is difficult to find examples of professional behavior that do not partake of good citizenship, and the correlations between the two concepts bear this out; about 83% of the variance is shared.

It is not surprising that the academic press and organizational citizenship of the school are so highly correlated. The central function of the school is the academic enterprise. When teachers are committed to academic press of the school, they often go beyond the narrow confines of the role by exerting extra effort to help students achieve intellectually. When the focus of the school is academic and achievement oriented, students typically respond by valuing academic excellence and the academic achievements of their peers. Such a climate sets the stage for behavior in which teachers voluntarily go out of their way to help students, colleagues, and others as they engage in the work of teaching and learning. In a word, academic press promotes organizational citizenship, and organizational citizenship reinforces academic press.

School mindfulness and organizational citizenship support each other. Mindful schools promote an atmosphere in which administrators and teachers are encouraged to be creative, that is, to do what it takes to help students achieve. With their attention to mistakes, reluctance to simplify, and their sensitivity to the day-to-day operations, mindful schools embrace a citizenship or organizational perspective. When the unexpected occurs, mindful schools are quick to move expertise to the site of the problem. Schools that are actively willing to exert extra effort in a conscientiousness attempt to solve problems without complaint readily work with colleagues and put the interests of the school before personal interest. School citizenship and mindfulness are inextricably bound together.

Effective schools are efficient, flexible, adaptable, and innovative (Mott, 1972; Uline et al., 1998). Good school citizens look for ways to make the school work effectively. Not every act of organizational citizenship, however, contributes to effectiveness. But in general, over time and across people, organizational citizenship behaviors facilitate the effectiveness of the organization (Bolino & Turnley, 20003; Dipaola & Hoy, 2004; Organ, 1997). Overall conscientiousness of the teachers, who used time wisely to help students and colleagues succeed, promotes school effectiveness, a proposition supported by the results in both elementary and middle schools.

In brief, organizational citizenship of a school is a key in promoting professionalism, academic excellence, mindfulness, supportive leadership of the principal, and effectiveness. Of course, it is also likely that each of these organizational properties in turn promotes organizational citizenship of the school. The relationships are clearly reciprocal. The saliency of organizational citizenship behavior is clear, and we now have a valid and reliable measure of the concept for schools.

FUTURE RESEARCH

Organizational citizenship of public schools is a new concept to educational researchers. Further analysis of the effects of organizational citizenship behaviors and the contexts in which they are found is of value to both researchers and practitioners.

In effective schools there is a high level of student achievement. Although only two studies of the relationships between organizational citizenship and student achievement have been conducted (DiPaola & Hoy, 2004; Juriewicz, 2004), both studies indicate significant relationships between citizenship behaviors and achievement. It seems that organizational citizenship works in concert with other school properties to enhance student achievement. Just how that dynamic occurs is an important topic for further research.

Most mental tests are highly correlated, a fact that led Spearman (1927) to posit the existence of general ability, a g-factor of intelligence. Organ and Ryan (1995), in a similar vein, raise the question of the existence of a general psychological state of the organization, an analogous m-factor, which stands for morale. This psychological state should include a host of such attitudinal variables as fairness, satisfaction, commitment, efficacy, and mindfulness. If organizational citizenship is "performance that supports the social and psychological environment in which the task performance takes place" (Organ, 1997, p. 95), then a useful area of inquiry would be the relationships between OCB and such systems variables as supportive leader behavior, commitment, organizational justice, school size, and morale. There is little information on the relationship of OCB to system performance in schools. Further investigations would then explore school output variables such as student achievement, student absenteeism, dropout rate, student alienation, and school quality.

Over time individual employees may be rewarded for nontask performance or performance that contributes to organizational maintenance (Organ, 1995). There are no studies at the organizational level that speak to the rewards for citizenship behavior; thus, such inquiry is warranted to understand the relationship of individual schools to the district, especially in terms of resource allocation. In other words, to what extent does the organizational citizenship of a school affect the allocation of resources to that school?

The unit of analysis for studying organizational citizenship is important. The current study is one of the few that focuses on the organization rather than the individual. Our OCB measure is worded to capture the collective sense of citizenship of the school. Most research on organizational citizenship, however, focuses on the individual (Organ, 1997; Organ & Ryan, 1995), not the organization. The relationship between individual and collective citizenship is worthy of careful analysis; in fact, it is no easy task to separate the influences of individual and collective organizational citizenship behavior. Such discrimination requires a sophisticated analysis that is likely a combination of structural equation and multilevel modeling.

The current research provides a perspective of social contexts of schools with implications for educational planning and school improvement. The social structures of schools should be interpreted as "levers" (Scheerens, 2000, p. 73) for change and improvement. For decades, the private sector has recognized the critical influence of organizational citizenship behaviors to employee performance, organizational effectiveness, and efficiency (Bateman & Organ, 1983; Moorman; 2003; Niehoff, 2000; Podsakoff, MacKenzie, Paine, & Bachrach, 2000). Until recently, organizational citizenship behavior had not been considered an important "lever" for school effectiveness. What can be done to influence the organizational citizenship of schools? For example, to what extent are organizational climate, organizational trust, culture, and leadership antecedents for developing organizational citizenship? When principals are concerned about the welfare of teachers and show support, consideration, and helpfulness, will teachers go the extra mile to help students be successful? From the perspective of practice, the school leader should have a valuable role as a cultivator of citizenship behaviors. What are the leader dynamics that pro-

OCB-SCALE

Indicate the extent to which you disagree or agree with the following statements about your school.

	Strongly Disagree					Strongly Agree
1. Teachers help students on their own time	1	2	3	4	5	6
2. Teachers waste a lot of class time	1	2	3	4	5	6
3. Teachers voluntarily help new teachers	1	2	3	4	5	6
4. Teachers volunteer to serve on new committees	1	2	3	4	5	6
5. Teachers volunteer to sponsor extracurricular activities	1	2	3	4	5	6

Table continues on next page.

OCB-SCALE

Indicate the extent to which you disagree or agree with the following statements about your school.

	Strongly Disagree				Strongly Agree	
6. Teachers arrive to work and meetings on time	1	2	3	4	5	6
7. Teachers take the initiative to introduce themselves to substitutes and assist them	1	2	3	4	5	6
8. Teachers begin class promptly and use class time effectively	1	2	3	4	5	6
9. Teachers give colleagues advance notice of changes in schedule or routine	1	2	3	4	5	6
10. Teachers give an excessive amount of busywork	1	2	3	4	5	6
11. Teacher committees in this school work productively	1	2	3	4	5	6
12. Teachers make innovative suggestions to improve the overall quality of our school	1	2	3	4	5	6

* © DiPaola & Hoy, 2003.

duce high organizational citizenship behaviors of schools? A qualitative approach to the exploration of schools with high and low norms of organizational citizenship behaviors would also help to identify other characteristics of schools in which these behaviors are present and would provide a richer description of the social context.

The questions above suggest a few of the research directions that might be used to investigate the significance of organizational citizenship behavior. The OCB is a reliable, valid, and useful tool in the study of such questions.

REFERENCES

Bateman, T. S., & Organ, D.W. (1983). Job satisfaction and the good soldier: The relationship between affect and employee citizenship. *Academy of Management Journal, 26*, 587–595.

Bolino, M., & Turnley, B. (2003, April). *Neglected issues in citizenship research. In R. H. Moorman (Chair), New frontiers for OCB research: An examination of four research directions.* Symposium conducted for the Midwest Academy of Management, St. Louis, MO.

Cantrell, S. M., Lyon, N., Valdes, R., White, J., Recio, A., & Matsum, L. U. (2001). *Pilot study report: The local district performance measures* (Tech. Report for the Los Angeles Unifed School District). Los Angeles, CA.

DiPaola, M. F., & Hoy, W. K. (2004, October/November). Organizational citizenship of faculty and achievement of high school students. *The High School Journal*.

DiPaola, M. F., & Tschannen-Moran, M. (2001, September). Organizational citizenship behavior in schools and its relationship to school climate. *Journal of School Leadership, 11*, 424–447.

Hoy, W. K., & Ferguson, J. (1985). A theoretical framework and exploration of organizational effectiveness in schools. *Educational Administration Quarterly, 21*, 117–134.

Hoy, W. K., & Miskel, C. G. (2001). *Educational administration: Theory, research, and practice* (6th ed.). New York: McGraw-Hill.

Hoy, W. K., & Sabo, D. (1998). *Quality middle schools: Open and healthy*. Thousand Oaks, CA: Corwin.

Hoy, W. K., Gage, C. Q., & Tarter, C. J. (2004). Theoretical and empirical foundations of mindful schools. In W. Hoy & C. Miskel (Eds.), *Educational administration, policy, and reform: Research and measurement* (pp. 305–335). Greenwich, CT: Information Age.

Hoy, W. K., Smith, P. A., & Sweetland, S. R. (2002). The development of the organizational climate index for high schools: Its measure and relationship to faculty trust. *The High School Journal High School Journal, 86*(2), 38–49.

Hoy, W. K., Tarter, C. J., & Kottkamp, R. B. (1991). *Open schools/healthy schools: Measuring organizational climate*. Newbury Park, CA: Sage.

Jurewicz, M. (2004). *Organizational citizenship behaviors of Virginia middle school teachers: A study of their relationship to school climate and student achievement*. Unpublished doctoral dissertation, College of William and Mary, Williamsburg, VA.

Karambayya, R. (1989). *Organizational citizenship behavior: Contextual predictors and organizational consequences*. Unpublished doctoral dissertation, Northwestern University, Evanston, IL.

Miskel, C., Fevurly, R., & Stewart, J. (1979). Organizational structures and processes, perceived school effectiveness, loyalty, and job satisfaction. *Educational Administration Quarterly, 15*, 97–118.

Miskel, C., McDonald, D., & Bloom, S. (1983). Structural and expectancy linkages within schools and organizational effectiveness. *Educational Administration Quarterly, 19*, 49–82.

Moorman, R. H. (2003, April). Refining our understanding of the mechanisms the link perceived fairness and OCB. In R. H. Moorman (Chair), *New frontiers for OCB research: An examination of four research directions*. Symposium conducted for the Midwest Academy of Management, St. Louis, MO.

Moorman, R. H., & Blakely, G. L. (1995). Individualism-collectivism as an individual difference predictor of organizational citizenship behavior. *Journal of Organizational Behavior, 16*(2), 127–142.

Mott, P. E. (1972). *The characteristics of effective organizations*. New York: Harper & Row.

Niehoff, B. P. (2000). *A motive-based view of organizational citizenship behaviors: Applying an old lens to a new class of organizational behaviors*. Paper presented at the Midwest Academy of Management Behavior Conference, Chicago.

Organ, D. W. (1988). *Organizational citizenship behavior.* Lexington, MA: D.C. Heath.

Organ, D. W. (1997). Organizational citizenship behavior: It's construct clean-up time. *Human Performance, 10,* 85–97.

Organ, D. W., & Ryan, K. (1995). A meta-analytic review of attitudinal and dispositional predictors of organizational citizenship behavior. *Personnel Psychology, 48,* 775–802.

Podsakoff, P. M., MacKenzie, S. B., Paine, J. B., & Bachrach, D. G. (2000). Organizational citizenship behaviors: A critical review of the theoretical and empirical literature and suggestions for future research. *Journal of Management, 26,* 513–563.

Rowan, B., Raudenbush, S. W., & Cheong, Y. F. (1993). Teaching as a nonroutine task: Implications for the management of schools. *Educational Administration Quarterly, 29,* 479–499.

Scheerens, J. (2000). *Improving school effectiveness* (Fundamentals of Educational Planning No. 68). Paris: UNESCO.

Scott, W. R. (2003). *Organizations: Rational, natural, and open systems* (5th ed.). Englewood Cliffs, NJ: Prentice Hall.

Skarlicki, D., & Latham G. (1995). Organizational citizenship behavior and performance in a university setting. *Canadian Journal of Administrative Sciences, 12,* 175–181.

Smith, C. A., Organ, D. W., & Near, J. P. (1983). Organizational citizenship behavior: It's nature and antecedents. *Journal of Applied Psychology, 68,* 653–663.

Spearman, C. (1927). *The abilities of man: Their nature and measurement.* New York: Macmillan.

Uline, C. L., Miller, D. M., & Tschannen-Moran, M. (1998). School effectiveness: The underlying dimensions. *Educational Administration Quarterly, 34,* 462–483.

Williams, L. (1988). *Effective and noneffective components of job satisfaction and organizational commitment as determinants of organizational citizenship and in-role behaviors.* Unpublished doctoral dissertation, Indiana University, Bloomington.

Yukl, G. A. (2002). *Leadership in organizations* (4th ed.). Upper Saddle, NJ: Prentice Hall.

CHAPTER 11

SCHOOL CHARACTERISTICS THAT FOSTER ORGANIZATIONAL CITIZENSHIP BEHAVIOR

Michael F. DiPaola and Wayne K. Hoy

After a theoretical analysis of the concept of organizational citizenship is elaborated, we complete an empirical analysis of the characteristics of school organization that promote citizenship behaviors. We assume that the leadership of the principal is critical in such an endeavor as well as the trust that colleagues have in each other and the extent to which there is a school press for academic achievement. Using a sample of 75 middle schools, our hypotheses were supported; all of these factors both individually and collectively have positive influences on organizational citizenship. Finally, the implications of the findings are considered.

Reprinted by permission from the *Journal of School Leadership*, Vol. 15, pp. 391-410.
Copyright © 2005. All rights reserved.

SCHOOL CHARACTERISTICS THAT FOSTER ORGANIZATIONAL CITIZENSHIP BEHAVIOR

Organizational citizenship as it is applied to schools is a relatively recent concept. The few studies that have examined organizational citizenship behavior report the significance of the concept because it relates to both student achievement (DiPaola & Hoy, in press) and the openness of the school climate (DiPaola & Tschannen-Moran, 2001). This inquiry explores the concept further by examining its relationship to three important aspects of schools: the leadership of the principal, trust of the faculty, and the achievement press of the school. The purpose of this research is twofold: to elaborate and explain the concept of organizational citizenship, and to identify features of the school that foster organizational citizenship behavior. We postulate that the leadership of the principal, the relationships among colleagues, and the general orientation of the school community either facilitate or hinder the development of organizational citizenship behavior.

CONCEPTUAL FRAMEWORK

We begin with an analysis of organizational citizenship. Then we move to three concepts that we predict will facilitate the development of citizenship behavior: collegial principal leadership, teacher trust in colleagues, and the achievement press of the school

Organizational Citizenship Behavior (OCB)

Bateman and Organ (1983) were the first to use the phrase "organizational citizenship behavior" (OCB) to denote organizationally beneficial behavior of workers that was not prescribed but occurred freely to help others achieve the task at hand. Research on organizational citizenship behavior has produced some intriguing insights in a variety of organizational settings (Organ, 1988; Organ & Ryan, 1995), but until recently, the concept has been neglected in the study of schools. Teachers perform the task of teaching. They are professionals in the sense that they study a relatively long time to master the fundamentals of teaching (expertise) and their primary commitment is to their students (service to clients). Teaching is a complex activity that requires professional judgments; it cannot adequately be prescribed in teachers' job descriptions or contracts. Voluntary teacher behavior that goes the "extra mile" to help students and colleagues succeed, that is, organizational citizenship behavior, seems an especially important aspect of the performance of school faculties.

Organizational citizenship behavior (OCB) is defined as "performance that supports the social and psychological environment in which task performance takes place" (Organ, 1997, p. 95). Such behavior is said to "lubricate the social machinery of the organization" (Bateman & Organ, 1983, p. 588). The willingness of participants to exert effort beyond the formal obligations of their positions has long been recognized as an essential component of effective organizational performance. For example, more than a half century ago, Barnard (1938) stated that the willingness of individuals to contribute cooperative efforts to the organization was indispensable to effective attainment of organizational goals.

Organizational citizenship was initially conceptualized along two basic dimensions—altruism and generalized compliance (Smith, Organ, & Near, 1983). Altruism is helping behavior directed at specific individuals. When individuals have specific problems, need assistance, or seek help, altruistic people go the extra mile to assist them. The other class of citizenship behavior is generalized compliance, which is a more impersonal conscientiousness: doing things "right and proper" to help achieve organizational goals rather than for any specific person. Conscientiousness in use of time is the hallmark of this dimension. Organizational participants' behavior far surpasses any enforceable minimum standards; workers willingly go far beyond stated expectations.

In attempting to further define organizational citizenship behavior, Organ (1988) highlights five specific categories of discretionary behavior and explains how each helps to improve efficiency in the organization.

- Altruism (e.g., helping new colleagues and freely giving time to others) is typically directed toward other individuals, but contributes to group efficiency by enhancing individuals' performance.
- Conscientiousness (e.g., efficient use of time and going beyond minimum expectations) enhances the efficiency of both an individual and the group.
- Sportsmanship (e.g., avoids complaining and whining) improves the amount of time spent on constructive endeavors in the organization.
- Courtesy (e.g., advance notices, reminders, and communicating appropriate information) helps prevent problems and facilitates constructive use of time.
- Civic Virtue (e.g., serving on committees and voluntarily attending functions) promotes the interests of the organization.

Empirical research on the dimensions of organizational citizenship behaviors has generated somewhat conflicting results. A few researchers have been successful in identifying four categories of OCB (Moorman & Blakely, 1995), but the weight of the factor analytic evidence suggests a two-factor structure. For example, Williams (1988) found a two-dimensional definition of OCB: 1) benefits to the organization in general, such as volunteering to serve on committees (OCBO), and 2) benefits directed at individuals within the organization, such as altruism and interpersonal helping (OCBI). More recently, Skarlicki and Latham (1995) examined OCB in a university setting; their data also supported a two-factor structure, (organizational and interpersonal) which underlies organizational citizenship behavior.

Organizational citizenship behavior in schools, however, departs from most of the earlier research in that all aspects of OCB fold into a single integrated conception of citizenship. In two separate factor analytic studies, DiPaola and Tschannen-Moran (2001) found that there are not five separate dimensions of the construct, or even two for that matter, but rather that a single dimension captures all aspects of organizational citizenship in schools. In other words, both benefits to the organization (helping the organization) and benefits to the individual (helping individuals) combine into a single, bipolar construct.

These results in schools are not surprising for at least two related reasons. First, the evidence suggests that organizational citizenship behaviors are context specific, that is, the behaviors inherent to organizational citizenship vary from one type of organization to another (Karambayya, 1989; Organ, 1988). Second, public schools are quite different from most private sector organizations. Schools are service organizations staffed by teacher professionals who are generally committed to doing what is best for their students. The client (students in the case of schools) is the prime beneficiary of the organization (Blau & Scott, 1962). Thus, in service organizations like schools, both the professional workers and the organization are committed to what is in the best interests of the client. Consequently, there is a high degree of congruence between professional goals and organizational goals. The distinction between helping individuals and furthering the organizational mission is blurred because in schools the mission is synonymous with helping people—schools are people-helping organizations. Most previous studies were performed in private sector organizations where altruistic behavior towards coworkers was not necessarily intertwined with behaviors that support the organization and its mission. Teachers routinely perform behaviors directed toward helping individuals, both students and colleagues, as part of their professional identity (DiPaola & Tschannen-Moran, 2001).

Teachers who voluntarily go out of their way to help their students, colleagues, and others as they engage in the work of teaching and learning defines organizational citizenship behaviors in schools. Teachers in such schools take it upon themselves to make innovative suggestions, to volunteer to sponsor extracurricular activities, and to volunteer to serve on new committees. Moreover, teachers help students on their own time, stay after school to help if necessary, and resist the temptation to give students busy work. Organizational citizenship behavior in schools connotes a serious educational context in which teachers are rarely absent, make efficient use of their time while at school, work productively with their colleagues, and give high priority to professional activities over personal ones while in school. They use their talents and efforts to help both students and the school to achieve.

Collegial Principal Leadership

A principal's day-to-day behaviors have a dramatic impact on a school and members of the school community. A major challenge of all principals is to create and nurture a climate in which teachers and staff members identify and affiliate with the school and its mission. The principal's leadership style is critical in this regard, and we postulate that a collegial style is especially important in generating such affiliation.

Collegial principal leadership is characterized by behavior of the principal that is supportive and egalitarian. The principal is considerate, helpful, and genuinely concerned about the welfare of teachers. At the same time, the principal lets faculty know what is expected of them and maintains definite standards of performance. The principal is open to exploring all sides of topics, admits that divergent opinions exist, and is willing to make changes. Moreover, the principal is friendly and approachable and teachers don't hesitate to make suggestions; in fact, the principal often implements constructive suggestions made by faculty members. In sum, collegial principal behavior is supportive yet communicates high expectations of performance.

Teacher Trust in Colleagues

Trust is a critical element in any relationship. Without it, individuals are guarded and unwilling to take risks or be vulnerable in any way. The work done in schools is too often simply described as a teacher working with students. However, in order for teachers in a school to serve their students well, teachers must collaborate, communicate, cooperate, help one another, and take full advantage of their collective expertise. To work effectively as a team, teachers must trust one another. Constant communication, data analysis, and brainstorming are hallmarks of schools where teachers work together to serve their clients well.

Teacher trust in colleagues is one of the dimensions of overall faculty trust. Trust is an individual's or group's willingness to be vulnerable to another party based on the confidence that the latter party is benevolent, reliable, competent, honest, and open (Hoy & Tschannen-Moran, 2003; Hoy & Tschannen-Moran, 1999; Tschannen-Moran & Hoy, 1998). When a high level of teacher trust in colleagues exists, all of the facets of trust – benevolence, reliability, competence, honesty, and openness—work together. Each facet merits further discussion.

- Benevolence—teachers perceive benevolence when they believe their colleagues will behave in their collective best interests. Teachers are considerate to the needs and interests of their colleagues. They can count on one another and look out for one another.

- Reliability—trust is nurtured when teachers are confident that they can reliably predict the behavior of their colleagues. Teachers sense reliability when their colleagues behave consistently. They know they can count on them in a time of need.

- Competence—teachers are professionals with a high degree of specialized training. They expect their colleagues to have comparable knowledge and skills and feel betrayed in their collective effort to serve their clients well when colleagues do not demonstrate competence. Trust is contingent on the ability to count on colleagues to make contributions to the collective effort and have the competence to help clients.

- Honesty—trust is built on the expectation that others will be honest and truthful. Teachers cannot trust if they cannot rely on their colleagues to be honest. There must be consistent congruence between words and actions. They can only trust colleagues who not only "talk the talk" but also "walk the talk."

- Openness—finally, teachers trust colleagues by openly sharing information, control, or influence. This openness is a gesture of extending trust, since it is extended with the confidence that neither the information nor individual will be exploited. Openness is a way of building trust by taking action that makes one vulnerable with the expected outcome that it will build more trust.

Thus, *faculty trust is the general willingness of teachers to be vulnerable to their colleagues based on the confidence that their colleagues are benevolent, reliable, competent, honest, and open.*

Achievement Press

Achievement press is another important aspect of the school. When there is a strong press for academic success, students achieve at higher levels (Goddard, Sweetland, & Hoy, 2000; Hoy & Sabo, 1998; Hoy & Hannum, 1997; Hoy & Tarter, 1997; and Hoy, Tarter, & Kottkamp, 1991). *Achievement press is the extent to which the school community (students, teachers, administrators, and parents) is driven by a quest for academic excellence.* Teachers and administrators in such schools set a tone that is serious, orderly, and focused on academics. High but achievable goals are set for students, and students respond positively to the challenge of these goals: they work hard and respect the academic accomplishments of their peers. Parents as well as teachers and the principal have high academic expectations.

Theoretical Rationale and Hypothesis

Organizations have been defined as systems of formal positions and roles (Blau & Scott, 1962) in which participants conform to the expectations of their positions. Organizational citizenship behaviors go beyond the official blueprint of the organization; they are extra behaviors, that is, they are not officially prescribed. Such behaviors do not directly conform to the usual notion of job performance, but nevertheless they tend to be functional for the organization. Indeed, adherence to only the letter of the formal role is typically not sufficient to promote effectiveness and efficiency. Organizations need participants who go beyond formally prescribed roles. Unexpected and unique situations arise in organizations that require spontaneous, creative, and new behaviors. Flexibility and extra effort are required (Hoy & Sweetland, 2000, 2001). Borman and Motowidlo (1993) have proposed that individuals contribute to organizational effectiveness by doing things that are not necessarily their main task functions but are important because they shape the organizational and social context that supports task activities.

In general, citizenship behaviors contribute to organizational performance because these behaviors provide an effective means of managing the interdependencies between members of a work unit and, as a result, increase the collective outcomes achieved (Organ, 1988, 1990, 1997; Smith, Organ, & Near, 1983). Organizational citizenship also reduces the need for an organization to commit scarce resources to maintenance functions, thus freeing up more resources for goal-related activities. Moreover, administrators, for example, are able to devote a greater proportion of their time to important activities such as planning, problem solving, and instructional leadership.

Individual, group, and organizational characteristics all influence organizational citizenship behaviors (Koberg, Boss, Bursten, & Goodman, 1999). Citizenship behaviors are not inspired by the same motivations that induce people to join, stay, and perform within the contractual, formal role definitions (Smith, Organ, & Near, 1983). Research shows that organizational citizenship behaviors are positively related to organizational outcomes and group-level performance in a variety of organizations (George & Bettrnhausen, 1990; Graham, 1986; Karambayya, 1989; MacKenzie, Podsakoff, & Fetter, 1991; Podsakoff & MacKenzie, 1994; Smith, Organ, & Near, 1983).

Organizational citizenship behaviors are not only perceived to make important contributions to organizational performance but are regarded by leaders as significant in the performance of individuals (Borman, White, & Dorsey, 1995; MacKenzie, Podsakoff, & Fetter, 1991; Orr, Sackett, & Mercer, 1989; Werner, 1994). A key to overall performance in the minds of many managers was the extra things people did well above and beyond the call of duty. Workers perceived to be the most effective by managers were individuals who were not only productive themselves but also made those around them more productive "by helping, by being good sports, and/or exhibiting civic virtue" (Podsakoff & MacKenzie, 1994, p. 359).

Another factor in the resultant efficiency and effectiveness derived by organizations with greater citizenship behaviors is a reduction in employee turnover. The cost of employee turnover is reduced in organizations that foster citizenship behaviors; in fact, individuals who exhibit such behaviors are less likely to leave the organization (Chen, Hui, & Sego, 1998; Koberg, Boss, Bursten, & Goodman, 1999). Clearly a construct related to so many positive individual and organizational outcomes is worthy of study. Identifying school characteristics that foster such positive behaviors can assist school leaders in creating and fostering a context in which citizenship behaviors are commonplace.

Thus far, our analysis of the general literature on organizational citizenship behavior paints a positive picture. In schools with such faculties, teachers should exert extra effort and be willing to try innovative approaches; principals should be supportive, should implement appropriate teacher suggestions, should set high standards, should be able to devote more resources and energy to teaching-related issues rather than routine management and monitoring; when trust exists, teachers should be more likely to engage in cooperative activities like helping colleagues and promoting behavior that is good for the collective; and teachers should be more likely to remain in such schools and thus minimize the costs of recruitment, selection, and socialization of new faculty.

In addition to these general positive outcomes, organizational citizenship behaviors should also have more direct influences on the school goal of increasing student learning. Faculty citizenship behavior should promote more responsibility, persistence, and resilience in teaching—all of which should lead to higher student performance (Bandura, 1997). Teachers who are willing to go the extra mile with students by working with students on their own time and staying after school to help are accepting personal responsibility for student achievement and are persistent in their teaching efforts. They help one another in devising instructional strategies to help students succeed. Such teachers are also more likely to be resilient and to try different curricular approaches and teaching strategies to improve their teaching effectiveness.

There seems to be little doubt that organizational citizenship behavior is an important aspect of school life for faculty and students alike. What are the school properties that promote and enhance organizational citizenship? We assume that citizenship is dependent on the principal, the faculty, and the interaction of both working together toward the common goal of student success. Hence, we focus our analysis on collegial leadership of the principal, teacher trust in colleagues, and the achievement press of the school.

Principals who model supportive behavior and set clear expectations provide a context that should encourage teachers to help one another and their students to achieve schools goals. In brief, principals who go the extra mile in helping teachers should provide positive models for teachers to do the same. When teachers trust their colleagues, they do not have to work in isolation, but rather they can function as a professional community that cooperates to serve their students. In such a community, teachers are more likely to go the extra mile because trust provides the security and confidence they need to extend themselves to outsiders, such as substitute teachers, to parents, and to others who share school goals. When parents and students join with teachers and principals all intent upon high academic achievement, then it seems likely that students will seek extra help and teachers will give it freely, that is, teachers are willing to give of their own time to enhance student achievement. In such schools, with a clear focus on academic achievement, organizational participants behave like citizens rather than tourists. Finally, not only do we expect that each of these three important features of schools to work independently but also to work together to promote organizational citizenship behavior. Hence, we predict:

Collegial leadership, teacher trust, and achievement press together form a linear composite that is positively related to organizational citizenship behavior of teachers.

Methods

Next, we turn to the methods, and describe the sample, data collection procedures, and the operational measures.

Sample of Schools

A diverse sample of 75 middle schools was selected to examine the hypothesized relationships. These schools were distributed in eleven counties in a Midwestern state. Although the sample selected was not random, care was taken to insure participation of urban, suburban, and rural schools. The current distribution of middle schools in the state is 39% rural, 34% urban, and 27% suburban. Correspondingly, the study's schools are distributed across 19% rural, 41% urban, and 40% suburban settings. Of the 612 school districts in the state, 43 participated in the study. Staff completed a total of approximately 1,300 usable surveys. The sample was similar to the population of middle schools in the state in terms of student enrollment, average teacher salary, average teacher experience, and the size of the faculty. In brief, the sample of schools was fairly typical of middle schools in the state. See Table 11.1 for a summary of the characteristics of the sample.

Table 11.1.   Demographic Characteristics of the Sample

Demographic Indicator	Current Study	State Average
Student Enrollment	596	518
Average Teacher Salary	$44,886	$43,016
Average Teacher Experience	12	13
Average Number of Teachers on Staff	39 teachers	35 teachers
Percentage of Teacher Attendance	96%	96%
Middle Schools	$n = 75$	N (State) = 788

Data Collection

Data were collected from the middle schools at regularly scheduled faculty meetings. A member of the research team explained the general purpose of the study, assured the confidentiality of all responses, and asked teachers to complete the questionnaires. Because this project was part of a larger study of organizational properties, and because the unit of analysis was the school, a random group of half of the teachers in each school was selected to respond to the measures.[1] No attempt was made to gather data from faculty who were not present at the meeting, but virtually all teachers returned usable questionnaires.

Measures

The scales[2] used to measure the variables of this study are now described.

Organizational Citizenship Scale (OCS)

The organizational citizenship scale (OCS) was administered to teachers in each school. The scale consisted of 12 Likert items with a 6-point scale in which the response choices ranged from strongly disagree to strongly agree. The scale is a shortened version of the Organizational Citizenship Behaviors Scale (DiPaola & Tschannen-Moran, 2001). Teachers were asked to describe the extent to which they agree with such statements as, "Teachers voluntarily help new teachers," "Teachers volunteer to sponsor extra-curricular activities," "Teachers volunteer to serve on new committees," and "Teachers help students on their own time."

The OCB measures the citizenship behavior of the school faculty; it is a collective not an individual measure. Scores are aggregated to the school level. A copy of the entire scale can be obtained from the first author (http://mfdipa.people.wm.edu) and schools are invited to use the scale without cost to assess the organizational citizenship of their schools. There is strong reliability and validity evidence supporting the Organizational Citizenship Behavior Scale (DiPaola & Tschannen-Moran, 2001). In the present sample, the reliability coefficient for the scale was also strong (alpha = .93). The complete scale can be found on line at http://mfdipa.people.wm.edu.

Collegial Principal Leadership Behavior

The Organizational Climate Index (OCI) measures the four dimensions of climate including collegial leadership of the principal and academic achievement. The OCI has good validity and high reliability coefficients (Hoy, Smith, & Sweetland, 2002). The scales are comprised of 4-point Likert items, ranging from "Rarely Occurs" to "Very Frequently Occurs". The subscale Collegial Leadership consists of seven items, which include the following sample items, "The principal treats all faculty members as his or her equal," "The principal is friendly and approachable," "The principal lets faculty know what is expected of them," and "The principal puts suggestions made by the faculty into operation." In the present sample, the reliability coefficient for the leadership subscale was also strong (alpha = .96). The complete scale can be found on line at www.coe.ohio-state.edu/whoy.

Teacher Trust in Colleagues

The measure of teacher trust in colleagues is a subscale of the Omnibus Trust Scale. The Omnibus T-Scale is a 26-item measure consisting of three subscales: Faculty Trust in the Principal, Faculty Trust in Clients, and Faculty Trust in Colleagues. Factor analytic studies of the Omnibus T-Scale support the construct and discriminant validity of the concept (Hoy & Tschannen-Moran, 2003). The scale was administered to teachers in each school and a school score was calculated. The format of the Trust Scale is a 6-point Likert response set, from strongly agree to strongly disagree. Teachers were asked to indicate the extent to which they agreed with the 8 subscale items. In the present sample, the reliability coefficient for the scale was also strong (alpha = .93). Sample items of the scale measuring faculty trust in colleagues included, "Teachers in this school trust each other," "Teachers in this school typically look out for each other," "Teachers in this school have faith in the integrity of their colleagues," and "Teachers in this school are open with each other." The complete scale can be found on line at www.coe.ohio-state.edu/whoy.

Achievement Press

Another subscale of the OCI measured the achievement press of the school; the scale consists of eight items including such sample items as, "The school sets high standards for academic performance," "Students respect others who get good grades,"

"Students seek extra work so they can get good grades," and "Academic achievement is recognized and acknowledged by the school." In the present sample, the reliability coefficient for the scale was also strong (alpha = .96). The complete scale can be found on line at www.coe.ohio-state.edu/whoy.

Control Variable

Socioeconomic status (SES) is often related to school outcomes; hence, in our regression analysis, we control for SES. The socioeconomic level of the school was determined using State Department of Education data. Specifically, the proportion of students receiving a free and reduced lunch was our index of the socioeconomic status of the school; the greater the proportion, the lower the socioeconomic status.

Results

We turn to the descriptive statistics and intercorrelations among the variables of the study and then to a multivariate analysis of the relationships.

Descriptive Statistics and Intercorrelations

The focus of this study is the aggregate—the collective faculty perceptions of organizational citizenship behavior of each school. Organizational citizenship is one descriptor of the school milieu. Accordingly, analyses were performed on school means; that is, individual teacher responses were aggregated to the school level. Moreover, collegial principal leadership, teacher trust in colleagues, and achievement press, as noted above, were also school properties because they were measured as the collective perceptions of teachers in the schools sampled.

The collegial principal leadership-organizational citizenship relationship was supported in this study. A significant and positive correlation was found between organizational citizenship behavior of the faculty of a school and the collegial leadership of the principal. Organizational citizenship behavior and collegial leadership were correlated ($r = .66$, $p < .01$); the higher the level of collegial leadership of the principal, the greater the amount of faculty organizational citizenship behavior.

Likewise, the trust-citizenship relationship was supported in this study. A significant and positive correlation was found between organizational citizenship behavior of the faculty of a school and the level of teacher trust in colleagues ($r = .67$, $p < .01$); the higher the level of teacher trust in colleagues, the greater the amount of faculty organizational citizenship behavior.

Table 11.2.   Descriptives and Intercorrelations

Variable	Mean	Standard Deviation	Organizational Citizenship	Collegial Leadership	Teacher Trust in Colleagues	Achievement Press
Organizational Citizenship	3.74	.241	.93[a]			
Collegial Leadership	3.83	.461	.66**	.96[a]		
Teacher Trust in Colleagues	4.46	.442	.67**	.43**	.93[a]	
Achievement Press	3.48	.445	.77**	.59**	.69**	.96[a]
SES	.28	.20	-.15	-.01	-.16 [a]	-.12

a = coefficient of reliability (on the diagonal)
**$p < .01$

The achievement press-organizational citizenship relationship was also supported in this study. A significant and positive correlation was found between organizational citizenship behavior of the faculty of a school and the achievement press of the school. Organizational citizenship behavior and achievement press were correlated ($r = .77$, $p < .01$), the greater the achievement press of the school, the higher the level of faculty organizational citizenship behavior.

Finally, no relationship was found between the socioeconomic status of students in the school and the organizational citizenship or to the independent variables: achievement press, collegial leadership, or teacher trust. The descriptive statistics and intercorrelations are reported in Table 11.2.

Multiple Regression Analysis

To test our general hypothesis we turn to multiple regression analysis to get a finer picture of the relationships. Multiple regression analysis permits us to analyze the impact of all of the independent variables simultaneously on the dependent variable as well as the individual contribution that each makes controlling for all the others. In the regression analysis, the set of three school variables was used to explain the variance in organizational citizenship behavior of teachers while controlling for the SES of the school. Thus, we entered SES into the regression equations first followed by a block of the other three independent variables to predict organizational citizenship. For collegial leadership and teacher trust in colleagues, the standardized beta weights were significant in predicting

Table 11.3. Descriptives and Intercorrelations

Model	Unstandardized Coefficients		Standardized Coefficients				Adjusted
	B	Std. Error	Beta	t	Sig.	R	R Square
1. (Constant)[a]	3.79	.048	-.15	79.56	.000	.150	.009
SES	-.18	.138		-1.29	.200		
2. (Constant)[b]	1.46	.174	-.103	8.389	.000		
SES	.123	.074		-1.664	.101		
Collegial Leadership	.113	.042	.217	2.718	.008**		
Teacher Trust in Colleagues	.095	.046	.175	2.068	.043*		
Achievement Press	.413	.072	.564	5.739	.000**	.860	.725

a Predictor: (Constant) SES
b Predictors: (Constant) SES, collegial leadership, teacher trust, achievement press
$*p < .05$, $**p < .01$

OCB—(Beta = .22, $p < .01$ for collegial leadership of the principal and Beta = .18 for teacher trust in colleagues, $p < .05$), with collegial leadership slightly higher. For achievement press, the standardized beta weight was higher (Beta = .56, $p < .01$) in predicting organizational citizenship. The conclusion is clear: *Collegial principal behavior, the level of trust teachers have in their colleagues, and the achievement press of the school are important factors in the level of organizational citizenship in schools.* These three independent variables form a linear composite that fosters organizational citizenship behavior that explains more than two-thirds of the variance in organizational citizenship (Adjusted $R^2 = .73$). Moreover, each of the three independent variables had a significant affect on citizenship controlling for all the other variables. The standardized beta weights enable the reader to compare the relative influence of each independent variable controlling the influence of all the others independent variables (Kerlinger & Lee, 2000). The results of the statistical analysis may be viewed in Table 11.3.

DISCUSSION

Our findings support the contention that there are organizational factors that foster organizational citizenship in schools. This study builds on the strong link between citizenship and school climate (DiPaola & Tschannen-Moran, 2001). One of the dimensions of school climate is the collegial leadership of the principal. Collegial principals support teacher professionalism by treating teachers as the professionals they are. It is not surprising that greater organizational citizenship is a natural consequence. In contrast, leaders who are directive and restrictive in their leadership style inhibit professional behaviors that contribute to organizational citizenship. Another aspect of school climate is achievement press. Schools with a strong press for academic achievement are places in which the professional goal of service to clients is congruent with the organizational goal of high levels of achievement for all students. Consequently, teachers' energy and efforts are focused on serving their professional ideals while enhancing the organizational mission. Our empirical evidence demonstrates that this is the case. We found, as expected, a strong correlation between achievement press and organizational citizenship behavior.

Trust is increasingly regarded as a critical mediating variable in the social processes of schools. Faculty trust is a complex construct with multiple facets. A prior study linked teacher trust in the principal and organizational citizenship (Tschannen-Moran, 2002). This study examined the relationship of another facet of trust, teacher trust in colleagues, to organizational citizenship behavior. As predicted, we found that teacher trust in colleagues was positively related to the cultivation of citizenship behaviors in schools. When teachers trust their colleagues, they apparently are willing to perform more altruistic acts. They feel the support of their colleagues and are more confident in taking risks.

Each of these three characteristics of the school (principal leadership, trust, and achievement press) has a significant, independent effect on organizational citizenship. That is, although the three variables are correlated significantly with each other, each is related to organizational citizenship even when controlling for the impact of all the others as well as socioeconomic status. Together the three variables explain about two-thirds of the variance in citizenship. The conclusion is clear: the collegial leadership of the principal, the trust of teachers in each other, and the achievement press of the school, individually as well as collectively, produce an organizational environment that fosters citizenship behavior regardless of the socioeconomic level of the school.

A caveat, however, is in order. Although our theory explains why each of the independent variables affects organizational citizenship behavior, we assume that the relationships are reciprocal. That is, the collegial leadership of the principal fosters citizenship behavior, but citizenship behavior of teachers enables the principal to be collegial. Similarly, teacher trust promotes citizenship behavior, but such behavior fosters trust among colleagues; and although achievement press of the school promotes citizenship behavior, such behavior reinforces a strong school press for achievement.

IMPLICATIONS

There are only a few organizational properties that seem to make a difference in school achievement beyond socioeconomic status: faculty trust in students and parents (Goddard, Tschannen-Moran, & Hoy, 2001; Bryk & Schneider, 2002), collective efficacy (Goddard, Hoy, & Woolfolk, 2000), academic emphasis (Goddard, Sweetland, & Hoy, 2000), and organizational citizenship behavior (DiPaola & Hoy, in press); each have an independent effect on school achievement (controlling for SES). Fostering these organizational properties should be the goal of school administrators.

We have identified three organizational characteristics that foster citizenship behavior. We theorized that collegial leadership of the principal, teacher trust in colleagues, and achievement press of a school would have a positive impact on organizational citizenship. In such schools expectations are clear and the principal is considerate, helpful, and fair. The school is orderly, focused on academics, and strives for excellence. Teachers are more confident and willing to take risks. As a result, teachers in such schools should spontaneously reach out to students and colleagues, exert extra effort, and be more willing to try innovative approaches to curriculum and instruction. It appears that such teachers are personally invested in the success of students and take responsibility for student learning. Consequently, their practice reflects more persistence in their teaching efforts. Teachers who are willing to go the extra mile with students by working with students on their own time and by staying after school to help students, demonstrate personal responsibility for student achievement and persist in their teaching efforts. Such teachers are also more likely to try different teaching strategies when their regular teaching tactics are not effective.

Schools with a high degree of organizational citizenship also free administrators from routine monitoring and checking and enable them to engage in more productive activities in support of teaching and learning. With organizational citizenship behaviors come a number of related activities that focus on teaching and learning and make schools more productive.

Organizational citizenship behavior of faculty is an important characteristic that is directly and indirectly linked to school achievement. The findings of this study were for middle schools. We suspect the results will be the same for elementary and high schools, but that remains an empirical question. A systematic agenda of research is needed to examine both the antecedents and consequences of organizational citizenship behavior. Consider only a few of the research questions in need of answers:

- What are the other factors that facilitate the development of organizational citizenship behaviors?
- Is gender an important variable in the development of organizational citizenship? How do the variables of collective efficacy interact with organizational citizenship to produce student achievement?
- To what extent do organizational politics impede or facilitate the development of organizational citizenship behaviors?
- To what extent are teacher empowerment and shared decision making important to the development of organizational citizenship behaviors?
- To what extent are reflective and mindful administrators necessary to the promotion of a culture of organizational citizenship?

The list goes on and on, but the preceding set of questions illustrates the heuristic nature of the concept and the need for further study.

One of the keys of achieving the primary school goal of improving student learning is to find ways to help teachers to exert extra effort, persist in their teaching, innovate, and to persevere despite initial failure. Strong organizational citizenship is quite consistent with such behavior. Moreover, the fact that such behavior is an organizational feature suggests that these schools have cultures that encourage and support behavior that goes far beyond routine and formal expectations. Teachers who find themselves in such schools are likely to discover that citizenship behaviors are the norm rather that the exception; consequently, individuals will feel the subtle pressure of their colleagues to follow that norm.

CONCLUSION

Clearly, the style of principal leadership, the level of academic focus, and the trust teachers have in their colleagues are factors that promote citizenship behaviors. Identifying others would help administrators in cultivating organizational citizenship in schools. The benefits are obvious: most of the teachers voluntarily expend extra effort and time to make the school a better place. We suspect that once some of the contextual factors that promote citizenship exist, a critical mass of teachers will be engaged in organizational citizenship behavior. The rest are sure to soon follow.

NOTES

1. This study was part of a larger study in which the other half of each faculty responded to a different set of measures.

2. The complete measures for each scale can be found at www.coe .ohio-state.edu/whoy.

REFERENCES

Bandura, A. (1997). *Self-efficacy: The exercise of control*. New York: W. H. Freeman & Co.

Barnard, C. I. (1938). *The functions of the executive*. Cambridge, MA: Harvard University Press.

Bateman, T. S., & Organ, D.W. (1983). Job satisfaction and the good soldier: The relationship between affect and employee citizenship. *Academy of Management Journal, 26*, 587-595.

Blau, P., & Scott, R. (1962). Formal organizations: A comparative approach. San Francisco: Chandler.

Borman, W. C., & Motowidlo, S. J. (1993). Expanding the criterion domain to include elements of contextual performance. In N. Schmitt & W. C. Borman, (Eds.), *Personality selection* (pp. 71–98). San Francisco: Jossey-Bass.

Borman, W. C., White, L. A., & Dorsey, D. W. (1995). Effects of task performance and interpersonal factors on supervisors and peer ratings. *Journal of Applied Psychology, 80*, 168-177.

Bryk, A. S., & Schneider, B. (2002). *Trust in schools*. New York: Russell Sage Foundation.

Chen, X. P., Hui, C., & Sego, D. J. (1998). The role of organizational citizenship behavior in turnover: Conceptualization and preliminary tests of key hypotheses. *Journal of Applied Psychology, 83*, 922-931.

DiPaola, M. F., & Hoy, W. K. (in press). Organizational citizenship of faculty and achievement of high school students. *The High School Journal*.

DiPaola, M. F., & Tschannen-Moran, M. (2001, September). Organizational citizenship behavior in schools and its relationship to school climate. *Journal of School Leadership, 11*, 424-447.

George, J. M., & Bettrnhausen, K. (1990). Understanding prosocial behavior, sales performance, and turnover: A group level analysis in a service context. *Journal of Applied Psychology, 75*, 698-709.

Goddard, R. D., Hoy, W. K., Woolfolk, A. (2000). Collective teacher efficacy: Its meaning, measure, and effect on student achievement. *American Educational Research Journal, 37*, 479-507.

Goddard, R. D., Sweetland, S., & Hoy, W. K. (2000). Academic emphasis of urban elementary schools and student achievement in reading and mathematics: A multilevel analysis. *Educational Administration Quarterly, 36*, 683-702.

Goddard, R. D., Tschannen-Moran, M., & Hoy, W. K. (2001). Teacher trust in students and parents: A multilevel examination of the distribution and effects of teacher trust in urban elementary schools. *Elementary School Journal, 102*, 3-17.

Graham, J. W. (1986). *Organizational citizenship informed by political theory.* Paper presented at the Academy of Management meeting, Chicago, Il.

Hoy, W. K., & Hannum, J. (1997). Middle school climate: An empirical assessment of organizational health and student achievement. *Educational Administration Quarterly, 33*, 290-311.

Hoy, W. K., & Sabo, D. J. (1998). *Quality middle schools: Open and healthy.* Thousand Oaks, CA: Corwin.

Hoy, W. K., Smith, P. A., & Sweetland, S. R. (2002). The development of the organizational climate index for high schools: Its measure and relationship to faculty trust. *The High School Journal High School Journal, 86(2)*, 38-49.

Hoy, W. K., & Sweetland, S. R. (2000). Bureaucracies that work: Enabling not coercive. *Journal of School Leadership, 10*, 525-541.

Hoy, W. K., & Sweetland, S. R. (2001). Designing better schools: The meaning and nature of enabling school structure. *Educational Administration Quarterly, 37*. 296-321.

Hoy, W.K., & Tarter, C.J. (1997). *The road to open and healthy schools: A handbook for change.* Thousand Oaks, CA: Sage.

Hoy, W. K., Tarter, C. J., & Kottkamp, R. (1991). *Open schools/healthy schools: Measuring organizational climate.* Thousand Oaks, CA: Sage.

Hoy, W. K. & Tschannen-Moran, M. (1999). Five faces of trust: An empirical confirmation in urban elementary schools. *Journal of School Leadership, 9*, 184-208.

Hoy, W. K., & Tschannen-Moran, M. (2003). The conceptualization and measurement of faculty trust in schools. In Wayne K. Hoy & Cecil Miskel (Eds.). *Studies in leading and organizing schools* (pp. 181-207).

Karambayya, R. (1989). *Organizational citizenship behavior: Contextual predictors and organizational consequences.* Unpublished doctoral dissertation, Northwestern University, Evanston, Il.

Kerlinger, F. N., & Lee, H. B. (2000). *Foundations of behavioral research* (4th ed.). Belmont, CA: Wadsworth.

Koberg, C., Boss, R., Bursten, R., & Goodman, E. (August, 1999). *Getting more than you bargained for: Empirical evidence of organizational citizenship behavior from the health care industry?* Paper presented at the annual meeting of the Academy of Management, Chicago.

MacKenzie, S. B., Podsakoff, P. M., & Fetter, R. (1991). Organizational citizenship behavior and objective productivity as determinants of managerial evaluations of salespersons' performance. *Organizational Behavior and Human Decision Processes, 50*, 123-150.

Moorman, R. H., & Blakely, G. L. (1995). Individualism-collectivism as an individual difference predictor of organizational citizenship behavior. *Journal of Organizational Behavior, 16(2)*, 127-142.

Organ, D. W. (1988). *Organizational citizenship behavior.* Lexington, MA: D.C. Heath and Co.

Organ, D. W. (1990). The motivational basis of organizational citizenship behavior. *Research in Organizational Behavior, 12*, 43-72.

Organ, D. W. (1997). Organizational citizenship behavior: It's construct clean-up time. *Human Performance, 10* , 85-97.

Organ, D. W., & Ryan, K (1995). A meta-analytic review of attitudinal and dispositional predictors of organizational citizenship behavior. *Personnel Psychology, 48,* 775-802.

Orr, J. M., Sackett, P. R., & Mercer, M (1989). The role of prescribed and nonprescribed behaviors in estimating the dollar value of performance. *Journal of Applied Psychology, 74,* 34-40.

Podsakoff, P. M., & MacKenzie, S. B. (1994). Organizational citizenship behaviors and sales unit effectiveness. *Journal of Marketing Research, 31,* 351-363.

Skarlicki, D., & Latham G. (1995). Organizational citizenship behavior and performance in a university setting. *Canadian Journal of Administrative Sciences, 12,* 175-181.

Smith, C. A., Organ, D. W., & Near, J. P. (1983). Organizational citizenship behavior: It's nature and antecedents. *Journal of Applied Psychology, 68,* 653-663.

Tschannen-Moran, M., (2002). Fostering organizational citizenship in schools: Transformational leadership and trust. In W. Hoy & C. Miskel (Eds.), *Studies in leading and organizing schools* (pp. 157-179), Greenwich, CT: Information Age Publishing.

Tschannen-Moran, M., & Hoy, W. K. (1998). Trust in schools: a conceptual analysis. *Journal of Educational Administration, 36,* 4, 334-352.

Werner, J. M. (1994). Dimensions that make a difference: Examining the impact of in-role and extra-role behaviors on supervisory ratings. *Journal of Applied Psychology, 79,* 98-107.

Williams, L. (1988). *Effective and noneffective components of job satisfaction and organizational commitment as determinants of organizational citizenship and in-role behaviors.* Unpublished doctoral dissertation, Indiana University, Bloomington, IN.

CHAPTER 12

ORGANIZATIONAL CITIZENSHIP OF FACULTY AND ACHIEVEMENT OF HIGH SCHOOL STUDENTS

Michael F. DiPaola and Wayne K. Hoy

All successful organizations, including successful high schools, have employees who go beyond their formal job responsibilities and freely give of their time and energy to succeed. Organ was the first to use the phrase "organizational citizenship behavior" (OCB) to denote organizationally beneficial behavior of workers that was not prescribed but occurred freely to help others achieve the task at hand (Bateman & Organ, 1983). The willingness of participants to exert effort beyond the formal obligations of their positions has long been recognized as an essential component of effective organizational performance.

Research on organizational citizenship behavior has produced some intriguing insights in a variety of organizational settings (Organ, 1988; Organ & Ryan, 1995), but it has been neglected in the study of schools. In

Reprinted with permission of *The High School Journal*, "Organizational citizenship of faculty and student achievement" by M. F. DiPaola & W. K. Hoy, Vol. 88, Issue 3. Copyright © 2005 by the University of North Carolina Press. All rights reserved.

an earlier paper (DiPaola & Tschannen-Moran, 2001), Organ's concept of organizational citizenship (Organ, 1988; Organ & Ryan, 1995) was developed and applied to public schools. This analysis builds on that earlier work.

In this analysis, the concept of organizational citizenship behavior is reviewed and then applied to schools. A set of hypotheses linking organizational citizenship behavior with student achievement in high schools is developed and tested. A significant relationship was found between student achievement on standardized tests and the level of organizational citizenship behaviors of the faculty in the high school sample studied. The relationship remained significant even after controlling for socioeconomic status (SES). Finally, a set of suggestions for further research and a series of practical suggestions for high school administrators are provided.

Successful organizations have employees who go beyond their formal job responsibilities and freely give of their time and energy to succeed at the task at hand. Such altruism is neither prescribed nor required; yet it contributes to the smooth functioning of the organization. In an earlier paper (DiPaola & Tschannen-Moran, 2001), Organ's concept of organizational citizenship (Organ, 1988; Organ & Ryan, 1995) was developed and applied to public schools. The current analysis builds on that earlier work. First, we review the concept of organizational citizenship behavior, then we apply the concept to schools, and finally, we develop and test a set of hypotheses linking organizational citizenship behavior with student achievement.

CONCEPTUAL FRAMEWORK

The three major variables of this study are organizational citizenship behavior, student achievement, and socioeconomic status.

Organizational Citizenship Behavior

Organ was the first to use the phrase "organizational citizenship behavior" (OCB) to denote organizationally beneficial behavior of workers that was not prescribed but occurred freely to help others achieve the task at hand (Bateman & Organ, 1983). Research on organizational citizenship behavior has produced some intriguing insights in a variety of organizational settings (Organ, 1988; Organ & Ryan, 1995), but it has been neglected in the study of schools. Teachers perform the task of teaching. They are professionals in the sense that they study a relatively long time to master the fundamentals of teaching (expertise) and their primary commitment is to their students (service to clients). Teaching is a complex activity that requires professional judgments; it cannot adequately be prescribed in teachers' job descriptions or contracts. Thus organizational citizenship behavior is an especially important aspect of the performance of faculty in schools.

Organizational citizenship behavior (OCB) is defined as "performance that supports the social and psychological environment in which task performance takes place" (Organ, 1997, p. 95). Such behavior is said to "lubricate the social machinery of the organization" (Bateman & Organ, 1983, p. 588). The willingness of participants to exert effort beyond the formal obligations of their positions has long been recognized as an essential component of effective organizational performance. For example, more than a half century ago, Barnard (1938) stated that the willingness of individuals to contribute cooperative efforts to the organization was indispensable to effective attainment of organizational goals.

Organizational citizenship behavior was described by Organ and his colleagues (Smith, Organ, &Near, 1983) as having two basic dimensions—altruism and generalized compliance. Altruism is helping behavior directed at specific individuals. When individuals have specific problems, need assistance, or seek help, altruistic people go the extra mile in assisting them. The other class of citizenship behavior is generalized compliance, which is a more impersonal conscientiousness: doing things "right and proper" for their own sake rather than for any specific person. Conscientiousness in use of time is the hallmark of this dimension. Organizational participants' behavior far surpasses any enforceable minimum standards; workers willingly go far beyond stated expectations.

In attempting to further define organizational citizenship behavior, Organ (1988) highlights five specific categories of discretionary behavior and explains how each helps to improve efficiency in the organization.

- Altruism (e.g., helping new colleagues and freely giving time to others) is typically directed toward other individuals, but contributes to group efficiency by enhancing individuals' performance.
- Conscientiousness (e.g., efficient use of time and going beyond minimum expectations) enhances the efficiency of both an individual and the group.
- Sportsmanship (e.g., avoids complaining and whining) improves the amount of time spent on constructive endeavors in the organization.

- Courtesy (e.g., advance notices, reminders, and communicating appropriate information) helps prevent problems and facilitates constructive use of time.

- Civic Virtue (e.g., serving on committees and voluntarily attending functions) promotes the interests of the organization.

Empirical research on the dimensions of organizational citizenship behaviors (OCB) has generated somewhat conflicting results. A few researchers have been successful in identifying four categories of OCB (Moorman & Blakely, 1995), but the weight of the factor analytic evidence suggests a two-factor structure. For example, Williams (1988) found a two-dimensional definition of OCB: 1) benefits to the organization in general, such as volunteering to serve on committees (OCBO), and 2) benefits directed at individuals within the organization, such as altruism and interpersonal helping (OCBI). More recently, Skarlicki and Latham (1995) examined OCB in a university setting; their data also supported a two-factor structure, (organizational and interpersonal) that underlies organizational citizenship behavior.

Organizational citizenship behavior in schools, however, departs from most of the earlier research in that all aspects of OCB fold into a single integrated conception of citizenship. In two separate factor analytic studies, DiPaola and Tschannen-Moran (2001) found that there are not five separate dimensions of the construct, or even two for that matter, but rather that one dimension captures all aspects of organizational citizenship in schools. In other words, both benefits to the organization (helping the organization) and benefits to the individual (helping individuals) combine into a single, bipolar construct.

These results in schools are not surprising for at least two related reasons. First, the evidence suggests that organizational citizenship behaviors are context specific, that is, the behaviors inherent to organizational citizenship vary from one type of organization to another (Karambayya, 1989; Organ, 1988). Second, public schools are quite different from most private sector organizations. Schools are service organizations staffed by teacher professionals who are generally committed to doing what is best for their students. The client (students in the case of schools) is the prime beneficiary of the organization (Blau & Scott, 1962). Thus, in service organizations like schools, both the professional workers and the organization are committed to what is in the best interests of the client. Consequently, there is a high degree of congruence between professional goals and organizational goals. The distinction between helping individuals and furthering the organizational mission is blurred because in schools the mission is synonymous with helping people—schools are people-helping organizations. Most previous studies were performed in private sector

organizations where altruistic behavior towards coworkers was not necessarily intertwined with behaviors that support the organization and its
mission. Teachers routinely perform behaviors directed toward helping
individuals, both clients and colleagues, as part of their professional identity (DiPaola & Tschannen-Moran, 2001).

Teachers who voluntarily help their new colleagues and go out of their
way to introduce themselves to others define organizational citizenship
behaviors in schools. Teachers in such schools take it upon themselves to
make innovative suggestions, to volunteer to sponsor extra-curricular
activities, and to volunteer to serve on new committees. Moreover, teachers help students on their own time, stay after school to help if necessary,
and resist the temptation to give students busy work. Organizational citizenship behavior in schools connotes a serious educational context in
which teachers are rarely absent, make efficient use of their time while at
school, work productively with their colleagues, and give high priority to
professional activities over personal ones while in school. They use their
talents and efforts to help both students and the school to achieve.

Student Achievement

One of the hallmarks of school effectiveness is student achievement in
academic disciplines. How well students are achieving is determined by
judgments of teachers, teacher-made tests, grades, and standardized
tests. In this era of standards and accountability, most states now employ
a standardized set of tests to assess the performance of schools within
their state. Schools and districts get "report cards" based on these tests
that indicate the school's performance and progress. The Ohio Department of Education has developed a set of proficiency tests to assess the
success of schools. The focus of the current study is mathematics and
reading achievement, two hallmarks of educated students. These two
indicators are not the only criteria of school effectiveness, but they are by
all accounts important ones.

Socioeconomic Status (SES)

Socioeconomic status (SES) is another important variable to consider
when looking at school achievement because it is invariably a strong predictor of student success (Coleman, et al., 1966), in fact, it is difficult to
find organizational variables that are as potent in predicting achievement. The wealth associated with high SES is generally a predictor of
high achievement in schools. Students from higher SES schools have

many of the important ingredients for success as part of their home environment— books; computers; and educated parents who help, support, and reinforce academic and intellectual pursuits, to mention only a few advantages. No study of student achievement of schools is complete without considering the impact of SES on student achievement. What educational researchers are seeking are variables that are malleable, that is, that can be changed relatively easily because SES is not amenable to much change. The challenge is to find factors that have as strong an influence on student achievement as SES.

ORGANIZATIONAL CITIZENSHIP AND STUDENT ACHIEVEMENT

There has been no research that we know of that links organization citizenship behavior and student achievement in school. In particular, this inquiry is concerned with three questions:

- Does the organizational citizenship behavior facilitate student achievement within a school?
- If so, how does such behavior work to improve achievement?
- How can the school improve the organizational citizenship behavior of faculty?

An Organizational Citizenship-Student Achievement Hypothesis

Organizations have been defined as systems of formal positions and roles (Blau & Scott, 1962) in which participants conform to the expectations of their positions. Organizational citizenship behaviors go beyond the official blueprint of the organization; they are extra behaviors, that is, they are not officially prescribed. Such behaviors do not directly conform to the usual notion of job performance, but nevertheless they tend to be functional for the organization.

Indeed, adherence to only the letter of the formal role is typically not sufficient to promote effectiveness and efficiency. Organizations need participants who go beyond formally prescribed roles. Unexpected and unique situations arise in organizations that require spontaneous, creative, and new behaviors. Flexibility and extra effort are required (Hoy & Sweetland, 2000, 2001). Borman and Motowidlo (1993) have proposed that individuals contribute to organizational effectiveness by doing things that are not necessarily their main task functions but are important because they shape the organizational and social context that supports task activities.

In general, citizenship behaviors contribute to organizational performance because these behaviors provide an effective means of managing the interdependencies between members of a work unit and, as a result, increase the collective outcomes achieved (Organ, 1988, 1990, 1997; Smith, Organ, & Near, 1983). Organizational citizenship also reduces the need for an organization to commit scarce resources to maintenance functions, thus freeing up more resources for goal-related activities. Moreover, administrators, for example, are able to devote a greater proportion of their time to important activities such as planning, problem solving, and organizational analysis.

Individual, group, and organizational characteristics all influence organizational citizenship behaviors (Koberg, Boss, Bursten, & Goodman, 1999). Citizenship behaviors are not inspired by the same motivations that induce people to join, stay, and perform within the contractual, formal role definitions (Smith, Organ, & Near, 1983). Research shows that organizational citizenship behaviors are positively related to organizational outcomes and group-level performance in a variety of organizations (George & Bettrnhausen, 1990; Graham, 1986; Karambayya, 1989; MacKenzie, Podsakoff, & Fetter, 1991; Podsakoff & MacKenzie, 1994; Smith, Organ, & Near, 1983).

Organizational citizenship behaviors are not only perceived to make important contributions to organizational performance but are regarded by leaders as significant in the performance of individuals (Borman, White, & Dorsey, 1995; MacKenzie, Podsakoff, & Fetter, 1991; Orr, Sackett, & Mercer, 1989; Werner, 1994). A key to overall performance in the minds of many managers were the extra things people did well above and beyond the call of duty. Workers perceived to be the most effective by managers were individuals who were not only productive themselves but also made those around them more productive "by helping, by being good sports, and/or exhibiting civic virtue" (Podsakoff & MacKenzie, 1994, p. 359).

Another factor in the resultant efficiency and effectiveness derived by organizations with greater citizenship behaviors is a reduction in employee turnover. The cost of employee turnover is reduced in organizations that foster citizenship behaviors; in fact, individuals who exhibit such behaviors are less likely to leave the organization (Chen, Hui, & Sego, 1998; Koberg, Boss, Bursten, & Goodman, 1999). Clearly a construct related to so many positive individual and organizational outcomes is worthy of study. In schools, is citizenship behavior related to student achievement? And, if so, why?

Thus far, our analysis of the general literature on organizational citizenship behavior paints a positive picture. In schools with such faculties, teachers should exert extra effort and be willing to try innovative approaches; administrators should be able to devote more resources and energy to teaching-related issues rather than routine management and monitoring; teachers and administrators should be more likely to engage in cooperative activities like helping colleagues and promoting behavior that is good for the collective; and teachers should be more likely to remain in such schools and thus minimize the costs of recruitment, selection, and socialization of new faculty.

In addition to these general positive outcomes of organizational citizenship behaviors, such behavior should also have more direct influences on student learning. Faculty citizenship behavior should promote more responsibility, persistence, and resilience in teaching—all of which should lead to higher student performance (Bandura, 1997). Teachers who are willing to go the extra mile with students by working with students on their own time and staying after school to help are accepting personal responsibility for student achievement and are persisting in their teaching efforts. Such teachers are also more likely to be resilient and to try different curricular approaches and teaching strategies to improve their teaching effectiveness.

Hence, *we hypothesize that: Faculty organizational citizenship behavior is positively associated with student achievement in both mathematics and reading.* Although the hypothesis is stated as an association between citizenship behavior of the schools and achievement, we believe that the relationship is an instance of reciprocal causality, that is, organizational citizenship behavior produces higher student achievement, and conversely, higher student achievement reinforces and produces greater organizational citizenship behaviors.

A Test of the Organizational Citizenship-Student Achievement Hypothesis

To test this hypothesis, data were collected and analyzed from a typical set of high schools in Ohio.

Sample

The current study consisted of a sample of 97 high schools in Ohio. Although procedures were not used to ensure a random sample from the population of high schools, care was taken to select urban, suburban, and rural schools from diverse geographic areas of the state. Only schools with 15 or more faculty members were candidates for the study. One hundred and forty-nine high schools were invited to participate, but for a variety of reasons only 97 agreed to be in the study (65%). High schools were defined by grade configurations that included grades 9-12 and grades 10-12. The high schools in the sample represented the entire range of socioeconomic status (SES); in fact, data from the Ohio Department of Education support the representativeness of the sample in terms of size, socioeconomic status, and urban-rural balance.

Organizational Citizenship Behavior in School Scale (OCBSS)

An organizational citizenship behaviors scale (OCBSS) was administered to teachers in each school. The scale consisted of 15 Likert items with a 4-point scale in which the response choices included rarely occurs, sometimes occurs, often occurs, and very frequently occurs (DiPaola & Tschannen-Moran, 2001). Teachers were asked to describe the extent to which they agree with such statements as

"Teachers voluntarily help new teachers."
"Teachers volunteer to sponsor extra-curricular activities."
"Teachers volunteer to serve on new committees."
"Teachers leave immediately after school is over (score is reversed)."

The OCBSS measures the citizenship behavior of the school faculty; it is a collective not an individual measure. Scores are aggregated to the school level.

A copy of the entire scale can be obtained from the first author and schools are invited to use the scale without cost to assess the organizational citizenship of their schools. There is strong reliability and validity evidence for the scale (DiPaola & Tschannen-Moran, 2001). In the present sample, the reliability coefficient for the scale was also strong (alpha = .87).

School Achievement

School achievement in mathematics and reading was measured by the Ohio Department of Education. Each year students take a 12th-grade proficiency test in mathematics and reading. Content validity evidence is provided by the extensive involvement of expert educators in the development and selection of items. Reliabilities of the test for the past five years have ranged from .91 to .92. The state establishes passing rates for all schools in Ohio. Because we were interested in the school as the unit of analysis, we focused on the percentage of students that passed these exams.

Socioeconomic Status (SES)

An index of SES was created by the Ohio Department of Education based on a composite measure of the inhabitant's typical income, overall level of education, and their professional leanings. The state's index was used as a measure of socioeconomic status for the high school.

DATA COLLECTION AND ANALYSIS

Data for faculty organizational citizenship behavior were collected from the faculty members of each school, during a regularly scheduled faculty meeting, as part of a larger study. A trained researcher personally administered the research instrument in each school. All teacher responses were anonymous, and because the unit of analysis was the school, data were aggregated to the school level. SES and proficiency test data for each high school were collected from the Ohio Department of Education.

Statistical Analyses

The focus of this study is the aggregate—the collective faculty perceptions of organizational citizenship behavior for each school. Organizational citizenship is a description of the school. Accordingly, analyses were performed on school means; that is, individual teacher responses were aggregated to the school level. Moreover, student achievement, as noted above, was also a school property because it was measured as the percent of students in each school passing the 12th-grade proficiency test in mathematics.

RESULTS

The organizational citizenship-achievement hypothesis was supported in this study. A significant and positive correlation was found between organizational citizenship behavior of the faculty of a school and the student achievement of the schools for both reading and mathematics. Organizational citizenship behavior and the percentage of students passing the 12th grade proficiency test were correlated for reading ($r = .30$, $p < .01$) and for mathematics ($r = .34$, $p < .01$); the greater the amount of faculty organizational citizenship behavior, the higher the level of student achievement.

The one school property, however, that consistently predicts student achievement in school is the SES of the parents and community. Wealthier school districts have higher academic achievement than poorer ones.

Indeed that was the case for schools in this sample; the higher the SES, the higher the student achievement in reading ($r = .27$, $p < .01$) and mathematics reading ($r = .37$, $p < .01$). If we control for SES, does citizenship behavior still make a significant impact on student achievement? The answer is yes! We controlled for SES and calculated the partial correlation of organizational citizenship and student achievement. The correlation remained substantial and significant (partial $r = .28$, $p < .01$) for reading and (partial $r = .30$, $p < .01$) for mathematics.

One more statistical analysis was performed to compare the relative importance of the impact of SES and organizational citizenship on student achievement. We entered both SES and organizational citizenship simultaneously into a regression equation predicting school achievement in reading and mathematics. For reading, the standardized beta weights were similar in predicting achievement—(beta $= 27$, $p < .01$ for organizational citizenship and beta $= .23$ for SES, $p < .01$), with organizational citizenship slightly higher. For mathematics, the standardized beta weights, again, were similar in predicting achievement—(beta $= 28$, $p < .01$ for organizational citizenship and for SES beta $= .33$, $p < .01$), with SES slightly more important. The conclusion is clear: Faculty organizational citizenship of a school is an important factor in the level of student achievement in schools. Faculty organizational citizenship has a significant independent effect on school student achievement in addition to the effect of SES on achievement; in fact, faculty citizenship behavior has approximately the same impact as SES. The results of the statistical analysis may be viewed in Table 12.1.

Discussion

There are only a few organizational properties that seem to make a difference in school achievement beyond socioeconomic status: faculty trust in students and parents (Goddard, Tschannen-Moran, & Hoy, 2001; Bryk & Schneider, 2002), collective efficacy (Goddard, Hoy, & Woolfolk, 2000),

Table 12.1.   Correlations and Standardized Beta Weights for the Relationship Between Faculty Organizational Citizenship and School Student Achievement

Achievement	r	Partial r Controlling For SES Weight	Standardized Beta Weight
Reading	.27*	.28*	.28*
Mathematics	.37*	.29*	.33*

$* p < .01$

and academic emphasis (Goddard, Sweetland, & Hoy, 2000) each have an independent effect on school achievement (controlling for SES). To that small list, we may now add faculty organizational citizenship behavior.

The theoretical rationale for linking organizational citizenship behavior to student achievement was also supported by the results. We theorized that organizational citizenship of a school would impact the achievement of students because teachers in such schools would spontaneously reach out to students and colleagues, exert extra effort, and be more willing to try innovative approaches to curriculum and instruction. It appears that such teachers are personally invested in the success of students and take responsibility for student learning. Consequently, their practice reflects more persistence in their teaching efforts. Teachers who are willing to go the extra mile with students by working with students on their own time and staying after school to help students demonstrate personal responsibility for student achievement and persist in their teaching efforts. Such teachers are also more likely to be resilient and to try different curricular approaches and teaching strategies when their regular teaching tactics are not effective.

Schools with a high degree of organizational citizenship also free administrators from routine monitoring and checking and enable them to engage in more productive activities in support of teaching and learning. With organizational citizenship behaviors come a number of related activities that focus on teaching and learning and make schools more productive.

Research Questions

Organizational citizenship behavior of faculty is a new concept that has received little attention in the research literature on schools. Yet, the concept seems an important one that is directly and indirectly linked to school achievement. A systematic agenda of research is needed to examine both the antecedents and consequences of organizational citizenship behavior. Consider only a few of the research questions in need of answers:

- The findings of this study were for high schools. We suspect the results will be the same for elementary and middle schools, but that remains an empirical question.
- What factors facilitate the development of organizational citizenship behaviors? For example, how is organizational citizenship related to the development of faculty trust in colleagues, in parents,

in students, and in the principal? How pivotal is the development of teacher trust?

- Is gender an important variable in the development of organizational citizenship?
- How do the variables of academic press, trust in parents, and collective efficacy interact with organizational citizenship to produce student achievement? In other words, how do these important organizational features work together?
- To what extent do organizational politics impede or facilitate the development of organizational citizenship behaviors?
- To what extent are teacher empowerment and shared decision making important to the development of organizational citizenship behaviors?
- To what extent are reflective and mindful administrators necessary to the promotion of a culture of organizational citizenship?

The list goes on and on, but the preceding set of questions illustrate the heuristic nature of the concept and the need for further study.

Practical Suggestions

Both the current study and the earlier one on citizenship behavior (DiPaola & Tschannen-Moran, 2001) provide enough information to begin to formulate some suggestions for practice. One of the keys to improving student learning is to find ways to help teachers to exert extra effort, persist in their teaching, innovate, and to persevere despite initial failure. Strong organizational citizenship is quite consistent with such behavior. Moreover, the fact that such behavior is an organizational feature suggests that these schools have cultures that encourage and support behavior that goes far beyond routine and formal expectations. Teachers who find themselves in such schools are likely to discover that citizenship behaviors are the norm rather that the exception; consequently, individuals will feel the subtle pressure of their colleagues to follow that norm.

Cultivating organizational citizenship in schools is like changing the culture of the school; it is slow, and not a simple process. The key is that most of the teachers voluntarily expend extra effort and time to make the school a better place. We suspect that once a critical mass of the teachers is engaged in organizational citizenship behavior, then the rest will follow. We offer the following suggestions for principals:

- Lead by example; be a good organizational citizen and reinforce those behaviors when you observe them in your school.
- Be supportive and flexible in dealing with your teachers; principals who focus on enforcing the rules and regulations will not be successful in motivating teachers to go the extra mile.
- Have as few formal rules as possible; formality breeds rule-oriented behavior and rigidity.
- Try not to permit the teaching contract to get too specific in terms of what teachers can and cannot do. If the contract is specific, work with the union leadership to enhance flexibility.
- Nurture the informal organization; work with the informal teacher leaders, and encourage novel solutions to problems. Limit your use of the formal apparatus.
- Praise your teachers when they demonstrate good organizational citizenship behavior; informal praise may be the best. Simply let your teachers know that you appreciate their extra efforts.
- Treat teachers as professionals, that is, as individuals with expertise in teaching and commitment to their students. Give them autonomy to experiment and to make important decisions about teaching and learning.
- Design a mentoring system in which experienced teacher, who routinely demonstrate organizational citizenship behaviors socialize new teachers.
- Protect your teachers from administrative trivia—unnecessary meetings, too much paper work, silly rules, busy work, etc.
- With your teachers, develop high levels of academic success, and then support and help teachers achieve those goals.

In brief, principals should develop an organizational structure and school culture that helps teachers do their jobs unfettered by bureaucratic rules and procedures (Hoy & Sweetland, 2000, 2001). The focus of the school should be collegiality, informality, professionalism, and volunteerism.

REFERENCES

Bandura, A. (1997). *Self-efficacy: The exercise of control.* New York: W. H. Freeman & Co.

Barnard, C. I. (1938). *The functions of the executive.* Cambridge, MA: Harvard University Press.

Bateman, T. S., & Organ, D. W. (1983). Job satisfaction and the good soldier: The relationship between affect and employee citizenship. *Academy of Management Journal, 26*, 587-595.

Blau, P., & Scott, R. (1962). *Formal organizations: A comparative approach.* San Francisco: Chandler.

Borman, W. C., & Motowidlo, S. J. (1993). Expanding the criterion domain to include elements of contextual performance. In N .Schmitt, & W.C. Borman, (Eds.), *Personality Selection* (pp. 71–98). San Francisco: Jossey-Bass.

Borman, W. C., White, L. A., & Dorsey, D. W. (1995). Effects of task performance and interpersonal factors on supervisors and peer ratings. *Journal of Applied Psychology, 80*, 168-177.

Bryk, A. S., & Schneider, B. (2002). *Trust in schools.* New York: Russell Sage Foundation.

Chen, X. P., Hui, C., & Sego, D. J. (1998). The role of organizational citizenship behavior in turnover: Conceptualization and preliminary tests of key hypotheses. *Journal of Applied Psychology, 83*, 922-931.

Coleman, J. S., Campbell, E. Q., Hobson, C. J., McPartland, J., Mood, A. M., Weinfeld, F. D., & York, R. L, (1966). *Equality of educational opportunity.* Washington, DC: National Center for Educational Statistics.

DiPaola, M. F., & Tschannen-Moran, M. (2001, September). Organizational citizenship behavior in schools and its relationship to school climate. *Journal of School Leadership, 11*, 424-447.

George, J. M., & Bettrnhausen, K. (1990). Understanding prosocial behavior, sales performance, and turnover: A group level analysis in a service context. *Journal of Applied Psychology, 75*, 698-709.

Goddard, R. D., Hoy, W. K., Woolfolk, A. (2000). Collective teacher efficacy: Its meaning, measure, and effect on student achievement. *American Educational Research Journal, 37*, 479-507.

Goddard, R. D., Sweetland, S., & Hoy, W. K. (2000). Academic emphasis of urban elementary schools and student achievement in reading and mathematics: A multilevel analysis. *Educational Administration Quarterly, 36*, 683-702.

Goddard, R. D., Tschannen-Moran, M., & Hoy, W. K. (2001). Teacher trust in students and parents: A multilevel examination of the distribution and effects of teacher trust in urban elementary schools. *Elementary School Journal, 102*, 3-17.

Graham, J. W. (1986). *Organizational citizenship informed by political theory.* Paper presented at the Academy of Management meeting, Chicago, Il.

Hoy, W. K., & Sweetland, S. R. (2000). Bureaucracies that work: Enabling not coercive. *Journal of School Leadership, 10*, 525-541.

Hoy, W. K., & Sweetland, S. R. (2001). Designing better schools: The meaning and nature of enabling school structure. *Educational Administration Quarterly, 37*, 296-321.

Karambayya, R. (1989). *Organizational citizenship behavior: Contextual predictors and organizational consequences.* Unpublished doctoral dissertation, Northwestern University, Evanston, Il.

Koberg, C., Boss, R., Bursten, R., & Goodman, E. (August, 1999). Getting more than you bargained for: Empirical evidence of organizational citizenship behavior from the health care industry? Paper presented at the annual meeting of the Academy of Management, Chicago.

MacKenzie, S. B., Podsakoff, P. M., & Fetter, R. (1991). Organizational citizenship behavior and objective productivity as determinants of managerial evaluations of salespersons' performance. *Organizational Behavior and Human Decision Processes, 50,* 123-150.

Moorman, R. H., & Blakely, G. L. (1995). Individualism-collectivism as an individual difference predictor of organizational citizenship behavior. *Journal of Organizational Behavior, 16*(2), 127-142.

Organ, D. W. (1988). *Organizational citizenship behavior.* Lexington, MA: D.C. Heath and Co.

Organ, D. W. (1990). The motivational basis of organizational citizenship behavior. *Research in Organizational Behavior, 12,* 43-72.

Organ, D. W. (1997). Organizational citizenship behavior: It's construct clean-up time. *Human Performance, 10,* 85-97.

Organ, D. W., & Ryan, K. (1995). A meta-analytic review of attitudinal and dispositional predictors of organizational citizenship behavior. *Personnel Psychology, 48,* 775-802.

Orr, J. M., Sackett, P. R., & Mercer, M. (1989). The role of prescribed and nonprescribed behaviors in estimating the dollar value of performance. *Journal of Applied Psychology, 74,* 34-40.

Podsakoff, P. M., & MacKenzie, S. B. (1994). Organizational citizenship behaviors and sales unit effectiveness. *Journal of Marketing Research, 31,* 351-363.

Skarlicki, D., & Latham G. (1995). Organizational citizenship behavior and performance in a university setting. *Canadian Journal of Administrative Sciences, 12,* 175-181.

Smith, C. A., Organ, D. W., & Near, J. P. (1983). Organizational citizenship behavior: It's nature and antecedents. *Journal of Applied Psychology, 68,* 653-663.

Werner, J. M. (1994). Dimensions that make a difference: Examining the impact of in-role and extra-role behaviors on supervisory ratings. *Journal of Applied Psychology, 79,* 98-107.

Williams, L. (1988). *Effective and noneffective components of job satisfaction and organizational commitment as determinants of organizational citizenship and in-role behaviors.* Unpublished doctoral dissertation, Indiana University, Bloomington, IN.

PART IX

ON ORGANIZATIONAL JUSTICE

CHAPTER 13

ORGANIZATIONAL JUSTICE IN SCHOOLS

No Justice Without Trust

Wayne K. Hoy and C. John Tarter

The concept of organizational justice is defined, and, based on a review of the literature, ten principles of organizational justice are elaborated. Similarly, the elements of faculty trust are conceptualized and discussed. Then, a model of organizational justice and trust is proposed and tested using path analysis. The results underscore the symbiotic relations between trust and justice. The paper concludes with a few suggestions for future research and recommendations for practice.

There is little question that justice has become a touchstone in contemporary American society. Students of educational administration have seized on the notion of social justice as a topic for discussion, analysis, and reform. One only has to examine the program of the last two meetings of the American Educational Research Association (AERA) and the Univer-

Reprinted by permission from the *International Journal of Educational Management,* Vol. 18, pp. 250-259. Copyright © 2004. All rights reserved.

sity Council for Educational Administration (UCEA) to see its pervasiveness. Moral philosophers beginning with Aristotle and continuing with the work of Rawls (1971) have defined and examined justice from a number of vantage points (for a review, see Cohen & Greenberg, 1982). The focus of this analysis is not on the grand scheme of social justice in American society, but rather on the system of justice in schools that educational leaders are responsible for creating. We are concerned with whether teachers perceive that they are being treated fairly. Questions of justice and fairness are fundamental whenever resources are distributed, that is, "Is who gets what fair?"(Greenberg & Lind, 2000).

The topic of organizational justice is not new in the administrative literature (Beugre, 1998; Cobb et al., 1995; Cohen & Greenberg, 1982; Greenberg, 1990, 1996; Greenberg & Lind, 2000), but it is a neglected concept in educational administration. Our essential argument is that matters of justice and fairness in the school workplace should not be taken lightly. Anyone who doubts the validity of this statement simply needs to visit a school and to question teachers about how fairly they are treated on the job; then stand back and listen to the lively discussion that ensues. Explaining the special significance that the concept of justice has taken in organizations, Greenberg (1996) coined the term organizational justice, which refers to individuals' perceptions of fairness in organizations—the topic of the present inquiry. We turn to an analysis of the concept in schools by first sketching ten "principles," then developing a measure and a model, and finally, testing the empirical nature of organizational justice in schools.

PRINCIPLES OF ORGANIZATIONAL JUSTICE

Rather than reviewing the literature on organizational justice in detail, we seek to summarize it with a series of principles that capture the essence of that literature. These principles highlight the well-established tenets of distributive justice—the fairness of the who gets what—and procedural justice—the fairness of the mechanisms of distribution (Greenberg, 1996). The principles discussed below come from two sources: Greenberg and Lind (2000) and Leventhal et al. (1980).

The Equity Principle: What Individuals Receive From the Organization Should be Proportional to Their Contributions

The rewards that teachers get for their contributions to the school should reflect balance; teachers should not feel that their contributions are undervalued or unrewarded. Although the equity principle is easy to state, it is not as readily applicable as one might suspect. In general, teachers expect that compensation, recognition, and the trappings of status will be distributed commensurate with their work, skill, and responsibility. Justice is a broad principle of which equity is an element. Too much emphasis on a few individual successes can breed jealousy and invidious comparisons. Equity requires an evenhanded fairness that balances equity and equality.

The Perception Principle: Individual Perception of Fairness Contributes to the General Sense Of Justice

Justice is both a public event and an individual judgment. Teacher perception of fairness is a key to satisfaction. Objective judgment is not the issue. What is critical is that teachers perceive that their principal is "following the rules" fairly, that is, following the procedures that everyone has tacitly accepted. For example, many districts require teachers to have lunch duty, a task most would rather pass on; however, as long as the teachers see assignments as fair, they will accept them with little criticism. It is important that the principal let everyone know by word and deed that fair procedures were followed. In the final analysis, public perception of justice becomes justice; "justice is in the eye of the beholder" (Greenberg, 1990).

The Voice Principle: Participation in Decision Making Enhances Fairness

Participation is especially important when teachers have a personal stake in the outcome because such decisions affect them. Principals should involve teachers in decision making when they have a personal stake in the outcome and when they have the expertise to contribute to the decisions (Hoy & Tarter, 2003). The issue of voice in decision making, however, becomes more problematic when there is a personal stake but no knowledge or when the principal does not trust teachers.

Principals cannot be invisible. They need to cultivate both informal and formal mechanisms to elicit teacher voice. A cup of coffee with teachers in the faculty lounge or simply "walking around" provides opportunities for informal voice. Formal voice occurs at faculty meetings, department meetings, in written communication, and in an authentic "open door" policy. For example, a principal at school every Saturday morning from 9.00 to 12.00 offers formal or informal opportunity for any faculty member to call or just drop by (Hoy, 2003).

The Interpersonal Justice Principle: Providing Sensitive, Dignified, and Respectful Treatment Promotes the Judgment of Fairness

No one likes bad news, but if given respectfully and with sufficient information, it conveys a sense of fair treatment. One of the most difficult things a principal must do is to communicate negative information to teachers, whether it is about teaching performance or an unpopular assignment. Timing, background, and delivery of such information are crucial; principals must strive to be open, sensitive, and authentic in their treatment of teachers. Buffering teachers from embarrassment and treating them as professionals with respect and dignity are paramount. Sound interpersonal skills and collegial interactions are likely to create a sense of trust in the principal by teachers; consequently, trust in turn should promote a strong sense of organizational justice. These last two propositions will be examined more closely in the empirical phase of this study.

The Consistency Principle: Consistent Leadership Behavior is a Necessary Condition for Subordinate Perception of Fairness

Consistency in behavior is not sufficient for the generation of a sense of fairness. Being consistently wrong, arbitrary, or political will not instill confidence, trust, or the acceptance of administrative impartiality. Consistent behavior is not necessarily identical behavior in all situations, but rather it is action that consistently fits the situation. Thus, in one situation the behavior may call for direct action whereas another situation may require a soft touch or a more democratic approach. Effective leadership is matching appropriate leader behavior with the characteristics of the situation (Yukl, 1998). Authenticity and procedural justice should guide consistency. Application of rules, regulations, and policies must be fair, visible, and consistent, yet flexible enough to take into account individual needs and extraordinary circumstances. Teachers should have a good idea of how the principal will react in a variety of situations and believe that his or her judgments and behavior will be both predicable and just. Leaders who "lose their cool" in difficult situations or hide behind their formal position, pass the buck, or manipulate teachers will not command trust, loyalty, or respect (Hoy &

Miskel, 2001; Hoffman et al., 1994). To paraphrase Thomas Jefferson, nothing gives a leader so much advantage over another as to remain cool, unruffled, and fair under all circumstances.

The Egalitarian Principle: Decision Making Should be Free of Self-interest and Shaped by the Collective Mission of the Organization

No one's interests take precedence over the needs of the collective. Treating everyone equally is not equal. Individuals have different needs and talents; thus, rigidly treating everyone the same is not equal. A balanced treatment, dependent on needs, should be a hallmark of egalitarian decision making. Self-interest is subordinated to the good of the whole.

The mission of the organization takes precedence over individual benefits, which are thought to ow out of the general success of the organization. For example, the practice of assigning beginning teachers to the more difficult classes seems to violate the egalitarian principle. Such practices are not in the best interest of the school or teachers. Rather, they are in the best interests of a few with power. The guiding mission of public schools is to provide a thorough and efficient education for all students, not to benefit the few and compromise the quality of instruction. Self-interest and internal politics are corrosive elements that erode egalitarianism.

The Correction Principle: Faulty or Poor Decisions Should be Corrected

Correction depends on feedback and willingness to reverse a bad decision. Some administrators believe that to admit a mistake is to somehow undermine their authority. To the contrary, a willingness to review a poor decision and correct it in all likelihood develops in teachers a trust in the fairness of the principal. The correction principle underscores the need for feedback and accurate information. For example, when teachers disagree with an evaluation, there should be provisions for challenge. New evidence should guide the principal's reappraisal in a fair and balanced way. Two-way communication is critical in any attempt to correct the record.

Flexibility in the structure of the school should explicitly promote feedback and reevaluation of important decisions. Moreover, the principal must have the personal security and confidence to retreat from a poor decision and embrace the possibility of error. A "humble decision making" strategy (Etzioni, 1989) uniting rationality with flexibilty emphasizes a series of techniques to deal with error, complexity, and uncertainty; tentative and reversible decisions avoid overcommitment to a course of action based on partial or inaccurate information (Hoy & Miskel, 2001). It behoves all administrators to recognize that virtually all complex decisions are made with incomplete data.

The Accuracy Principle: Decisions Should be Based on Accurate Information

Correction is inextricably tied to accuracy. The accuracy principle promotes a sense of justice by demonstrating that decisions are based on sound evidence. Research has shown that fairness of performance evaluations is enhanced by procedures such as diaries that insure the accuracy of performance judgment. Rumor and innuendo are poor substitutes for accurate information. Principals who base their judgments on systematic evidence rather than stories or fragmentary hearsay are likely to reinforce the belief that the principal is searching for the truth and is open to new information. Accuracy promotes fairness in the same way that correction insures that the organization can respond justly in the light of new information.

The Representative Principle: Decisions Must Represent the Interests of Concerned Parties

Organizational decisions affect many constituencies. Decision making that elicits the opinions of those affected fulfills the representative principle. For example, changing curriculum in the school affects what teachers teach. This is a case where teachers should be represented in the decision-making process because they not only have a personal stake in the outcome but they have also the knowledge to contribute to a good decision. Indeed, it is imperative that teachers have a strong role in such decisions especially if they are guided by the egalitarian principle that makes them willing to subordinate their self-interest to the good of the school. Representation is achieved, as teachers believe their ideas are being represented and have influence on outcomes.

The Ethical Principle: Follow Prevailing Moral and Ethical Standards

Justice is preeminently an ethical standard. Honesty, integrity, authenticity, sincerity, equality, impartiality, trustworthiness, and honor are contemporary ethical and moral standards that should guide behavior in decision making in school organizations. Some might argue about the need to include other standards, but few would disagree with the proposed ethical standards. School administrators will not go far afield in creating a just school climate if they have the courage to adhere to these ethical standards. A commitment to the other principles of organizational justice is a commitment to an ethical principle of fairness. Indeed, one standard for training prospective educational leaders underscores administrative action characterized by integrity, fairness, and ethical behavior (available at: www.ccsso.org/ standrds.html).

In summary, a sense of justice in the school workplace is dependent on leader behavior that is consistent with these ten principles. Leader behavior that is equitable, sensitive, respectful, consistent, free of self-interest, honest, and ethical is likely to create a perception of fair and balanced treatment. Moreover, the principles of voice, egalitarianism, and representativness are crucial in any attempt to empower teachers. Teachers want to participate in decisions that affect them (voice), but they must be willing to put the interests of the school ahead of their own (egalitarianism) and yet feel that their views are being authentically represented in the process of deciding (representativness). These three principles work together to promote a sense of fairness among teachers. Finally, leaders must have the good sense and confidence to reverse and correct poor decisions as they get feedback and more accurate information.

Faculty Trust: the Keystone to Organizational Justice

Trust is a little like air—we all pay little attention to it until it is not there. Yet, if schools are to prosper and succeed, trust is essential. Trust, like credibility, is a perishable commodity within any organization; it must be continually nurtured and renewed if it is to survive and grow (Schulman, 1993). Too often, however, trust is reduced to a slogan. Principals admonish teachers, "just trust me," and teachers exhort parents to trust them because they "know what is best for their children." Trust can be an empty slogan or a fundamental aspect of a school's culture. We plan to demonstrate in this inquiry that trust is fundamental to organizational justice in schools. We focus on two important aspects of organizational trust—faculty trust in the principal and faculty trust in colleagues, but first we must develop the conceptual underpinnings of trust in schools.

Most people have an intuitive sense of what is meant when we say that we trust someone, yet trust is complex with many layers. Despite its complexity, there are reoccurring themes that emerge from a review of the

philosophic, economic, organizational, individual, and empirical literature on trust.

Vulnerability is a general element that surfaces in most discussions of
trust (Tschannen-Moran & Hoy, 2000; Hoy & Tschannen-Moran, 1999).
The comfort a person or group feels in the midst of vulnerability speaks
to the degree of trust; in fact, there is little need for trust without a sense
of vulnerability. Comfort is confidence that another party is concerned
with protecting the well-being of the trusting party and that the other
party will be reliable and competent in fulfilling one's expectations
(Mishra, 1996). For example, when it comes to schooling, parents often
feel vulnerable to teachers because teachers have the power to make life
difficult for their children. Conversely, teachers feel vulnerable to parents
because they have the power to make life difficult for teachers. Thus, it
should not be surprising to learn that trust is critical in student-teacher-
parent interactions concerned with student learning (Bryke & Schneider,
2002; Goddard et al., 2001; Hoy, 2002). Honesty, openness, benevolence,
competency, and reliability are other aspects of the trust relationship. Our
earlier analyses of trust in organizations led to the following multifaceted
definition of trust:

> Trust is one party's willingness to be vulnerable to another party based on
> the confidence that the latter party is benevolent, reliable, competent, hon-
> est, and open (Hoy, 2002; Hoy & Tschannen-Moran, 1999; Tschannen-
> Moran & Hoy, 1998).

We turn to a brief examination of each of these facets of trust.

Vulnerability

A necessary condition for trust is interdependence. Trust is important
when the interests of one party cannot be achieved without reliance on
another. Without interdependence there is no need for trust (Rousseau et
al., 1998). Parents depend on teachers to act in the best interests of their
children and teachers depend on the good will and cooperation of students
and parents in the teaching and learning process. Interdependence produces vulnerability in the relationship, and vulnerability leads to reliance
and risk. Risk moderates the trust relationship—trust is supported and
buttressed when expected behaviors occur but is diminished and undermined when they do not. Trust ultimately rests with the degree of confidence one holds in the face of vulnerability and risk (Rousseau et al., 1998).

Schools ask for the trust of parents in assuming the responsibility in
protecting their children and in shaping their thinking, learning, and

behavior. Schools also ask their communities to risk vulnerability by requesting millions of dollars of resources in the form of tax dollars for buildings, supplies, curriculum materials, and the employment of professional staff. Administrators and teachers in turn invest their talents and professional lives in the hope of earning the confidence, good will, and trust of the community (Tschannen-Moran & Hoy, 2002).

Benevolence

Perhaps the most commonly recognized facet of trust is a sense of benevolence, that is, *confidence that one's well being or something one cares about will be not harmed by the trusted party* (Cummings & Bromily, 1996; Hosmer, 1995; Mishra, 1996). Trust is the assurance that another party will not exploit one's vulnerability and that one can rely on the good will of the other to act in one's best interest. In an ongoing relationship, there will be a mutual attitude of good will even though future actions may not be specified (Putnam, 1993). Benevolence is the "accepted vulnerability to another's possible but not expected ill will" (Baier, 1986, p. 236). Parents who trust educators to care for their children are confident that teachers will be consistently fair, compassionate, and benevolent. Likewise, teachers who trust students and parents believe that neither will undermine the teaching-learning process nor do them harm.

Reliability

Trust also has to do with predictability, that is, consistency in knowing what to expect from others (Butler & Cantrell, 1984; Hosmer, 1995). However, predictability alone is unsatisfying as an aspect of trust. One can expect a person to be invariably late, consistently malicious, self-serving, or dishonest. Clearly, when our well-being is diminished in a predictable way, trust is undermined. Reliability is more than dependability; in fact, it combines a sense of dependability and predictability with benevolence. In brief, *reliability is confident that others will consistently act in ways that are beneficial to the trustee.*

Competence

Good intentions often are not enough to produce trust. When a person is dependent on another and expertise and skill are required, individuals who mean well are not always trusted (Baier, 1986; Butler & Cantrell,

1984; Mishra, 1996). Many school tasks require competence. When a teacher's or team's project depends on the contribution of others, trust will depend on an "assured confidence" that deadlines will be met, the task will be accomplished, and the work will be of adequate quality to meet goals.

Principals and teachers depend on one another to accomplish teaching and learning goals. Students rely on the competence and skill of their teachers. A student may feel that her teacher wants to help her learn, but if the teacher lacks knowledge or skill, then student trust will likely wane. Competence is the ability to perform as expected and consistent with standards appropriate to task, and is a critical ingredient of trust. If the public loses confidence in the competence of an administrator or a teacher, then trust in the school is eroded, regardless of good intentions and benevolence of those involved. Just as people are unwilling to trust a surgeon with a poor performance record so, too, are they reluctant to trust administrators and teachers whose competence is questionable.

Honesty

Not surprisingly honesty is another critical facet of trust (Baier, 1986; Cummings and Bromily, 1996); in fact, Rotter (1967, p. 651) defined trust as "the expectancy that the word, promise, verbal or written statement of another individual or group can be relied upon." *Honesty is the truthfulness, integrity, and authenticity of a person or group.* A consistency between words and actions is the heart of truthfulness and integrity. Moreover, accepting responsibility for one's actions and not distorting the truth in order to shift blame is the essence of authenticity (Tschannen-Moran & Hoy, 1998). Honesty is a necessary, but not sufficient condition for trust.

Openness

Openness is the *extent to which relevant information is shared.* In the process of being open, people make themselves vulnerable by sharing personal or organizational information. Openness is a giving of oneself (Butler & Cantrell, 1984; Mishra, 1996); it signals reciprocal trust and a confidence that the shared information will not be exploited by either party. Furthermore, individuals who are guarded in their interactions often provoke suspicion because people wonder what they are hiding and why. Openness breeds trust, just as trust creates openness. People who are unwilling to extend trust through openness end up living in isolated prisons of their own making (Kramer et al., 1996). Principals in closed school climates engender distrust by unsuccessful attempts to spin the truth to make their view of reality the accepted standard (Sweetland & Hoy, 2001). In contrast, productive organizations have cultures of openness in which mistakes are freely admitted and addressed rather than hidden and ignored (Weick & Sutcliffe, 2001).

Trust: A Complex and Integrated Whole

In sum, trust is a multifaceted phenomenon with at least six faces. Although all of these faces of trust are significant, their relative importance is dependent on the situation, the nature of the interdependence, and the vulnerability of the relationship. For example, one is differentially vulnerable to a stranger, a friend, an investment broker, or a surgeon. Notwithstanding, in schools all these facets of trust are important; in fact, they combine into an integrated whole. Vulnerability, benevolence, reliability, competence, honesty, and openness form a single, unitary and coherent concept of trust in schools whether the referent is trust in teachers, principal, students, or parents (Hoy & Tschannen-Moran, 1999). Hence, administrators who neglect any of these facets of trust are jeopardizing the entire trust relationship.

ORGANIZATIONAL JUSTICE AND FACULTY TRUST: AN EXPLANATORY MODEL

Thus far, our analysis has been on justice and trust—two constructs that we argue are pivotal properties of schools. We now turn to the development of a model that links them and suggests their antecedents. The relationship between organizational justice and faculty trust is a reciprocal one: we postulate that faculty trust promotes organizational justice, but that justice in return reinforces trust. The notion of organizational justice that we are attempting to explain in this analysis is circumscribed; that is, it pertains to the just and fair treatment of the faculty. Two sets of questions are addressed:

1. What school characteristics are necessary for organizational justice?
2. What are the antecedents that promote these school characteristics?

Two referents of faculty trust are of special significance to our theoretical rationale. First, faculty trust in colleagues is central to and, perhaps, a necessary condition for organizational justice. Trust is an important component of interpersonal relationships; in fact, the very survival of a social group may depend on the members' willingness to exercise trust with one another (Rotter, 1967). When colleagues trust one another, it enhances the openness and authenticity of interpersonal relations (Hoffman et al., 1994), and provides a climate where members will likely treat one another with respect, honesty, and altruism—all aspects of a just and caring workplace. The ability to establish a sense of self-worth, to enjoy healthy social relations, and to have the respect of colleagues is anchored in trust (Hodson, 2001). Thus, it should come as no surprise that we predict that faculty trust in colleagues promotes a fair and just workplace; and in turn, that justice in the school workplace reinforces an atmosphere of trust among teachers.

Second, faculty trust in the principal also seems central to the emergence of a sense of justice in the school workplace. Just as teachers trusting one another is important in generating fairness in the workplace, so too is faculty trust in the principal; in fact, the rationale for predicting a close connection between faculty trust in the principal and organizational justice is similar. When teachers trust the principal, it promotes open interactions between teachers and the principal (Hoffman et al., 1994) and signals that the principal is dependable, honest, competent, and concerned about teachers (Geist & Hoy, 2003). When principals earn the trust of the faculty, they bolster a sense of human dignity in the workplace (Hodson, 2001). We hasten to add that the relationship is reciprocal, that is, faculty trust enhances school justice, but justice promotes trust. Our argument thus far is that faculty trust in colleagues and faculty trust in the principal are independent sources of organizational justice in schools, and that such justice reinforces both aspects of faculty trust.

But what are the antecedents of each aspect of faculty trust? Earlier research has shown that faculty trust in colleagues is best predicted by characteristics of the group, whereas faculty trust in the principal is best predicted by the leadership behavior of the principal (Geist & Hoy, 2003; Smith et al., 2001). Thus, we predict that professional faculty behavior marked by competence, commitment to students, autonomous judgment, and respect for colleagues (Smith et al., 2001) is positively related to trust in colleagues. Similarly, principals generate trust by behaving in ways that foster both the achievement of school goals and social needs teachers. Such principal behavior has been termed collegial leadership (Geist & Hoy, 2003; Smith et al., 2001) and is characterized by warm, supportive expressive behavior as well as the instrumental behavior of setting clear teacher expectations and standards of performance. These hypothesized relationships are summarized in the model depicted in Figure 13.1.

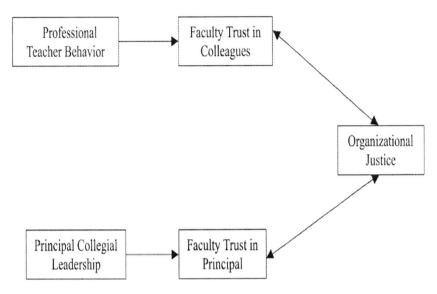

Figure 13.1.   Proposed trust-justice model.

The model predicts that professional teacher behavior is directly related to faculty trust in colleagues, which in turn promotes organizational justice in the workplace and reinforces trust. The collegial leadership of the principal generates faculty trust in the principal, which independently enhances organizational justice in the school and reinforces trust. Thus, both teacher and principal behavior develop a system of organizational justice, and trust is pivotal in the process.

METHOD

Having developed a model of organizational justice, the next step was to develop a research plan to test the model. We turn to the sample, instruments, and data collection.

Sample

Data from 75 middle schools in the state of Ohio were collected to test the model. The schools were distributed in 11 counties. Although the sample selected was not a random one, care was taken to insure participation of urban, suburban, and rural schools. Currently, the distribution of middle schools in Ohio is 39 percent rural, 34 percent urban, and 27 percent suburban. Correspondingly, the study's schools are distributed across 19 percent rural, 41 percent urban, and 40 percent suburban settings. Of the 612 school districts in the state, 43 participated in the study. Staff completed a total of approximately 2,600 usable surveys. The sample was also similar to the population of middle schools in Ohio in terms of student enrollment, average teacher salary, average teacher experience, and the size of the faculty. In brief, the sample of schools was fairly typical of middle schools in Ohio.

Data Collection

Data were collected from the middle schools at regularly scheduled faculty meetings. A member of the research team explained the general purpose of the study, assured the confidentiality of all responses, and asked teachers to complete the questionnaires. Because this project was part of a larger study of organizational properties and because the unit of analysis was the school, two random groups of teachers responded to different surveys. One set of teachers responded to a climate index that included measures of collegial leadership of the principal and professional teacher behavior, and the second random group of teachers described other school properties, including trust and justice. The unit analysis was the school; hence, all data were aggregated to the school level. No attempt was made to gather data from faculty who were not present at the meeting, but virtually all teachers returned usable questionnaires.

Measures

Five organizational behaviors were measured in this research—organizational justice, faculty trust in the principal, faculty trust in colleagues, collegial leadership of the principal, and professional teacher behavior.

Organizational Justice Index (OJI)

An organizational justice index was created by summing responses to items based on organizational justice principles. Teachers were asked to describe the behavior of teachers and administrators along a seven-point Likert scale from strongly disagree to strongly agree; the higher the score, the greater the extent of behavior in the school. Examples of items included the following: "Teachers are involved in decisions that affect them (voice principle)," "The principal adheres to high ethical standards (ethical principle)," "The principal treats everyone with respect and dignity (interpersonal justice principle)," and "educators in this school follow courses of action that are generally free of self-interest (egalitarian principle)."

Factor analysis of the ten items of the index indicated a strong single factor of organizational justice with all the items loading strongly on that factor. All the items had factor loadings greater than 0.77 and explained 78 percent of the variance. The results of the analyses supported the construct validity of organizational justice. Moreover, the alpha coefficient of reliability was 0.97.

Faculty Trust in the Principal and Trust in Colleagues

The two referents of organizational trust were measured with the Omnibus t-Scale, a trust scale developed by Hoy and Tschannen-Moran (1999).

A ten Likert-item subtest of the t-Scale that tapped the facets of trust discussed earlier measured faculty trust in the principal. Sample items for trust in the principal include: "Teachers in this school trust the principal," "The principal doesn't really tell teachers what is going on (score reversed)," "The principal in this school is competent in doing his or her job." The alpha reliability coefficient for the subtest with the current sample was 0.98.

Faculty trust in colleagues was similarly measured with a separate eight Likert-item subtest of the Omnibus T-Scale. Examples of the items included: "Teachers in this school trust each other," "Teachers in this school are open with each other," Teachers in this school do their jobs well," and "Teachers in this school are suspicious of each other (score reversed)." The alpha reliability coefficient for the subtest with the current sample was 0.94. Further reliability evidence as well as predictive and construct validity for both measures of faculty trust are provided by Hoy and Tschannen-Moran (1999, 2003).

Collegial Leadership and Professional Teacher Behavior

Teacher and principal behaviors were measured with subtests from the organizational climate index (Hoy, Smith, & Sweetland, 2002).

Collegial leader behavior is measured by a seven-item subtest, which gauges the extent to which the principal helps teachers meet their needs and treats them as professional colleagues while simultaneously setting clear goals and standards of performance. Examples of the Likert items include: "The principal treats all faculty members as his or her equal," "The principal is willing to make changes," "The principal lets faculty know what is expected of them," and "The principal is friendly and approachable." The alpha coefficient of reliability for the current sample is 0.96.

Teacher professional behavior was also measured by a subtest of the OCI, a seven-item subtest that determines which faculty engages in professional behavior such as respect for colleague competence, commitment to students, autonomous decision making, and mutual cooperation and support of colleagues. Examples of items include, "Teachers respect the professional competence of their colleagues", "Teachers help and support each other", and "Teachers in this school exercise professional judgment". Predictive and construct validity is provided in a factor analytic study by Hoy et al. (2002) for both OCI subtests. Reliability is typically strong; in the current study the alpha coefficient of reliability was 0.98.

AN EMPIRICAL TEST OF THE TRUST-JUSTICE MODEL

The trust-justice model was tested using multiple regression techniques and path analysis. As predicted, both aspects of trust – faculty trust in the principal (beta = 0.72, p, 0.01) and faculty trust in colleagues (beta = 0.31, p, 0.01) had significant independent effects on organizational justice; that is, faculty trust in the principal was significantly related to organizational justice controlling for trust in colleagues, and faculty trust in colleagues was significantly related to organizational trust controlling for trust in the principal. Moreover, as expected, professional teacher behavior was significantly related to trust in colleagues (beta = 0.77, $p < 0.01$) controlling for collegial leadership, and collegial leader behavior was significantly related to trust in the principal (beta = 0.66, $p < 0.01$) controlling for professional teacher behavior. The results of the path analysis are summarized in Figure 13.2. The adjusted R^2 for organizational justice is 0.90, $p < 0.01$, that is, faculty trust in colleagues and trust in the principal explains 90 percent of the organizational justice variance. The path model was supported by the empirical data.

DISCUSSION AND CONCLUSIONS

Even though we predicted the strong relationship between trust and justice, we were surprised to discover its strength. The data demonstrate that trust and justice are inextricably linked; you cannot have one without the other. Although we used faculty trust in colleagues and faculty trust in the principal to predict organizational justice, the relationship clearly can be seen as going the other way, that is, as justice producing trust. On the one hand, if teachers trust the principal, then they are likely to perceive the principal as acting in a fair and just way (believing is seeing); on the other hand, if the teachers perceive their principal as acting ethically and fairly,

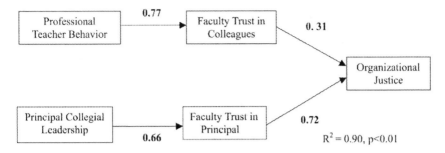

Note: All the regression coefficients are significant.

Figure 13.2. A test of the trust-justice model: a path analysis.

then they are more likely to trust him or her. The conceptual facets of trust—benevolence, reliability, competence, honesty, and openness—are certainly consistent with the underlying conceptual foundations of organizational justice—equity, equality, voice, fairness, dignity, and consistency. In fact, the two sets of conceptual underpinnings are so consistent that they vary together in harmony; they are different but they are intertwined and likely not separable.

The strong influence of principal trust on organizational justice was not surprising. Clearly, the principal is the single most important person in developing a sense of organizational justice in school. The principal of the school is much more important than the faculty in creating a just and fair school at least with respect to professional interactions; however, trust of teachers in their colleagues is not an inconsequential factor. Faculty trust in colleagues makes a substantial independent effect on the school's justice system. Even so, it is within the principal's power to forge a climate of justice by demonstrating in word and deed a commitment to the ten principles of justice articulated earlier. The leader leads by example, and there may be no more important role than fair and just interactions with teachers, students, and parents, that is, to be a moral leader.

Our results also suggest that the principal can lead in a way that directly influences faculty trust in the principal and indirectly affects a sense of organizational justice through such trust. Collegial principal leadership captures three critical concerns of leadership – concern for people, concern for the task, and concern for change. The principal whose behavior is expressive, instrumental, and change-oriented, that is, who leads with friendly, supportive behavior, sets clear teacher expectations and standards of performance, and is open to change, is likely to be successful (Yukl, 1998). Moreover, such collegial principal behavior cultivates a culture of trust and justice.

The faculty clearly has an independent role to play in generating a culture of trust and justice in the school workplace. The principal gets the starring role, but the faculty gets a strong supporting role. The faculty through its professional behavior—treating one another as competent professionals, making autonomous judgments, showing a commitment to students, and engaging in cooperation and support—learn to rely and trust one another, which also indirectly influences a sense of organizational justice in the school.

In sum, the collegial leadership of the principal is critical in fostering a trusting relationship with the faculty and such trust is pivotal in nurturing a sense of organizational justice. Professional teacher relationships are significant in facilitating trust among teachers, which in turn enhances a sense of fairness in the school. Although the trust-justice relationship for faculty was not as strong as for the principal, faculty trust in colleagues does make a significant independent contribution in the explanation of organizational justice. Perhaps the most surprising findings of the study was the strength of the trust-justice relationship; both aspects of trust combine to explain 90 percent of the variance in organizational justice. Faculty trust and organizational justice are inextricably related and perhaps inseparable, which leads to our final caveat: the relationship between trust and justice is clearly reciprocal with each influencing and reinforcing the other.

IMPLICATIONS

Although this is one of the few studies to examine organizational justice in the school workplace, there are a number of practical and research implications that can be sketched. First, the concept of organizational justice as it was defined and measured in this research seems useful, especially the ten principles of organizational justice that we articulated at the beginning of this inquiry. Those ten principles serve as a framework for guiding the administrative behavior of principals. Principals who are guided by them will not go far afield in generating a sense of fairness and justice among their teachers as well as cultivating a culture of trust.

The research on faculty trust continues to grow. This study focused on only two aspects of faculty trust—in colleagues and the principal. If principals are to command faculty trust, they must demonstrate behavior that is collegial, enabling (Geist & Hoy, 2003), and supportive (Hoy et al., 2002). The generation of faculty trust in colleagues, however, is more closely related to the interactions among teachers themselves and only indirectly related to the principal's behavior (Geist & Hoy, 2003; Smith et al., 2001). Principals who can create a climate with high morale and strong teacher professionalism can set the stage for the growth trust among teachers. There is little evidence that principals can directly facilitate faculty trust in colleagues.

This study did not deal with the generation of faculty trust in parents and students because attention was on fair and just relations between the principal and teachers and among teachers themselves. The concept of organizational justice should be expanded to relationships between teachers and students. Here we predict that the teachers will have the starring role and the principal the supporting one and that faculty trust in students will be inextricably related to organizational justice for students. The moral leadership of teachers is no less important than the moral leadership of the principal.

We conclude with a few suggestions for principals based on our analysis of organizational justice, trust, and leader behavior:

- be equitable, sensitive, respectful, unbiased, honest, and ethical in your relationships with teachers and parents;
- involve teachers in decisions that affect them, especially when they are willing to put the interests of the school ahead of their own and they have the knowledge to improve the quality of the decision;
- have the good sense and confidence to reverse and correct poor decisions as feedback informs the decision;
- show concern for the needs of teachers;
- show concern for the task at hand;
- show concern for the need to change;
- help teachers cultivate a sense of trust among
- themselves by trusting them to make autonomous decisions in the best interests of their students; and
- remember that justice and trust are inseparable; you cannot have one without the other.

REFERENCES

Baier, A. C. (1986). Trust and antitrust. *Ethics, 96,* 231-60.

Beugre, C. C. (1998), *Managing fairness in organizations.* Westport, CT: Quorum.

Bryke, A. S., & Schneider, B. (2002). *Trust in schools: A core resource for improvement.* New York: The Russell Sage Foundation.

Butler, J. K., & Cantrell, R. S. (1984). A behavioral decision theory approach to modeling dyadic trust in superiors and subordinates. *Psychological Reports, 55*, 81-105.

Cobb, A. T., Wooten, K. C., & Folger, R. (1995). Justice in the making: Toward understanding the theory and practice of justice in organization change and development. In W. A. Pasmore & R. W. Woodman (Eds.), *Research in organizational change and development* (Vol. 8, pp. 243-95.). Greenwich, CT: JAI Press.

Cohen, R. L., & Greenberg, J. (1982). The justice concept in social psychology. In J. Greenberg & R. L. Cohen (Eds.), *Equity and justice in social behavior* (pp. 1-41). New York: Academic Press.

Cummings, L. L., & Bromily, P. (1996). The Organizational Trust Inventory (OTI): Development and validation. In R. Kramer & T. Tyler (Eds.), *Trust in Organizations*.Thousand Oaks, CA: Sage.

Etzioni, A. (1989). Humble decision making. *Harvard Business Review, 67*, 122-126.

Geist, J., & Hoy, W. K. (2003). *Cultivating a culture of trust: Enabling school structure, teacher professionalism, and academic press.* Unpublished working paper, Ohio State University, Columbus, OH.

Goddard, R. D., Tschannen-Moran, M., & Hoy, W. K. (2001). Teacher trust in students and parents: A multilevel examination of the distribution and effects of teacher trust in urban elementary schools. *Elementary School Journal, 102*, 3-17.

Greenberg, J. (1990). Looking fair versus being fair: management impressions of organizational justice. In B. M. Staw & L. L. Cummings (Eds.), *Research in organizational behavior and development* (Vol. 12, pp. 111-157). Greenwich, CT: JAI Press.

Greenberg, J. (1996). *The quest for justice on the job.* Thousand Oaks, CA: Sage.

Greenberg, J., & Lind, E. A. (2000). The pursuit of organizational justice: from conceptualization to implication to application. In C. L. Cooper & E. W. Locke (Eds.), *Industrial and organizational psychology.* Malden, MA: Blackwell Press.

Hodson, R. (2001). *Dignity at work.* Cambridge, MA: Cambridge University Press.

Hoffman, J. D., Sabo, D., Bliss, J., & Hoy, W. K. (1994). Building a culture of trust. *Journal of School Leadership, 3*, 484-501.

Hosmer, L. T. (1995). Trust: The connecting link between organizational theory and philosophical ethics. *Academy of Management Review, 20*(2), 379-403.

Hoy, W. K. (2002). Faculty trust: A key to student achievement. *Journal of School Public Relations, 23*(2), 88-103.

Hoy, W. K. (2003). An analysis of enabling and mindful school structures: some theoretical, research, and practical considerations. *Journal of Educational Administration, 41*, 87-108.

Hoy, W. K., & Miskel, C. G. (2001). Educational administration: Theory, research, and practice (6th ed.). New York: McGraw-Hill.

Hoy, W. K., & Tarter, C. J. (2003). *Administrators solving the problems of practice: Concepts, cases, and consequences* (2nd ed.). Boston: Allyn and Bacon.

Hoy, W. K., & Tschannen-Moran, M. (1999). Five faces of trust: An empirical conrmation in urban elementary schools. *Journal of School Leadership, 9*, 184-208.

Hoy, W. K., Smith, P. A., & Sweetland, S. R. (2002). The development of the organizational climate index for high schools: Its measure and relationship to faculty trust. *The High School Journal, 86*(2), 38-49.

Kramer, R. M., Brewer, M. B., & Hanna, B. A. (1996). Collective trust and collective action: the decision to trust as a social decision. In R. Kramer & T. Tyler (Eds.), *Trust in organizations.* Thousand Oaks, CA: Sage.

Leventhal, G. S., Karuza, J., & Fry, W. R. (1980). Beyond fairness: A theory of allocation of preferences. In G. Mikula (Ed.), *Justice and social interaction.* New York: Springer-Verlag Press.

Mishra, A. K. (1996). Organizational responses to crisis: The centrality of trust. In R. Kramer & T. Tyler (Eds.), *Trust in organizations.* Thousand Oaks, CA: Sage.

Putnam, R D. (1993). The prosperous community: Social capital and public life. *The American Prospect, 13,* 35-42.

Rawls, J. (1971). *A theory of justice.* Cambridge, MA: Harvard University Press.

Rotter, J. B. (1967). A new scale for the measurement of interpersonal trust. *Journal of Personality, 35,* 651-65.

Rousseau, D., Sitkin, S. B., Burt, R., & Camerer, C. (1998). Not so different after all: A cross-discipline view of trust. *The Academy of Management Review, 23*(3), 393-404.

Schulman, P. R. (1993). The negotiated order of organizational reliability. *Administration and Society, 25,* 353-72.

Smith, P. A., Hoy, W. K., & Sweetland, S. R. (2001). Organizational health of high schools and dimensions of faculty trust. *Journal of School Leadership, 11,* 135-51.

Sweetland, S. R., & Hoy, W. K. (2001). Varnishing the truth: Principals and teachers spinning reality. *Journal of Educational Administration, 39,* 282-93.

Tschannen-Moran, M., & Hoy, W. K. (1998). Trust in schools: A conceptual analysis. *Journal of Educational Administration, 36,* 334-335.

Tschannen-Moran, M., & Hoy, W. K. (2000). A multidisciplinary analysis of the nature, meaning, and measurement of trust. *Review of Educational Research, 70,* 547-93.

Tschannen-Moran, M., & Hoy, W. K. (2002). Trust: A key to quality schools. Unpublished working paper, Ohio State University, Columbus, OH.

Tschannen-Moran, M., & Hoy, W. K. (2003). The conceptualization and measurement of faculty trust in schools: The Omnibus-T-Scale. In W. K. Hoy & C. G. Miskel (Eds.), *Studies in leading and organizing schools.* Greenwich, CT: Information Age Press.

Weick, K. E., & Sutcliffe, K. M. (2001). *Managing the unexpected.* San Francisco, CA: Jossey-Bass.

Yukl, G. A. (1998). *Leadership in organizations* (4th ed.). Englewood Cliffs, NJ: Prentice-Hall.

Wayne K. Hoy *is Fawcett Professor of Educational Administration at The Ohio State University, School of Policy and Educational Leadership, Columbus, Ohio, USA.*

C. John Tarter *is Professor of Educational Administration at St John's University, School of Education, Jamaica, New York, USA.*

PART X

ON ORGANIZATIONAL MINDFULNESS

CHAPTER 14

SCHOOL MINDFULNESS AND FACULTY TRUST

Necessary Conditions for Each Other?

Wayne K. Hoy, Charles Quincy Gage, III, and C. John Tarter

Background: *The paradox of relying on routines and standard practices, which protect institutional functioning from the vagaries of personality, often comes at the cost of thoughtful adaptability.*

Purpose: *The objectives are to conceptualize and apply the construct of mindfulness to schools and to explore trust as a school condition that fosters mindful actions.*

Setting: *A diverse sample of 75 middle schools was selected for study.*

Participants: *Twenty-six hundred teachers responded to survey instruments in 75 schools.*

Research Design: *An ex post facto test of a theoretical set of hypotheses was performed.*

Reprinted by permission from the *Educational Administration Quarterly*, Vol. 42, pp. 236-255. Copyright © 2006. All rights reserved.

Data Collection and Analysis: Data were collected by researchers in regular faculty meetings and assessed using correlational, regression, and factor analyses.

Findings: Faculty trust and school mindfulness seemed necessary conditions for each other.

Conclusions: Mindfulness is a concept every school administrator should understand and practice, and a culture of trust seems necessary to achieve both the ends of understanding and practice. Principals need to lead in mindful ways. By encouraging faculty to play with ideas, to create novelty in their classrooms, to feel safe to take reasonable risks, to experiment, and to be resilient, the principal can have profound effects on school mindfulness.

"Avert the danger not yet risen" is an old Vedic proverb with contemporary meaning for school administrators. It is an injunction to catch the early signs of trouble before small difficulties become major crises. Early signals of change are harbingers of opportunity or catastrophe. Mindful administrators seize the moment of opportunity, but inattentive ones, having missed the subtleties of change, find themselves unpleasantly surprised and trapped by the unexpected. Mindful management of the unexpected is heeding early warnings of trouble.

The paradox of relying on routines and standard practices, which protect institutional functioning from the vagaries of personality, often comes at the cost of thoughtful adaptability. People are so accustomed and so efficient at one way of behaving that they become seduced by the nominal success of their routines. When the routines don't work well, their typical response is to do more of the same. Once habits are formed, it is difficult to break set and respond in novel ways, especially if the routines have been successful. Mindful behavior of individuals and organizations is more than simply being alert; it is a habit of mind that scans for subtle changes that cause trouble. The notion of individual mindfulness has been developed by Langer (1989) in a series of thoughtful and careful research studies. Weick and Sutcliffe (2001) move the level of discourse from the individual to the organization. We draw extensively from both as we theoretically and empirically apply the notion of mindfulness to schools.

There is likely an organizational environment that cultivates mindful actions. We expect that rigid bureaucracies are not conducive to mindfulness; in fact, they may produce a mindless standardization (Hoy, 2003). To develop habits of mindfulness, individuals need situations where they are not afraid to make mistakes and feel free to experiment. A culture of trust should provide a setting in which people are not afraid of breaking new ground, taking risks, and making errors. The objective of this inquiry is twofold: (a) to conceptualize and apply the construct of mindfulness to schools and (b) to explore trust as a school condition that fosters mindful actions.

CONCEPTUAL FRAMEWORK

The central concepts of this investigation are mindfulness and trust. We begin with a theoretical discussion of each and then turn to a theoretical rationale that links the two. Finally, we propose hypotheses to test our theory.

Mindfulness: Individual and Organizational

First, we consider the developmental evolution from individual mindfulness, associated with Langer's (1989) work, through organizational mindfulness (Weick & Sutcliffe, 2001), to school mindfulness (Hoy, 2003; Hoy, Gage, & Tarter, 2004).

Individual Mindfulness

People use information more or less mindfully, much the same way as they act with differing degrees of reflection. Too often, individuals seize on standard classifications, use routine rules and procedures, and then proceed to become seduced by habits. On the other hand, it is overly simplistic to maintain that the use of rules and procedures can be equated to mindlessness. Blindly following rules and procedures is different from following reasonable rules and challenging unreasonable ones. There is in all of us an inclination toward a "habit of mind" that adopts sets of routine categories to order and simplify experience. Habit is a reason people find formal rules and regulations so appealing. Dogmas of all kinds justify our behavior because they provide us with identities, rules of action, and standard interpretations (Trungpa, 1973). Mindlessness relies on old categories, whereas mindfulness is the creation of new ones.

When teachers and administrators simply follow rules or comply with senseless orders, they are mindless; they turn mindful as they substitute their judgments for routine responses. Mindlessness grows out of routine and general comfort that things are being done "correctly," that is, according to standard procedures. The single-minded pursuit of outcomes typically promotes mindlessness unlike an emphasis on process. For example, focusing on the outcome of tests often obscures the process of teaching. Process defines steps to achieve goals and is guided by the general principle, "There are no failures, only ineffective solutions" (Langer, 1989, p. 34). A process approach is conditional; that is, facts are true in only some situations but not in others. Thoughtful inquiry searches for appropriate conditions and encourages playfulness with ideas.

Context controls our reactions and interpretations. When people confuse the context controlling the behavior of another with the context determining their own behavior, that is, assuming that motives of others are the same as their own (often not the case), they fall prey to what Langer (1989) calls "context confusion." The consequence is narrowness in perspective, which impedes understanding behavior. Contextual confusion reinforces action viewed from one perspective only and limits the use of multiple perspectives. In sum, the causes of mindlessness that influence daily behavior are repetition, narrow mindsets, preoccupation with ends rather than means, and context confusion.

Mindfulness is continuous scrutiny and refinement of expectations based on new experiences, appreciation of the subtleties of context, and identification of novel aspects of context that can improve foresight and functioning (Hoy, 2003; Langer, 1989). Mindfulness requires flexibility, vigilance, openness, and the ability to break set.

Just as mindlessness is rooted in rigid categories, mindfulness blossoms in the creation of new ones. Mindfulness requires openness to new information and different points of view. Events have multiple interpretations, and mindful individuals search for variation and subtlety in meaning; impulsive can be spontaneous, rigid can be consistent, and weak can be sensitive. Mindfulness is playful and nimble and avoids the traps of narrow contexts and the anesthetic of routine by trying to notice the new and different.

Overall, individual mindfulness is a habit of mind that continuously seeks disconfirming evidence to test assumptions. Mindful administrators know that "believing is seeing," and they are on guard—wary of the obvious and searching for "the danger not yet arisen." They are suspicious of facile explanation as well as their own success.

Organizational Mindfulness

Just as individuals vary in their mindfulness, so too do organizations; that is, mindfulness can be a collective property as well as an individual one. But a mindful organization is more than the sum of mindful individuals (Hoy, 2003).

Weick and Sutcliffe (2001) first sketched the characteristics of mindful organizations by analyzing high reliability organizations, ones that consistently avoided major mistakes and failure. Five processes promote mindfulness in organizations: preoccupation with failure, reluctance to simplify, sensitivity to operations, commitment to resilience, and deference to expertise (Weick & Sutcliffe, 2001).

Preoccupation with failure is counterintuitive. At first blush, it suggests a dysfunctional pessimism, but first impressions are often wrong. The key to this preoccupation is to identify small mistakes before they become major problems. Mindful organizations continuously scan for problems, large and small, but mostly small. Because success breeds complacency and sometimes arrogance, preoccupation with failure prevents being lulled into a false sense of organizational confidence. For example, when 90% of the students meet the state achievement standards, mindful schools focus on the 10% who failed rather than indulge in celebration.

Reluctance to simplify is another aspect of mindful organizations that promotes an understanding of the subtleties of the situation. Schools need to simplify less and see more. Knowing that life in schools is complex, teachers and administrators need to adopt multiple perspectives to understand the shadings that are hidden below the surface of the obvious. Reconciliation of different interpretations runs the risk of losing the nuances of diversity and complexity. The difference in perceptions between students and teachers toward fairness is best understood by considering rival explanations, each of which should be tested.

Sensitivity to operations means staying close to the core function of the organization, which in the case of schools is the teaching-learning process. Mindful organizations continuously search for problems in day-to-day operations. Surprises are not unexpected; mindful organizations anticipate them. Sensitivity to operations nurtures sensitivity to interpersonal relations. The continuous scan for problems requires a close relationship between teachers and administrators; teachers who refuse to act freely enact a system that knows less than it needs to know to be effective (Hoy, 2003). Lack of sensitivity to teaching and learning causes an information gap, which delays timely response.

Commitment to resilience is also a characteristic of mindful organization. No organization or school is perfect, and mindful principals know better than most that they must develop a capacity not only to identify mistakes early but also to bounce back and overcome them. No amount of anticipation is going to prevent mistakes, so resilience is critical. Schools must deal with the unexpected both by anticipation and by resilience (Wildavsky, 1991). School leadership and teachers must be strong and flexible enough to cope with the consequences of bad surprises.

Deference to expertise is the final property of mindful schools. Mindful schools avoid the error of embracing standard rules and rigid structures. Instead, the focus is on matching expertise with the problem regardless of rank and status. Decision making is fluid and defers to knowledge. Rigid structures are replaced by enabling ones, in which consulting with and listening to those with expertise are fundamental to problem solving (Hoy, 2003; Hoy & Sweetland, 2001).

In brief, mindful schools have teachers and administrators who develop the ability to anticipate surprise by focusing on failure, avoiding simplification, and remaining sensitive to operations. But when the unexpected happens, the organization rebounds with persistence, resilience, and expertise. Table 14.1 summarizes the characteristics of mindfulness.

Trust: Its Elements and Referents

Trust is a global concept with at least five facets; benevolence, predictability, competence, honesty, and openness are the elements of trust most frequently identified in the literature (Hoy & Tschannen-Moran, 1999, 2003; Tschannen-Moran & Hoy, 2000). All these elements are based on common beliefs that individuals or groups act in ways that are in the best interest of the concerned parties. Trust involves taking risks and making oneself vulnerable to another in the confidence that the other will act in ways that are not detrimental to the trusting party.

Benevolence may be the most common element of trust; it is confidence that those things one cares about will not be harmed (Baier, 1986; Cummings & Bromily, 1996). Benevolence is the "accepted vulnerability to another's possible but not expected ill will" (Baier, 1986, p. 236). When there is no trust in the benevolence of the principal, teachers become excessively concerned about both real and imagined harm.

Reliability is the extent to which behavior is predictable and benefits the other party (Butler & Cantrell, 1984; Hosmer, 1995). It is not simply

Table 14.1.   Characteristics of Mindfulness and Mindlessness

Characteristics of Mindfulness	Characteristics of Mindlessness
Individual	Individual
Creation of new categories	Use of standard categories for analysis
Open to new information	Reliance of current information
Considers multiple perspectives	Trapped in a single perspective
Organizational	Organizational
Preoccupation with mistakes	Complacency
Reluctance to simplify	Oversimplification
Sensitivity to day-to-day operations	Insulated from day-to-day operations
Resilience	Rigidity
Deference to expertise	Reliance on formal authority

consistent behavior; it is behavior that combines with benevolence to be predictably well intentioned.

Competence is the ability to perform according to appropriate standards. Good intentions are not enough (Baier, 1986; Butler & Cantrell, 1984; Mishra, 1996). Trust depends on organizational tasks being carried out competently. The disorganized administrator, for example, is unlikely to elicit trust from the faculty.

Honesty refers to an individual's character, integrity, and authenticity. Rotter (1967) defined trust as "the expectancy that the word, promise, verbal or written statement of another individual or group can be relied upon" (p. 651). Integrity is shown when statements correspond to deeds. Authentic behavior neither distorts the truth nor shifts responsibility (Tschannen-Moran & Hoy, 2000). Honesty and trust are inextricably part of one another (Baier, 1986; Cummings & Bromily, 1996).

Openness is a process in which relevant information is shared and often creates a vulnerability to another (Butler & Cantrell, 1984; Mishra, 1996). Openness signals confidence in both parties that neither the information nor the individual will be exploited. Principals and teachers who guard information provoke suspicion, not openness and trust. The preceding analysis leads to the following definition: Trust is an individual's or group's willingness to be vulnerable to another party based on the confidence that the latter party is benevolent, reliable, competent, honest, and open (Hoy & Tschannen-Moran, 2003).

Because trust is relational, the referent (individual or group) of trust influences its meaning. In this analysis, three referents of faculty trust are of interest: faculty trust in colleagues, faculty trust in the principal, and faculty trust in clients (parents and students).

Theoretical Rationale

We have conceptualized school mindfulness as a collective capability to anticipate surprise by focusing on failure, avoiding simplification, and remaining sensitive to day-to-day operations. But when the unexpected happens, as it inevitably will, mindful schools are committed to resilience; they rebound with confidence and expertise. The general question of this inquiry is, What organizational conditions foster mindfulness in schools?

There is not an abundance of research on organizational mindfulness because it is a relatively new construct (Hoy, 2003; Weick & Sutcliffe, 2001); however, those few empirical studies that deal with organizational mindfulness provide some useful clues to its nature. Weick and Sutcliffe (2001) have analyzed high reliability organizations (HROs), which they view as prototypes of organizational mindfulness. They conclude that

HROs are characterized by "an underlying style of mental functioning that is distinguished by continuously updating and deepening of increasingly plausible interpretations of what the context is, what problems define it, and what remedies it contains" (p. 3). In a word, mindful organizations are reliable.

Mindful organizations also manage the unexpected in its earliest stages, when the signals of trouble are subtle and weak. They encourage the reporting of errors and any failure, no matter how small, as a window to the functioning of the system as a whole (Weick & Sutcliffe, 2001). Managers in these organizations cultivate an atmosphere of openness and teamwork and encourage individuals to challenge each other's thought and behavior. The openness and trust, however, must be strong enough so the organization can use mistakes and failures as learning experiences rather than cause for censure and punishment. Weick and Sutcliffe (2001) identify several studies (Edmonson, 1999; Landau & Chisholm, 1995; Westrum, 1992) that are particularly relevant in this regard.

Westrum (1992) describes the Redstone missile development headed by Wernher Von Braun. After careful and painstaking preparation and much to the chagrin and puzzlement of everyone, an early test of the Redstone missile went out of control. It was surprising that one of the engineers reported that he may have accidentally caused a short circuit during the prelaunch testing. Further investigation revealed that indeed the engineer had caused the accident. His openness and honesty in confessing his mistake in the end saved time and money. Costly retesting and expensive redesigns were unnecessary. Upon hearing that the engineer had voluntarily reported the mistake that had caused the out-of-control missile, Von Braun sent the man a bottle of champagne. In many organizations, such mistakes are routinely hidden rather than admitted because punishment, not reward, is the typical consequence. It is in organizations that focus on uncovering failure for the sake of improvement that such open and honest behavior of subordinates is rewarded.

A similar incident is reported by Landau and Chisholm (1995). A seaman on the nuclear carrier Carl Vinson reported that he had lost a tool on the deck of the carrier. Unfortunately, all aircraft were aloft. The captain immediately diverted all planes to land bases, and a systematic search for the tool was conducted because an errant tool on the deck of a carrier is potentially dangerous for both men and planes. Only after the tool was found were the planes allowed to return and land. The next day, in a formal ceremony, the seaman was commended for his action. Again, we have the triumph of openness and honesty, and the reinforcement of catching mistakes early.

Finally, Edmonson's (1999) study of psychological safety and learning in work teams produced an unexpected finding; she found that high-performing nurses' units reported higher (not lower) rates for adverse drug use than low-performing units. She interpreted her surprising finding, however, not to mean that the higher performing units actually committed more mistakes, but rather that more mistakes were reported in those units because of the openness and trust. Edmonson theorized that mistakes were hidden in poor-performing units, whereas a culture of openness made nurses in the high-performing units more willing to admit and discuss mistakes, correct them, and learn from them. The message is similar: Openness, competence, and trust enable subordinates to engage in problem solving rather than defensive behavior.

There are a number of themes that run through these studies. First, the workers are competent, expert, and reliable. Their managers are benevolent and constructive in their interactions. Finally, an atmosphere of honesty and openness pervades a work environment that is focused on finding mistakes early, and correcting and learning from them. In fact, these studies strongly suggest that a work environment characterized by competence, reliability, benevolence, honesty, and openness fosters mindful thought and action. Thus, we postulate that an atmosphere of trust is a necessary condition for school mindfulness. We hasten to add that mindfulness reinforces trust in schools, that is, the trust-mindfulness relation is a reciprocal one. In particular, we will test the relationships between three types of faculty trust—trust in the principal, trust in colleagues, trust in clients—and school mindfulness.

METHOD

We turn next to the methods used to test the relationships between trust and mindfulness. In particular, we describe the sample, data collection, and measures.

Sample of Schools

A diverse sample of 75 middle schools was selected for study because middle schools have the properties of both elementary and high schools (Herriott & Firestone, 1984). We also wanted to avoid the confounding effects of multiple school levels or types. These schools were distributed in 11 counties. Although the sample selected was not random, care was taken to ensure participation of urban, suburban, and rural schools. The current distribution of middle schools in Ohio is 39% rural, 34% urban, and 27% suburban. Correspondingly, the study's schools are distributed across 19% rural, 41% urban, and 40% suburban settings. Of the 612 school districts in the state, 43 participated in the study. Staff completed a total of approximately 2,600 usable surveys. The sample was similar to the population of middle schools in Ohio in terms of student enrollment, average teacher salary, average teacher experience, and the size of the faculty. In brief, the sample of schools was fairly typical of middle schools in Ohio.

Data Collection

Data were collected from the middle schools at regularly scheduled faculty meetings. A member of the research team explained the general purpose of the study, assured the confidentiality of all responses, and asked teachers to complete the questionnaires. Because this project was part of a larger study of organizational properties and because the unit of analysis was the school, a random group of teachers was selected to respond to the measures. No attempt was made to gather data from faculty who were not present at the meeting, but virtually all teachers returned usable questionnaires.

Measures

Two instruments, the School Mindfulness Scale and the Omnibus T-Scale, were administered to the teachers in each middle school.

School Mindfulness Scale (M-Scale)

Hoy et al. (2004) used the conceptual framework of mindfulness summarized earlier in this article as a basis for developing the scale; that is, school mindfulness rested on five properties—a focus on mistakes, reluctance to simplify, sensitivity to teaching and learning, commitment to resilience, and deference to expertise in problem solving. The M-Scale is a 20-item Likert-type scale. Teachers are asked to respond to each item, descriptions of behavior, along a 6-point scale from *strongly disagree* (1) to *strongly agree* (6).

A series of factor analytic studies demonstrated that the M-Scale had two significantly correlated factors: mindfulness of the principal and mindfulness of the faculty, each measured by 10 items. Both factors measure all five elements of mindfulness for the principal and faculty, respectively. Samples of items are as follows.

Focus on Mistakes and Failure

- In my building, teachers hide mistakes (reversed).
- Teachers in my building learn from their mistakes and change things so they do not happen again.

Reluctance to Simplify

- My principal negotiates differences among faculty without destroying the diversity of opinions.
- Teachers negotiate differences among each other without destroying the diversity of opinions.

Sensitivity to Teaching and Learning

- My principal is an expert on teaching and learning.
- In this school, teachers welcome feedback about ways to improve.

Commitment to Resilience

- When a crisis occurs, the principal deals with it so we can get back to teaching.
- When things don't go well, the teachers bounce back quickly.

Deference to Expertise

- The principal of this school does not value the opinions of the teachers (reversed).
- Teachers in this school value expertise more than authority.

The construct and predictive validity of the scale has been supported in a comprehensive factor-analytic study (Hoy et al., 2004). Likewise, reliability coefficients for all the scales are consistently high, that is, .90 or greater. Similarly, a factor analysis of data for the middle schools in this sample supported the factor structure of the instrument and the high reliabilities (see Table 14.2). Finally, as expected, the variance of school mindfulness was greater across all schools (.60) than it was within schools (.31), which suggests that school mindfulness is a collective property.

Omnibus Trust Scale (Omnibus T-Scale)

The Omnibus T-Scale is a measure of faculty trust, which has three subtests: faculty trust in colleagues, in principal, and in clients (parents and

**Table 14.2.   Factor Analysis of the 20-Item
School Mindfulness Scale (M-Scale)**

Item	Principal Mindfulness	Faculty Mindfulness
Principal		
The principal welcomes challenges from teachers.	.88	
When a crisis occurs, the principal deals with it so we can get back to teaching.	.81	
My principal negotiates faculty differences without destroying the diversity of opinions.	.83	
The principal of this school does not value the opinions of the teachers.	−.92	
My principal is an expert on teaching and learning.	.87	
My principal often jumps to conclusions.	−.75	
Teachers do not trust the principal enough to admit their mistakes.	−.87	
Mistakes are seen as important sources of information.	.56	
In times of crisis, it takes my principal too much time to effectively deal with the situation.	−.58	
My principal does not really know what is happening in most classrooms.	−.76	
Faculty		
When things don't go well, teachers bounce back quickly.		.77
Teachers in my building learn from their mistakes and change so they do not happen again.		.91
In this school, teachers welcome feedback about ways to improve.		.78
Teachers negotiate differences among each other without destroying the diversity of opinions.		.74
Too many teachers in my building give up when things go bad.		−.80
Teachers in this school value expertise more than authority.		.62
Most teachers in this building are reluctant to change.		−.55
Teachers in this school often jump to conclusions.		−.55
People in this school respect power more than knowledge.		−.64
In my building, teachers hide mistakes.		−.67
Cumulative variance	52.61	66.16
Alpha coefficient.	.96	.93

students). Each measure is grounded in the faculty's willingness to be vulnerable to one group or individual in the confidence that the other party would be benevolent, reliable, competent, honest, and open. The Omnibus T-Scale is a 26-item scale. Teachers were asked the extent to which each statement characterizes their school along a 6-point scale from *strongly disagree* to *strongly agree*.

A series of factor analytic studies has supported the validity and reliability of the three faculty trust subtests of the Omnibus T-Scale for elementary and high schools (Hoy & Tschannen-Moran, 2003). Alpha coefficients of reliability for each scale are consistently above .90. To check the consistency of the factor structure for our sample of middle schools, we replicated the factor analysis with our current sample (see Table 14.3). The results confirm the factor structure of the Omnibus T-Scale for middle schools. The three factors of trust explain about 86% of the variance, and all the alpha coefficients of reliability are strong (.98 for trust in principal, .97 for trust in colleagues, and .98 for trust in clients).

DATA ANALYSIS

We turn to the descriptive statistics and intercorrelations among the variables of the study and then to a multivariate analysis of the relationships.

Descriptive Statistics and Intercorrelations

The descriptive statistics and intercorrelations between the major variables are summarized in Table 14.4. As expected, the two aspects of school mindfulness—principal and faculty—were significantly correlated with each other ($r = .59$, $p < .01$), which supported our decision to compute an overall measure of school mindfulness by combining principal and faculty mindfulness. Also, as expected, the three aspects of faculty trust were significantly correlated with each other; faculty trust in clients was related to trust in principal ($r = .49$, $p < .01$) and trust in colleagues ($r = .78$, $p < .01$), and faculty trust in principal and in colleagues were related to each other ($r = .49$, $p < .01$).

As predicted, school mindfulness and aspects of faculty trust were strongly correlated with each other: $r = .67$, $p < .01$ for faculty trust in clients; $r = .90$, $p < .01$ for faculty trust in principal; and $r = .73$, $p < .01$ for faculty trust in colleagues. Faculty trust in principal was a very strong predictor of principal mindfulness ($r = .97$, $p < .01$), and faculty trust in colleagues was likewise a strong predictor of faculty mindfulness ($r = .90$, $p < .01$). Faculty trust in clients, however, was moderately related to principal mindfulness ($r = .49$, $p < .01$) but strongly related to faculty mindfulness ($r = .78$, $p < .01$).

Table 14.3. Trust Factor Structure Compared to Hoy and Tschannen-Moran (2003)

Item	Elementary School	High School	Current Middle School
Trust in Principal			
The teachers in this school have faith in the integrity of the principal.	.92	.92	.92
The principal in this school typically acts in the best interests of the teachers.	.94	.94	.92
The principal doesn't tell the teachers what is really going on.	−.89	−.84	−.79
Teachers in this school trust the principal.	.88	.97	.90
The principal of this school does not show concern for the teachers.	−.91	−.84	−.83
The teachers in this school are suspicious of most of the principal's actions.	−.86	−.91	−.89
Teachers in this school can rely on the principal.	.94	.97	.94
The principal in this school is competent in doing his or her job.	.92	.91	.92
Alpha coefficient	.98	.98	.98
Trust in Colleagues			
Teachers in this school typically look out for each other.	.91	.83	.88
Teachers in this school trust each other.	.91	.74	.88
Even in difficult situations, teachers in this school can depend on each other.	.93	.79	.85
Teachers in this school have faith in the integrity of their colleagues.	.92	.73	.77
Teachers in this school are suspicious of each other.	−.89	−.66	−.64
Teachers in this school do their jobs well.	.71	.43	.57
When teachers in this school tell you something, you can believe it.	.84	.63	.67
Teachers in this school are open with each other.	.91	.74	.81
Alpha Coefficient	.93	.93	.97
Trust in clients (students and parents)			
Teachers in this school trust their students.	.79	.72	.80
Students in this school can be counted on to do their work.	.90	.83	.84
Students in this school care about each other.	.89	.80	.84
Students here are secretive.	−.75	−.30	−.56
Teachers here believe that students are competent learners.	.75	.81	.82
Teachers can count on parental support.	.91	.82	.89

Table continues on next page.

Table 14.3. Trust Factor Structure Compared to Hoy and Tschannen-Moran (2003) Continued

Item	Elementary School	High School	Current Middle School
Teachers in this school believe what parents tell them.	.84	.72	.79
Teachers think that most of the parents do a good job.	.90	.90	.85
Parents in this school are reliable in their commitments.	.91	.81	.89
Teachers in this school trust the parents.	.89	.89	.83
Alpha coefficient	.94	.94	.97
Cumulative percentage of variance	a	a	85.66

Note: Numbers represent the factor loadings.
a. Not reported.

Multiple Regression Analysis

In some contrast to the explanation of faculty mindfulness, but not unexpected, faculty trust in the principal is the strongest predictor of principal mindfulness (beta = .95, $p < .01$); in fact, the other two faculty trust variables have no effect on principal mindfulness (beta = −.04, *ns* and beta = .08, *ns*). More than 90% of the variance of principal mindfulness is explained by faculty trust in the principal.

Table 14.4. Means, Standard Deviations, Reliabilities, Correlations

Variable	M	SD	SM	PM	FM	TCl	TP	TCo
School mindfulness (SM)	4.11	.44	.95[a]					
Principal mindfulness (PM)	4.13	.59	.94*	.96[a]				
Faculty mindfulness (FM)	4.09	.38	.84*	.59*	.93[a]			
Trust in clients (TCl)	3.53	.62	.67*	.49*	.78*	.97[a]		
Trust in principal (TP)	4.42	.73	.90*	.97*	.57*	.49*	.98[a]	
Trust in colleagues (TCo)	4.46	.44	.73*	.50*	.90*	.78*	.47*	.97*

a. Alpha coefficient of reliability.
* $p < .01$.

Overall school mindfulness is explained by faculty trust in the principal (beta = .72, $p <$ .01) and faculty trust in colleagues (beta = .36, $p <$ .01). The combined prediction of the faculty trust variables on school mindfulness was very strong (R = .97, adjusted R^2 = .94), with virtually all the variance explained by faculty trust in principal and colleagues. The results of the regression analyses are summarized in Table 14.5.

DISCUSSION

This inquiry focused on two constructs: school mindfulness and faculty trust. Our initial task was to examine the theoretical and empirical components of each. We did factor analyses of each measure to ensure that the factor structures were stable and consistent with both the theoretical underpinnings and empirical outcomes. The 20-item mindfulness measure (M-Scale) was consistent with earlier analyses (Hoy et al., 2004). School mindfulness was made up of two highly related concepts—principal mindfulness and faculty mindfulness—that combine to provide a good index of overall school mindfulness.

A factor analysis of the Omnibus T-Scale also supported the validity of faculty trust and the reliability of its measure. In fact, the factor structure was stable and the results demonstrated that the scale worked as well or better in this sample of middle schools than it did in samples of elementary and high schools. Both scales appear to be valid and reliable measures of the two constructs.

Next, we examined the interrelationships between the components of school mindfulness and the aspects of school trust. As expected, the cor-

Table 14.5. Multiple Regressions of Teacher, Principal, and School Mindfulness on Dimensions of Trust

	Standardized Beta		
Variable	Faculty Mindfulness	Principal Mindfulness	School Mindfulness
Trust in clients	.15*	−.04	.04
Trust in colleagues	.71**	.08	.36**
Trust in principals	.17**	.95**	.72**
R	.92**	.97**	.97**
Adjusted R^2	.85**	.94**	.94**

Note: N = 75 schools.
* $p <$ .05. ** $p <$ .01.

relations between the faculty trust variables and mindfulness variables were strong. In fact, faculty trust in clients and faculty mindfulness shared 61% of the variance with each other, and the shared variance of faculty trust and principal mindfulness was even stronger (94%). Both of these findings supported our theoretical rationale that trust and mindfulness were inextricably related and were likely necessary conditions for each other.

The multiple regression analyses also supported this conclusion. Trust in clients had limited influence on mindfulness; in fact, only with respect to faculty mindfulness did it have a significant independent effect, that is, controlling for the influence of the other two types of faculty trust. Overall school mindfulness is best explained by both trust in colleagues and trust in the principal; together, they explain almost 94% of the shared variance. It seems unlikely that schools can be mindful without a school environment in which teachers trust the principal and each other. Faculty trust in the school principal is most important, but teachers' trusting each other is a strong complementary buttress for school mindfulness.

Are trust and mindfulness necessary conditions for each other? Our results provide a resounding yes to the question; trust and mindfulness go hand in hand. Faculty trust promotes school mindfulness and mindfulness reinforces trust. Both the theoretical and empirical underpinnings for this relationship are strong. Trust requires a group's willingness to be vulnerable to another party based on the confidence that the latter party will be benevolent, reliable, competent, honest, and open. These same characteristics of trust are necessary for school mindfulness. Recall, the prototype for organizational mindfulness was the high reliability organization; reliability is critical (Weick & Sutcliffe, 2001). Moreover, creating an atmosphere in which members, including leaders, are competent, open, honest, and benevolent is important. Trust is essential if errors are to be openly and honestly admitted rather than hidden, if catching mistakes early is the objective rather than only celebrating success, and if mistakes are to be perceived as learning opportunities rather than times for censure. Openness, honesty, competence, reliability, and benevolence enable organizational members to be continuously attentive to small mistakes and multiple interpretations of events. A productive climate of rival explanations is possible only when competent individuals respect each other and are open and honest (Edmonson, 1999; Landau & Chisholm, 1995; Westrum, 1992). It seems axiomatic that trust is essential if the organization's objectives are focusing on mistakes, discussing them, learning from them, and engaging in successful problem solving. The results of the research clearly support this conclusion. In addition, when things go wrong and surprises occur, trust is critical in creating an organizational resilience to bounce back and work together with problem solving anchored in expertise regardless of rank or status. Theoretically and empirically, trust is necessary for school mindfulness and school mindfulness reinforces a culture of trust.

IMPLICATIONS

The significance of both trust and mindfulness in schools is indisputable. They are inextricably related, and both create a climate for success. Both have reliable and valid measures, which should encourage their research use in schools. The conceptualization and measure of mindfulness of schools is in its early stage. We invite other researchers to use and refine the concept. Qualitative case studies, for example, would be helpful in demonstrating specific examples of mindful and mindless behavior. The concept needs to be fleshed out.

Trust has already been linked to student achievement (Bryk & Schneider, 2002; Goddard, Tschannen-Moran, & Hoy, 2001; Hoy, Smith, & Sweetland, 2002), leadership success (Bennis, 1989; Zand, 1997), moral authority (Sergiovanni, 1992), and sound, healthy interpersonal relationships in schools (Hoy & Sabo, 1998). Organizational mindfulness has received much less attention (Hoy, 2002; Weick & Sutcliffe, 2001), yet the construct has the potential to make schools more productive workplaces. For example, consider the following sample of research questions:

- What structural properties foster mindfulness in organizations?
- How do organizational politics improve or distract from school mindfulness?
- What individual motivations enhance or hinder mindfulness?
- What climate properties promote mindfulness?
- To what extent is school mindfulness related to student achievement?
- What personality traits of principals promote and impede mindfulness?
- To what extent do mindful teachers promote mindful students?
- Is school mindfulness a necessary condition for effective school reform?

Mindfulness in schools warrants more attention and has strong potential to increase our understanding of effective school organizations. We suspect that positive school leadership is pivotal in promoting mindful and productive school operations.

Weick and Sutcliffe (2001) offer several practical suggestions for mindful leadership, some of which are particularly germane to schools and school leaders. Building on Weick and Sutcliffe (2001), here are a few recommendations for school leaders:

1. Restate goals as failures that must not occur; this will focus the lens of the organization more directly on unexpected events and reliability.

2. Create an awareness of vulnerabilities in the school. Teachers need to be aware of weaknesses so they are not surprised and overwhelmed by the unexpected.

3. Inculcate humility so educators are not blinded by successes. Although success is good, it can be damaging because it often ushers in complacency.

4. Welcome the bad day. None of us particularly likes bad days, yet they provide experiences inherently filled with learning opportunities.

5. Create a mistake-friendly learning atmosphere. Teachers and administrators need to be free to experiment, make mistakes, and learn from them.

6. Cultivate skepticism in the school. This might at first seem unproductive; skepticism, however, is the opposite of complacency. Skeptical teachers will make an effort to refute information, which in the end is a positive form of redundancy.

7. Reinvent the wheel periodically. Most of us do not want to reinvent the way we do things; however, each time a task is revisited, the process can be improved, and experiences since the last revisit are brought to bear on the process.

8. Embrace uncertainty. Uncertainty is a good sign that you are in touch with reality because there is little that is certain in school organizations.

9. Test your assumptions. It is easy to overestimate the accuracy of your information and expectations, so don't assume, test.

10. Encourage rival hypotheses. There are usually competing explanations for events. Encourage others to find and test them.

Mindful schools develop open and trusting relationships between administrators and teachers. Both faculty and principal mindfulness are important, but principal mindfulness is especially critical. Principals need to lead in mindful ways. By encouraging faculty to play with ideas, to create novelty in their classrooms, to feel safe to take reasonable risks, to experiment, and to be resilient, the principal can have profound effects on school mindfulness.

CONCLUSION

Mindfulness is a concept every school administrator should understand and practice, and a culture of trust seems necessary to achieve both the ends of understanding and practice. Mindfulness may seem like common sense and good practice, but it is much more. The focus on failure is an abrupt departure from common practice; the news of mistakes is typically not well received.

With the recent growth of high stakes tests, unfunded mandates from legislators, and a shrinking pool of resources, the five elements of mindfulness should aid administrators in their quest to improve teaching and learning. Educators who can implement novel ideas with a fresh perspective, who can take the old ways of doing things and reframe them to make them new, and who challenge others to search out the latent failures in the system will achieve higher levels of mindfulness. Although this study was not concerned with student achievement, a strong case can be made that mindful schools facilitate higher student achievement. Thus, the development and elaboration of school mindfulness should be seen as a beginning, not an end. Ultimately, designing schools to improve student learning is a continuing challenge, and school mindfulness seems an important piece of the puzzle.

REFERENCES

Baier, A. C. (1986). Trust and antitrust. *Ethics, 96,* 231-260.

Bennis, W. G. (1989). *On becoming a leader.* Reading, MA: Addison-Wesley.

Bryk, A. S., & Schneider, B. (2002). *Trust in schools: A core resource for improvement.* New York: Russell Sage Foundation.

Butler, J. K., & Cantrell, R. S. (1984). A behavioral decision theory approach to modeling dyadic trust in superiors and subordinates. *Psychological Report, 55,* 19-28.

Cummings, L. L., & Bromily, P. (1996). The organizational trust inventory (OTI): Development and validation. In R. Kramer & T. Tyler (Eds.), *Trust in organizations* (pp. 302-330). Thousand Oaks, CA: Sage.

Edmonson, A. C. (1999). Psychological safety and learning behavior in work teams. *Administrative Science Quarterly, 44,* 350-383.

Goddard, R. D., Tschannen-Moran, M., & Hoy, W. K. (2001). Teacher trust in students and parents: A multi-level examination of the distribution and effects of teacher trust in urban elementary schools. *Elementary School Journal, 102,* 3-17.

Herriott, R. F., & Firestone, W. A. (1984). Two images of schools as organizations: A refinement and elaboration. *Educational Administration Quarterly, 20,* 41-58.

Hosmer, L. T. (1995). Trust: The connecting link between organizational theory and philosophical ethics. *Academy of Management Review, 20*(2), 379-403.

Hoy, W. K. (2003). An analysis of enabling and mindful school structures: Some theoretical, research and practical considerations. *Journal of EducationalAdministration, 41*(1), 87-108.

Hoy, W. K., Gage, C. Q., & Tarter, C. J. (2004). Theoretical and empirical foundations of mindful schools. In W. K. Hoy & C. Miskel (Eds.), *Educational organizations, policy and reform: Research and measurement* (pp. 305-335). Greenwich, CT: Information Age.

Hoy, W. K., & Sabo, D. (1998). *Quality middle schools: Open and healthy.* Thousand Oaks, CA: Corwin Press.

Hoy, W. K., Smith, P. A., & Sweetland, S. R. (2002). The development of the organizational climate index for high schools: Its measure and relationship to faculty trust. *High School Journal, 86,* 38-49.

Hoy, W. K., & Sweetland, S. R. (2001). Designing better schools: The meaning and measure of enabling school structures. *Educational Administration Quarterly, 37*(3), 296-321.

Hoy, W. K., & Tschannen-Moran, M. (1999). Five faces of trust: An empirical confirmation in urban elementary schools. *Journal of School Leadership, 9,* 184-208.

Hoy, W. K., & Tschannen-Moran, M. (2003). The conceptualization and measurement of faculty trust in schools: The omnibus t-scale. In W. K. Hoy & C. Miskel (Eds.), *Theory and research in educational administration* (pp. 181-208). Greenwich, CT: Information Age.

Landau, M., & Chisholm, D. (1995). The arrogance of optimism: Notes of failure avoidance management. *Journal of Contingencies and Crisis Management, 3,* 67-80.

Langer, E. J. (1989). *Mindfulness.* Cambridge, MA: Perseus Books.

Mishra, A. K. (1996). Organizational responses to crisis: The centrality of trust. In R. Kramer & T. Tyler (Eds.), *Trust in organizations* (pp. 261-287). Thousand Oaks, CA: Sage.

Pedhazur, E. J. (1982). Multiple regression in behavioral research (2nd ed.). New York: Holt, Rinehart and Winston.

Rotter, J. B. (1967). A new scale for the measurement of interpersonal trust. *Journal of Personality, 35,* 651-665.

Sergiovanni, T. J. (1992). *Moral leadership: Getting to the heart of school improvement.* San Francisco: Jossey-Bass.

Trungpa, C. (1973). *Cutting through spiritual materialism.* Boulder, CO: Sambhala.

Tschannen-Moran, M., & Hoy, W. K. (2000). A multidisciplinary analysis of the nature, meaning, and measurement of trust. *Review of Educational Research, 70,* 547-593.

Weick, K. E., & Sutcliffe, K. M. (2001). *Managing the unexpected.* San Francisco: Jossey-Bass.

Westrum, R. (1992). Cultures with requisite imagination. In J. A. Wise, D. Hopkin, & P. Stager (Eds.), *Verification and validation of complex systems: Human factors issues* (pp. 402-405). Berlin, Germany: Springer-Verlag.

Wildavsky, A. (1991). *Searching for safety.* New Brunswick, NJ: Transaction.

Zand, D. (1997). *The leadership triad: Knowledge, trust, and power.* New York: Oxford University Press.

Wayne K. Hoy *is the Novice Fawcett Chair in Educational Administration at The Ohio State University. His research interests include school properties that enhance teaching and student learning, especially organizational structure, culture, motivation, and leadership.*

Charles Quincy Gage, III, *is the assistant principal of Barrington Elementary School in Upper Arlington, Ohio. His main fields of interest are leadership, motivation, and innovative school structures.*

C. John Tarter *is a professor of educational administration at St. John's University in New York. He teaches courses in organizational theory, politics of education, and educational leadership. His research interests are organizational climate, decision making, and school leadership.*

PART XI

ON ENABLING STRUCTURE

CHAPTER 15

DESIGNING BETTER SCHOOLS

The Meaning and Measure of Enabling School Structures

Wayne K. Hoy and Scott R. Sweetland

Common usage of the term bureaucracy is pejorative. To most people, bureaucracy is synonymous with red tape, rigid rules, autocratic superiors, and alienated and apathetic employees. But organizations of any size, including schools, have bureaucratic structures because they need appropriately designed formal procedures and hierarchical structures to prevent chaos and promote efficiency. Two conflicting views of the consequences of bureaucracy emerge from the literature. Some studies demonstrate that structure alienates and frustrates, whereas other research finds structure increases satisfaction and innovation. This study is consistent with an earlier attempt to reconcile these two theoretically opposing perspectives by creating and testing a new construct termed enabling structure. Evidence is mounting that schools can be designed with formalized procedures and hierarchical structures that help rather than hinder.

Reprinted by permission from the *Educational Administration Quarterly,* Vol. 37, pp. 296-321. Copyright © 2001. All rights reserved.

Essential Ideas for the Reform of American Schools, pp. 339–365

Like it or not, schools are bureaucracies—they are structures with hierarchy of authority, division of labor, impersonality, objective standards, technical competence, and rules and regulations (Weber, 1947). Weber claimed that bureaucracies are capable of attaining the highest degree of administrative efficiency. Yet, bureaucracies are criticized and even demonized as structures that produce overconformity and rigidities (Gouldner, 1954; Merton, 1957), block and distort communication (Blau & Scott, 1962), alienate and exploit workers (Aiken & Hage, 1968; Scott, 1998), stifle innovation (Hage & Aiken, 1970), and are unresponsive to its publics (Coleman, 1974; Scott, 1998). Moreover, feminists attack bureaucracy as a male invention that rewards such masculine virtues as competition, power, and hierarchy and eschews such feminine values as collaboration, care, and equality (Ferguson, 1984; Martin & Knopoff, in press). Administrators and teachers and school executives fault state bureaucracies for impeding and preventing local districts from delivering educational programs that meet community needs. What these criticisms have in common is the human frustration with unresponsive structures and unfair and rigid rules and policies.

Clearly bureaucratic structures can be detrimental to their participants and publics, but that is only half the picture. Research also shows that bureaucracies can also enhance satisfaction (Michaels, Cron, Dubinsky, & Joachimsthaler, 1988), increase innovation (Craig, 1995; Damanpour, 1991), reduce role conflict (Senatra, 1980), and lessen feelings of alienation in schools (Moeller & Charters, 1966) as well as other organizations (Jackson & Schuler, 1985). Indeed, research paints two conflicting pictures of human response to bureaucracy. The dark side reveals a bureaucracy that alienates, breeds dissatisfaction, hinders creativity, and demoralizes employees. The bright side shows a bureaucracy that guides behavior, clarifies responsibility, reduces stress, and enables individuals to feel and be more effective (Adler, 1999; Adler & Borys, 1996; Hoy & Miskel, 2001). The purposes of this study are, first, to examine the positive and negative consequences of bureaucratic school structures, then to theoretically reconcile these two contrasting views, and finally, to refine and test a new construct of school structure—*enabling bureaucracy*.

FUNDAMENTAL FEATURES OF BUREAUCRACY

Two salient aspects of bureaucratic organization are formalization (formal rules and procedures) and centralization (hierarchy of authority). We examine each property with the goal of sorting out the features that capture positive outcomes of bureaucracy while preventing negative consequences.

Formalization

Formalization is the degree to which the organization has written rules, regulations, procedures, and policies. Gouldner's (1954) classic analysis of bureaucracy advanced two types of formalization—representative and punishment-centered. Adler and Borys (1996) posited a more comprehensive and contemporary theoretical analysis of formalization—enabling and coercive. They develop a deeper theoretical analysis of how work practices are affected by the features, design, and implementation of these two contrasting types of formalization. We start with their theoretical framework to build a conceptual model for analyzing bureaucratic properties in schools.

Coercive formalization more often than not generates alienation at the expense of commitment. Coercive rules and procedures punish subordinates rather than reward productive practices. Instead of promoting organizational learning, coercive procedures force reluctant subordinates to comply. The consequences are not surprising. For example, formalization promoted alienation (Kakabadse, 1986) and undermined job satisfaction (Arches, 1991) and was positively associated with absenteeism and stress and negatively related to job satisfaction and innovation (Rousseau, 1978). Likewise, school formalization is typically related to negative consequences (Anderson, 1968; Hoy, Blazovsky, & Newland, 1983; Hoy & Sweetland, 2000; Isherwood & Hoy, 1973). Rules simply cannot be designed to make work foolproof; in fact, the more restrictive the procedures, the more hindering they are in dynamic situations.

Enabling formalization assists employees with solutions to problems in their work. Enabling rules and procedures are flexible guidelines that reflect "best practices" and help subordinates deal with surprises and crises (Adler & Borys, 1996). For example, a stimulus for problem solving is not to adhere blindly to rules but to reflect on innovative ways to respond to novel situations. Indeed, what is often required is flexibility to substitute judgment for rigid rules. Hence, a general rule that professional judgment is encouraged and acceptable enables rather than hinders problem solving.

Enabling procedures invite interactive dialogue, view problems as opportunities, foster trust, value differences, capitalize on and learn from mistakes, and delight in the unexpected; in brief, they facilitate problem solving. Coercive procedures, however, frustrate two-way communication, are autocratic, see problems as obstacles, foster mistrust, demand consensus, suspect differences, punish mistakes, and fear the unexpected; in sum, they demand blind obedience to the rules. Enabling strategies require participation and collaboration. Trust is required, and improvement is the objective. In contrast, coercive procedures are top-down, unilateral, and unyielding. The coercive system is designed to monitor and control teachers. The point we are making is that adverse consequences are not necessarily inherent in rules themselves, but rather are due to the decisions that administrators make in establishing rules and procedures (Adler, 1999). The differences in the two approaches are summarized in Table 15.1.

Not surprisingly, implementation of enabling and coercive formalization has similar differences. Blau's (1955) classic analysis of the dynamics of bureaucracy is instructive. He suggested that if practices are to be effectively implemented, organizations must have five characteristics: employment security, a professional perspective, cohesive work groups, little management-labor conflict, and pressure to change. To this list, Adler (1993) added three additional features: employee participation, employee skills, and coordination for improvement. Flexibility in the implementation is also critical.

Coercive rules and procedures are difficult to change because revision is typically viewed as a threat to the existing power balance. Moreover, the context for implementation of coercive procedures is usually one that limits employee security, voice, skills, and promotes employee apathy, conflict, and rigidity (Adler & Borys, 1996). The contrasts in contexts are summarized in Table 15.2. In brief, enabling and coercive formalization have different features and are implemented in different organizational contexts.

Centralization

Centralization of authority is the locus of control for organizational decision making; it is the degree to which employees participate in decision making. High centralization means that decisions are concentrated at the top in the hands of a few, whereas low centralization indicates that

Table 15.1.   Contrasting Enabling and Coercive Formalization

Characteristics of Enabling Rules and Procedures	Characteristics of Coercive Rules and Procedures
Interactive dialogue	Frustrate two-way communication
View problems as opportunities	View problems as obstacles
Foster trust	Foster mistrust
Value differences	Demand consensus
Learn from mistakes	Punish mistakes
Delight in the unexpected	Fear the unexpected
Facilitate problem solving	Blindly follow the rules

Table 15.2.   Contrasting Enabling and Coercive Contexts

Characteristics of Enabling Contexts	Characteristics of Coercive Contexts
Employment security	Employee insecurity
Professional perspective	Autocratic perspective
Cohesive work groups	Divisive relationships
Limited management-labor conflict	Management-labor conflict
Pressures for change	Maintenance of status quo
Employee participation	Administrative control
Employee skills	Limited employee expertise
Coordination for improvement	Layers of control

the authority for making decisions is diffuse and shared among many. Hierarchy of authority, high centralization, is a classic characteristic of structure; authority is concentrated at the top and flows down the chain of command. High centralization often is coercive. Directives from superiors are to be followed without question. The central purpose of hierarchy is to guarantee disciplined compliance.

Hindering centralization refers to a hierarchy and administration that gets in the way rather than helps its participants solve problems and do their work. In such structures, the hierarchy obstructs innovation, and administrators use their power and authority to control and discipline teachers. In schools where professional work is controlled in top-down fashion, the consequence is often resistance by teachers who are coerced to play the bureaucratic game of satisfying artificial standards rather than serving the needs of their student clients (Hoy, Blazovsky, & Newland, 1983). Hierarchies typically respond to outside pressures in such dysfunctional ways as increasing autocratic supervision, overstandardizing work processes, and standardizing outputs (Mintzberg, 1979, 1989)—all of which can hinder the effective operation of the organization. Organizations require direction, coordination, and compliance, and hierarchy is central to these efforts. Yet, participants usually react negatively to unilateral attempts to control them because it is a violation of the norm of egalitarianism that is so pervasive in American society. The ubiquitous control mentality that pervades many hierarchies produces dissatisfaction, alienation, and hostility (Aiken & Hage, 1968; Hoy, Blazovsky, & Newland, 1983; Mintzberg, 1989).

Enabling centralization helps employees solve problems rather than obstructing their work. The authority structure of an organization can help superiors and subordinates work across recognized authority boundaries while retaining their distinctive roles (Hirschhorn, 1997).

Enabling hierarchy is an amalgam of authority in which members feel confident and are able to exercise power in their professional roles. We conceive of enabling centralization as flexible, cooperative, and collaborative rather than rigid, autocratic, and controlling. Administrators use their power and authority to buffer teachers and design structures that facilitate teaching and learning.

Structure in schools is inevitable. Schools have boards, superintendents, assistant superintendents, principals, assistant principals, teachers, and students. For all the talk about flat structures, empowerment, teacher participation, and reform, schools like all organizations have hierarchies. In spite of all the reform rhetoric, the evidence has suggested that hierarchy of authority in schools will continue. Indeed, the accountability movement itself demands more not less hierarchy. The key to avoiding the dysfunctions of centralization is to change the kind of hierarchy rather than to try to eliminate it. We need to develop structures that enable rather than hinder, or as Hirschhorn (1997) has suggested, we must embrace hierarchy and enliven it with feelings and passion. Participants don't like to be controlled, especially by an arbitrary and autocratic hierarchy. But just as formalization can be enabling rather than coercive, we postulate that hierarchy can be enabling rather than hindering. Again, we reiterate that adverse consequences of hierarchy are not inherent in structure itself but rather are due to the decisions of administrators in implementing their authority.

We are not simply advocating decentralization of authority as enabling; the problem is more complicated. Our argument is not against hierarchy per se but rather against a specific kind of centralization—hierarchy that hinders. Our conceptualization of hierarchy of authority is along a continuum from enabling at one pole to hindering at the other. Again, we are referring to the kind not the amount of centralization (Hoy & Sweetland, 2000). The contrasting characteristics of enabling and hindering centralization are summarized in Table 15.3.

Two fundamental features of bureaucracy are formalization and centralization. Our conceptualizations of these features lead to the generation of four kinds of bureaucratic structures. These structures are theoretical; that is, pure types in the Weberian sense. Whether they exist in the actual world of schools is an empirical question, one that will be examined later.

Four types of structure are developed by cross partitioning the dimensions of formalization and centralization in a 2 x 2 crossbreak (see Figure 15.1). Enabling bureaucracy is a structure that is formed by enabling formalization and enabling centralization—the rules, regulations, and procedures are helpful and lead to problem solving among members rather than rigid, coercive activities that demand conformity. Complementing enabling formalization is a hierarchical structure that helps rather than

Table 15.3.   Contrasting Enabling and Hindering Centralization

Characteristics of Enabling Hierarchy	Characteristics of Hindering Hierarchy
Facilitates problem solving	Frustrates problems solving
Enables cooperation	Promotes control
Collaborative	Autocratic
Flexible	Rigid
Encourages innovation	Discourages change
Protects participation	Disciplines subordinates

hinders subordinates in their jobs, what we have called enabling centralization. These two bureaucratic features provide an integrated and effective structure—enabling bureaucracy.

When formalization and centralization coerce and hinder rather than help, the other extreme is found. Mintzberg (1989) called such structures machine bureaucracies and Gouldner (1954) described them as punishment-centered bureaucracies, but we prefer the term *hindering bureaucracy* because they not only control and punish but also hinder the effective and efficient operation of the organization.

If formalization and centralization are independent dimensions, then two additional structures are possible, one in which there is enabling for-

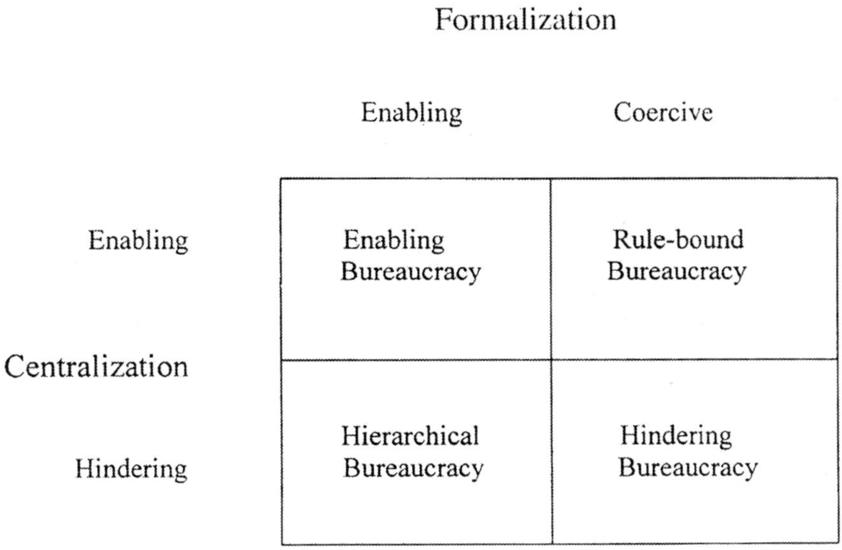

Formalization

	Enabling	Coercive
Centralization Enabling	Enabling Bureaucracy	Rule-bound Bureaucracy
Hindering	Hierarchical Bureaucracy	Hindering Bureaucracy

Figure 15.1.   A typology of school bureaucracy.

malization but hindering centralization and another that has coercive formalization and enabling centralization. We call the first *hierarchical bureaucracy* because the focus is on hierarchy. In such organizations, we would expect administrators to "ride rough shod" over any and all rules, including enabling ones. Indeed, there may be little need for rules because the administration would make all decisions; rules would be superfluous. The second pattern we term *rule-bound bureaucracy* because of its unyielding attention to rules and regulations. In this case, administrators would be rigid bureaucrats that enforce the rules to ensure disciplined compliance. The rules rule. Thus, four types of bureaucracy are generated: enabling bureaucracy, hindering bureaucracy, hierarchical bureaucracy, and rule-bound bureaucracy.

Thus, we have developed a theoretical argument for four types of school structures based on the bureaucratic dimensions of formalization and centralization. Do these four types of structures exist in the real world of schools? We turn next to an empirical assessment of this question in three separate studies.

PRELIMINARY STUDIES

In the first two studies (Hoy & Sweetland, 2000), we attempted to develop a set of reliable and valid measures for formalization and centralization. The theoretical framework developed above was used to generate a series of descriptive statements describing the formalization and centralization of schools.

Item Generation

Initially, a 24-item questionnaire was developed to measure the two bureaucratic dimensions of formalization and centralization (Hoy & Sweetland, 2000). The task was to develop four sets of Likert-type items— items to measure the degree of enabling formalization, coercive formalization, enabling centralization, and hindering centralization. For example, items to measure enabling formalization included the following:

- Administrative rules in this school are guides to solutions rather than rigid procedures.
- The administrators in this school use their authority to enable teachers to do their jobs.

- Administrative rules help rather than hinder.

Items to measure coercive formalization included the following:

- Administrative rules in this school are coercive.
- Administrative rules in this school are substitutes for professional judgment.
- Administrative rules in this school are used to punish teachers.

Items to measure enabling centralization included the following:

- The administrative hierarchy of this school facilitates the mission of the school.
- Administrators in this school are effective buffers for teachers.
- The administrative hierarchy of this school enables teachers to do their job.

Items to measure hindering centralization included the following:

- The administrative hierarchy of this school obstructs innovation.
- In this school the authority of the principal is used to undermine teachers.
- The administrative hierarchy of this school causes more problems than it solves.

Twenty-four items were generated for testing with teachers currently teaching in the public schools of Ohio. All items were 5-point Likert-type items on which teachers were asked to describe the extent to which each item described behavior in their school from *never* to *always* occurs.

Sample 1

Responding to the questionnaire were 61 teachers in three educational administration courses at the Ohio State University. The teachers represented 61 different schools and worked in a diverse set of urban, rural, and suburban schools. If one group is overrepresented, it is likely the urban group because a majority of the teachers taught in the urban area. Participation in the study was voluntary, yet more than 90% of the teachers returned usable questionnaires. All responses were anonymous and all respondents were teachers.

Exploratory Factor Analysis

Using a principal-axis factor analysis, we searched for two independent factors, one for centralization and another for formalization. The two-factor solution with a varimax rotation revealed that many items loaded strongly on both factors rather than two distinct factors. Thus we turned to a one-factor solution. The factor loadings ranged from .40 to .81. All the enabling items loaded positively as predicted, and the hindering or coercive items, as anticipated, had negative loadings. The one-factor solution was clearly the better solution both conceptually and empirically (Hoy & Sweetland, 2000).

In this sample of schools, when the hierarchy was enabling, so were rules and vice versa. Conceptually, we did not find the four types of bureaucracy described earlier. Rather, school bureaucracy varied along a single continuum with enabling bureaucracy at one extreme and hindering bureaucracy at the other; enabling bureaucracy was a bipolar construct. The 24 items used to measure enabling formalization and enabling centralization combined to form a single scale of enabling bureaucracy with strong internal consistency (alpha = .94).

Some Validity Evidence

To assess the validity of enabling bureaucracy, we tested two relationships. Aiken and Hage (1968), in their seminal study of bureaucracy, found that a hierarchy that made organizational participants dependent on superiors produced alienated and dissatisfied professionals in social welfare agencies. The same was true for organizations in which job incumbents were required to consult rules in fulfilling their professional responsibilities; that is, organizations with a high level of job codification. Similar results have been confirmed in high schools (Hoy, Blazovsky, & Newland, 1983). The critical features of enabling bureaucracy are their enabling centralization and enabling formalization; hierarchy and rules help rather than constrain participants. Thus, we theorized that enabling bureaucracies would not be characterized by hierarchical structures that promoted dependence or constrained professional decisions by rule consultation (high job codification). Indeed, that was the case; dependence on the hierarchy ($r = -.62$, $p < .01$) and dependence on rules ($r -.25$, $p < .05$) were negatively related to our measure of enabling bureaucracy; the more enabling the school structure was, the less constrained teachers were by either the hierarchy or the rules. These results offered some initial evidence for the validity of enabling bureaucracy.

Sample 2

One of the limitations with the first sample was both the small number of schools and the location of the schools in one state. The second sample of schools was much broader: 116 different schools were represented, one teacher for each school. The sample was diverse, representing schools in the five states of Ohio, Michigan, New Jersey, Virginia, and New York. Professors of educational administration collected data from teachers who were graduate students in five major universities. All responses were anonymous, and more than 89% returned usable questionnaires.

Factor Analysis

The new data were subjected to a principal-axis factor analysis. Consistent with the results of the first sample, we expected all the items to array themselves along a bipolar continuum from enabling at one extreme to hindering at the other. In fact, all the items did load strongly on the factor (range .53 to .81), and the alpha coefficient of reliability was .96. Thus, the data from the second sample had the same factor structure as the initial sample.

Additional Validity Evidence

We theorized that enabling bureaucracy should promote a sense of trust between teachers, and conversely, teacher trust of colleagues should promote a climate in which enabling bureaucracy could function effectively. Trust is a critical aspect of organizational life; it enables a leader to innovate and cope with confusion that often accompanies change (Bennis & Nanus, 1985). Moreover, Covey (1990) argued that trust is critical for productivity because it enables the organization to function effectively. Hence, we predicted that the more enabling the structure of schools, the greater the extent of collegial trust between teachers.

Etzioni (1961) built an entire theory of complex organization on the assumption that coercive organizations tend to alienate workers, which finds strong support in the empirical literature (Etzioni, 1975). Our conceptualization of enabling bureaucracy is the antithesis of a coercive organization; therefore, we hypothesized that the more enabling the bureaucratic structure of schools, the less the sense of powerlessness among teachers.

Both of these hypotheses were supported. Collegial trust and teacher sense of powerlessness were related to enabling bureaucracy as predicted;

the more enabling the bureaucracy, the more trust teachers have in their colleagues ($r = .61$, $p < .01$) and the less the sense of powerlessness among teachers ($r = -.74$, $p < .01$).

Summary

The theoretical dilemma, that sometimes bureaucracy frustrates organizational participants (Scott, 1998; Martin & Knopoff, in press) but at other times facilitates innovation and enhances organizational life (Adler & Borys, 1996; Craig, 1995), provided the impetus for this series of studies. Two classic structural aspects of bureaucracy—formalization and centralization—were measured.

Formalization was conceptualized along a continuum from enabling at one extreme to coercive at the other. Similarly, centralization can help or hinder the operations of an organization; hence, it was viewed along a continuum from enabling hierarchy at one extreme to hindering at the other. If formalization and centralization are two independent dimensions of organizational structure, then at least four types of schools can be theoretically formulated—enabling bureaucracy (enabling hierarchy, enabling rules), hindering bureaucracy (hindering hierarchy, coercive rules), hierarchical bureaucracy (hindering hierarchy, enabling rules), and rule-bound bureaucracy (enabling hierarchy, coercive rules). The results of two empirical studies, however, demonstrated that enabling formalization and enabling centralization were not independent, but rather formed a unitary bipolar factor. The factor was measured reliably and validly with a 24-item Likert-type scale.

THE CURRENT STUDY

The preliminary studies provided evidence of the nature, meaning, and measure of enabling school structures. There was, however, a major limitation to this early research. The measure of bureaucracy was determined by the perceptions of only one faculty member per school. Although this is fine for exploratory purposes, we wanted to replicate the results with a sample of schools in which there were multiple respondents for each school, consistent with Halpin's (1959) research on reliable perceptual measures for groups.

A second problem with the instrument is its length. Originally, we had anticipated measuring two dimensions of bureaucracy, but the results demonstrated one unitary dimension, which suggested that perhaps half as many items could be used to measure reliably and validly the concept

Table 15.4.   Items to Measure Enabling School Structure

Enabling formalization items

1. Administrative rules in this school enable authentic communications between teachers and administrators.
2. Administrative rules help rather than hinder.
3. Administrative rules in this school are guides to solutions rather than rigid procedures.

Coercive formalization items

4. Administrative rules in this school are used to punish teachers.
5. In this school red tape is a problem.
6. Administrative rules in this school are substitutes for professional judgement.

Enabling centralization items

7. The administrative hierarchy of this school enables teachers to do their job.
8. The administrative hierarchy of this school facilitates the mission of the school.
9. The administrators in this school use their authority to enable teachers to do their job.

Hindering centralization items

10. The administrative hierarchy obstructs student achievement.
11. The administrative hierarchy of this school obstructs innovation.
12. In this school the authority of the principal is used to undermine teachers.

of enabling school structure. To that end, we selected the 12 items with the strongest factor loadings, making sure that enabling, hindering, and coercive items were represented. The items selected are found in Table 15.4.

The purpose of this phase of the investigation was threefold: (a) check the stability of the factor structure of enabling bureaucracy, (b) increase the number of respondents from each school, and (c) test a number of original theoretical hypotheses in order to explore the relationships of enabling bureaucracy with other important school variables.

Sample

The sample for the current study consisted of 97 high schools in Ohio. Although procedures were not used to ensure a random sample from the population of high schools, care was taken to select urban, suburban, and rural schools from diverse geographic areas of the state. Only schools with 15 or more faculty members were considered candidates for the study. We selected high schools for two reasons: Their structures are typically more developed and complex than elementary and middle schools, and we wanted to control the level of the school. A total of 150 high schools were contacted and invited to participate, but for a variety of reasons only 98 agreed to participate (65.3%). One of the 98 high schools, however, did not meet the criteria for inclusion in the current sample. The high schools were defined by grade-span levels that included Grades 9 to 12 and Grades 10 to 12. Schools in the sample represented the entire range of socioeconomic status (SES); in fact, data from the Ohio Department of Education support the representativeness of the sample in terms of SES and urban-rural balance. Indeed, the sample of high schools was quite representative of Ohio high schools in terms of SES and urban-rural balance, but sample schools were a little smaller on average than were schools in the population. (See Table 15.5 for a comparison of the sample with the population.) The state indices on SES and urbanicity are reported in standard scores with 0 equal to the mean and a standard deviation of 1.

Data were collected from the teachers in each school at a regularly scheduled faculty meeting. A trained researcher during regular faculty meetings administered research instruments. All responses were anonymous. Because the unit of analysis of this study was the school, two groups of faculty were selected at random, and teachers were asked to respond to separate questionnaires; that is, some teachers received one set of questionnaires, and the others received a second set of questionnaires. For example, the enabling bureaucracy scores were on one questionnaire and the faculty trust score on the other; hence, the structural and trust variables were methodologically independent of each other, but both were measures of school properties. The items were written to capture school characteristics; hence, they were aggregated at the school level for each variable to provide school scores.

Factor Stability, Reliability, and Validity of the Enabling Bureaucracy Scale

The 12-item enabling bureaucracy scale was assessed for its factor stability, validity, and reliability. To that end, we did a principal-axis factor

Table 15.5.   A Comparison Between the Population and Sample

School Property	State Parameters		Sample Characteristics	
	M	SD	M	SD
School size	891	490	727	465
Socioeconomic status	0	1.00	-0.01	0.91
Urban-rural	0	1.00	-0.03	0.96

analysis of the selected 12 items for each of the earlier samples and the current sample so that we could compare the factor structures in each of the three samples. The results were encouraging. In the first sample, the factor loadings ranged from .52 to .80. The items loaded as predicted; that is, all enabling items loaded positive, and all coercive and hindering items loaded negative. The single factor explained 46.8% of the variance. The second sample provided similar results. Factor loadings ranged from .55 to .85 and again loaded as predicted, and the factor explained 53.6% of the variance. Finally, the current sample replicated the results of the earlier two samples in an even stronger fashion. The loadings were stronger (range .69 to .86); in fact, 10 of the 12 loading were .8 or greater. The variance explained by the factor was greater (64.4%), and only the first factor had an eigenvalue greater than 1. In addition, the alpha coefficients for the scale in each sample were strong (.90, .93, and .95, respectively for the three samples). See Table 15.6 for a comparison of the results of the three factor analyses.

The 12-item short form is a good parsimonious measure of enabling bureaucracies: It is a balanced measure with 6 enabling items (positive loadings) and 6 hindering items (negative loadings), it has high reliability in all samples (never lower than .9), it correlates almost perfectly with its longer version in the first two samples (.96 and .99 respectively), and finally, it has good factor and predictive validity. All validity evidence mounted in the first two studies is relevant for the new 12-item measure because the correlations between the two forms are near 1.

Hypotheses

The next phase of the investigation was to generate a set of hypotheses relating enabling school structures with important school outcomes. We theorized that for enabling organizations to be genuine and effective, they needed to be anchored in trust. Earlier research (Hoy & Sweetland, 2000) demonstrated that trust between teachers was strongly related to enabling bureaucracy. Trust is a key aspect of organizational life; it enables a leader to innovate and deal with resultant confusion that often accompanies change (Bennis & Nanus, 1985). Moreover, Covey (1990) argued that trust is critical for a productive environment because it enables the bureaucracy to function effectively. But teachers need to do more than trust each other if they are to be innovative and effective; they must trust their leader. Finally, enabling structures are characterized by principals who are disposed to help teachers solve problems, encourage open communication, and help teachers do their jobs. Hence, we hypothesized the following:

Table 15.6.   A Comparison of Factor Loadings for the Three Samples

Item Number	Number Statement	Factor 1 Enabling Bureaucracy		
		S_1	S_2	S_3
1.	Administrative rules in this school enable authentic communications between teachers and administrators.	.71	.85	.85
2.	The administrative hierarchy of this school enables teachers to do their job.	.76	.83	.83
3.	Administrative rules help rather than hinder.	.72	.75	.80
4.	The administrative hierarchy obstructs student achievement.	-.80	-.75	-.81
5.	Administrative rules in this school are used to punish teachers.	-.70	-.74	-.81
6.	Administrative rules in this school are guides to solutions rather than rigid procedures.	.52	.74	.81
7.	The administrative hierarchy of this school facilitates the mission of the school.	.69	.69	.86
8.	In this school red tape is a problem.	-.53	-.75	-.71
9.	The administrative hierarchy of this school obstructs innovation.	-.79	-.72	-.83
10.	In this school the authority of the principal is used to undermine teachers.	-.75	-.75	-.81
11.	The administrators in this school use their authority to enable teachers to their job.	.76	.61	.69
12.	Administrative rules in this school are substitutes for professional judgement.	-.53	-.55	-.81
	Percentage of variance	46.80	53.60	64.40
	Alpha coefficient	.90	.93	.95

Hypothesis 1:   The more enabling the bureaucratic structure of the school, the greater the extent of faculty trust in the principal.

This relationship is likely reciprocal; that is, enabling structure facilitates faculty trust in the principal, and conversely, faculty trust in the principal reinforces enabling bureaucracy.

Similarly, we expected enabling structures to facilitate authenticity in schools because authenticity and trust go hand in hand. The open communication encouraged in enabling organizations helps participants to be straight with each other and limits the need to hide or spin the truth (Nyberg, 1993, Sweetland & Hoy, in press). Spinning the truth is the adding, subtracting, partially displaying, or concealing what one person believes to be true while communicating with another (Nyberg, 1993). Truth spinning is the other side of the authenticity coin. Enabling bureaucracies foster trust and help participants learn from mistakes. Such behaviors should promote open and authentic interactions, not concealment, deception, or delusion. Hence, spinning the truth should be limited in enabling organizations. The reciprocal nature of truth spinning and enabling structures seems clear: Enabling structures dampen truth spinning, and truth spinning undermines enabling bureaucracy. Thus, we hypothesize the following:

Hypothesis 2:   The more enabling the bureaucratic structure of the school, the less the degree of truth spinning in school.

Conflict can be destructive or constructive in schools, but role conflict typically undermines the efficient operation of organizations by confusing participants (DiPaola & Hoy, 2001). Role conflict creates inconsistent behavior because the employee tries to do things accepted by one person but not by another, hence creating a tension and destructive edge in organizational relationships (Rizzo, House, & Lirtzman, 1970). We postulate that such inconsistency, tension, and negative conflict will be much less evident in enabling school structures because of the flexibility, openness, and problem-solving orientation found in such schools. Moreover, enabling bureaucracies encourage cooperation and broad professional discretion rather than narrow organizational control. Therefore, we hypothesized the following:

Hypothesis 3:   The more enabling the bureaucratic structure of the school, the less the extent of role conflict in the school.

Once again, we assumed reciprocal causality. Although enabling organizations should limit role conflict, it also seems likely that role conflict will undermine enabling organization and promote coercion and control.

Measures

To test these hypotheses, we needed reliable and valid measures. The measure of enabling bureaucracy has already been discussed at length; thus, we turn directly to the indicators of faculty trust in the principal, truth spinning, and role conflict.

Trust in the Principal

Trust in the principal was measured by a subtest of the Faculty Trust Survey designed to measure collective perceptions of faculty trust. The construct validity of the scale has been supported in two factor analytic studies (Hoy & Tschannen-Moran, 1999). Reliabilities are consistently high, always in the .90 range; in the current sample, the alpha coefficient of reliability was .98. Teachers respond to the Faculty Trust Survey by describing faculty behaviors along a 6-point Likert-type response set ranging from *strongly agree* to *strongly disagree*. Sample items include, "The principal in this school is unresponsive to teachers' concerns," (score reversed), and "Teachers in this school can rely on the principal."

Spinning the Truth

To measure truth spinning in schools, we used a set of items developed by Sweetland and Hoy (in press) to create a truth-spinning index for each school. Teachers were asked how much deception and spinning of the truth characterized the interpersonal relations in their schools—for example, "In this school the principals deceptions are intentional," and "In this school the principal is shrewd and artful at alternatively revealing and obscuring information." Similarly, teachers were asked to describe their interpersonal relations with each other—for example, "In this school the truth is hedged," and "In this school teachers are afraid to tell the truth." Evidence of the predictive validity of truth spinning is presented in earlier research (Sweetland & Hoy, in press). The alpha coefficient of reliability in the current study was .87.

Role Conflict

Role conflict is a 6-item Likert-type scale developed by Rizzo, House, and Lirtzman (1970) to measure inconsistent behavior. The measure has good validity and strong reliability. In this study, the alpha coefficient of reliability was .88. Sample items include, " I receive incompatible requests from two or more people," and "I do things that are apt to be accepted by one person and not by others."

RESULTS

We tested the three original hypotheses of this study by subjecting the relationships to correlational analysis. All three of the hypotheses were supported. The more enabling the school bureaucracy, the greater the degree of faculty trust in the principal ($r = .76$, $p < .01$), the less the truth spinning ($r = -.74$, $p < .01$) and the less role conflict ($r = -.71$, $p < .01$). Enabling schools, as predicted, were imbued with faculty who trusted their principals, who were disinclined to spin the truth, and who suffered from much less role conflict than did their colleagues in schools with hindering structures.

Next, we examined the combined influence of the variables under study in predicting enabling bureaucracy. To that end, we regressed enabling structure on faculty trust in the principal, truth spinning of the faculty, and perceived role conflict in the school. As expected, the three independent variables had a major relationship with enabling bureaucracy; in fact, the three variables combined ($R = .89$, $p < .01$) explained 78% of the variance (adjusted R^2) of enabling bureaucracy. Moreover, each predictor made a significant independent contribution to enabling structure with standardized beta weights of $-.30$ ($p < .01$) for role conflict, $.39$ ($p < .01$) for trust in the principal, and $-.38$ ($p < .01$) for teachers spinning the truth. Because size, urbanicity, and SES are three demographic variables that are often related to school outcomes, we decided to control these variables by simultaneously entering them in the regression equation together with the initial three independent variables. The results were relatively unaffected because none of the demographic variables made a significant contribution to enabling bureaucracy, whereas all three of the original variables continued to have significant independent effects. The regression and correlational results are summarized in Table 7. Note that entering the three demographic variables had negligible effects on the results.

DISCUSSION

The empirical phase of the study demonstrated that enabling structure is a unitary construct that can be measured reliably and validly with a 12-item Likert-type scale. In three separate samples, the factor structure of the construct was confirmed. Construct and predictive validity were supported in all three analyses. We purposefully used different variables in each succeeding study to demonstrate the validity of enabling bureaucracy. All of the predictor variables were ones for which we developed a priori theoretical rationales, and the confirmation of each hypothesis provided further evidence to bolster the idea of enabling structures. Hence, in the first sample, enabling structure was negatively related to dependence of teachers on the hierarchy and rules. In the second sample, enabling structure was positively related to trust between teachers and between teachers and the principal but negatively related to a sense of powerlessness among teachers. In the third sample, enabling structure was positively related to faculty trust in the principal and negatively related to both role conflict and truth spinning in schools.

Enabling schools encourage trusting relations between teachers and between teachers and the principal; facilitate telling the truth and make it unnecessary, and likely dysfunctional, to spin the truth; and limit the degree of role conflict because we suspect trust and truthfulness make rigid roles obsolete. Trust, truthfulness, and limited role conflict are hallmarks of enabling organizations; indeed, they are central to enabling schools regardless of size, SES, and urbanicity.

The theoretical rationale for the hypotheses assumed that trust was a key ingredient of organizational life because it enables a leader to innovate without fear of creating destructive conflict (De Dreu & Van De Vliert, 1997). The findings of this study support the argument that enabling structures are characterized by principals who help teachers solve problems, encourage openness, and support teachers to do their jobs without undue concern for conflict and punishment. Enabling organizations foster trust and help teachers learn from mistakes. Such behaviors should promote truthful and authentic interactions and limit concealment, deception, and delusion; in fact, the evidence supports the notion that enabling structures dampen truth spinning, and truth spinning undermines enabling bureaucracies. Research is beginning to show the pivotal importance of organizational trust in facilitating student achievement (Goddard, Tschannen-Moran, & Hoy, in press). The strong link between faculty trust and enabling organization found in this study suggests that such structures will also aid student achievement.

Role conflict typically undermines efficient operation by confusing participants (DiPaola & Hoy, 2001) and creating tension and a destructive edge in organizational relations (Rizzo, House, & Lirtzman, 1970).

Table 15.7.   of Correlational and Regression Analyses of Enabling Structure

Independent Variables	Zero-Order Correlations (r)	Regression 1 Standardized Beta Weights	Regression 2 Standardized Beta Weights
Role conflict	-.71**	-.30**	-.30**
Trust in principal	.74**	.39**	.40**
Truth spinning	-.78**	-.38**	-.40**
Demographic variables			
Socioeconomic Status	-.01	—	-.07
Size	-.18	—	.05
Urbanicity	-.22*	—	.01
Multiple correlation		$R = .789**$	$R = .801**$
		(Adjusted $R^2 = .78$)	(Adjusted $R^2 = .79$)

$*p < .05. **p < .01.$

Because enabling structures encourage cooperation, flexibility, problem solving, and broad professional autonomy, it is not surprising that enabling structures are relatively free of role conflict and are in a stronger position to deal with emerging professional problems than are hindering structures. Furthermore, the finding that enabling structure is negatively related to sense of powerlessness (Hoy & Sweetland, 2000) suggests that enabling structure empowers rather than alienates teachers.

One of the limitations with our analysis is that we have sketched enabling bureaucracy in broad and general strokes. The items that measure the concept are general. For example, teachers say, "Administrative rules are guides to solutions rather than rigid procedures" and "substitutes for professional judgments." But what solutions and what judgments? Enabling structures seem to be humanistic; that is, ones that are concerned as much with causes of behavior as the actual act. The focus of enabling rules is on helping not punishing. Thus, deviation from the rules likely triggers a search for the cause rather than simple punishment. When teachers, for example, do not comply with the administrative rule that students must be in class before the bell rings, or they are sent to the office, then the critical question is why. Is the time too short? Are teachers simply indifferent? Is teacher noncompliance a symbolic act of resentment? Is there no follow-up from the office? Is the rule a meaningless ritual? The point is that in hindering bureaucracies, the emphasis is on compliance, whereas in our conceptualization of enabling school structures, the deviation is seen as a problem to be understood and solved. Deviation from the tardy rule can be used as a way to punish teachers, or it can be seen as an opportunity to solve a problem. The kind of school structure, enabling or hindering, will define which type of rule it is.

We also suspect that in schools where administrative rules are used to coerce teachers to comply, there may be a cascading effect. Teachers may be tempted to turn their frustrations with the administration toward their students by treating their students the same way they are treated by their superiors. Unconditional and absolute rules imposed on teachers may lead to unconditional and absolute rules imposed on students. Indeed, the rigid rules may become part of a culture of coercion that permeates relationships at all levels in the school including teacher-administrator, student-teacher, and student-administrator. The picture we are sketching is extreme. The issue is a matter of degree rather than dichotomy. The point is that as we search for examples, those that come to mind are extreme, and we have only scratched the surface.

As we have seen, rules and hierarchy vary together. When the rules are enabling, so is the hierarchy and vice versa. In high schools, the principal and assistants represent the hierarchy. What are examples of enabling hierarchies? When teachers describe the administration as one that helps them do their job or facilitates the mission of the school, What specifically does that mean? Clearly, it means different things in different schools, but it is likely that teachers are describing an administration that is sympathetic, supportive, and perhaps collegial. The principal in an enabling school is one who finds ways to help teachers succeed rather than one who monitors teacher behavior to ensure compliance. For example, in one school where there was tremendous pressure on everyone to get student proficiency tests above the state average, we found a principal with an open door policy with teachers. She cared for teachers and respected their professional judgments. She was unwilling to tell teachers how to get the scores up, and instead was a colleague working with them on this difficult problem. She demonstrated her commitment to them and problem solving by working long and hard with teachers. One hallmark of her supportive behavior was that teachers knew that they could always find this principal in her office every Saturday from 9:00 a.m. until 12:00 p.m. There was no press for teachers to be in school on Saturdays, but everyone knew that this principal was always available and ready to talk either on the phone or in person. She enabled. No secretaries, no students, no guidance counselors, no other administrators, just the principal was their every Saturday. Leading by example was evident; her standards for her own behavior were higher than those she held for her teachers, and teachers respected her for it. We suspect that transformational leadership (Bass & Avoilio, 1994; Leithwood & Duke, 1999) is strongly related to the creation of enabling school structures, but of course, that remains an empirical question.

The examples that we have provided for enabling school structures are modest at best. Quantitative approaches can be used to identify schools with enabling and hindering structures, but what is needed at this juncture are also qualitative studies to map specific examples of enabling rules and enabling hierarchy, as well as the internal dynamics of such structures. In this way, we will learn the specifics of enabling authority and enabling rules in schools, which will aid in the suggestion of strategies of action for school principals and teachers.

The conceptualization and measure of school structures along an enabling-hindering continuum is useful and sets the frame for a host of research questions. We have already suggested the need for qualitative studies to enhance and enrich the concept of enabling school structure. We now turn to a few examples of the kind of quantitative studies that are needed to move this line of inquiry forward. First, the structure of schools is likely related to the effectiveness of schools. Teachers are more likely to enjoy and be professionally challenged by enabling structures than by hindering ones; hence, teacher morale and job satisfaction should be higher. But, furthermore, enabling school structures should be places where professional relations are open, collegial, supportive and empowering. Such organizations should have high collective efficacy. Collective efficacy should give teachers purpose, encourage them to plan and take responsibility for student achievement, and foster persistence in teaching to overcome temporary setbacks (Bandura, 1997; Sweetland & Hoy, 2000). Such planning, persistence, purpose, and responsibility should promote higher levels of student achievement in schools (Bandura, 1997).

Enabling school structures should generate enabling knowledge. Enabling knowledge has at least two meanings. First, it refers to knowledge that enables one to solve problems, and second, it refers to the creation of knowledge by organizations. We predict that enabling school structures are critical in both of these enterprises: enabling problem solving and the creation of knowledge by organizations. Hence, enabling bureaucracy should be directly associated with the school as a learning organization. Knowledge needs to be supported by a number of activities that enable it to develop in spite of obstacles, and we predict that enabling structures provide such a context for schools. Knowledge enabling involves both deliberate activities—those that can be planned and directed by the administration and emergent ones that are the unintended consequence of intended actions or the discovery after the fact that a particular activity enhances knowledge creation (Von Krogh, Ichijo, & Nonaka, 2000). In sum, we hypothesize that enabling school structures are important to the development of effective learning organizations (Senge, 1990) and to the creation of enabling knowledge.

Another significant series of research questions revolves around the conditions that are necessary to facilitate the emergence of enabling school structures. What environmental constraints enhance and prevent the development of enabling structures? To what extent do recent efforts to make schools more accountable to the public impede or enhance the development of such organizations? What kind of educational leadership is necessary for enabling schools? Is transformational leadership a necessary condition? How do race (Larson, 1997) and gender (Capper, 1993) affect school organization? To what extent is enabling structure related to a culture of openness? To motivation of teachers? To power and politics? To constructive and destructive conflict? To open patterns of communication? To shared decision making? And the list goes on. There seems to be little question that enabling bureaucracy is a heuristic construct, one that is pivotal in designing and building better schools.

CONCLUSION

We have conceptualized enabling school bureaucracy along a continuum with enabling at one pole and hindering at the other. Rules and hierarchy are the two major aspects of the school structure, which combine to form a unitary, bipolar construct. Furthermore, we have operationalized school structure with a 12-item Likert-type scale that measures the degree to which a school structure is enabling or hindering. The reliability of the scale has been high and the validity strong in three separate samples.

The prototype for an enabling bureaucracy is a hierarchy that helps rather than hinders and a system of rules and regulations that guides problem solving rather than punishes failure. Although hierarchy can hinder, that need not be the case; in fact, in enabling school structures principals and teachers work cooperatively across recognized authority boundaries while retaining their distinctive roles. Similarly, rules and regulations are flexible guides for problem solving rather than constraints that create problems. In brief, both hierarchy and rules are mechanisms to support teachers rather than vehicles to enhance principal power.

The prototype for a hindering bureaucracy is a hierarchy that impedes and a system of rules and regulations that is coercive. The basic objective of hierarchy is disciplined compliance of teachers. The underlying administrative assumption in hindering structures is that teacher behavior must be closely managed and strictly controlled. To achieve the goal of disciplined compliance, the hierarchy and rules are used to gain conformity. Indeed rules and regulations are used to buttress administrative control, which in turn typically hinders the effectiveness of teachers. In sum, the roles of hierarchy and rules are to assure that reluctant, incompetent, and irresponsible teachers do what administrators prescribe. The power of the principal is enhanced but the work of the teachers is diminished.

The picture that emerges in enabling bureaucracy is an organization imbued with trust; faculty trust the principal and each other. There is no need for varnishing the truth, and indeed, little truth spinning is found. On the other hand, a hindering structure (the other end of the enabling continuum) is characterized by teacher sense of powerlessness, role conflict, and dependence on rules and the hierarchy. We suspect that teachers in hindering structures try to avoid conflict and play it safe by hiding behind rules and demonstrating blind obedience to authority. Moreover, when teachers are confronted with coercive rules, they likely defend their actions by spinning the truth in ways to satisfy their superiors and avoid conflict and punishment.

In this analysis, our major concern was exploring the theoretical and empirical roots of a new construct of school structure, one that enables rather than hinders. In this regard, our work is encouraging, but it is merely a beginning of what we hope will be a new and important line of inquiry about school structure, school improvement, and student achievement. We postulate that better schools are possible, and one key ingredient to more effective schools is a school structure that enables participants to do their jobs more creatively, cooperatively, and professionally. Designing better schools seems inextricably bound to creating enabling school structures.

REFERENCES

Adler, P. S. (1993). The "learning bureaucracy": New United Motors Manufacturing Incorporated. In B. M. Staw & L. L. Staw (Eds.), *Research in organizational behavior* (Vol. 12, pp. 111-194). Greenwich, CT: JAI.

Adler, P. S. (1999). Building better bureaucracies. *The Academy of Management Executive, 13*, 36-49.

Adler, P. S., & Borys, B. (1996). Two types of bureaucracy: Enabling and coercive. *Administrative Science Quarterly, 41*, 61-89.

Aiken, M., & Hage, J. (1968). Organizational interdependence and intra-organizational structure. *American Sociological Review, 33*, 912-930.

Anderson, J. G. (1968). *Bureaucracy in education*. Baltimore: Johns Hopkins Press.

Arches, J. (1991). Social structure, burnout, and job satisfaction. *Social Work, 36*(3), 202-206.

Bandura, A. (1997). *Self-efficacy: The exercise of control*. New York: Freeman.

Bass, B. M., & Avolio, B. J. (1994). Introduction. In B. M. Bass & B. J. Avolio (Eds.), *Improving organizational effectiveness through transformational leadership* (pp. 1-10). Thousand Oaks, CA: Sage.

Bennis, W., & Nanus, B. (1985). *Leaders: The strategies for taking charge*. New York: Harper & Row.

Blau, P. M. (1955). *The dynamics of bureaucracy*. Chicago: University of Chicago Press.

Blau, P. M., & Scott, W. R. (1962). *Formal organizations: A comparative approach*. San Francisco: Chandler.

Capper, C. (1993). *Educational administration in a pluralistic society*. Albany: State University of New York Press.

Coleman, J. S. (1974). *Power and structure of society*. New York: Norton.

Covey, S. R. (1990). *The seven habits of highly effective people: Restoring the character ethic*. New York: Simon & Schuster.

Craig, T. (1995). Achieving innovation through bureaucracy. *California Management Review, 38*(10), 8-36.

Damanpour, F. (1991). Organizational innovation. *Academy of Management Journal, 34*, 555-591.

De Dreu, C., & Van De Vliert, E. (1997). *Using conflict in organizations*. Thousand Oaks, CA: Sage.

DiPaola, M. F., & Hoy, W. K. (2001). *School structure and conflict: Constructive and destructive consequences of conflict in schools*. Unpublished manuscript.

Etzioni, A. (1961). *A comparative analysis of complex organizations*. New York: Free Press.

Etzioni, A. (1975). *A comparative analysis of complex organization* (Rev. ed.). New York: Free Press.

Ferguson, K. E. (1984). *The feminist case against bureaucracy.* Philadelphia: Temple University Press.

Goddard, R. D., Tschannen-Moran, M., & Hoy, W. K. (in press). Teacher trust in students and parents: A multilevel examination of the distribution and effects of teacher trust in urban elementary schools. *Elementary School Journal.*

Gouldner, A. (1954). *Patterns of industrial bureaucracy.* New York: Free Press.

Hage, J., & Aiken, M. (1970). *Social change in complex organizations.* New York: Random House.

Halpin, A. W. (1959). *The leader behavior of school superintendents.* Chicago: Midwest Administrative Center.

Hirschhorn, L. (1997). *Reworking authority: Leading and following in a post-modern organization.* Cambridge, MA: MIT Press.

Hoy, W. K., Blazovsky, R., & Newland, W. (1983). Bureaucracy and alienation: A comparative analysis. *The Journal of Educational Administration, 21,* 109-121.

Hoy, W. K., & Miskel, C. G. (2001). *Educational administration: Theory, research, and practice* (6th ed.). New York: McGraw-Hill.

Hoy, W. K., & Sweetland, S. R. (2000). School bureaucracies that work: Enabling, not coercive. *Journal of School Leadership, 10,* 525-541.

Hoy, W. K., & Tschannen-Moran, M. (1999). Five faces of trust: An empirical confirmation in urban elementary schools. *Journal of School Leadership, 9,* 184-208.

Isherwood, G., & Hoy, W. K. (1973). Bureaucracy, powerlessness, and teacher work values. *Journal of Educational Administration, 9,* 124-38.

Jackson, S., & Schuler, R. S. (1985). A meta-analysis and conceptual critique of research on role ambiguity and role conflict in work settings. *Organizational Behavior and Human Decision Processes, 36,* 17-78.

Kakabadse, A. (1986). Organizational alienation and job climate. *Small Group Behavior, 17,* 458-471.

Larson, C. L. (1997). Is the land of Oz an alien nation? A sociopolitical study of school community conflict. *Educational Administration Quarterly, 33,* 312-350.

Leithwood, K., & Duke, D. L. (1999). A century's quest to understand school leadership. In J. Murphy & K. S. Louis (Eds.), *Handbook of research on educational administration* (pp. 45-72). San Francisco: Jossey-Bass.

Martin, J., & Knopoff, K. (in press). The gendered implications of apparently gender-neutral theory: Rereading Weber. In E. Freeman & A. Larson (Eds.), *Ruffin lectures series: Business ethics and women's studies* (Vol. 3). Oxford: Oxford University Press.

Merton, R. (1957). *Social theory and social structure.* New York: Free Press.

Michaels, R. E., Cron, W. L., Dubinsky, A. J., & Joachimsthaler, E. A. (1988). Influence of formalization on the organizational commitment and work alienation of salespeople and industrial buyers. *Journal of Marketing Research, 25,* 376-383.

Mintzberg, H. (1979). *The structuring of organizations.* Englewood Cliffs, NJ: Prentice Hall.

Mintzberg, H. (1989). *Mintzberg on management.* New York: Free Press.

Moeller, G. H., & Charters, W. W., Jr. (1966). Relation of bureaucratization to sense of power among teachers. *Administrative Science Quarterly, 10*, 444-465.

Nyberg, D. (1993), *The varnished truth: Truth telling and deceiving in ordinary life.* Chicago: University of Chicago Press.

Rizzo, J., House, R., & Lirtzman, S. (1970). Role conflict and ambiguity in complex organizations. *Administrative Science Quarterly, 15*, 150-163.

Rousseau, D. M. (1978). Characteristics of departments, positions, and individuals: Contexts for attitudes and behavior. *Administrative Science Quarterly, 23*, 521-540.

Scott, W. R. (1998). *Organizations: Rational, natural, and open systems* (4th ed.). Englewood Cliffs, NJ: Prentice Hall.

Senatra, P. T. (1980). Role conflict, role ambiguity, and organizational climate in a public accounting firm. *Accounting Review, 55*, 594-603.

Senge, P. M. (1990). *The fifth discipline: The art and practice of the learning organization.* New York: Doubleday.

Sweetland, S. R., & Hoy, W. K. (in press). Varnishing the truth in schools: Principals and teachers spinning reality. *Journal of Educational Administration.*

Sweetland, S. R., & Hoy, W. K. (2000). School characteristics and educational outcomes: Toward an organizational model of student achievement in middle schools. *Educational Administration Quarterly, 36*, 703-729.

Von Krogh, G., Ichijo, K., & Nonaka, I. (2000). *Enabling knowledge creation.* New York: Oxford University Press.

Weber, M. (1947). *The theory of social and economic organizations.* (A. M. Henderson & T. Parsons, Trans.) New York: Free Press.

CHAPTER 16

AN ANALYSIS OF ENABLING AND MINDFUL SCHOOL STRUCTURES

Some Theoretical, Research, and Practical Considerations[1]

Wayne K. Hoy

This inquiry is a theoretical analysis that attempts to identify the features of school structure that efficiently promote positive outcomes of organization while limiting negative consequences that are often associated with bureaucratic structures. To that end, the concepts of enabling structures and mindful organizations are developed, contrasted, and synthesized. Then, the research and practical implications of enabling and mindful school structures are proposed and discussed.

Common usage of the term bureaucracy is pejorative, but like it or not, most schools are bureaucracies because they possess a hierarchy of

Reprinted by permission from the *Journal of Educational Administration*, Vol. 41, pp. 87-108. Copyright © 2003. All rights reserved.

authority, division of labor, impersonality, objective standards, technical competence, and rules and regulations—classic characteristics of bureaucracy (Weber, 1947). Weber claims such structures are capable of reaching the highest degree of administrative efficiency. Yet, bureaucracies are criticized because they produce overconformity and rigidities (Gouldner, 1954; Merton, 1957), block and distort communication (Blau & Scott, 1962), alienate and exploit workers (Aiken & Hage, 1968; Scott, 1998), stifle and eliminate innovation (Hage & Aiken, 1970), and are passive and indifferent to their publics (Coleman, 1974; Scott, 1998). Feminists assault bureaucracy as an invention of men that rewards the masculine virtues as competition and power and eschews the feminine values such as collaboration and equality (Ferguson, 1984; Martin & Knopoff, 1999). Principals, teachers, and school executives blame state bureaucracies for artificial barriers, which hinder the development of educational programs to meet community needs. The common thread running through all these criticisms is human frustration with unresponsive structures, rigid rules, and mindless policies.

Notwithstanding these criticisms, organizations of any size, including schools, have bureaucratic features because they need appropriately designed formal procedures and hierarchical structures to prevent chaos and promote efficiency. This inquiry has a number of purposes: first, to describe a different kind of bureaucratic structure in schools, one that enables teachers rather than hinders or punishes them; second, to begin to flesh out some specific examples of enabling structures; third, to develop construct of organizational mindfulness in schools; fourth, to compare and contrast mindful and enabling school structures; and finally, to consider the research and practical implications of enabling and mindful structures.

SCHOOL STRUCTURES

There is little doubt that bureaucratic structures can be detrimental to participants and publics, but that is only half the picture. Bureaucracies can increase satisfaction (Michaels, Cron, Dubinsky, & Joachimsthaler, 1988), support innovation (Damanpour, 1991; Craig, 1995), reduce role conflict (Senatra, 1980), as well as diminish alienation in organizations including public schools (Moeller & Charters, 1966; Jackson & Schuler, 1985). The extant literature paints two contrasting pictures of human response to bureaucracy. The dark side reveals alienation, discontent, rigidity, and dullness, but the bright view highlights commitment, flexibility, responsibility, and effectiveness (Adler, 1999; Adler & Borys, 1996; Hoy & Miskel, 2001, Hoy & Sweetland, 2001; Sinden, Hoy, & Sweetland,

2002). It is the dark view, however, that is emphasized and demonized in education.

Consider the bright side of the picture for schools. What kind of school configurations can achieve the positive outcomes of structure and avoid the negative ones? Earlier research (Hoy & Sweetland, 2000, 2001) has shown that school structures vary along a continuum from enabling at one extreme to hindering at the other. Formalization and centralization are the fundamental features of structure that define the two extremes of this continuum.

Formalization

Formalization is the extent to which the organization has written rules, regulations, procedures, and policies. Gouldner's (1954) classic analysis of rules and regulations offers two kinds of formalization—punishment-centered and representative. Building upon Gouldner's earlier work, Adler and Borys (1996) present a more comprehensive and contemporary theoretical analysis of formalization—coercive and enabling—which offers a deeper analysis of how work practices are affected by the features, design, and implementation of enabling and coercive structures.

Coercive formalization tends to generate alienation at the expense of commitment. Coercive rules and procedures constrain and even punish subordinates for deviance rather than reward unusual and productive practices. Instead of promoting flexibility and organizational learning, coercive procedures force reluctant subordinates to acquiesce and comply with formal routines. The consequences are not that surprising. For example, formalization is positively associated with absenteeism, stress, alienation, and negatively related to job satisfaction and innovation (Arches, 1991; Kakabadse, 1986; Rousseau, 1978). Similar relations are found in schools (Anderson, 1968; Isherwood & Hoy, 1973; Hoy, Blazovsky, & Newland, 1983; Hoy & Sweetland, 2000).

Rules cannot be designed to make behavior foolproof; moreover, the more restrictive the procedures, the more hindering they are in dynamic situations. Coercive procedures frustrate two-way communication, are rigid and autocratic, define problems as restraints, foster mistrust, demand consensus, punish mistakes, and fear the unexpected. In sum, they demand blind obedience to the rules.

Enabling formalization, in contrast, helps participants find solutions to problems because here the rules and procedures are viewed as flexible guidelines that reflect "best practices" rather than rigid rules. Enabling procedures help subordinates deal with surprises and crises (Adler & Borys, 1996) because flexibility is often required, for example, substituting expert judgments for rules. Loyally adhering to the rules may be safe organizational behavior, but it dampens innovative ways to respond to novel situations. Indeed, as a general rule, professional judgment is encouraged and acceptable when it enables problem solving.

Successful enabling procedures invite open communication and encourage viewing problems are opportunities. Procedures that foster trust and value differences help organizations anticipate the unexpected and learn from their mistakes; that is, they facilitate problem solving and organizational learning. Enabling strategies require participation and collaboration and improvement is the goal, whereas coercive procedures are autocratic and unyielding. Adverse consequences are not necessarily inherent in rules themselves, but rather are a function of the kind of decisions that administrators make in establishing rules and procedures (Adler, 1999).

Centralization

Centralization of authority is the locus of control for organizational decision making; it is the degree to which employees participate in decision making (Aiken & Hage, 1968). In highly centralization organizations, decision making is concentrated at the top in the hands of a few, whereas, low centralization depicts a decision-making structure that is diffuse and shared. Hierarchy of authority, high centralization, is a classic characteristic of bureaucracy; authority is concentrated at the top and flows down the chain of command. Centralization can be viewed along a continuum from hindering at one pole to enabling at the other.

Hindering centralization is a structure and administration that impede rather than help subordinates solve problems and do their work. The hierarchy obstructs innovation, and administrators use their power to control and to discipline teachers. In schools when professional work is controlled by an autocratic administration, the consequence is often resistance by teachers who are coerced to play the game of satisfying artificial standards rather than making independent judgments about the needs of their students (Hoy, Blazovsky, & Newland, 1983). Such hierarchies typically respond to outside pressures in such dysfunctional ways as increasing autocratic supervision, overstandardizing work processes, and standardizing outputs (Mintzberg, 1979, 1989), all of which can hinder the effective operation of the organization. Make no mistake, schools like all complex organizations require direction, coordination, and compliance, and hierarchy is central to these efforts. But the ubiquitous control mentality that pervades hindering structures produces dissatisfaction, alienation, and hostility (Aiken & Hage, 1968; Hoy, Blazovsky, & Newland, 1983; Mintzberg, 1989).

Enabling centralization helps solve problems rather than getting in the way. The authority structure of an organization can help superiors and subordinates work across recognized authority boundaries while retaining their distinctive roles (Hirschhorn, 1997). Enabling hierarchy is an amalgam of authority where members feel confident and are able to exercise power in their professional roles. Enabling centralization is flexible, cooperative, and collaborative rather than rigid, autocratic, and controlling. Administrators use their power and authority to buffer teachers and design structures that facilitate teaching and learning.

School Structures: Enabling to Hindering

Organizational structure is inevitable. Schools have boards, superintendents, assistant superintendents, curriculum directors, principals, department heads, assistant principals, teachers, and students. Regardless of all the talk about flat structures, empowerment, teacher participation, and reform, schools like all formal organizations have hierarchical structures. In spite of all the reform rhetoric, hierarchy of authority in schools will inevitably continue. In fact, the accountability movement itself demands more not less hierarchy. The key, however, is to avoid the dysfunctions of centralization by changing the *kind* of hierarchy rather than eliminating it.

Schools need structures that enable rather than hinder, or as Hirschhorn (1997) suggests, organizations must both embrace hierarchy and enliven it with feelings and passion. Organizational members don't like to be manipulated and controlled. But just as formalization can be enabling rather than coercive, hierarchy can be enabling rather than coercive or hindering. The adverse consequences of hierarchy are not inherent in hierarchy itself but rather are a function of the decisions administrators make as they implement their authority. Decentralization of authority is not synonymous with enabling; the problem is more complicated. The argument is not against hierarchy per se but rather against a specific kind of centralization—hierarchy that hinders. Again, the issue is the *kind* not the *amount* of centralization (Hoy & Sweetland, 2000).

Although centralization and formalization were conceptualized as two separate dimensions of structure, several empirical factor analytic studies of schools have shown that not to be the case; in fact, the two variables vary together and form a single, unitary continuum of structure (Hoy & Sweetland, 2000; Hoy & Sweetland 2001). When rules are enabling so is the hierarchy and vice versa. At the extremes, enabling structures have both enabling rules and hierarchies, whereas hindering structures have both coercive rules and hindering hierarchies.

Research (Hoy & Sweetland, 2001) also suggests that enabling school structures encourage trusting relations among teachers and between teachers and the principal. Such structures facilitate telling the truth and make it unnecessary and likely dysfunctional to spin the truth. Moreover, enabling school structures limit the degree of role conflict because trust and truthfulness make rigid roles obsolete. In brief, trust, truthfulness, and limited role conflict were hallmarks of enabling organizations; indeed, they were central to enabling schools regardless of size, socioeconomic status, and urbanicity (Hoy & Sweetland, 2001). Also, as theoretically expected, enabling school structure correlated positively with collegial trust in teachers and negatively with hierarchical dependence, rule dependence, and teacher sense of powerlessness (Hoy & Sweetland, 2000). In other words, when school structure was enabling, teachers trust each other, demonstrate professional autonomy, are not bound by rigid rules, and do not feel powerlessness.

The prototype for an **enabling structure** is a hierarchy of authority and a system of rules and regulations that help rather than hinder the teaching-learning mission of the school. Although hierarchy often hinders, that need not be the case; in fact, in enabling structures, principals and teachers work cooperatively across recognized authority boundaries while retaining their distinctive roles. Similarly, rules and regulations are flexible guides rather than restraints to problem solving. Both the authority hierarchy and the rules and procedures are mechanisms that support the work of the teachers rather than means to enhance the power of the principal. Enabling schools develop an atmosphere of trust and teacher commitment to the school and its mission.

The prototype for a **hindering structure** is a hierarchy of authority that hinders and a system of rules and regulations that is coercive. The hierarchy has as its primary goal controlled and disciplined compliance of teachers. The underlying assumption in these organizations is that teacher behavior must be closely supervised and tightly regulated. In order to achieve that goal not only is the hierarchy of authority used to gain compliance but also the system of rules and regulations is used to buttress control and punish deviance. The consequence typically hinders and restrains the performance of teachers. In brief, the role of authority, rules, procedures, and policy is to assure that potentially reluctant and irresponsible teachers do what is prescribed by the administration. The power of the principal is enhanced and the work of the teachers is hindered. A culture of trust and cooperation is undermined and eventually replaced by one of conflict and alienation. Key features of the two types of structures are summarized in Table 16.1.

Table 16.1.   Contrasting Characteristics of Enabling and Hindering Structures

Characteristics of Enabling Structures	Characteristics of Hindering Structures
View problems as opportunities	View problems as obstacles
Foster trust	Produce mistrust
Value differences	Demand consensus
Learn from mistakes	Punish mistakes
Anticipate the unexpected	Fear the unexpected
Facilitate problem solving	Frustrate problems solving
Enable cooperation	Promote control and compliance
Encourage innovation	Bound to the status quo
Flexible	Rigid

Some Illustrations

Professors speak in abstractions and generalizations; practitioners want specifics and concrete examples. Let's see if we can come up with a few examples of enabling administrative behavior. In high schools, the principal and assistants represent the hierarchy. Teachers describe the administration as enabling (Hoy & Sweetland, 2001) when it "helps them do their job" or "facilitates the mission of the school." But what specifically does that mean?

It means different things in different schools, but in general, teachers are describing an administration that is flexible, sympathetic, supportive, and perhaps collegial. Principals in an enabling school find ways to help teachers succeed rather than being obsessed with control and compliance. For example, in one school (Hoy & Sweetland, 2001) there was tremendous pressure on everyone to get student proficiency tests above the state average. The principal had an open door policy, and she cared for teachers and respected their professional expertise. She would not and did not tell teachers how to get the scores up. Instead she viewed herself as colleague working with teachers on this difficult problem. She demonstrated her commitment to teachers and problem solving by working long and hard with teachers. A hallmark of her enabling behavior was that teachers knew that they could always find her at work and in her office every Saturday from nine-to-noon. There was no press, however, for others to be in school on Saturdays, but everyone knew the principal was available and ready to talk either on the phone or in person every Saturday mornings. No secretaries, no students, no guidance counselors, no other administrators, just the principal. She enabled. Leading by example was evident; her standards for her own behavior were higher than those she held for her teachers, and teachers respected her for it. We suspect that transformational leadership (Bass & Avoilio, 1994; Leithwood & Duke, 1999) is strongly related to the creation of enabling school structures, but of course, that remains an empirical question.

Another example of enabling administrative behavior comes from a superintendent who enabled by bending rigid rules. In an interview with him in a study of tacit knowledge, he gave the following account:

> Certain policies are mandated by state, such as special education or whatever. To give you an illustration of "doing what is right"—In my state, if you have twenty kids with the same language, you have to set up a separate program and teach them in their native language. The parents didn't want that; the kids didn't want it; and the teachers didn't want it. But that was a rule I had to live with. When the director of bilingual education would come to me and say, "We have 19 Koreans and a 20th Korean just enrolled, now we have to end English as a second language." I would say, "I think that kid is Japanese." And she would leave and understand what I was saying. So, I did some things that were against the rules ... but I did them for two reasons. One, the programs we had in place were much more successful for those kids. And two, I knew that the parents themselves were never lobbying for it. In fact, you would have to say to 20 Korean parents, we now have to teach your children in Korean. And they would insist, we want English. And I have to say, "I'm sorry, that's the law." So, I deliberately ignored the rules and regulations.... And took some risks.

Although this is an extreme example and we are not advocating violating the law or questioning the value of bilingual education, the example does illustrate bending the rules for good purpose. The superintendent explained:

> As long as there was no personal gain on my part or the people around me ... the motivation was one that I believed in and the participants believed in and it was a silly, stupid rule that shouldn't have been there in the first place, I believed justified in bending the rule for the good of the kids.

He told that story around the state, and it was common knowledge to the county superintendent and the state department of education. The state officials did nothing because they knew there was implicit agreement in this case that strict adherence to this rule did not make sense, and they did not want to make an issue of the matter because it might be embarrassing for a lot of important people; thus they ignored the matter. The superintendent enabled his school to move forward by promoting flexibility and preventing a problem.

What about examples of enabling rules? Consider the following examples. A famous basketball coach suggested to the NCAA some twenty years ago a rule to enhance graduation rates of basketball players. He proposed that schools should not be permitted to use scholarship monies of players who did not graduate until the time at which they would have graduated. Such a rule would refocus attention on players as students not merely athletes and have enabling benefits on their education.

Here is another example. Many agencies and universities operate on annual budgets. They must expend all their monies by the end of the fiscal year or lose it. Thus, there is often a flurry of unnecessary and wasteful spending near year's end. Moreover, not spending all your money suggests that your unit or agency does not need that much money and becomes grounds for budget reduction in the next budget cycle. Imagine replacing that rigid rule with an enabling one that guaranteed the agency the same budget plus half of what they had not expended the previous year—both the agency and the funding agent would profit and the rule would enable healthy budgets and sensible spending (Langer, 1989). There seems little doubt that rules can hinder wise educational decision making, especially if they are narrowly conceived and rigidly interpreted and enforced as they are in hindering structures.

A Caveat on Enabling Structures

Enabling structures are not panaceas; they do not guarantee positive outcomes. Consider this recent example that occurred just prior to 9/11. An instructor at a Phoenix flight school called the Federal Aviation Administration (FAA) to report a student in his school who claimed he was French but refused to converse with his French speaking flight instructor. Suspicion grew as the student repeatedly failed to understand basic flying techniques but still insisted on learning how to fly a 747, the largest commercial jet. What was the FAA response to the report from the flight school? Newspaper accounts suggest the FAA responded to this and similar incidents in an "enabling way," that is, the Agency offered to provide a tutor to help the students learn English, a requirement for all commercial pilots. The point is that an enabling response can be detrimental and sometimes disastrous. If organizations have the suspect goals, enabling structures can be dysfunctional.

INDIVIDUAL AND ORGANIZATIONAL MINDFULNESS

Individuals and organizations are easily seduced by routine ways of doing things that worked at one time. There is much dependence on the use of standard categories and automatic responses to events; indeed habit itself can become mindless. This section of the analysis examines mindfulness of individuals and organizations and is based upon Langer's (1989) seminal work on individual mindfulness and Weick and Sutcliffe's (2001) more recent analysis of mindful organizations.

Individual Mindfulness

Individuals take in information either mindfully or mindlessly and in much the same way they act with or without much reflection. Too often our initial mindsets form before we do much reflection, what psychologists call *premature cognitive commitment*. We seize on standard classifications, use routine rules and procedures, and then proceed to become seduced by our habits. Even when the routine ways don't work, we often respond by simply by doing more of the same in belief that more is the key to fixing the problem. It is easy to get trapped by absolute categories and routines and difficult to break set and respond to a dynamic world in different and novel ways.

There is in all of us a "habit of mind" that adopts sets of routine categories that serve as ways of ordering and managing phenomena as we make sense out of complexity. Such habit is one of the reasons organizational participants find formal rules and regulations so appealing. Ideologies of all kinds rationalize and justify our behavior; they provide us with identities, rules of action, and standard interpretations (Trungpa, 1971). Once formed, it is difficult to break these mindsets; we act like there is only one set of rules. Yet it is the very creation of new categories and novel perspectives that characterizes mindfulness, and it is rigid reliance on old categories and distinctions that reinforces mindlessness. When teachers and administrators ritually follow rules or comply with senseless orders, they are mindless, but when they substitute their judgments for routine responses, they turn mindful.

Mindlessness grows out of repetition; individuals get used to doing things the same way; their responses become routine, automatic, and secure. Indeed much organization behavior is routinized. People do things a certain way because "that is the way it is done here." Rules and routines bring stability, efficiency, predictability, and a general comfort that things are being done "correctly," that is, according standard rules and procedures.

Concentration on goals and the single-minded pursuit of outcomes also hinder mindfulness whereas an emphasis on process promotes mindfulness. For example, teachers and administrators often emphasize goals and outcomes at the expense of process, that is, they are concerned with

"Can I do it?" rather than "How can I do it?" A process perspective focuses on defining steps to achieve goals and is guided by the general basic principle: "There are no failures, only ineffective solutions" (Langer, 1989, p. 34). In contrast, an outcome approach is narrow and generally presents facts as absolutes rather than conditionals, which further discourages alternative thoughts and novel interpretations. To break the tyranny of unreflective behavior, *facts* are better seen as statements that are *true only in some situations* but not in others. Such a stance promotes thoughtful inquiry, searches for appropriate conditions, and encourages playfulness with information and ideas.

Context is another powerful force that can lead to mindless behavior because it controls our reactions and interpretations and makes individuals susceptible to what Langer calls "context confusion." Individuals confuse the context controlling the behavior of another with the context determining their own behavior. Individuals assume that others' motives and intentions are the same as their own, which is frequently not the case. Such a perspective also promotes narrowness and rigidity because it impedes understanding behavior from different contextual perspectives. Contextual confusion reinforces action viewed from a single perspective.

Thus far, we have considered some the basic causes of mindlessness that influence our daily behavior—repetition, premature cognitive commitment, an emphasis on outcomes, and context confusion. But just what is mindfulness? *Mindfulness is ongoing scrutiny of existing expectations, continuous refinement of those expectations based on new experiences, appreciation of the subtleties of context, and identification of novel aspects of context that can improve foresight and funcitioning.*[2] Mindfulness is hard work because it requires flexibility, vigilance, openness, and the ability to break set.

Just as mindlessness relies on rigid old categories, mindfulness depends on the creation of new ones. New information must be continuously received and monitored. Mindfulness requires openness, not only to new information, but also to different points of view. Multiple perspectives and a playful approach can create novelty. Most events have many interpretations, and mindful individuals search for varied and subtle meanings. For example, behavior can usually be cast in positive or negative terms, that is, impulsive can be spontaneous, rigid can be consistent, and weak can be sensitive. Mindfulness calls for a playful and nimble state of mind.

Mindfulness can give individuals more control over their contexts by helping them create different and more useful perspectives. Langer (1989) gives the example of the Birdman of Alcatraz who was sentence to life in prison with no hope of parole. One day he found a crippled sparrow that happened in his cell. He nursed the bird back to health and thus began to cultivate an interest that led him to become a distinguished authority on bird diseases, by noticing more and more. Langer explains:

Instead of living a dull, stale existence in a cell for forty odd years, the Bird-man of Alcatraz found that boredom can be just another construct of the mind, no more certain than freedom. There is always something new to notice. And he turned what might have been absolute hell into, at the least, a fascinating, mindful purgatory. (p. 74)

The point is that mindful individuals need not be trapped in narrow contexts; there is always something new to notice. The trick is to notice and avoid the anesthetic of routine.

Mindfulness also requires that expectations be viewed as assumptions to be tested rather than givens to be accepted. Often, however, people make assumptions and then confirm them by searching only for confirming information. Overlooking disconfirming and highlighting confirming evidence means that over time, individuals see more and more confirmation based on less and less data, and their beliefs become more and more certain. The difficulty begins when individuals fail to notice that they only see what confirms their beliefs and the trouble is only acerbated by the belief that "seeing is believing." That is wrong. Weick and Sutcliffe (2001) have it right:

Believing is seeing. You see what you expect to see. You see what you have the labels to see. You see what you have the skills to manage. Everything else is a blur. And in that "everything else" lies (sic) the developing unexpected event that can bite you and undermine your best intentions. (p. 46)

In sum, mindfulness redirects attention from the expected to the unexpected, from the confirming to the disconfirming, from the comfortable to the uncomfortable, from the explicit to the implicit, from the manifest to the latent, from the factual to the probable, and from the simple to the complex. (Weick & Sutcliffe, 2001). Mindfulness is a paradox of sorts: it sees problems as opportunities and views successes as problematic; it is both optimistic and skeptical.

Organizational Mindfulness[3]

Clearly mindful organizations have mindful leaders and participants, but organizational mindfulness is an organization property—a description of the collective and not of individuals per se. Some organizations have to be mindful to survive. Consider the following:

Imagine it's a busy day, and you shrink San Francisco airport to only one short runway and one ramp and one gate. Make plans take off and land at the same time, at half the present time interval, rock the runway from side to side, and require that everyone who leaves in the morning returns the same day. Make sure the equipment is so close to the envelope that it's fragile. Then turn off the radar to avoid detection, impose strict controls on the radios, fuel the aircraft in place with their engines running, put an enemy in the air, and scatter love bombs and rockets around. Now wet the whole thing down with sea water and oil, and man it with twenty-year-olds, half of whom have never seen an airplane close-up. Oh, and by the way, try not to kill anyone.[4] (p. 357)

It is difficult to think of an environment that is so full of the unexpected and that requires mindful decision making and behavior to survive. Most organizations are not as precarious as this depiction of a working aircraft carrier. But Weick and Sutcliffe use the aircraft carrier as a prototype of highly reliable and mindful organization. They argue that five processes promote mindfulness in organizations: *preoccupation with failure, reluctance to simplify interpretations, sensitivity to operations, commitment to resilience, and deference to expertise*.

Preoccupied With Failure

To focus on failure at first blush seems defeating, yet such a preoccupation is indeed functional for the organization because it leads to continuous scanning for problems, large and small, but mostly small. Mindful leaders and organizations avoid preoccupation with their successes, in part, because success breeds contentment and sometimes arrogance, which ultimately leads to vulnerability. Instead, mindful organizations pay attention to small mistakes and seek to eliminate them. For example, if routine scanning of data shows high achievement levels for most students in their schools, then mindful organizations have leaders who examine the data to find reasons for why the few failed. An old Vedic proverb captures mindfulness, "Advert the danger not yet arisen." The word is "advert" not avert. To call attention and catch the early warning of trouble, organizations must be continuously open and alert to new information and subtle changes (Langer, 1989). Mindful organizations are sensitive to all mistakes, but especially small ones.

Reluctance to Simplify Interpretations

Mindful organizations and their leaders are also reluctant to accept simplifications because of the need to understand the subtleties of the situation. A basic goal of mindfulness is to simplify less and see more. Knowing that schools are complex and unpredictable, leaders and participants of mindful schools position themselves to see as much as possible and try to reconcile different interpretations without destroying the nuances of diversity and complexity. For example, differences in the perceptions between

African Americans and whites or between males and females toward shared decision making in the school need explanation and interpretation. Rival explanations should be developed, considered, and tested. The nuances of the situation are important and must not be overlooked.

Sensitivity to Operations

Mindful organizations signal a constant concern for the unexpected. Organizational surprises are not unexpected; they are inevitable and mindful decision makers know it. With the unexpected in mind, they try to see the "big picture." They detect problems, make continuous adjustments, and prevent them from enlarging. They are unremitting in their scan for problems and never so removed from the day-to-day operations that they have difficulty understanding what is happening and why. Thus it is especially important for school leaders to stay close teaching and learning in the classroom. Moreover, there is a close tie between sensitivity in operations and sensitivity in interpersonal relationships. Teachers who refuse to speak freely enact a system that knows less than it needs know to remain effective. Moreover, sensitivity to teaching and learning enables real-time information so there is little time lag in information processing. Preventing such an information lag means staying close to the teaching and learning.

Commitment to Resilience

Mindful organizations are committed to resilience. Because no organization or system is perfect, mindful school leaders know better than most that they must develop a capacity to detect and bounce back from mistakes. No amount of anticipation is going to prevent mistakes and surprises from occurring. Schools must not only deal with the unexpected by anticipation but also *by resilience* (Wildavsky, 1991), that is, schools and their leaders must learn to be sufficiently strong and flexible to cope with whatever negative outcomes emerge. Mindful organizations and leaders don't let failure paralyze; instead, they detect, contain, and rebound from mistakes.

Deference to Expertise

Finally, mindful school organizations avoid the mistake of embracing rigid administrative structures. Instead they search and hire people with the specific knowledge to solve their problems. To match expertise with problems, they encourage a fluid decision-making system by *deferring to expertise* not to status or experience. Rigid structures are replaced by enabling structures, in which consulting and listening to those with expertise are paramount. Authority is situational and anchored in expertise. Mindful organizations defer to expertise regardless of rank.

In sum, anticipating the unexpected means developing a state of organizational readiness in which scanning, anticipating, containing, removing, and rebounding from the unexpected are ever present. A well-developed organizational capability for mindfulness in schools has five hallmarks: it catches the unexpected early (focus on failure); it comprehends its potential importance despite its small size (reluctance to simplify); it is sensitive to the teaching and learning (sensitivity to technical operations); it removes, contains, or rebounds from the effects of the unexpected (resilience), and it embraces a structure and process that require decisions to migrate to expertise (deference to expertise). Table 16.2 summarizes the basic elements of mindfulness and mindlessness. The first three elements are individual properties and the last five are organizational ones.

MINDFUL AND ENABLING SCHOOL STRUCTURES

Thus far in this inquiry, enabling school structures and mindfulness have been examined separately, but it should be clear that conceptually these two constructs are related to each other and are perhaps complementary. The analysis continues with a discussion of some of the similarities and differences between the two concepts, proposes an integration, and develops a number of propositions. Finally a few realistic guidelines are considered to illustrate the practical as well as the theoretical significance of these constructs.

Table 16.2. Contrasting Features of Mindfulness and Mindlessness

Characteristics of Mindfulness	Characteristics of Mindlessness
Individual	Individual
• Continuous creation of new categories to interpret information	• Routine use of standard categories to interpret information
• Open to new information	• Closed to new information
• Use of multiple perspectives	• Use of a single perspective
Organizational	Organizational
• Preoccupied with failure	• Complacency
• Reluctance to simplify	• Propensity to oversimplify
• Sensitive to the unexpected	• Insensitivity to change
• Commitment to resilience	• Commitment to rigidity
• Deference to expertise	• Deference to the hierarchy

Complementary Concepts

There are certainly similarities between mindful and enabling structures. Both require trust, openness, flexibility, cooperation, and organizational learning. Both are concerned with problem solving, collaboration, and anticipating the unexpected. But it is mindfulness that directs attention to a preoccupation with failure, a characteristic not necessarily associated with enabling structures. Further, success can be a problem in enabling organizations because it breeds the seeds of its own destruction. For example, school administrators often attribute a school's success to themselves or at least to their teachers rather than to luck. As the school grows more confident in its administrators, teachers, and rules and procedures, it begins to rely on the procedures to warn them of potential problems, but the school and its procedures are usually more focused on its successes and tend to ignore its shortcomings. In the long run, such a stance undermines its effectiveness.

A common feature of both mindful and enabling perspectives is an emphasis on learning from mistakes. Hiding behind the rules and regulations is the antithesis of both enabling and mindful structures. When rules become the mechanism for feeling secure and comfortable, the perspective becomes one of protecting oneself rather than taking risks and engaging in problems solving activities. School administrators need to promote a mindful collective in which people are rewarded for questioning, for finding mistakes, for admitting their own mistakes, and for being open with each other, behaviors that can be cultivated through thoughtful leadership. Teachers need to feel safe enough to question the rules, the procedures, the principal, and each other.

Enabling structures have flexible hierarchies, which are attuned to expertise much in the same way that mindful organizations defer to expertise rather that status or experience. Both constructs stress dynamic structures that shift leadership and problem solving strategies in ways that match expertise with the problem at hand. Reliance on the hierarchy to solve emergent problems is neither enabling nor mindful; in fact, it is both hindering and mindless. The resilience of mindfulness complements the flexibility of enabling behavior just as the rigidity of mindlessness reinforces the inflexibility of hindering structures.

It is difficult to imagine a mindful organization that is not enabling, but it is possible to conceive of enabling organizations that are not mindful. Such enabling structures would be mindless in the sense that they would facilitate inappropriate procedures and behaviors. They would be flexible and supportive but misdirected, and their initial success would render them complacent and insensitive to changing conditions. Over time, pressure would develop to correct their performances. In fact, in the long-term, mindfulness might be the antidote for correcting for inappropriate goals, objectives, and behaviors. Mindfulness calls for continuous scanning and monitoring of activities and pays special attention to the smallest subtleties and deviations. Questioning and openness are encouraged; thus, inappropriate goals would likely to be identified and changed more quickly in structures that are mindful. Structures can enable the wrong thing, but mindful structures have a continuous process of scanning and checking built into their functioning that should provide a self-correction for errant ways.

In sum, for the most part the concepts of enabling and mindful structures are complementary; they have much more in common than differences. Although both focus on similar processes and procedures, there are a few contrasts. Mindful organizations have a preoccupation with failure, a resiliency, and a sensitivity to the unexpected that some enabling structures lack. Yet, the expectation is that mindfulness and enabling go together, that is, two concepts are expected to be strongly associated.

In Figure 16.1 we present a synthesis of the two constructs with predictions of their actual frequencies for schools. Organizations that are both mindful and enabling are the prototype for learning organization. Coercive organizations are both mindless and hindering; they are likely misdirected, rigid, autocratic structures that punish participants for questioning or noncompliant behavior. Both of these congruent types of organizations are likely occurrences because of their complementarity. Occasionally, enabling structures are mindless organizations in their pur-

Enabling Structure

	Enabling	Hindering
Mindful	Learning Organization **(Likely)**	Mindful, but Hindering Organization **(Least Likely)**
Mindless	Mindless Organization **(Less Likely)**	Coercive Organization **(Likely)**

Mindful Organization

Figure 16.1.   A typology of school organizations.

suit of the wrong strategies and objectives. Finally, although theoretically possible, it seems rare and least likely that organizations will be both mindful and hindering.

Some Hypotheses

Next, some hypotheses are proposed to illustrate the research potential of the constructs of mindfulness and enabling structure. Mindfulness can be examined at the individual level or the collective level. The exploration of administrator mindfulness is important, at least in part, because principals play such a crucial role in developing the organizational climate of schools. What personal traits facilitate the emergence of mindfulness in administrators and teachers? Because breaking mindset, being open to new information, and using multiple perspectives and conditional thinking are so pivotal in individual mindfulness, it seems reasonable to assume that personality traits that predispose people to act otherwise prevent mindful behavior. One such concept is the authoritarian personality.

Beginning with the classic studies of Adorno and his colleagues (1950) and continuing with contemporary analyses of Altemeyer (1996), the authoritarian personality has been a topic of interest to many social scientists. The underlying theory of the authoritarian personality is the assumption that some people have attitudinal predispositions or orientations to respond the same general way to authority, in particular, to submit to those who have legitimate authority (authoritarian submission), to be aggressive to groups and people targeted by the established authority (authoritarian aggression), and to be compliant with social conventions that are perceived to be endorsed by society (conventionalism). These three clusters of attitudes come together to define "right-wing authoritarianism" (Altemeyer, 1996). Such attitudinal predispositions should prevent the development of mindfulness because they foster general attitudes and behavior that are antagonistic to mindfulness; hence it is hypothesized that:

H1. Authoritarianism in personality is negatively associated with mindfulness.

The authoritarian personality refers to dispositions among individuals on the political right (Adorno et al., 1950; Altemeyer, 1996). Rokeach (1960) proposes a more general kind of authoritarianism regardless of political ideology, dogmatism, which he conceptualizes along a continuum from open to closed mindedness. Dogmatism refers to the openness of the structure of the belief system regardless of the content of the beliefs; it is not what you believe, but how you believe it. Openness in belief systems is a fundamental feature of mindfulness; hence, it is proposed that:

H2. The more open minded the belief system of the individual, the more mindful the behavior of the individual.

Both of the previous hypotheses are at the individual level and deal with administrators and teachers. Similar hypotheses can be developed at the collective or organizational level. Consider the following:

H3. The more open the organizational climate of a school, the greater the collective mindfulness of the school.

The earlier discussion of the nature of mindful and enabling organizations lead to the following two hypotheses:

H4. Enabling school structure is a necessary but insufficient condition for collective mindfulness, in other words, enabling structure aids in the development of organizational mindfulness but does not guarantee it.

H5. Organizational mindfulness, however, is both a necessary and sufficient condition for enabling structure, in other words collective mindfulness assures enabling school structures.

Is mindfulness in schools related to student achievement? Some hypotheses are offered in this regard. Teacher mindfulness should be directly related and collective mindfulness indirectly related to student outcomes.

Individual mindfulness in teachers should influence teaching in a number of ways. First, a mindful approach emphasizes continuous creating of new categories for analysis, openness to new information, and a awareness of multiple perspectives, all of which reduce boredom, create novelty, promote interest, and make learning more like play than work (Langer, 1989; Langer, 1997). Mindful teaching also encourages conditional teaching and thinking. When statements of fact are viewed as conditional, that is, "under what conditions" is the statement true, then conclusions are implicitly conditional and explicitly statements of uncertainty, at least for the moment (Langer, 1997). A mindful approach to teaching should produce a more creative and interesting perspective for learning, which should increase motivation, enhance perseverance, and promote critical thought and inquiry. Hence, is hypothesized that:

H6. Individual mindfulness in teachers produces a mindful approach to teaching.

H7. A mindful approach in teaching produces higher levels of student achievement than traditional top-down approaches.

H8. A mindful approach in teaching produces more creativity in students than traditional top-down approaches.

Bandura's (1986, 1997) social cognitive theory is useful in understanding how individuals exercise influence over what they do. The theory is anchored in human agency—the ways individuals act intentionally to gain some level of control over their lives. Teacher self-efficacy is a teacher's belief in his or her ability to organize and execute actions required to accomplish a specific teaching task (Bandura, 1997; Tschannen-Moran, Woolfolk Hoy, & Hoy, 1998). Teacher mindfulness should facilitate teacher self-efficacy because mindfulness promotes the reframing of problems in ways that make them amenable to successful solution, and thus should increase one's self- efficacy. Thus, the prediction that:

H9. Individual teacher mindfulness and teacher self-efficacy are positively related to each other.

Although sense of self-efficacy and individual mindfulness are important in the exercise of control, personal agency operates within a broad network of socio-structural influences; hence, the mechanisms of human agency also explain the exercise of collective agency, that is, how individuals' beliefs about a group's conjoint capability can work together to produce desired effects (Bandura, 1997). Collective efficacy in schools is the perceptions of teachers in a specific school that the faculty as a whole can execute courses of action required to positively affect student outcomes (Goddard, Hoy, & Woolfolk Hoy, 2000). Just as individual teacher mindfulness is thought to be linked to teacher self- efficacy, collective mindfulness is predicted to be related to collective efficacy, that is:

H10. Collective mindfulness and collective efficacy are positively related to each other.

Moreover, if collective mindfulness enhances collective efficacy, then it follows that organizational mindfulness working through collective efficacy, and perhaps independently, also influences student achievement because strong collective efficacy not only increases individual teacher performance but also affects the pattern of shared beliefs held by teachers. A teacher with average self-efficacy beliefs is likely to exert even more effort upon joining a faculty with high levels of collective efficacy. These behavioral changes reflect the normative effect of a school's collective efficacy on its individual members (Goddard, Hoy, & Woolfolk Hoy, 2000). In other words, the effect of an individual teacher's efficaciousness is strengthened by a strong collective efficacy of a school. Moreover, when teachers believe they can be effective in teaching, they often are. Such teachers are more persistent in their efforts, they set higher goals; they plan more; they accept personal responsibility for student achievement; and temporary setbacks or failures do not discourage them (Bandura, 1997; Hoy, Sweetland, & Smith, 2002).

The preceding hypotheses are only a few of the relationships that could be developed. For example, one could also examine the relationships between leadership style of the principal and mindfulness of the teachers or the leadership style of the principal and enabling school structures. Suffice it to say, both constructs provide heuristic means to study schools.

Some Practical Suggestions

Finally, a few practical suggestions are developed to demonstrate that mindful and enabling structures have practical as well as theoretical and research utility. A colleague recently told of an incident in his university that illustrates the futility of working in structures that hinder and promote a mindless compliance to rules and procedures. He had a Ph. D. student who had toiled five years on a difficult dissertation topic, and although near the completion, was out of time. The Graduate School had an automatic ten-week extension if the advisor recommended it. In the case in question, the advisor was on leave in Europe and in a rare circumstance the other two members of the committee were likewise not on campus. The advisor's attempt to get a longer extension for the student was rebuffed by the graduate dean. Indeed when the advisor made the case personally to the graduate dean he was told that, "You would be surprised at how many times we have cases just like this one. If your student cannot complete and defend his dissertation in the next ten-weeks, he must re-qualify as a candidate by taking a supplemental qualifying exam." When the professor suggested that if there were so many exceptions to the rule, then it might be wise to revisit the rule, the graduate dean hunkered down and proclaimed. "You can appeal my decision to the Provost, but rules are rules."

The point of recounting this story is to underscore the fact that often structures, even in loosely coupled systems like universities, do not enable but promote a mindless response to rigid procedures. Mindlessness abounds in our research universities as well as our public schools. As a general rule, the fewer explicit rules the better. But because organizational rules are necessary, the following ten guidelines on rules are offered to enable and promote mindfulness:

- There are exceptions to the most rules; find them.
- There are times when the rules don't work; suspend them.
- Some rules encourage mindlessness; avoid them.
- Some rules support mindfulness; seize on them.
- Some rules become unnecessary; eliminate them.
- Routine rules leads to mindlessness; question them.
- Some rules create dependence; beware of them.
- Some rules encourage a playful approach; invent them.
- Rules set precedents; if the precedents are bad, change the rules.
- Rules are best to guide but not to dictate.

Enabling administrators likely subscribe to the mindful edict: *there are no absolute rules*. Situations change, people change, needs change and so must rules. Change is that the heart of all mindful organizations.

Weick and Sutcliffe (2001) offer a host of practical suggestions for mindful leadership. Consider just a few of these suggestions for school leaders.

- *Cultivate humility*. Be aware of the traps of short-term success. School administrators need a healthy skepticism about their own accomplishments and concern about their potential for failure.
- *Welcome the bad day*. When things go bad, administrators can uncover more details and learn more about how things really work.
- *Speak up*. Just because the administrator sees something clearly, don't assume that teachers see the same thing.
- *Be wary of good news*. There is always enough bad news to go around. If school administrators are not getting any bad news, then teachers and subordinates are hiding it.
- *Develop skepticism in your teachers*. When information is met with skepticism, teachers make an independent effort to confirm the

information. Skepticism is a countervailing force for complacency; it is positive redundancy.

- *Embrace a soft vigilance.* Soft vigilance is a mindful state as contrasted with hypervigilance, which locks in attention. Soft vigilance keeps the administrator's mind open to novelty and new information (Langer, 1997).

Mindful leadership is not only possible but necessary for the development of a collective mindfulness, and these suggestions only sketch a few of the features of a mindful mindset.

CONCLUSION

This inquiry has examined two constructs as they apply to schools: mindful and enabling structures; in fact, the two perspectives share so much in common that they are viewed as highly compatible and complementary. Mindful organization is the more comprehensive concept because it seems to encompass enabling structure. But the road to mindful structures may first pass through hierarchies and rules that enable, that is, enabling structure may be an antecedent to collective mindfulness. The analysis also sketched the beginning of a research agenda that links mindful and enabling structures to important school outcomes.

School organizations can be mindful. They can organize themselves in such a way that they are better able to recognize the unexpected in the making and halt its development, but if it does develop, then contain it and focus on resilience and restoration of system functioning (Weick & Sutcliffe, 2001). Mindful organization needs mindful leadership, mindful administrators, mindful teachers, and mindful students. Such organizations are likely to have positive consequences for most of the important outcomes of schooling, including student learning and achievement.

NOTES

1. This theoretical analysis builds upon our earlier conceptual and empirical work (Hoy & Sweetland, 2000, 2001).
2. This definition of mindfulness is adapted from Langer (1989) and Weick and Sutcliffe (2001).
3. This section draws heavily on Hoy and Tarter (in press) and Weick and Sutcliffe (2001).
4. Weick and Roberts (1993).

REFERENCES

Adler, P. S. (1999). The "learning bureaucracy": New United Motors Manufacturing Incorporated. In B. M. Staw & L. L. Staw (Eds.), *Research in organizational behavior* (Vol. 12, pp. 111-194). Greenwich, CT: JAI Press.

Adler, P. S. (1999). Building better bureaucracies. *The Academy of Management Executive, 133*, 36-49.

Adler, P. S., & Borys, B. (1996). Two types of bureaucracy: Enabling and coercive. *Administrative Science Quarterly, 41*, 61-89.

Aiken, M., & Hage, J. (1968). Organizational interdependence and intra-organizational structure. *American Sociological Review, 33*, 912–930.

Altemeyer, B. (1996). *The Authoritarian Specter*. Cambridge, MA: Harvard University Press.

Anderson, J. G. (1968). *Bureaucracy in education*. Baltimore, MD: Johns Hopkins Press.

Arches, J. (1991). Social structure, burnout, and job satisfaction. *Social Work, 36*(3), 202-206.

Bandura, A. (1986). *Social foundations of thought and action: A social cognitive theory*. Englewood Cliffs, NJ: Prentice-Hall.

Bandura, A. (1997). *Self-efficacy: The exercise of control*. New York: Freeman.

Bass, B. M., & Avolio, B. J. (1994). Introduction. In B. M. Bass & B. J. Avolio (Eds.), *Improving organizational effectiveness through transformational leadership* (pp. 1-10). Thousand Oaks, CA: Sage.

Blau, P. M. (1955). *The dynamics of bureaucracy*. Chicago: University of Chicago Press.

Blau, P. M., & Scott, W. R. (1962). *Formal organizations: A comparative approach*. San Francisco: Chandler.

Coleman, J. S. (1974). *Power and structure of society*. New York: Norton.

Craig, T. (1995). Achieving innovation through bureaucracy. *California Management Review, 38*(10), 8-36.

Damanpour, F. (1991). Organizational innovation. *Academy of Management Journal, 34*, 555-591.

Ferguson, K. E. (1984). *The Feminist Case Against Bureaucracy*. Philadelphia: Temple University Press.

Goddard, R. D., Hoy, W. K., & Woolfolk Hoy, A. (2000). Collective teacher efficacy: Its meaning, measure, and impact on student achievement. *American Educational Research Journal, 37*, 479-508.

Gouldner, A. (1954). *Patterns of Industrial bureaucracy*. New York: Free Press.

Hage, J., & Aiken, M. (1970). *Social Change in complex organizations*. New York: Random House.

Hirschhorn, L. (1997). *Reworking authority: Leading and following in a post-modern organization*. Cambridge, MA: MIT Press.

Hoy, W. K., Blazovsky, R., & Newland, W. (1983). Bureaucracy and alienation: A comparative analysis. *The Journal of Educational Administration, 21*, 109–121.

Hoy, W. K., & Miskel, C. G. (2001). *Educational administration: Theory, research, and practice* (6th ed.). New York: McGraw-Hill.

Hoy, W. K., & Sweetland, S. R. (2000). School bureaucracies that work: Enabling, not coercive. *Journal of School Leadership, 10*, 525-541.

Hoy, W. K., & Sweetland, S. R. (2001). Designing better schools: The meaning and nature of enabling school structure. *Educational Administration Quarterly, 37.* 296-321.

Hoy, W. K., Sweetland, S. R., & Smith, P. A. (2002). Toward and organizational model of achievement in high schools: The significance of collective efficacy. *Educational Administration Quarterly, 38*, 77-93.

Hoy, W. K., & Tarter, C. J. (in press). *Administrators solving the problems of practice: Decision-making concepts, cases, and consequences* (2nd ed.). Boston: Allyn and Bacon.

Isherwood, G., & Hoy, W. K. (1973). Bureaucracy, powerlessness, and teacher work values. *Journal of Educational Administration, 9*, 124-38.

Jackson, S., & Schuler, R. S. (1985). A meta-analysis and conceptual critique of research on role ambiguity and role conflict in work settings. *Organizational Behavior and Human Decision Processes, 36*, 17-78.

Kakabadse, A. (1986). Organizational alienation and job climate. *Small Group Behavior, 17*, 458-471.

Langer, E. J. (1989). *Mindfulness.* Cambridge, MA: Perseus Books.

Langer, E. J. (1997). *The power of mindful learning.* Cambridge, MA: Perseus Books.

Leithwood, K., & Duke, D. L. (1999). A century's quest to understand school leadership. In J. Murphy and K. S. Louis (Eds.), *Handbook of research on educational administration* (pp. 45-72). San Francisco, CA: Jossey-Bass.

Martin, J., & Knopoff, K. (1999). The gendered implications of apparently gender-neutral theory: rereading Weber. In E. Freeman & A Larson (Eds.), *Ruffin lecture series, Vol. 3: Business ethics and women's studies.* Oxford: Oxford University Press.

Merton, R. (1957). *Social theory and social structure.* New York: Free Press.

Michaels, R. E., Cron, W. L., Dubinsky, A. J., & Joachimsthaler, E. A. (1988). Influence of formalization on the organizational commitment and work alienation of salespeople and industrial buyers. *Journal of Marketing Research, 25*, 376-383.

Mintzberg, H. (1979). *The structuring of organizations.* Englewood Cliffs, NJ: Prentice-Hall.

Mintzberg, H. (1989). *Mintzberg on management.* New York: Free Press.

Moeller, G. H., & Charters, W. W., Jr. (1966). Relation of bureaucratization to sense of power among teachers. *Administrative Science Quarterly, 10*, 444-465.

Rokeach, M. (1960). *The open and closed mind.* New York: Basic Books.

Rousseau, D. M. (1978). Characteristics of departments, positions, and individuals: Contexts for attitudes and behavior. *Administrative Science Quarterly, 23*, 521-540.

Scott, W. R. (1998). *Organizations: Rational, natural, and open systems* (4th ed.). Englewood Cliffs, NJ: Prentice-Hall.

Senatra, P. T. (1980). Role conflict, role ambiguity, and organizational climate in a public accounting firm. *Accounting Review, 55*, 594-603.

Sinden, J., Hoy, W. K., & Sweetland, S. R. (2002). *Enabling structures: Principal leadership and organizational commitment of teachers*. Working Paper, Educational Policy and Leadership, Ohio State University.

Sweetland, S. R., & Hoy, W. K. (2000). School characteristics and educational outcomes: Toward an organizational model of student achievement in middle schools. *Educational Administration Quarterly, 36*, 703-729.

Tschannen-Moran, M., Woolfolk Hoy, A. W., & Hoy, W. K. (1998). Teacher efficacy: Its meaning and measure. *Review of Educational Research, 68*, 202-248.

Trungpa, C. (1973). *Cutting through spiritual materialism*. Boulder and London: Shambhala.

Weber, M. (1947). *The theory of social and economic organizations*. [T. Parsons (Ed.), A. M. Henderson and T. Parsons (Trans.).] New York: Free Press.

Weick, K. W., & Roberts, K. H. (1993). Collective mind in organizations: Heedful interrelating on flight decks. *Administrative Science Quarterly, 38*, 351-381.

Weick, K. W. and Sutcliffe, K. M. (2001). *Managing the Unexpected*. San Francisco: Jossey-Bass.

Wildavsky, A. (1991). *Searching for safety*. New Brunswick, NJ: Transaction.

PART XII

ON ENPOWERMENT

CHAPTER 17

A NORMATIVE THEORY OF PARTICIPATIVE DECISION MAKING IN SCHOOLS

Wayne K. Hoy and C. John Tarter

Shared decision making has taken on added importance as reformers advocate teacher involvement in decision making. Involving subordinates in
decisions may improve the quality and acceptance of decisions when participation fits the constraints of the situation. A theory of participative decision
making is developed that suggests under what conditions subordinates
should be involved in decision making. The model describes not only when
teachers should be involved, but also the appropriate role for the administrator, which depends on the decisional situation. The model is applied to
several hypothetical cases in order to illustrate its use.

Shared decision making has taken on added importance as reformers
advocate teacher involvement in decision making. Always involving subordinates is as shortsighted as never involving them. Participation in decision
making (PDM) can improve the quality of decisions and promote co-oper-

Reprinted by permission frosm the *Journal of Educational Administration*, Vol. 31, pp. 4-
19. Copyright © 1993. All rights reserved.

Essential Ideas for the Reform of American Schools, pp. 395–415
Copyright © 2007 by Information Age Publishing

ation if the right strategy is linked to the right situation. That is, the decision of subordinate involvement is best made using a contingency model.

There are extant PDM models that deal with subordinate participation, [1-4] but they are either little known or unwieldy. For example, the Vroom-Yetton model, though well-known, is initially formidable. Nonetheless, PDM is becoming increasingly "fashionable," to use Mintzberg's [5] term, as school site management becomes more popular. "Should subordinates be involved in decision making?"

We propose a model which answers the question with a forthright, "It depends." But on what does it depend? Using theoretical concepts from Barnard[6], Simon[7], Bridges[8] and Hoy and Miskel[2] we develop a simplified, yet comprehensive, normative theory of shared decision making. The model suggests under what conditions subordinates should be involved in decision making and the frequency, nature, purpose and structure of their involvement. Further, the model analyzes differential roles of the administrator, depending on the situation. The analysis concludes with several examples of its use.

THE ZONE OF ACCEPTANCE

There are some decisions which employees simply accept because they are indifferent to them. As Barnard[6, p. 167] observed there is a zone of indifference "in each individual within which orders are accepted without conscious questioning of their authority." Simon[7] prefers the term "acceptance" rather than "indifference," but in point of fact they are used interchangeably in the literature on decision making[1,2]. Bridges[1] was first to develop a model of shared decision making using the zone to guide the extent of subordinate participation. Although his formulation was developed for use by school principals to involve teachers in the decision-making process, it is useful to extend PDM to educational administration in general. Drawing on the work of Barnard[6] and Chase[9], Bridges[1,8] advanced two propositions:

1. As subordinates are involved in making decisions located in their zone of acceptance, participation will be less effective.
2. As subordinates are involved in making decisions clearly outside of their zone of acceptance, participation will be more effective.

There are, however, decisions which fall neither clearly within nor outside the zone of acceptance. These marginal cases occur when subordinates have a personal stake in the outcome of the decision, but no expertise to contribute, or when they have expertise, but no personal stake. For example, teachers have a personal stake in the kind of payroll system that is to be implemented, but typically they do not have expertise in accounting systems. In this instance, they may want to be involved in the decision, but unfortunately, the technical aspects of the decision may not be informed by their involvement. Indeed, their involvement may complicate the issue because they are prone to protect their own interests at the expense of the welfare of the organization.

On the other hand, administrators who need expert help on problems which do not affect their subordinates may encounter resentment and even alienation as they force subordinates to participate. For example, the biology department may resent being asked to suggest office plants to decorate the foyer, or the maths department may bridle at being forced to make decisions about the layout of the landscaping for the new administration building. Thus, we advance two additional propositions:

1. As subordinates are involved in making decisions for which they have marginal expertise, their participation will be marginally effective.
2. As subordinates are involved in making decisions in which they have marginal interest, their participation will be marginally effective.

The involvement of subordinates in decision making assumes having sufficient time; in fact, time is nearly always a factor in decision making.

MAPPING THE ZONE OF ACCEPTANCE

How does an administrator know where a decision issue falls? Is it inside the zone, outside the zone, or one of the marginal cases? Concrete guidelines are required. Two decision rules have been developed and applied to this question[1,2]—the relevance rule and the expertise rule.

*   The relevance rule: Do subordinates have a personal stake in the decision outcome?
*   The expertise rule: Do subordinates have expertise to contribute to the decision?

These two rules define four decision situations as illustrated in Figure 17.1. As Figure 17.1 shows, the issue is not simply one of the decision falling inside or outside the zone. The zone is not conceived here as a continuous variable. Rather, it is a two-dimensional construct defined by relevance and expertise. There are two distinct types of marginality, each with different decisional constraints. It is tempting, but unproductive, to

RELEVANCE?

Yes   No

	Yes	No
Yes	**Outside Zone of Acceptance** (Definitely include)	**Marginal with Relevance** (Occasionally include)
No	**Marginal with Relevance** (Occasionally include)	**Inside Zone of Acceptance** (Do not include)

EXPERTISE?

Figure 17.1.   Decision Issues of the Zone of Acceptance.

view the zone as a unidimensional construct which measures the distance from inside to outside the zone. Depending on the absence or presence of each dimension, four discrete situations are identified, each requiring a different decision strategy.

SITUATION-PARTICIPATION MATCH

When the decision is outside the zone, subordinates should be involved in the decision-making process[1,2,4,10]. They have the knowledge and skill to improve the decision, and they want to be involved because of a personal stake in the outcome[11,12]. Subordinate involvement is appropriate.

The second situation is a marginal case. Where the subordinate has a personal stake but not the expertise, involvement should be limited. Subordinate participation in this case is dangerous; it may lead to frustration because teachers are asked to do a job for which they are ill-prepared[13-

15]. As a common consequence, either the decision will be uninformed by expertise, or it will be made by the administrator contrary to the wishes of those involved. In the first instance, bringing teachers into the process who lack expertise may reduce their resistance, but it cannot inform the substance of the decision. In the latter instance, the administrator makes a show of soliciting opinion, which is subsequently ignored. Such decisions give the appearance of manipulation and "game playing" and eventually produce teacher discontent and hostility[1,15-17].

Occasionally, however, teachers must be brought into the process to gain acceptance of the decisions, but only when the teachers know at the outset that their role is advisory. The role of the administrator is clearly educational, a point to be developed later.

The third situation is the marginal case of expertise and absence of a personal stake. Teachers involved in these instrumental decisions may feel that they are merely being used by their superiors[1,15-17]. They have little interest in the outcomes of the decisions because they are unaffected. Initially, they may feel a sense of worth as they are involved, but that quickly passes as they labour. The likely long-term response of such involvement is alienation. Teachers wonder aloud, "What does the principal get paid for doing?" and "What is my payoff?" No payoff, no personal stake, and no motivation produce eventual resentment and alienation. Nonetheless, a case will be made for occasional involvement of the teachers to improve the quality of the decision.

Teachers should not be involved in decision making when they have neither the inclination nor the skill to aid in the process. This fourth situation is clearly a case for unilateral administrative decision making[3,4]. These four situations are summarized in Figure 17.1.

THE EXTENT OF PARTICIPATION

Participation is not simply a yes or no decision; it varies along a continuum from extensive to limited. Extensive participation in decision making means involving individuals in the process as early and as long as possible. To illustrate, let us conceive of the decision-making process as a six-stage cycle:

1. Define the problem.
2. Specify reasonable alternatives.
3. Examine the consequences for each alternative.
4. Select a strategy for action.
5. Implement the plan.

6.   Monitor and evaluate the plan[18].

To maximize involvement, teachers or other administrators are brought into the process as early as possible. Extensive collaboration occurs when subordinates share in the definition and elaboration of the problem and then are involved in each successive step of the cycle. Participation is limited when people are involved in the later steps of the process. For example, if the problem has been defined, reasonable alternatives identified, and the consequences specified, then participation is limited to selecting a strategy for action. On the other hand, if teachers are provided with data, asked to define the problem, and are involved in each subsequent step of the decision-making process, then their participation is extensive. In practical terms, the steps in the decision-making process in which teachers or administrators are involved, as well as whether they recommend or actually select a strategy for action, depend on the subordinates' zone of acceptance and the area of freedom granted to the administrator by the district. It is important to make clear to teachers the boundaries of their authority and the area of freedom to decide[1].

When the decision is outside the zone of acceptance, participation is also mediated by commitment to the organization. To gauge subordinate commitment, we propose a third and final decision rule:

• The commitment trust rule: Are subordinates committed to the organizational goals [19]?

If the decision is outside the teachers' zone of acceptance and they share the administrative aims, then participation should be extensive. But if there is little commitment, then inclusion in the decision process should be restricted because, to do otherwise invites moving the decision in directions not consistent with the school's goal. Mintzberg[5, p. 183] explains that strong personal needs can be sufficient for ill-meaning employees to displace legitimate goals. The commitment rule applies only to those decisions that fall clearly outside the zone of acceptance. In all other situations, participation will be limited.

AN ELABORATION OF COLLABORATIVE SITUATIONS: SIX TYPES

The initial formulation of decision situations contained four types of collaborative opportunities—outside the zone, marginal with relevance, marginal with expertise, and inside the zone (see Figure 17.1). The commitment rule refines and elaborates situations outside the zone of acceptance. Subordinates may have expertise and a personal stake in the outcome, but may not be committed to the aims of the organization. Thus, there are at least two different situations outside the zone of acceptance, those with committed and those with uncommitted subordinates. Moreover, even when subordinates are committed, the resolution of the problem may require total consensus rather than a simple majority.

Unlike previous analyses[1,2], which fail to consider these subtleties, three distinct variations outside the zone of acceptance are identified and defined.

Collaborative decision making is called for when the teachers have expertise, a personal stake, and commitment. In fact, the only issue here is whether the decision should be a product of total consensus (a consensual situation) or a simple majority (a majoritarian situation). However desirable, consensus is not usually realistic. When the decision requires total acceptance (by law or for successful implementation), an administrator must hold out for unanimity. These situations are rare. More commonly, teachers and administrators seek a democratic solution.

Teachers are not always committed to the aims of the school. Sometimes, their personal agendas may be different from the school's goals. In these conflictual situations, unrestricted participation is counterproductive. Still, effective decision making requires using teacher expertise while allaying their anxieties about the consequences of the decision.

When teachers have a personal stake in the outcome, but no expertise to contribute, we have a marginal situation called the stakeholder situation. Whether or not teachers are committed to the aims of the school, unrestricted participation is dangerous because it may lead to frustration as teachers are asked to do a job for which they are ill-prepared.

When teachers have expertise to contribute to problems in which they have no interest, we have a marginal situation called the expert situation. Regardless of their commitment to the school, teachers involved in these instrumental decisions may feel that they are merely being used by their superiors.

Finally, when teachers have no expertise and no personal stake in the outcome, we have a non-collaborative situation. They have neither the inclination nor the skill to aid in the process. These six situations for collaborative decision making are summarized along a continuum in Table 17.1.

THE STRUCTURE OF PDM

Participation in decision making can be defined by five structural arrangements. These arrangements are the appropriate matchings

Table 17.1.   Situations for Collaborative Decision Making: A Continuum

Degree of Collaboration	Total ◀┄┄┄┄┄┄┄┄┄┄┄┄┄┄┄┄┄┄┄┄┄┄┄┄┄┄▶ None					
Situation	**Consensual**	**Majoritarian**	**Conflictual**	**Stakeholder**	**Expert**	**Noncollaborative**
Relevance?	Yes	Yes	Yes	Yes	No	No
Expertise?	Yes	Yes	Yes	No	Yes	No
Commitment?	Yes	Yes	No	Yes/No	Yes/No	NA

between administrative delegation and actual teacher involvement. Administrative delegation is the extent to which administrators give teachers the authority to make decisions. Teacher involvement is the degree to which teachers actually participate in decision making. Group consensus is the most extensive involvement and delegation possible within an organization, while unilateral decision making marks the least. There should be a congruence between teacher involvement and administrative delegation; in fact, we conceive the structures (see Figure 17.2) of the decision-making arrangements arrayed along the following continuum:

1. *Group consensus.* The administrator involves participants in the decision making, then the group decides. All group members share equally as they generate and evaluate a decision. Total consensus is required before a decision can be made.

2. *Group decision.* The administrator involves participants in the decision making, then the group decides, using parliamentary procedures. All group members share equally as they generate, evaluate and attempt consensus. Ultimately, though, a decision is usually made by the majority.

3. *Group advisory.* The administrator solicits the opinion of the entire group, discusses the implications of group suggestions, then makes a decision that may or may not reflect subordinates' desires.

4. *Individual advisory.* The administrator consults with relevant subordinates individually, who have expertise to assist in the decision, then makes a decision which may or may not reflect their opinion.

5. *Unilateral decision.* The administrator makes the decision without consulting or involving subordinates in the decision[20].

The successful use of these decision-making structures is contingent on the decision situation.

MATCHING DECISION STRUCTURES WITH SITUATIONS

In situations outside the zone of acceptance, there are three possibilities. Most frequently, a group decision is made. That is, each individual, including the administrator, has an equal voice as a majority decision is reached (majoritarian). Occasionally, a regulation mandates consensus, or the implementation of the decision requires consensus (consensual). In these relatively rare instances, group consensus is the necessary structure. A third possibility exists when employees are not committed to the organization (conflictual); their involvement is limited and the structure of the decision making is group advisory. The administrator solicits their opinions as the group is educated to the problem at hand, but eventually the administrator must act for the group. In these instances, the administra-

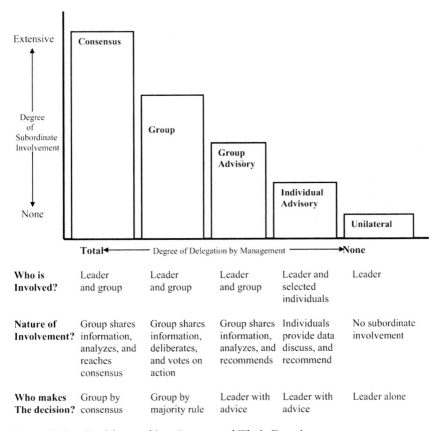

Figure 17.2. Decision-making Groups and Their Functions.

tor explains at the outset that he or she has the final responsibility for making the decision.

When subordinates have a stake but no expertise (stakeholder), the structure of decision making is always group advisory. The administrator requests opinions from the group, discusses the implications of group suggestions, then makes a decision which may or may not reflect their desires. This can be token participation which causes backlash.

When subordinates have expertise but are unaffected by the decision (expert), the structure of decision making is always individual advisory. The administrator consults individually with subordinates who have expertise to inform the decision, then makes a decision that may or may not reflect their opinion.

When the decision is inside the zone of acceptance (noncollaborative), the administrator uses existing information to make the decision alone; a unilateral decision is made.

ADMINISTRATIVE ROLES: INTEGRATOR TO DIRECTOR

Thus far, our analysis has focused on the subordinates in decision making, but what is the role of the administrator? What about the administrator's decision to be a member of the group? How well do groups function when there are differences in formal status? For example, if the administrator is a member of the group, does it function as effectively? A study by Bridges et al. [21] deals directly with this question in the context of public schools. In an experimental study of 20 groups of administrators and teachers, groups without administrators were significantly more productive, efficient, and showed greater propensity for risk-taking behavior than those groups in which an administrator was a group member. In this particular study, a group mode of decision making was used; other modes such as consensus, group advisory, and individual advisory were not tested.

Administrative involvement in group decision making may have dysfunctional consequences. The introduction of hierarchy into a group may complicate the social interactions by making subordinates reluctant to disagree with superiors (even if they are wrong), by fostering a desire for consensus at the expense of the divergent idea, and by nurturing competition for managerial favour rather than group respect[1-5,21,22]. As early as 1955, Torrance[23] found suggestions that lower status group members were often ignored, even when lower status members had correct solutions more frequently than other members of the group. This research is not cited to suggest that administrators should avoid involving either subordinates or themselves in decision making but rather to identify effective roles to improve decisions.

We conceive of five effective administrative roles for collaborative decision making. The principal is an integrator when bringing teachers together for consensus decision making. Here the task is to reconcile divergent opinions and positions. The principal as parliamentarian facilitates open communication by protecting the opinions of the minority and leads teachers through a democratic process to a group decision. The principal as educator reduces resistance to change by explaining and discussing with teachers the opportunities and constraints of the decisional issues. The principal as consultant solicits advice from teacher-experts. The quality of decisions is improved as the principal guides the generation of relevant information. The principal as director makes unilateral decisions in those instances where the teachers have no expertise or personal stake. Here the goal is efficiency. Principals lead using all five roles, but an effective strategy for collaborative decision making involves matching each role with the appropriate situation.

If consensus is required, then the group probably can best achieve it itself, that is, without the active intervention of the leader. If, however, consensus does not emerge, then the administrator functions as the integrator who brings together divergent positions. Divergent alternatives are integrated into still another proposal which includes the best of the competing views. If such accommodation fails, the administrator may either suggest experimental trials of the divergent approaches or continue to work with the group on decreasing the obstacles to consensus. The challenge one faces is in overcoming likely polarization within the group and bringing the group together.

If a group decision is required, then the appropriate administrative role is that of parliamentarian. The parliamentarian of the group guarantees open communication by protecting the opinions of the minority from a tyranny of the majority. Premature decision making reduces the quality of decisions[6,24]. The administrator must ensure that different ideas, regardless of the personalities holding them, get a thorough airing.

If a group-advisory decision is necessary, then the appropriate role of the administrator is one of educator. The purpose of participation in this case is to reduce resistance to change by educating the teachers or other administrators to the need for the decision. The subordinates have a personal stake in the outcome of the decision, but, by definition, they do not have the expertise to make the decision. The administrator makes the case by stipulating the problem, examining the difficulties, reviewing the opportunities and constraints, and developing the rationale for the final decision. The role is clearly educational.

If an individual-advisory decision is required, then the administrator is a consultant; advice is solicited from experts. The purpose of involvement in this case is to improve the quality of decision by using the skill of organizational members. The reluctance of faculty and staff to criticize the status quo must be overcome. The free flow of communication is nurtured by focusing on problem solving, risk taking, and divergent ideas.

If no participation is required, the administrator as a director simply makes the decision. From integrator to director, the role of the manager varies according to leadership function, purpose, and appropriate decision-making arrangements (see Figure 17.3).

USING THE MODEL

Principals are too often exhorted to involve teachers in all decisions. The more appropriate tack is to determine, "When should others be involved

Role	Function	Aim
Integrator	Brings together divergent positions	To achieve consensus
Parliamentarian	Facilitates open discussion	To support reflective deliberation
Educator	Explains and discusses issues	To insure acceptance of decisions
Consultant	Solicits advice from teachers	To improve quality of decisions
Director	Makes unilateral decisions	To attain efficiency

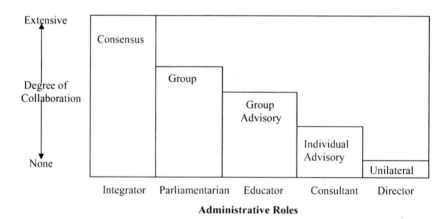

Figure 17.3.   Administrative Roles for Decision Making.

in decision making?" We have proposed a model that answers the question. The model has several advantages: it is built on sound organizational theory and research; its internal logic is clear; its applicability is extensive; and, it is easy for school administrators to use.

The key concept in the model, drawn from Barnard[6] and Simon[7], is the zone of acceptance. There are some decisions which subordinates simply accept and, therefore, in which they should not be involved. The administrator identifies those situations by asking two questions:

1. Do the subordinates have a personal stake in the outcome (Relevance)?
2. Can subordinates contribute expertise (Expertise)?

If the answer to both these questions is yes (outside the zone), the subordinates have both a personal stake in the outcome and expertise to contribute. They will want to be involved, and their involvement should improve the decision. However, one must next evaluate their commitment to the organization by asking the following question:

3. Are the subordinates committed to the goals of the organization (Commitment)?

If they are committed, their involvement should be extensive as the group tries to develop the "best" decision. In the process, the role of the administrator is to act either as an integrator (if consensus is essential) or as a parliamentarian (majoritarian situation). If subordinates are not committed (conflictual situation), their involvement should be limited: Here, the objectives are to educate others to the goals and demonstrate how the proposed decision helps to accomplish these goals. In this situation the administrator acts as an educator, and the group serves to advise and identify pockets of resistance.

If, however, subordinates have only a personal stake in the decision, but no expertise to contribute (stakeholder situation), their involvement should be occasional and limited. Subordinates are interested in the outcome, but they have little knowledge to bring to bear on the decision. The reason for occasional involvement in this situation is to lower resistance and educate participants. If the involvement is more than occasional, the danger is alienation as teachers feel manipulated because their wishes are not met. At the outset, all parties know that the group is clearly advisory to the principal. The administrator's role is to decide and educate.

If subordinates have expertise but no personal stake (expert situation), their involvement should also be occasional and limited as the school administrator attempts to improve the decision by tapping the expertise of significant individuals who are not normally involved in this kind of action. At first blush, one might think that expertise should always be consulted in a decision, but if workers have no personal stake in the outcomes, their enthusiasm will quickly wane. They may well grumble, "This isn't my job."

Paradoxically, when inside the zone of acceptance (non-collaborative situation), the decision to involve is the most difficult and easy case of the six. There is such a strong norm about involving teachers in all sorts of decisions, even when they have neither a personal stake nor expertise, that school administrators may feel constrained to involve teachers anyway. Such ritual is dysfunctional and illogical. Why would you involve someone in a decision when that person does not care and cannot help? Our model proposes that administrators make direct unilateral decisions when the issue is within the zone of acceptance of subordinates. The entire model is summarized in Figure 17.4.

In sum, the model we propose is simple to use. The analysis is logical and straightforward. One concept, the zone of acceptance, drives the analysis. Two tests determine whether subordinates should participate in the decision: the tests of relevance and of expertise. Four decisional situations readily emerge—outside zone of acceptance, marginal with relevance, marginal with expertise, inside zone (see Figure 17.4). The test of commitment then defines six collaborative situations. Finally, the model guides the decision maker in answering the questions of the extent, purpose, and manner of involvement.

AN APPLICATION OF THE MODEL

To illustrate the use of the model, we will apply it to several cases. We begin with a curriculum problem.

You are principal, and your school's social studies department is highly regarded for its innovative approach to teaching. The programme is oriented towards enquiry as a process, rather than the retention of historical fact. Typically, curriculum is made by the department as different concepts are developed. The teachers are enthusiastic about their programme and it is well received by the students. You respect all the members of the department and see it as one of the strongest departments in the school. You do not always agree with the direction of the curriculum, but there is little question that this is a highly skilled and professional group of teachers whom you respect.

Recent reform in the state has argued for back to basics and the use of curricular materials that stress recall of specific persons, places, and

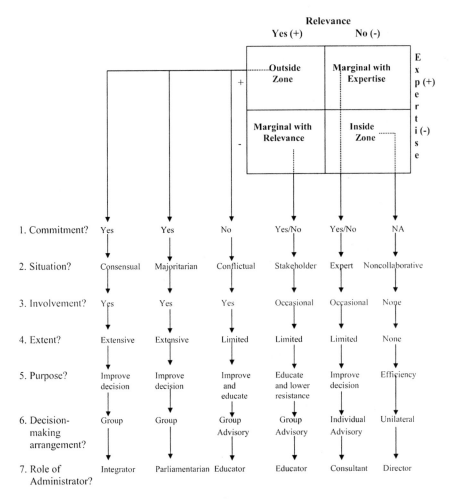

Figure 17.4.   A Normative Model for Shared Decision Making.

events in state and national history. The reform is supported by a battery of state tests, which have been used to compare the effectiveness of schools across the state. Although the state maintained that no invidious comparisons would be made, your community has made them. The superintendent has her feet to the fire on this issue, and now you are feeling the heat. Recent test scores show that your students are not doing nearly as well in history as they are in science and mathematics. The superintendent has "requested" that you integrate the state curricular materials into the history programme to correct the current deficiencies. Your history faculty, on the other hand, claim that this is exactly the wrong tack to take to develop enquiring minds. They are not overly concerned with the students' performance on the state tests because they claim the tests measure the wrong thing. There is strong pressure in the community, however, to do well on all tests. Parents cannot understand why their children are not doing as well in history as they are in math and science; in fact, at the last board meeting the superintendent promised, under pressure, that the scores would rise. There is no question that you as principal must help realign the history curriculum. You are troubled by the current state of affairs, but decisions must be made.

As the principal in this situation, the first question is whether the issue is within the teachers' zone of acceptance. Without question, the social studies teachers have a personal stake and expertise to contribute. The decision clearly falls outside the zone of acceptance; they should be involved. Are the teachers committed to the aims of the school? Yes. The model tells us that the teachers should be involved extensively because they have a personal stake, expertise, and are committed. The purpose of their involvement is to improve the quality and acceptance of the decision.

The manner of their involvement is also suggested by the model. The principal must work with teachers, first trying to integrate and achieve consensus and then, as a parliamentarian helping the group realize a majority decision. Is this too simple a solution to a complex problem? It is not a solution. It is a strategy of action to solve the problem, one which emphasizes teacher-administration collaboration.

We turn next to a sharply different issue involving the professional development of a principal:

> You are a high school principal who has done quite well in the administration of a large comprehensive high school. As both reward and as part of your professional development, the superintendent and the board of education have agreed to send you to a special management training seminar for school principals, sponsored by the Harvard Business School. The seminar will last three weeks and provides participants with five distinct curricular options:
>
> 1. Management-by-Objectives.
> 2. Instructional Improvement.
> 3. Participative Management.
> 4. Organizational Climate.
> 5. Organizational Design.
>
> Each participant is permitted to enrol in two of these elective options.

You are excited about the prospect, and you want to get the most benefit possible from the experience. All of the options sound intriguing. You have the pleasant task of deciding on your speciality. You have checked with the superintendent who agrees that any and all of the options are useful and encourages you to make your own decision. You have decided to participate in the Organizational Climate and Organizational Design tracks. You mentioned what you were going to do to your assistant who asked you if you had talked to any of the faculty about your choices. You had not even thought about it. Why?

At first, the case seems to dictate a unilateral decision. But, let us look at the problem by using the model. Is there anyone else who should be involved in this decision? Do your teachers have a personal stake or expertise? They may have. For instance, what you learn may very well affect your teachers. Courses in organizational climate and design will probably give you the incentive and means to change the nature of the school. Perhaps some staff members feel the principal should be more active as an instructional leader, prompting a course decision for instructional improvement.

Do the faculty and staff have a personal stake in the outcome of your decision of what to study? If you intend to alter the school based on what you learn, they will be affected, so they do have a stake. Their expertise is probably limited in each area. Thus, we have a situation in which the teachers have a personal stake in the outcome, but little expertise to contribute to the decision. The model advises limited involvement of teachers as a group. The purpose of the involvement is for the group to supply advice to the leader and for the leader to inform and educate the group.

In this instance, the principal will seek the advice of the faculty because he/she intends to use the information from the seminars to change administrative practice at the school. The personal stake of the teachers then becomes high enough to warrant their participation. But even here the participation is advisory and informational. In other cases, the principal might not involve teachers because no changes in school policy were being contemplated. The decision would be purely individual.

We conclude with a staff rather than a faculty example to demonstrate the general applicability of the framework.

You find yourself in an unusual, but fortunate, situation. The superintendent has informed you that there is some extra money in the budget which must be spent in the next three months. She remembered your complaining about the shabbiness of your secretarial suite. There is enough money for repainting and replacing the carpet.

As a first step, you have contracted with a painting and carpeting company to do the job. They have sent over some paint and carpet samples for your selection. You have examined the samples and made an initial selection. As you are walking out of the door, you are struck by your insensitivity to your secretary. You have not even told her about the redecoration. You rationalize that you are going to surprise her. But then you think that she may not be pleasantly surprised if she does not like the colors you have chosen. But, then again, she probably will. Why not ask her?

Once again the model provides direction. We first ask the question, "Does the secretary have expertise in the decision area?" In all likelihood, the secretary has no special expertise in interior design or color co-ordination. However, it is also obvious that the secretary, who works in the room every day, has a personal stake in the outcome. Thus, the decision is a stakeholder situation. The model suggests that some involvement is appropriate provided that it will not lead to alienation or backlash, a reasonable assumption in this case.

Ultimately, however, you will make the decision after deliberation with the assistant; a discussion should produce a better understanding for both parties of the constraints. We suspect that in most cases principals will affirm the wishes of their secretaries, but they do hold a veto over the final decision (e.g., no purple walls). Of course, if the answer to the expertise question is yes, that is, the secretary does have expertise in color selection, then the decision falls outside the zone of acceptance, and the decision should be delegated to the secretary.

We repeat, this model does not solve problems. It is no substitute for clear and reflective thinking. However, the model is a guide to participative decision making. Note that in the examples given above, no solutions are offered, for good reason. The framework simply addresses the following issues:

1. Under what conditions should subordinates be involved?
2. To what extent should they be involved?
3. What is the purpose of their involvement?
4. How should the process of decision making be structured?
5. What are the administrative and subordinate roles in the process?

As we examined a variety of school problems confronted by the principal, we were struck by the difficulty of finding decision areas where the principal should make unilateral decisions. Because the principal is a key figure in the organization, virtually every decision affects someone in the organization. Clearly, it is not possible for all subordinates to be involved in all decisions. Nor should subordinates be involved in the same ways. The model deals with these questions. However, time occasionally forces administrators to make unilateral decisions, thereby increasing the risk of a poor decision or a decision which will not be readily accepted by subordinates.

Some may object to the fact that the principal, rather than teachers, decides expertise, personal stake, and the commitment of the teachers. The decisions which we are considering are problems which the administrator must solve as part of the job. The model is an administrative tool. Its use can be no better than the skill, perception and sensitivity of the administrator. We assume that when administrators have questions about the criteria of inclusion they will consult with subordinates.

The best-known model of management of participation in organizations is the Vroom-Yetton formulation. After reviewing research evidence on normative leadership theories, Miner[25,26] concludes that no leadership theory surpasses the Vroom-Yetton model in either its validity or usefulness. Other researchers[10,27] argue that the model is too complex to be of much practical utility to the manager. In the latest iteration of the model, Vroom and Jago[4, p. 180] themselves suggest that, "as a practical matter, its use required an adaptation to some sort of computer or programmable calculator."

We examined the potential utility of our model by applying it to comparable cases presented by Vroom and Jago[4] and compared our decisions with theirs. Assuming that the manager has sufficient time to involve subordinates in the decision process, our results are typically congruent with the Vroom-Yetton model.

In those decisions which affect only one subordinate (individual problems) our model is more likely to call for a different decision than found with the Vroom-Yetton procedure. The "library space problem," for example, is one in which a manager and an assistant must decide what color to paint the walls of a new room being added to the library. The assistant has responsibility for the room. The Vroom-Yetton model directs delegation of the problem and its solution to the assistant or prompts a unilateral decision in the interests of time. Our model recommends that the manager consult with the assistant and then decides.

A CAUTION

Although our model has not been tested extensively, Schneider[28] found support for the zone of acceptance as a guide to participation in decision making. Principals who have used the model also attest to its ability, but testimonial is no substitute for systematic investigation. We hope other researchers will join us in testing the model. Clearly, the model is easier for practitioners to use than the Vroom-Yetton perspective, but is it as effective? That is an empirical question.

NOTES AND REFERENCES

1. Bridges, E. M. (1967). A model for shared decision making in the school principalship. *Educational Administration Quarterly, 3,* 49-61.

2. Hoy, W. K., & Miskel, C. G. (1991). *Educational administration: Theory, research, and practice* (4th ed.). New York: Random House.

3. Vroom, V. H., & Yetton, P. W. (1973). *Leadership and decision making.* Pittsburgh, PA: University of Pittsburgh Press.

4. Vroom, V. H., & Jago, A. G. (1988). *The new leadership: Managing participation in organizations.* Englewood Cliffs, NJ: Prentice-Hall.

5. Mintzberg, H. (1989). *Mintzberg on management.* New York: The Free Press.

6. Barnard, C. (1938). *The functions of the executive.* Cambridge, MA: Harvard University Press.

7. Simon, H. (1947). *Administrative behaviour.* New York: Macmillan.

8. Bridges, E. M. (1964). Teacher Participation in Decision Making. *Administrator's Notebook, 12,* 1-4.

9. Chase, F. S. (1952). The teacher and policy making. *Administrator's Notebook, 1,* 1-4.

10. Field, R. H. G. (1982). A test of the Vroom-Yetton model of leadership. *Journal of Applied Psychology, 67,* 523-32.

11. Alluto, J. A., & Belasco, J. A. (1972). A Typology of Participation in Organizational Decision Making. *Administrative Science Quarterly, 17,* 117-25.

12. Conway, J. A. (1976). A Test of linearity between teachers' participation in decision making and their perceptions of their schools as organizations. *Administrative Science Quarterly, 21,* 130-9.

13. Imber, M. (1983). Increased decision making involvement for teachers: Ethical and Practical Considerations. *Journal of Educational Thought, 17,* 36-42.

14. Imber, M., & Duke, D. L. (1984). Teacher participation in school decision making: A framework for research. *Journal of Educational Administration, 22,* 24-34.

15. Mulder, M. (1971). Power Equalization through Participation! *Administrative Science Quarterly, 16,* 31-8.

16. Duke, D. L., Showers, B. K., & Imber, M. (1980). Teachers and shared decision making: The costs and benefits of involvement. *Educational Administration Quarterly, 16,* 93-106.

17. Mintzberg, H. (1983). *Power in and around organizations.* Englewood Cliffs, NJ: Prentice-Hall.

18. This version of the decision-making process is fairly typical of decision processes reported broadly across the organizational literature.

19. This rule is not unlike Vroom and Yetton's[3] trust rule.

20. Our framework for distinguishing decision-making arrangements is similar to Vroom and Yetton's[3] management decision methods; however, we distinguish between consensus and majority rule because some situations require consensus, but we do not distinguish between sharing and obtaining information.

21. Bridges, E. M., Doyle, W. J., & Mahan, D. J. (1968). Effects of Hierarchical Differentiation on Group Productivity, Efficiency, and Risk Taking. *Administrative Science Quarterly, 13*, 305-319.

22. Blau, P., & Scott, W. R. (1962). *Formal organizations: A comparative approach.* San Francisco, CA: Chandler.

23. Torrance, E. P. (1955). Some consequences of power differences in decision making in permanent and temporary three-man groups. In A. P. Hare, E. F. Borgatta, & R. F. Bales (Eds), *Small groups* (pp. 482-92). New York: Alfred A. Knopf.

24. Nitzan, S., & Paroush, J., (1984). A general theorem and eight corollaries in search of correct decision. *Theory and Decision, 17*, 211-20.

25. Miner, J. B. (1984). The validity and usefulness of theories emerging in organizational science. *Academy of Management Review, 9*, 296-306.

26. Miner, J. B. (1988). *Organizational behaviour: Performance and productivity.* New York: Random House.

27. Filley, A. C., House R. J., & Kerr, S. (1976). *Managerial process and organizational behaviour* (2nd ed.). Glenview, IL: Scott, Foresman.

28. Schneider, G. T. (1984). teacher involvement in decision making: Zones of acceptance, decision conditions, and job satisfaction. *Journal of Research and Development in Education, 18*, 25-32.

Printed in the United States
130199LV00003B/3/A